Sonia Delaunay

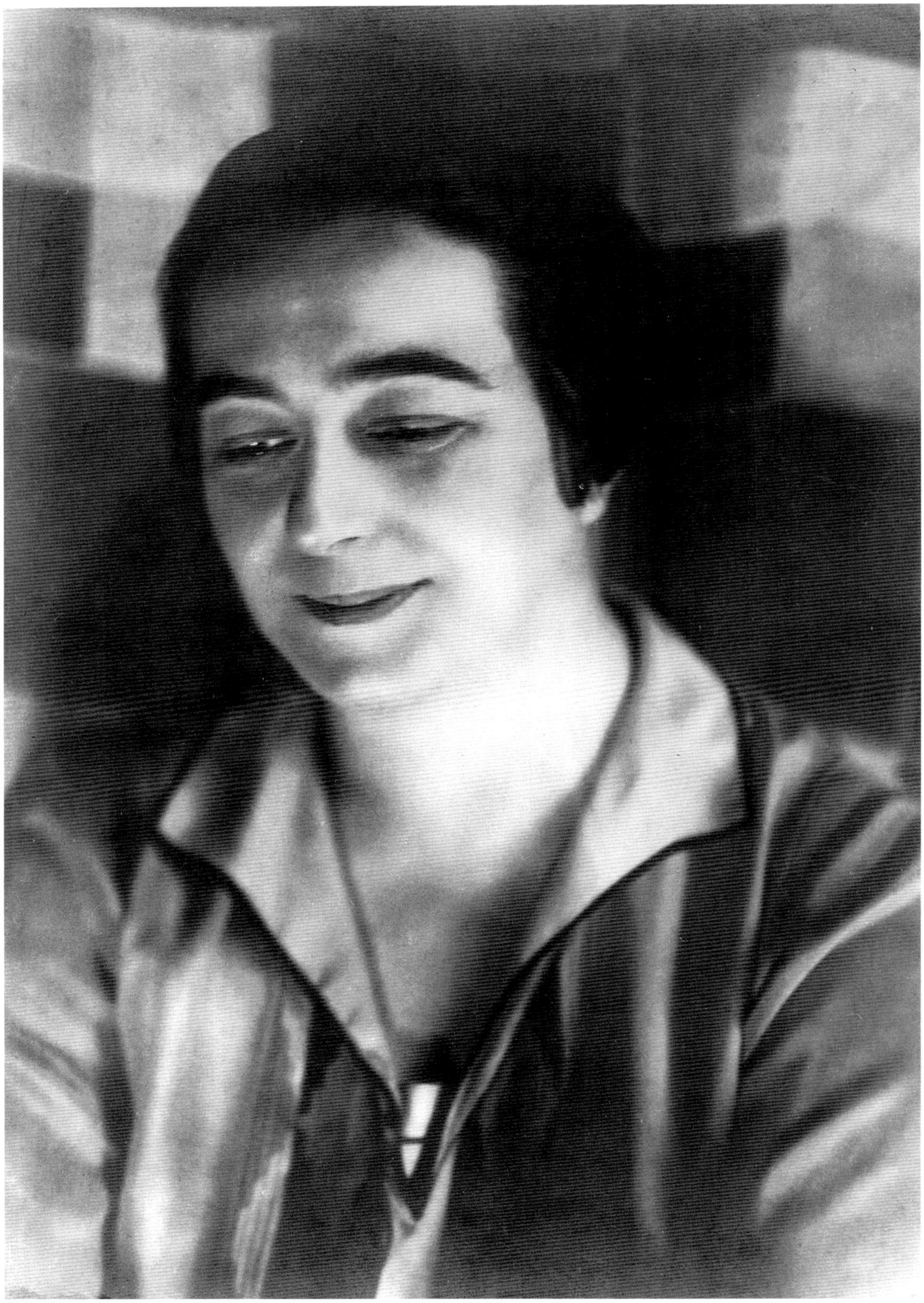

Sonia Delaunay

THE LIFE OF AN ARTIST

STANLEY BARON
in collaboration with
JACQUES DAMASE

with 203 illustrations, 115 in colour

THAMES AND HUDSON

Frontispiece: Portrait of Sonia Delaunay *c.* 1928 by Florence Henri

Right: Lithograph, 1960's

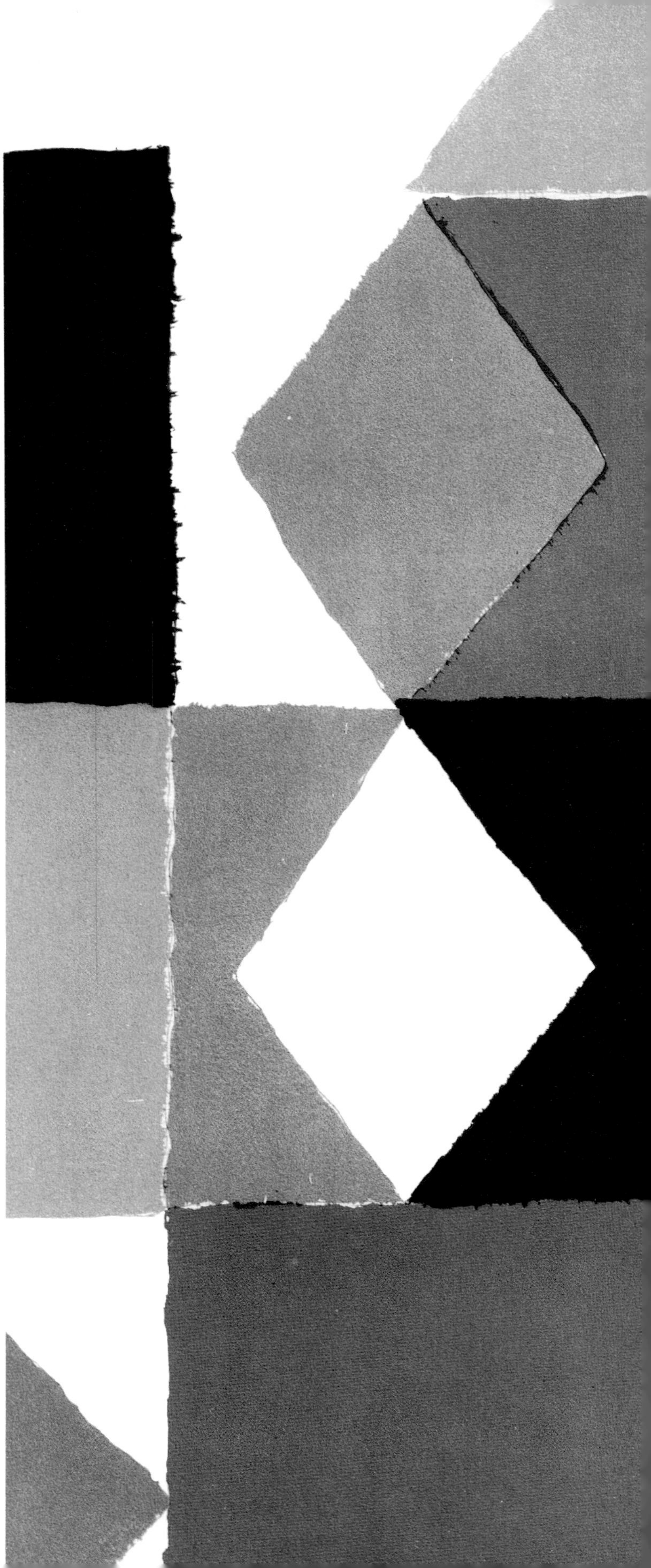

British Library Cataloguing-in-Publication Data
A catalogue record of this book is available from the British Library.
ISBN 0-500-23703-4

Printed and bound in Singapore

CONTENTS

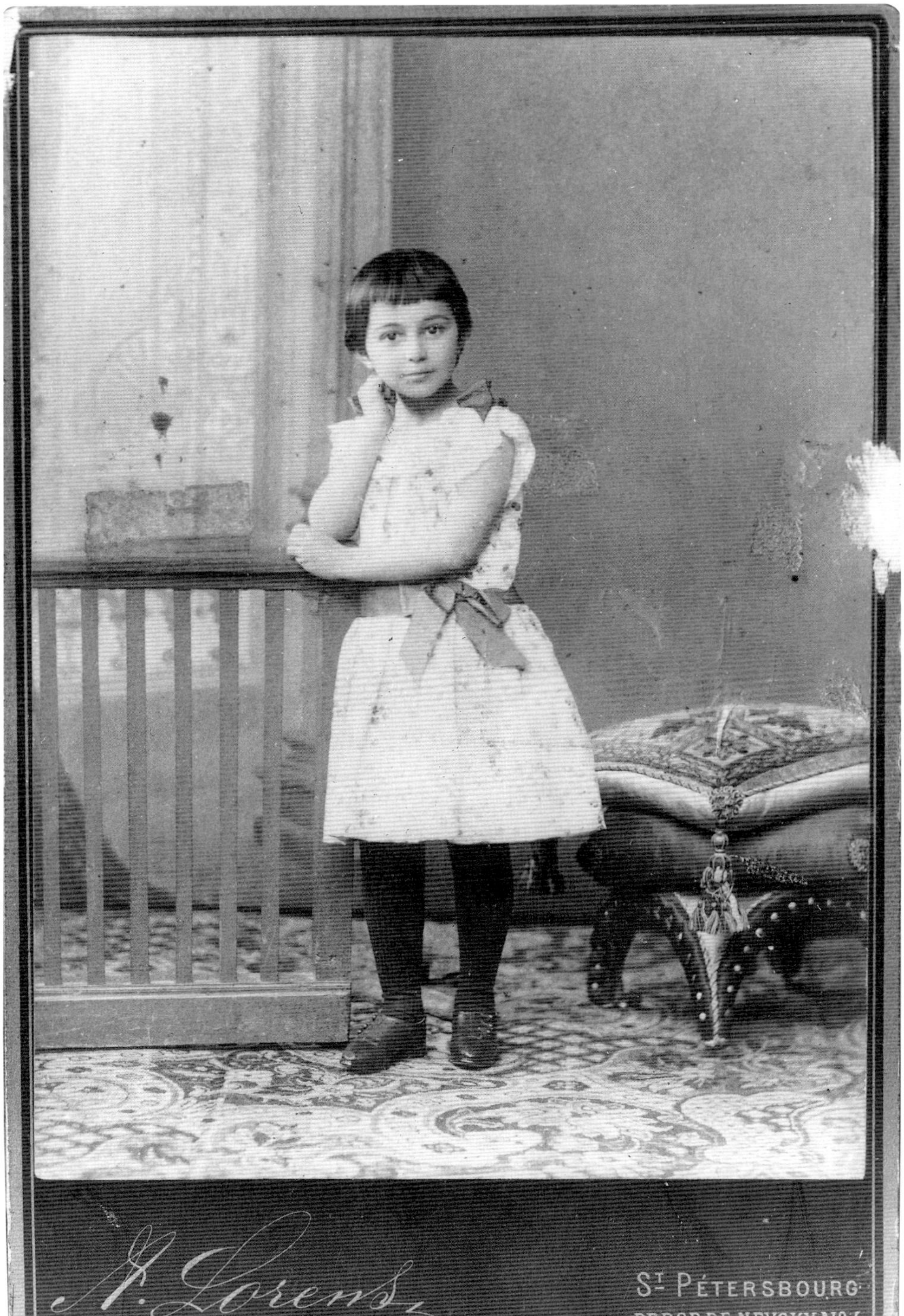
A. Lorens
St Pétersbourg
Persp. de Nevsky No. 4

CHAPTER 1

ORIGINS

SONIA DELAUNAY was an original. She was an innovator, an inventor, a fabricator, an artificer. She made things, and she made things happen. By instinct she was a passionate adept of the avant-garde, and yet the traditionally pure, unmodulated colours of her remembered childhood in the Ukraine are everywhere visible in her work. She was aesthetically uncompromising, but she felt at home in many worlds: the commercial, the theatrical, the literary, the social. Her range was immense, and at everything she attempted she sought excellence. First as a partner-wife, and then as a woman artist alone, she was in the forefront of cultural developments throughout the first half of the twentieth century, and her influence lives on far beyond her own life.

Her own life, however, was not an entirely open book. While she was an extremely generous and articulate woman, there were parts of her past that she did not easily discuss. In the autobiography she published in 1978, the first twenty years of her life occupy no more than seven pages and can hardly be called a detailed account.

Sonia Terk at the age of eight, when she had come to live with her relations in St Petersburg and had her name changed from Sarah Stern.

Even the actual date of her birth is ambiguous. Most of the official biographies and catalogues state that she was born in the Ukrainian town of Gradizhsk (sometimes given as Gradzinsk) on the Dnieper river on 14 November 1885; indeed, in her own book she speaks of that town, where her father was a labourer in a nail factory. And yet her will, signed and witnessed in the presence of a notary, gives the birthdate as 4 November 1885 and the place as Odessa. The discrepancy in dates may be explained by the gap that still existed at the time of her birth between the 'Old Style' calendar of the Russian Empire and the Gregorian calendar that had been adopted in most of Western Europe. In her own mind, the 14th was the date to celebrate; as late as 1946 she noted in her journal on Thursday, the 14th of November: 'Sixty-one years. I don't feel them . . .' The reason for the substitution of Odessa for Gradizhsk (or Gradzinsk) is less open to explanation.

We can assume that she was not an only child, since she refers in her book to 'her youngest brother'; but she appears to have lost contact with her immediate family early in life.The one thing she makes clear about her childhood is that she loved her father and hated her mother. In one place she writes of her 'aversion' to her mother, who was a whiner, constantly bewailing her fate. From her father she learned never to complain; and as an adult she did not suffer complainers gladly. Her fortitude, her lack of cupidity, her high assessment of honesty, she attributes to the example of her father, even though she left her parents as a child – probably before she was five years old.

It was a brother of her mother's, Henri Terk, a successful lawyer in St Petersburg, who took over her upbringing. He and his well-connected wife Anna wanted to adopt the child, but her mother would not permit it. What took place was in fact a virtual adoption; she not only assumed the name of Sonia Terk (she was born and remained legally Sarah Stern), but lived, apparently without interruption, in the privileged Jewish background of her uncle's affluent St Petersburg home where, according to her memoir, she was educated by a number of governesses, learned several foreign languages, and was exposed to an elevated milieu of music and art.

What she always recalled of her pre-adolescent life, aside from St Petersburg's great avenues and palaces and gardens, were the academic paintings in her uncle's house, his portfolios of prints after famous masterpieces, the colours of everything that struck her eyes, the summer house in Finland where she lay naked among the pine trees every morning from 9 to 12 and thus 'introduced naturism into Russia.'

The Terks spent a month or two each summer in their Finnish home, and each year they would also travel as a family to Germany, Italy, France, exploring the treasures of the stupendous museums and galleries in those countries, so that Sonia came to know not only the priceless collection in the

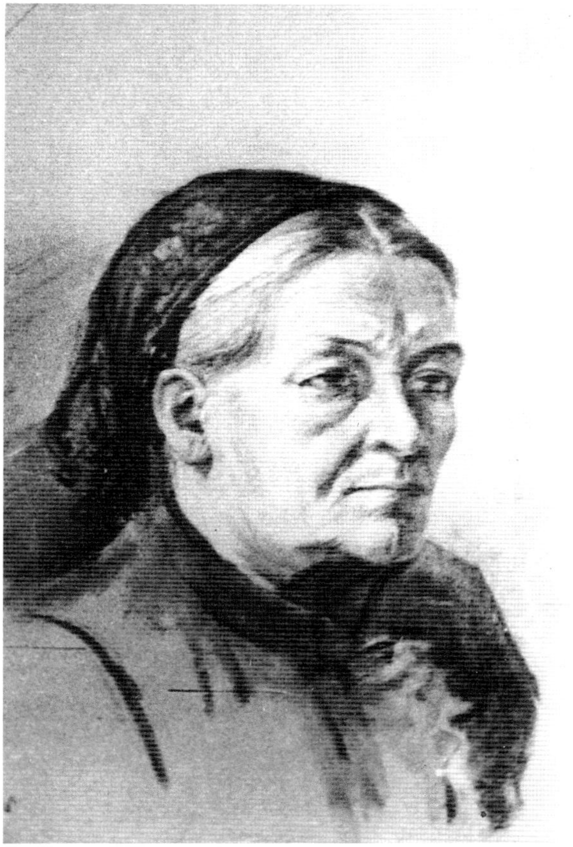

Two of the charcoal portraits Sonia Terk did in 1904, which showed her natural talent for drawing: the laundress in St Petersburg (left) and her aunt Anna Terk.

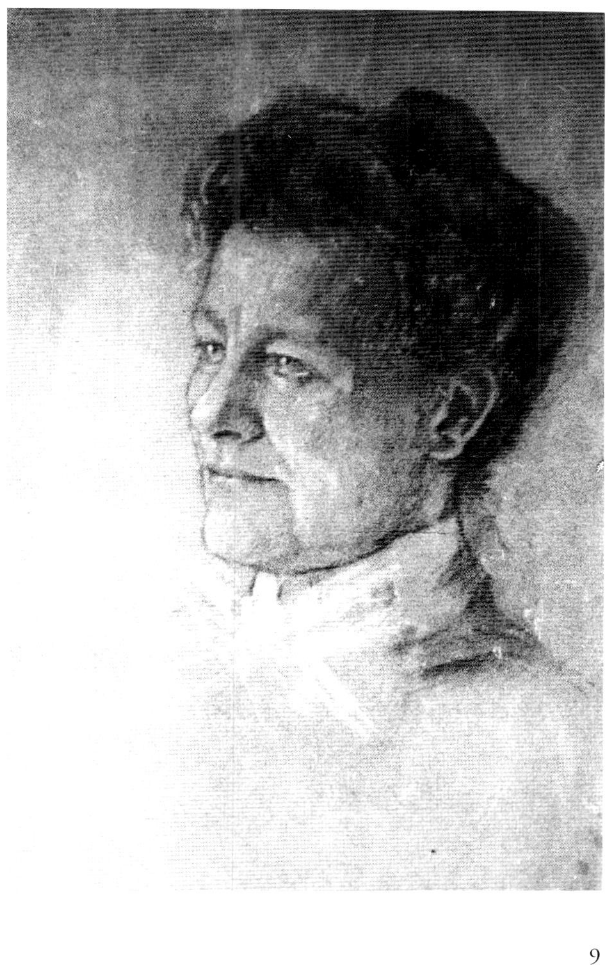

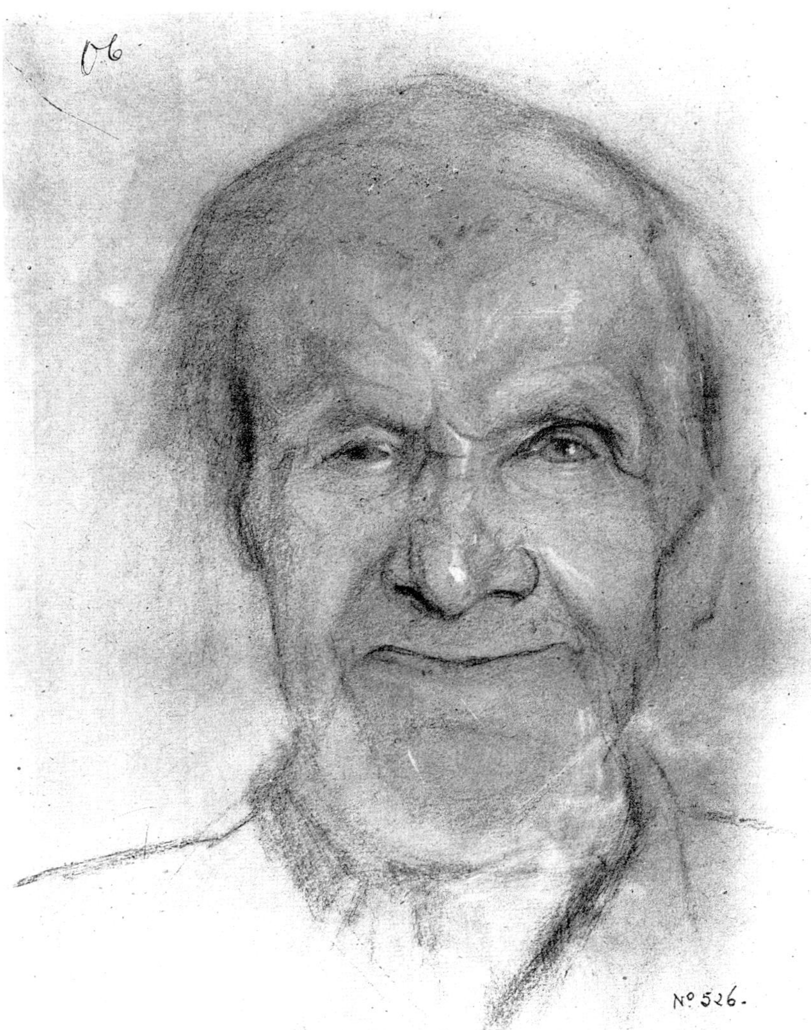

A charcoal and chalk drawing by Sonia of a Finnish peasant, 1904.

Hermitage, but those in the Uffizi, the Louvre and the Munich Pinakothek as well.

When she was sixteen, she attended a highly regarded secondary school in St Petersburg, and it was there that her gift for drawing was first encouraged. The art teacher, a woman, advised the Terks that Sonia was sufficiently talented to warrant more professional art training in Germany, where there were many excellent advanced schools at that time.

She was eighteen when she finished her studies at the St Petersburg lycée, and that same year, following the suggestion of her art teacher, she entered the academy of fine arts in Karlsruhe. That small city in the Land of Baden, near to the Rhine and famous for a variety of academic institutions, was chosen over Munich by her relations for the reason that a brother of Anna Terk's practised medicine in nearby Heidelberg. Sonia would therefore not be entirely free of family surveillance. Nevertheless, considering the period and the social conventions of bourgeois Jewish Russians, it was markedly unusual for a girl of eighteen to travel abroad alone, and it indicates perhaps that Sonia had given the Terks good reason to have confidence in her reliability and discretion.

During the winters from 1903 to 1905, Sonia attended the studio of a professor, sometimes spelt Schmidt-Reuter and sometimes Schmitt-Reuter, who had something of a reputation as a teacher. He was strict and reminded her later of the painter Fernand Léger. She claimed to have received from him 'a solid basis . . . an approach to art without false academism.' And when she vacationed in Finland between times, she began to produce a number of drawings in pastel and charcoal (portraits of her aunt, of their laundress, of a Finnish peasant and of herself) which show the results of her lessons – traditional, unexceptional, realistic studies with a good grounding in anatomy and technique.

The reason for her abandoning Germany for Paris is usually attributed to her reading of a book by the well-known art critic and sponsor of Art Nouveau, Julius Meier-Graefe. In *Manet und sein Kreis*, which appeared in Berlin in 1902, Meier-Graefe promoted the view that the centre of true art was now in Paris.

Decisions of this importance are usually the outcome of a variety of influences, but the Meier-Graefe book certainly played its part. Whatever the circumstances, Sonia Terk left Germany and Russia behind when she set out for Paris in 1905; except for two summer visits to the Terks' Finnish house, she never returned to Russia.

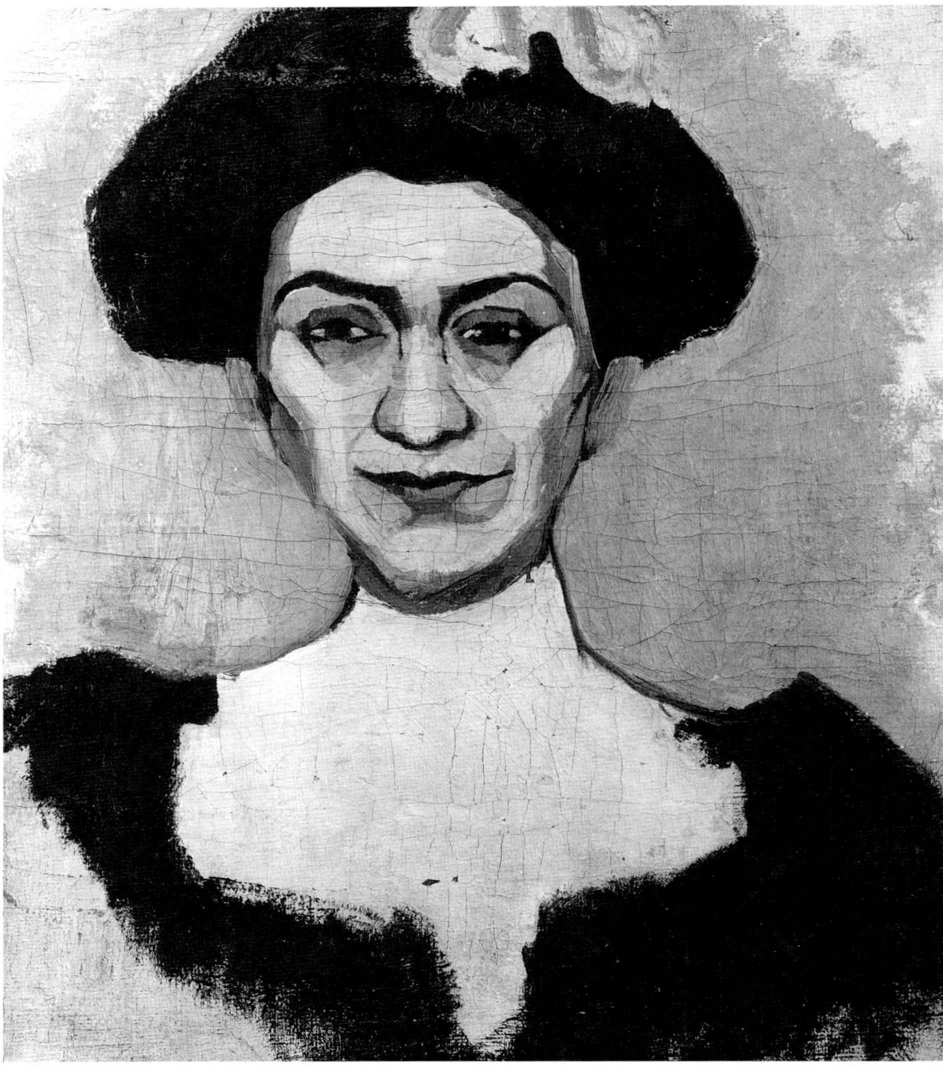

Portrait by Sonia of a Mme Minsky, oil on canvas, 1907.

CHAPTER 2

PARIS AND THE BEGINNINGS OF AN ARTIST'S CAREER

SHE WAS ALMOST TWENTY when she arrived in Paris – an attractive, solidly built young woman of average height, recognizably Slav, dark in colouring, with a well-shaped head, a good strong forehead and chin, knowing eyes and an expressive mouth. She wore her long straight hair swept to the back of her head in the style of the period and dressed quite conventionally. In Paris of the belle époque she was to breathe a new atmosphere of creativity, experimentation and the joy of living. In years to come, she frequently referred to the excitement, the light and the allure of Paris after the drab solidity of Germany.

With four other Russian girls she took up lodgings in a *pension* in the rue Campagne Premier (14th arrondissement), where every night there were gatherings of at least twenty acquaintances or friends. But she had come to Paris not for social entertainment or youthful revelry; as hers was a serious purpose, she enrolled in art courses at the Académie de la Palette in Montparnasse. There she received instruction from so-called masters like Jacques-Emile Blanche and Lucien Simon, but found that their style of teaching through criticism ended up by confusing and discouraging the students. She began to work on her own, and spent less time in the Académie than she did at exhibitions and galleries.

It was an interesting year to be in Paris. There were public showings of Cézanne's seminal painting *Les Grandes Baigneuses.* At the Salon des

Indépendants, Sonia came under the spell of Van Gogh, forty-five of whose paintings and drawings were on display. Works by Gauguin were being exhibited in the rue Laffitte, and in the windows of the Bernheim Gallery, near the Madeleine, she discovered the colourful, sophisticated art of Bonnard and Vuillard. Works by Matisse, Derain and others were exhibited at the first Salon d'Automne in October, and the influential critic Louis Vauxcelles, who obviously did not find their exuberant, vivid colours to his taste, named them 'the wild animals' – *Les Fauves* – and so they have been known ever since.

Surprisingly, her circle of Russian girls were critical of Matisse; they found him too bourgeois, not avant-garde enough for them. Sonia wrote later that 'It was out of this strong desire to go beyond Fauvism that my paintings of this period were born.' Yet Matisse's work can be seen to have had as great an influence on her earliest paintings as that of Van Gogh and Gauguin. From Van Gogh she retained the art of extracting the essential character of her models, whom she chose by preference for their expressive ugliness or provocative vulgarity. Gauguin's example taught her to suppress details in favour of the larger design and to use colours that were not found in nature. Both her *Young Finnish Girl* and *Philomène* of 1907 show these two influ-

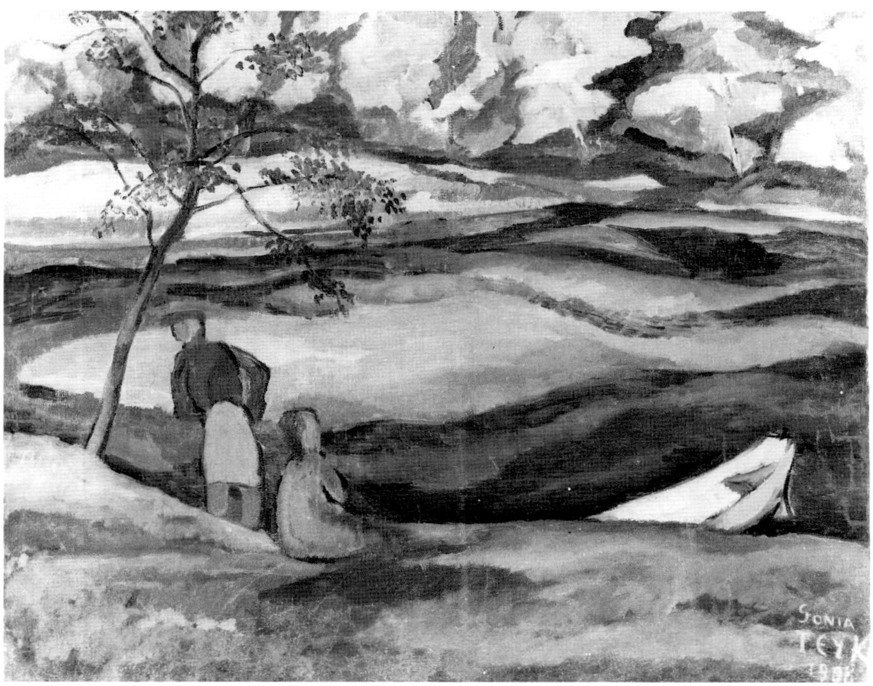

Finnish landscape, oil on canvas, 1906, a rather crude painting that shows how much Sonia was influenced by Gauguin and the Fauves in these early years of her career.

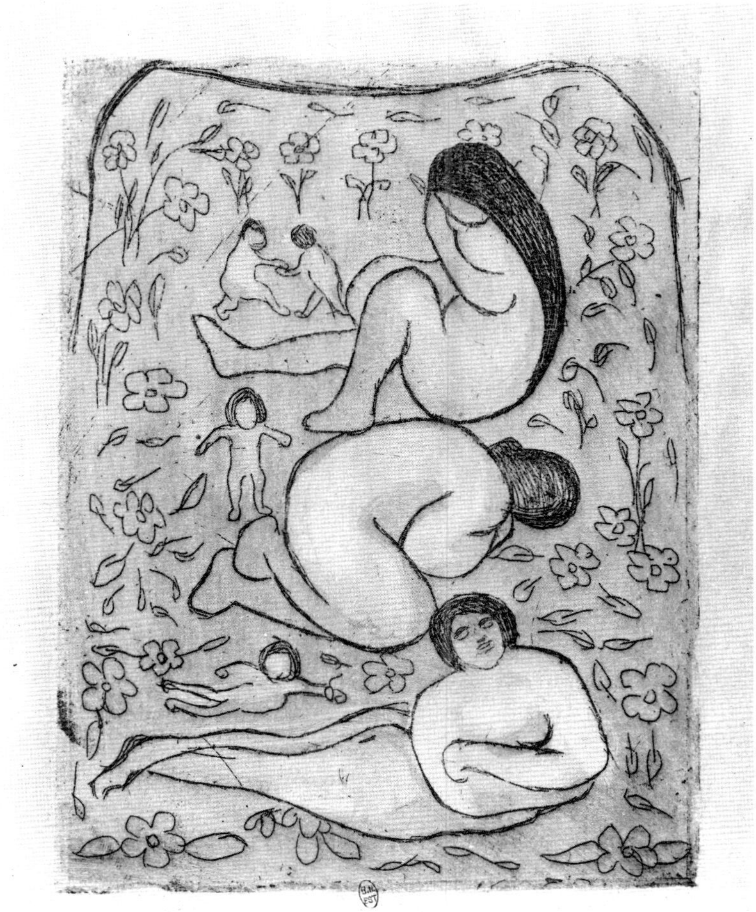

Three Nudes, engraving on copper, 1908

ences, as well as the secret she learned from Matisse in harmonizing her figures with their background.

But what these paintings mainly indicate is that she was groping to find her own art. In effect, like most fledgling artists, she was serving an apprenticeship, learning what she could from every available source or example, relying in her work on a heavy massing of shapes, strong outlines, even a kind of Expressionism (as in her *Nu jaune* of 1907-08) – none of which was to become her signature when she eventually forged her individual form of expression.

She was helped to some degree by an influential man whom she met during her first year in Paris. An acquaintance who lived along the quai aux

Fleurs on the Ile Saint-Louis introduced her to one of his neighbours, a German collector and art-dealer whose name was Wilhelm Uhde. Eleven years older than Sonia, Uhde had had a conventional bourgeois upbringing, and had studied law in several German and Swiss universities. An aesthete at heart, he came to realize in his late twenties that the law was not going to satisfy him; and an extended tour through Italy awoke his interest in art. He came to Paris in 1904, and was able to find his way fairly quickly into the art world, frequenting the popular cafés on the boulevard du Montparnasse and making friends with people like Leo Stein, who was as knowledgeable a collector as his more famous sister Gertrude. Uhde, exhibiting a flair for which he had not been trained, began to buy cheaply on his own, and to sell at a profit when he needed cash. Thus, almost accidently, he became a dealer.

When Sonia met him, he had opened a gallery in the Montparnasse area at 73 rue Notre-Dame des Champs, which was known simply as the Galerie Notre-Dame des Champs. His collection included magnificent works of the Fauve painters: Braque, Derain, Vlaminck, Dufy. Sonia, fascinated by his extensive knowledge of art and his 'nose' for new talent, became an habitué of the gallery as well as his apartment at 21 quai de la Tournelle.

On 5 December 1908, she and Uhde were unexpectedly married in a civil ceremony in the district of Holborn, London. Uhde identified himself to the authorities as a journalist and gave his age as thirty-four. The records show that they stayed at the Bucklers Hotel in Finsbury Square.

Both Sonia and Uhde eventually wrote autobiographical memoirs, but neither has much to say about the marriage. Uhde never mentions Sonia by name but writes, 'I learned to know a young Russian girl, who had become a good friend. She was clever and broad-minded, knew a bit about pictures, and had a talent for painting. Since she too desired a well-ordered and looked-after household with a seriously intellectual tenor, we agreed to give our existing comradeship the external form of a marriage.'

In her own memoir, Sonia barely mentions the marriage; and it is clear that it was not the result of a sudden rush of hot blood to the heart or head. It was a practical, calculated move, not at all out of character so far as Sonia was concerned. It is known that Uhde was homosexual – indeed, he had a male lover at the time. Bernard Dorival, in his book on her life and works, speculates that, even though she was over twenty-two years old, she was apprehensive lest the narrow mores of her St Petersburg relatives should induce them to

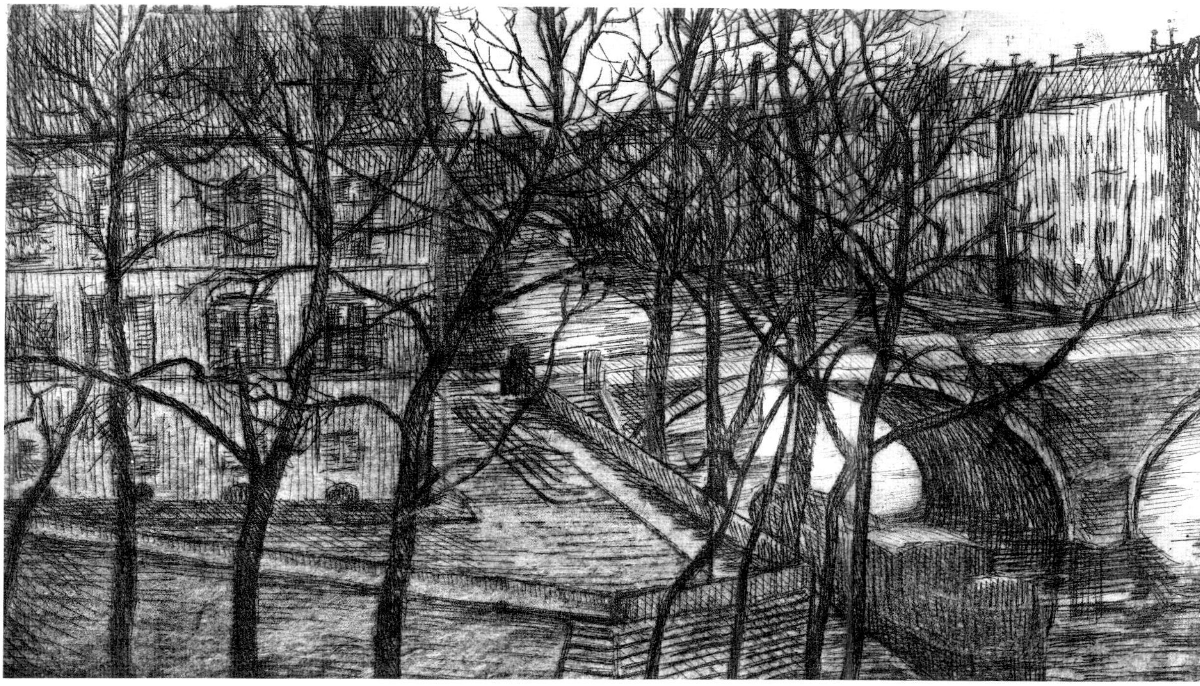

The first print made by Sonia, 1906; a drypoint etching of the Ile Saint-Louis, where she met her first husband, Wilhelm Uhde.

make her return to Russia before long and she was determined to stay 'at any cost'. Uhde, too, may have been under pressure from his extremely respectable family in Germany. As a marriage of convenience it was very convenient indeed. Uhde was able to conceal, at least from the outside world, an inclination which, even in the easy-going moral atmosphere of Paris before World War I, was not universally acceptable; Sonia's ability to remain in the city of her choice was assured for the time being; Uhde's profession and connections not only led to his giving her a one-person show in his gallery in 1908 but also introduced her to the artistic and literary elite of Paris. Indeed, he helped her to become a woman of the world.

One of Uhde's particular enthusiasms was the work of Henri Rousseau, *le Douanier* Rousseau. This was shared by an extremely *mondaine* divorced woman, Comtesse de Rose, described by Uhde as 'witty and talented', who was a frequent visitor to his gallery, accompanied sometimes by her twenty-three-year-old son, an aspiring painter whose name was Robert Delaunay.

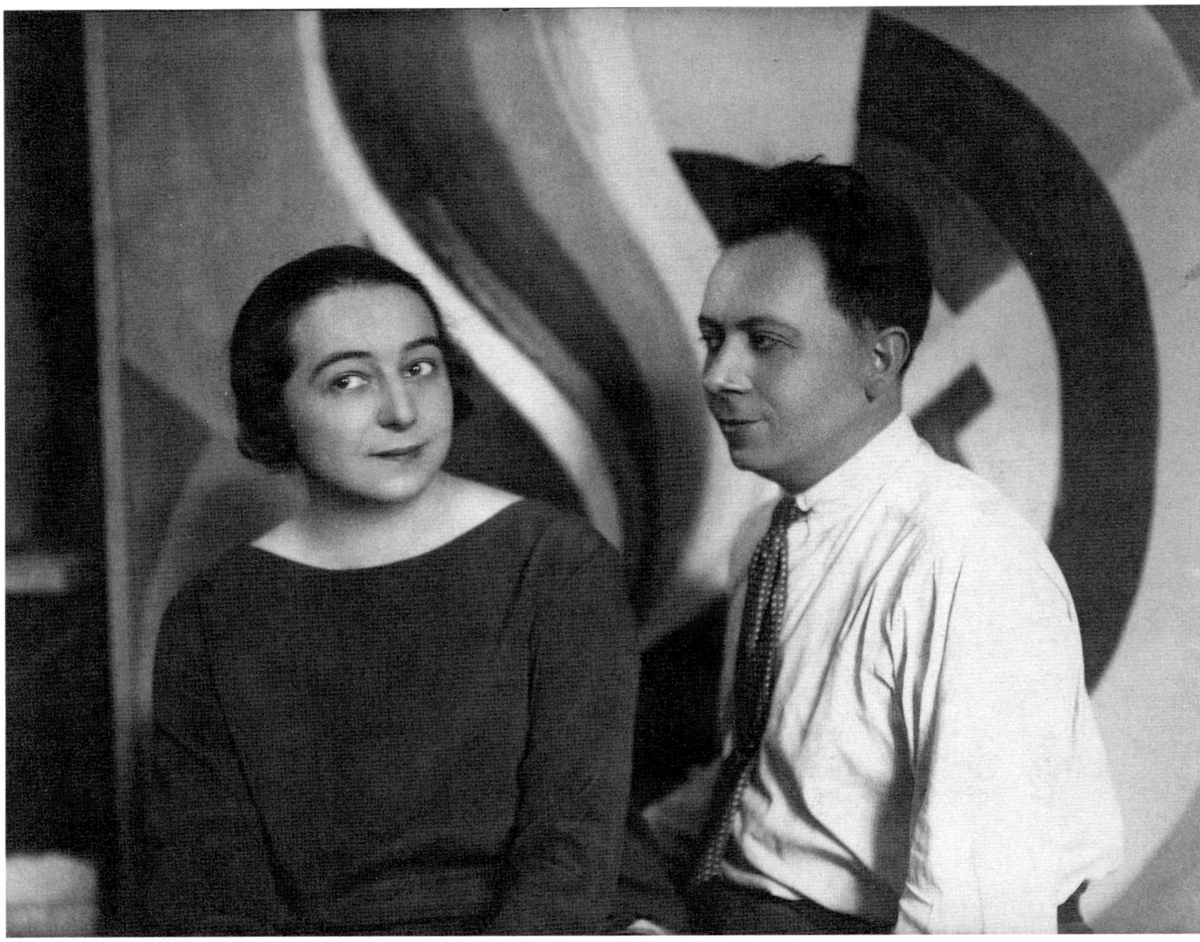

Sonia and Robert Delaunay in front of one of Robert's paintings, 1923.

CHAPTER 3

ROBERT

THE OPENING WORDS of Sonia Delaunay's autobiography read as follows: *I was born the same year as Robert Delaunay, under the same sun, some 3,000 versts away.*

There is no mistaking her intention to indicate that her life and his were intricately entwined. All the evidence implies that the thirty years they spent together, often working side by side, continually exchanging views and ideas, and feeding each other's talent, were filled with a sense of rare unity. It was all the more extraordinary because their heritage and background were in only few respects comparable; they seemed, all the same, to complement each other basically, to fulfil each other's needs, and to harmonize to a remarkable extent their ideas about the nature of art and their painting.

They met for the first time at the beginning of 1909, and by April they were lovers. Robert lived at 24 quai du Louvre, where she became an accustomed visitor, but during the early summer they were separated: Sonia had to accompany an aunt of hers to a resort near Genoa, while Robert spent some time in a hotel in the Drôme. But they met again in August at Chaville, where Robert was working in a villa rented by his uncle, Charles Damour.

Like Sonia, Robert had been virtually adopted by an aunt and uncle. His parents had been divorced when he was nine. His father seems to have vanished from his ken after that, and his eccentric, socially frivolous mother showed far greater interest in distant travel and intrigues than in bringing up her offspring. And so he was taken in by his mother's sister and her husband. Whereas the Delaunay parents, on both sides, came from distinguished families who had frittered away their inheritance, Damour was a businessman who had made his own fortune. Robert was nurtured in an atmosphere of bourgeois comfort, even luxury, but like Sonia he had in effect turned against that kind of life and was determined from an early age to devote himself to art. In this respect, he was very much indeed like Sonia.

For some reason, she refers to the episode at Chaville as their *true* meeting. She and Uhde were lodging in a family *pension* across the road. From there, she could watch Robert painting flowers in his uncle's garden, and when he came out of the garden he would take her for long walks in the woods. A few months later, as she puts it, they were 'engaged'.

Upon their return to Paris, they saw each other every day, visiting museums and churches. She would return to her husband's lodgings at 2 a.m. It was decided that she and Uhde should divorce. According to his discreet version, 'After a year had passed, our marriage was over. A friend of mine had reason to believe that he was better able than I to make my wife completely happy, and I had no wish to stand in the way of their beautiful future.'

Uhde – who remained a friend of Sonia's until he died – was obliging enough to arrange (as one commonly did in those days) a supposed adulterous assignation with another woman. Their divorce took place on 28 February 1910 and became final on 11 August. As she was pregnant, she and Robert waited no longer than 15 November (just after her birthday) to marry, and on 18 January she gave birth to their son, Charles.

Madame de Rose, who was by now no longer making romantic voyages to foreign places, had established herself in Paris and suddenly developed a maternal passion for her son. In the period before he and Sonia were married, she sought to devote her life to him; she kept in close touch with him, was eager to entertain his friends, expected him to have lunch with her every Sunday. But once he was married, he hardly ever saw her again. Sonia writes that, though he was not a strong-willed person, his decisions were unequivocal and he never reversed them. His mother laid the blame entirely on Sonia, but the fact was that, at the age of twenty-four, from one day to the next he had changed his life.

'In Robert Delaunay I found a poet. A poet who wrote not with words but with colours.' Thus Sonia describes the man who was to play such a strong catalytic role in her artistic development.

Robert's studies in art had been no more conventional or consistent than Sonia's. In his uncle's circle, contemporary art was an object of derision, and as a rebellious youth he had no hesitation, at his uncle's dinner parties, about supporting the work of Cézanne and Gauguin against the conventional output of the Salon academicians or the popular society painters. At his schools, he was interested in nothing but drawing and natural history; as a result he was more than once expelled for laziness. When his right-thinking uncle remonstrated with him, he said that nothing and no one was going to prevent him from being an artist. He agreed to become an apprentice in a studio of stage design at Belleville, and remained there for two years. That was where he developed the taste for large surfaces that later became characteristic of his major work.

During his vacations in Brittany in 1904 and 1905, he produced his first known pictures: Breton women painted on the spot, landscapes, flowers. In 1906 he spent his military service in the town of Laon, where he was fascinated by the cathedral and its towers, of which he did various studies. The next year he was in Paris, visiting the museums. At the Louvre it was not only the paintings that excited him, but also the antique objects. He was already acquainted with a group of young artists: Metzinger, Le Fauconnier, Léger, all artistic heirs of Cézanne and all searching for a new art.

That year, 1906, he offered a painting called *Le Manège électrique* to the Salon d'Automne, who turned it down. From then on, he never agreed to be shown at the Salon.

He was haunted by the towers of cathedrals, not only those of Notre-Dame in Laon, but those of Notre-Dame in Paris. The nave of Saint-Séverin in Paris fascinated him too, and he did repeated studies of all these subjects, until in due course the whole city of Paris became his subject in paintings called simply *Ville de Paris* or *La Ville*. His work was going through a post-Impressionist phase, and he even painted for a while in the *pointilliste* style of Seurat. A strong portrait he did of Wilhelm Uhde in 1907 was in this manner, though executed in much larger dabs of colour than Seurat used.

But in 1910, the first exhibition of a daring modernist art took place in Paris, its main proponents Braque and Picasso, but including also such friends of Robert's as Metzinger and Le Fauconnier; Matisse rather disapprovingly gave it the name of Cubism. No serious artist of the day could fail to be aware of the aims of Cubism, though few were tempted to copy its techniques. Delaunay, however, began towards the end of 1910 to veer away from his post-Impressionist manner to produce Cubist-style paintings that reduced the use of colour almost to monochrome. It was eventually Sonia who brought colour back into his life and his work.

The year they first met, 1909, Sonia was still painting under the influence of Van Gogh and Gauguin, but the work of Rousseau had also begun to fascinate her, as it did Uhde, Mme de Rose and Robert. Delaunay and his mother had been among the vanguard of Rousseau's supporters. They were regular visitors to the late-blooming artist's studio in the rue Perrel, along with other self-appointed representatives of the avant-garde. Mme de Rose was to commission one of Rousseau's most famous paintings, *The Snake Charmer*, which, after her death, graced the dining-room of Sonia and Robert's apartment until 1922. At that point they were sorely pressed for money and decided to sell the painting for 50,000 francs to the well-known entrepreneur of couture, bibliophile and art collector, Jacques Doucet, on the condition that he leave it to the Louvre upon his death. The deal was successfully negotiated by the arch-Surrealist writer André Breton, who was a friend of the Delaunays and, alongside his ardent promotion of the Surrealist cause, acted as Doucet's art adviser. (Two years later, Breton was similarly to arrange for the sale to Doucet of Picasso's *Les Demoiselles d'Avignon*.)

Delaunay was deeply affected by Rousseau's death in 1910, and after four years the *Douanier*'s daughter commissioned him to paint a portrait of her father on the basis of two photographs that she sent him: 'However, I beg you to show him wearing a black jacket, with an open waistcoat and black tie, which is what he usually wore when he came to see us – that is, very correct – and not in his working coat, as you were more accustomed to seeing him.' The portrait Delaunay accordingly painted is indeed very correct, simple, full of feeling, almost Cézannesque and quite unlike the pseudo-Cubist type of work he had been doing in that period.

Rousseau's influence on Sonia's early art is evident in an unusual work of 1909: an embroidery of wool on canvas called *Foliage*, in which can be seen the forest scenery that the old Rousseau introduced into so many of his paintings. In another work of the same year, she shows her admiration for Cézanne; it is a watercolour still-life with a bowl and a pitcher, the sort of subject dear to the aged master of Aix-en-Provence, in which she dispensed for once with the line she had been using to imprison the forms, and at the same time allowed the light to break up the objects in the picture.

Foliage, an embroidery of wool on canvas, 1909.

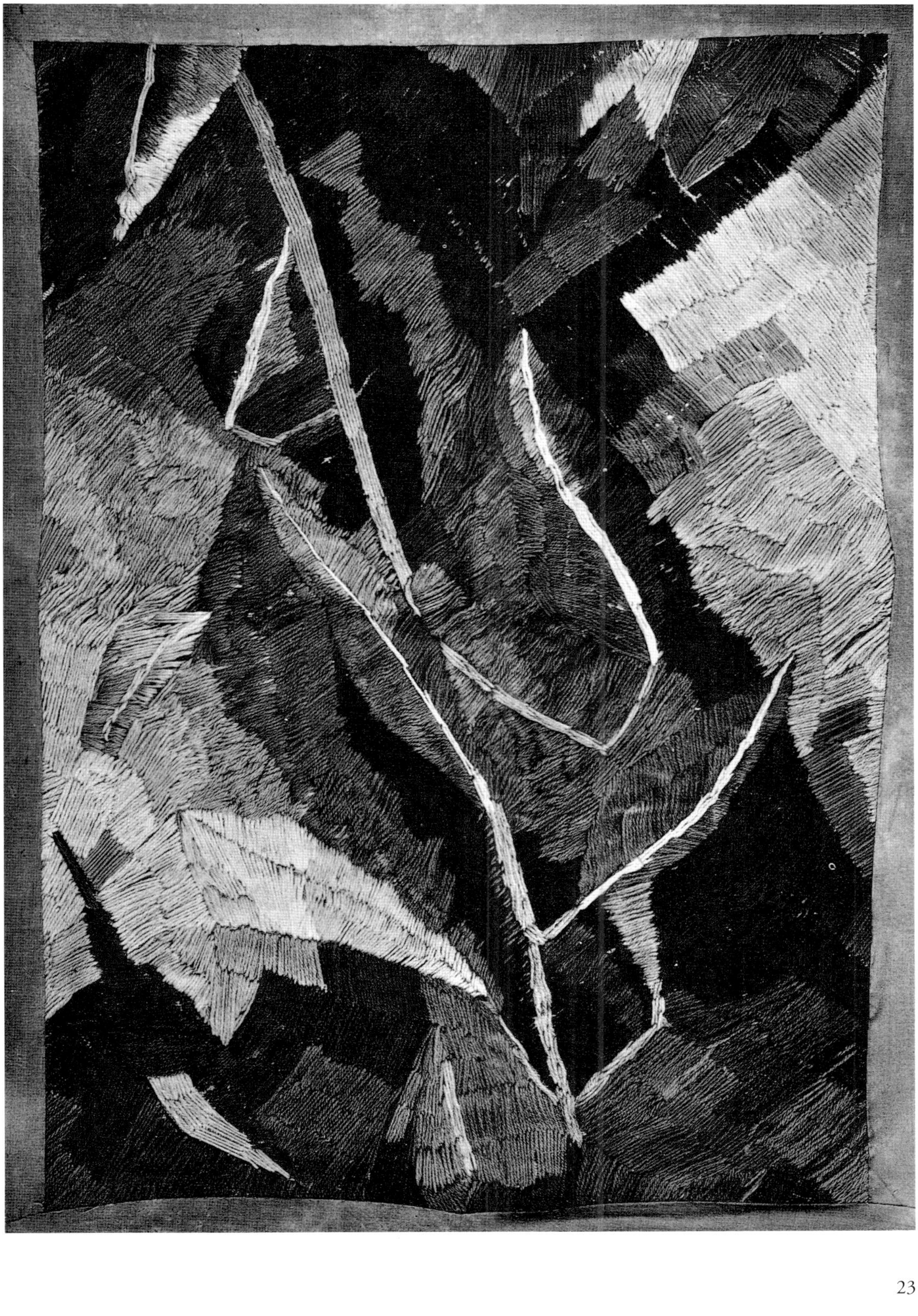

But Sonia's sense of colour, her passion for colour, went back to her childhood, to the robust primary colours of the Russian villages, peasant costumes and the fairs, like the one in Stravinsky's *Petrouchka*. Robert called her sense of colour 'atavistic'. It had been, perhaps inadvertently, suppressed in some of her early work, but it was alive and well, and simply waiting to be released into a new art.

In a curious way, the fact that she and Robert had to be separated soon after Charles's birth played its part in the development of their art. It may have been because of the baby's health that she took him first to Nice, to stay in the home of Russian relations there; then, to Villerville in Normandy, in a rented villa. In their absence, Robert was able to ponder the example of her pictures and to take advantage of them when he and Sonia were reunited in their apartment in the rue des Grands-Augustins. At that stage, in the tower paintings, the *Ville de Paris* paintings and especially the *Fenêtre* series (all 1910–12), he broke with Cubism and rediscovered colour. These free, spontaneous, untethered paintings of fragmented images, described by a recent art critic as 'lighter-than-air', were a vital bridge on his way to a completely abstract art; and this was a bridge that he and Sonia crossed together.

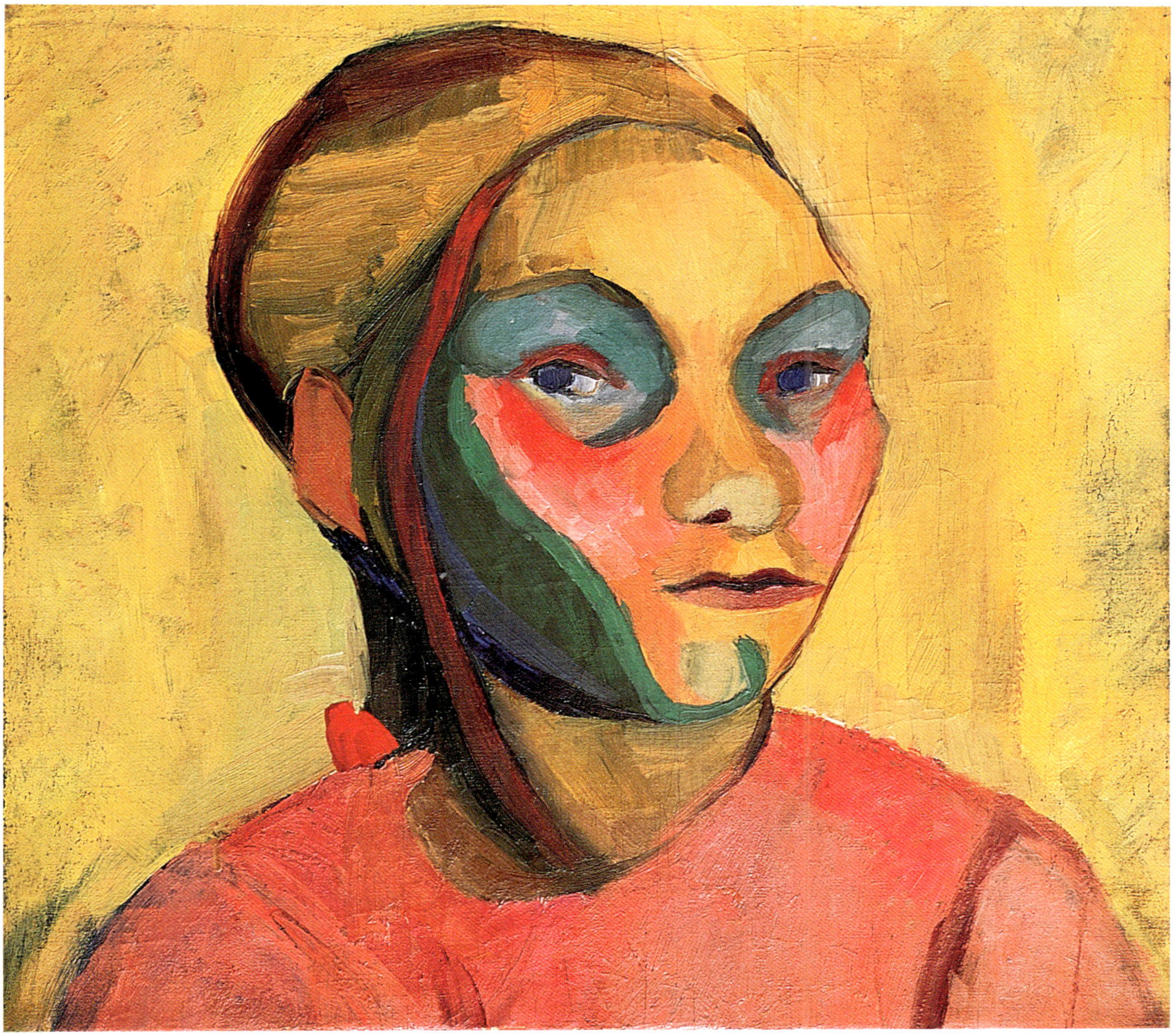

1 *Young Finnish Girl*, 1906; one of Sonia's earliest paintings after her arrival in Paris.

2,4 Study for *Philomène* and (opposite) the finished painting, 1907.

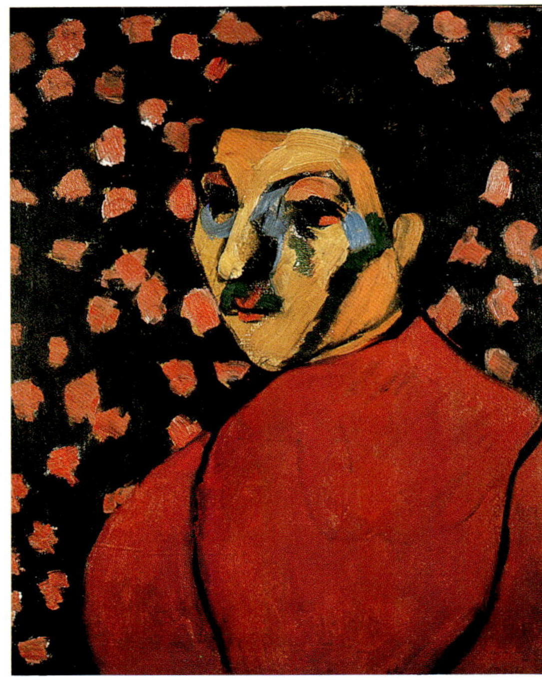

3 *Nu jaune*, an oil painting on canvas of 1907, which shows how distinctly Sonia had adopted some of the mannerisms of the Fauves, such as the dark outlining of forms and the application of bright colours.

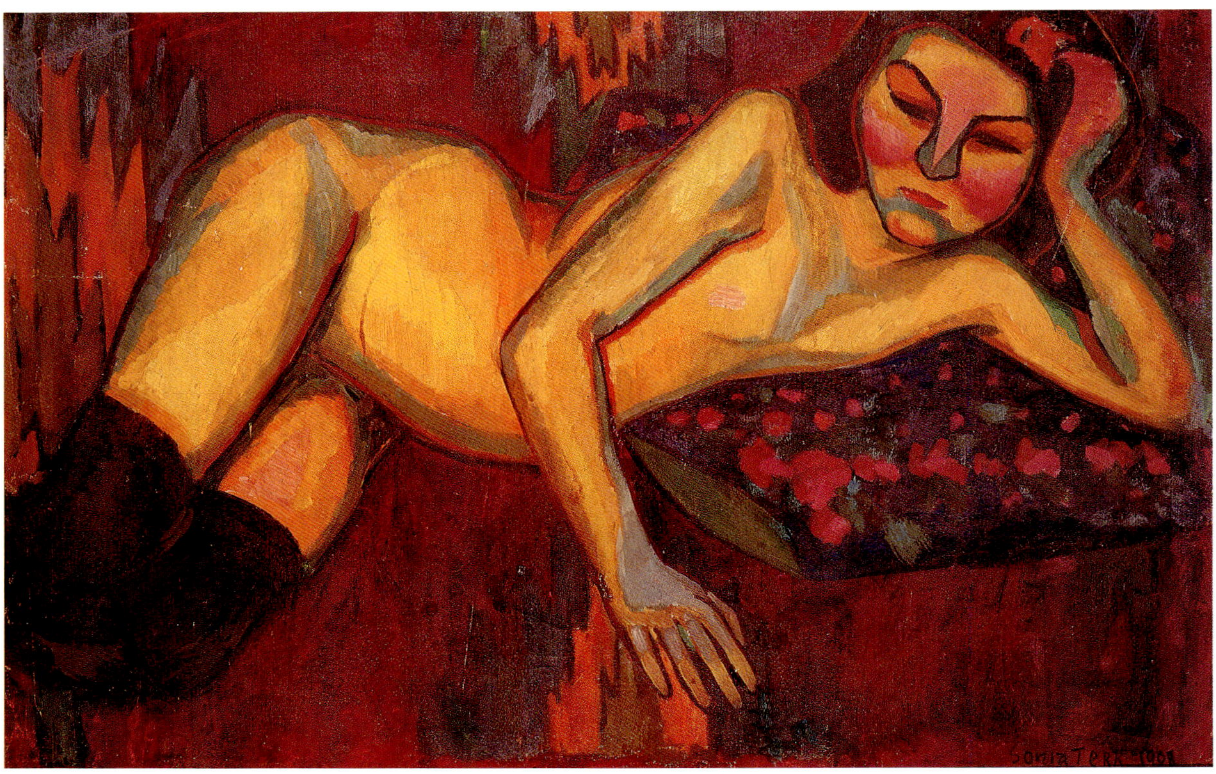

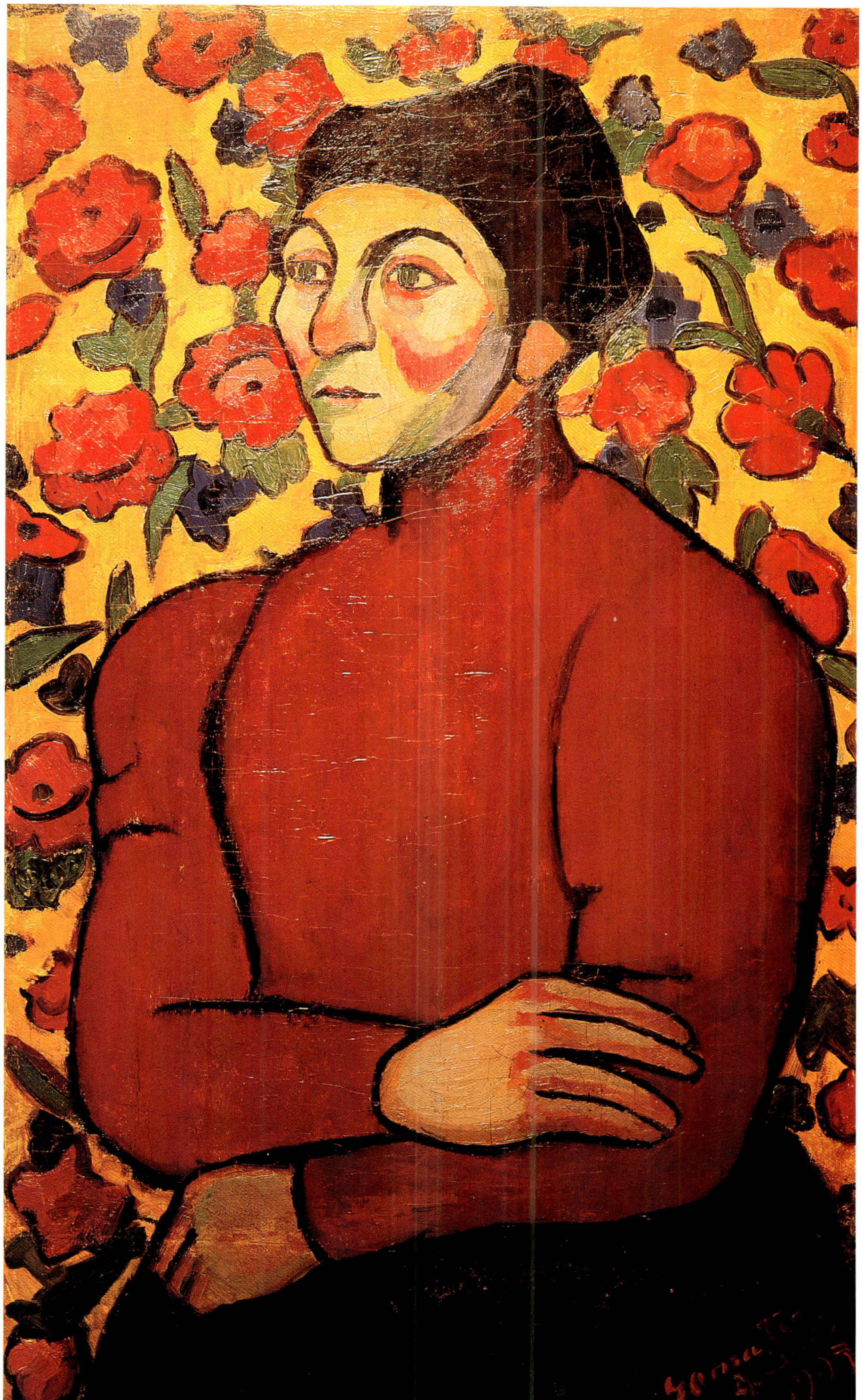

5 A self-portrait of 1906 (on the back of the *Young Finnish Girl*).

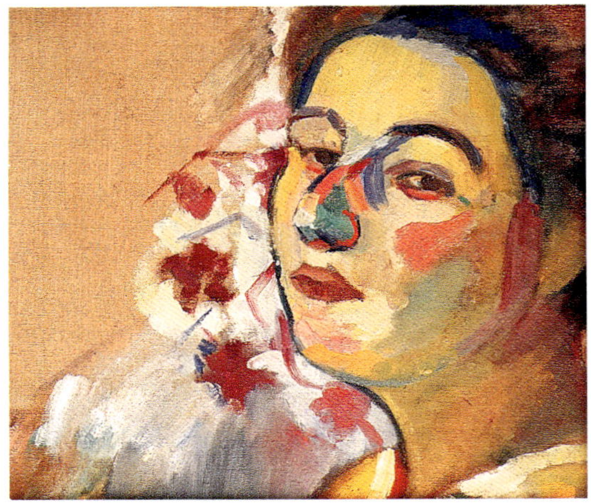

6 Sonia's portrait (1908) of the Russian poet (Vladimir Viktorovich?) Chuiko.

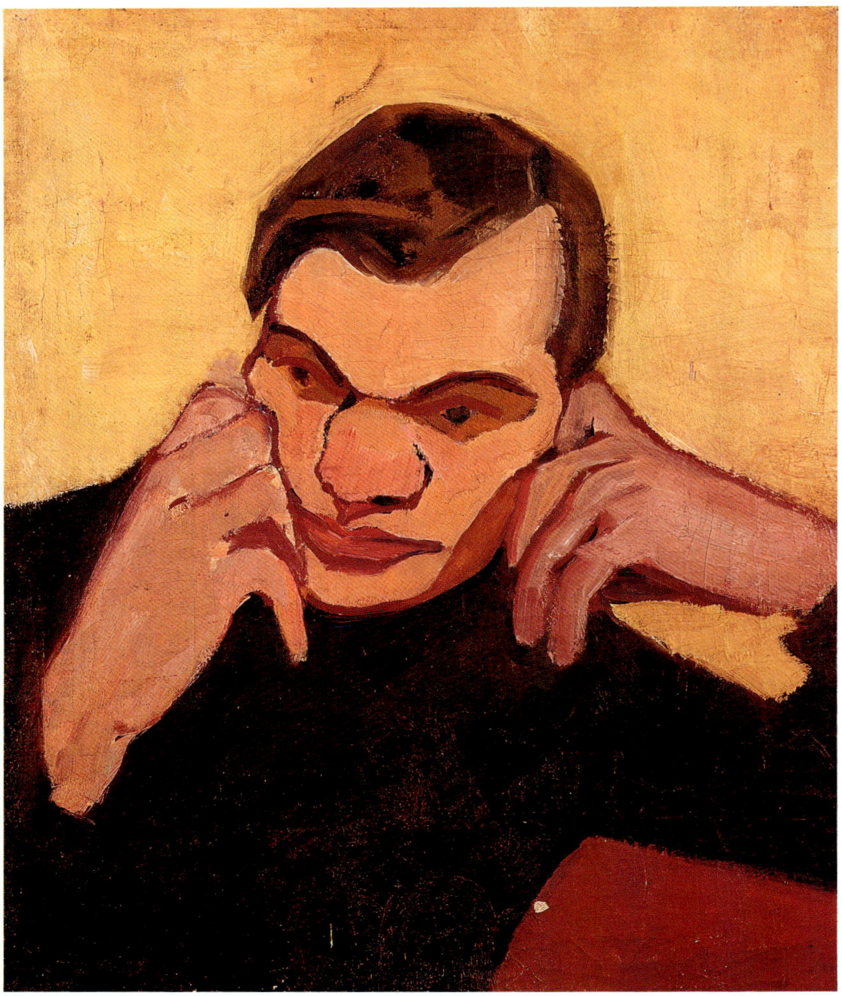

CHAPTER 4

WIFE AND ARTIST

At the start of their marriage, Sonia and Robert were 'playing house'. They lived well beyond their means, which comprised a monthly allowance from her aunt in St Petersburg. Robert's mother, in an access of generosity, promised to match the amount; but in the event, according to Sonia, she never contributed 'a sou'. In fact, she hid the fact that she had no money, and had been forced to sell her emeralds and even some of her furniture.

This made life difficult for Sonia, who had always been a bit extravagant by nature, and was known to lend money with unimpeded generosity to whoever was in need. She had to perform 'acrobatics' to make out on their income. Yet they were constantly entertaining in the rue des Grands-Augustins. On Sundays it was open house, and people visited from far and wide, both French and foreign, the latter largely Russians, and mostly young poets and painters who constituted the experimenters, the iconoclasts, the avant-garde.

Sonia gradually changed the decor of the apartment-studio, hunting out here and there handsome pieces of Empire furniture, which seemed to suit the place. She found that the walls were covered with 20 centimetres of wallpaper and had it replaced with white calico.

The baby's presence did not interfere with their working habits. For one thing, Charles was an unusually tranquil, quiet baby. For another, the studio was a long way from the nursery. Sonia's only cavil about the early months of her marriage is that Robert became so obsessed by whatever he was engaged in that he forgot about shaving or bathing. This drove her into a fury, but she did not mention it. Instead, at 4 in the afternoon, she would simply shove him out of the studio and force him to make his ablutions.

When Charles was born he had an Empire bed. She created for it a patchwork quilt (now in the collection of the Musée National d'Art Moderne in Paris) out of fabric remnants, in a style she remembered from the handiwork of Russian peasant women. Friends who saw it exclaimed that it was Cubist, though Sonia had put it together completely spontaneously. As she continued in other works to use this technique, art critics saw in it a kind of 'geometrization' of forms and a melody of colours which presaged the work she produced in the years that followed. In other words, the patchwork quilt led directly to her break with perspective and naturalism.

Another thread in this development was their (mostly Robert's) fascination by the research into colour of the nineteenth-century chemist Eugène Chevreul, who had been in charge of colours and dyes at the Gobelin tapestry works. Chevreul's findings on the subject of colour relationships, published in 1839 under the title *De la loi du contraste simultané des couleurs* (The Law of the Simultaneous Contrast of Colours), had already had their effect on Delacroix and particularly on the Impressionists. The Delaunays used certain aspects of Chevreul's theories as a basis for their own experimentation in the effects of simultaneous contrast. Robert's main interest was in applying these to painting, but for Sonia, it was a less a matter of experimenting; she could see and understand the effect of contrasting colours all around her in everyday life. She made collages, bookbindings out of paper and left-over pieces of material, she painted small boxes, she made cushions, waistcoats, lampshades – and all examples of simultaneous contrast. Their Sunday visitors were astonished by these things she made only to amuse herself. Her colour sense was completely instinctive, and remained with her all her life.

At that time, and indeed in all stages of her career, she refused to accept any facile distinction between fine art and the applied or decorative arts. She devoted her gifts equally to the design of a fabric or to a room-size oil painting. That may well be the reason why it took so long for her to receive the attention and recognition in France that her work had always deserved.

One of her first large-scale works in this new style of '*simultanéisme*' was her painting of the *Bal Bullier* (1912-13). The Bal Bullier was a well-

Sonia in street clothes photographed in the apartment in the rue des Grands-Augustins before World War I.

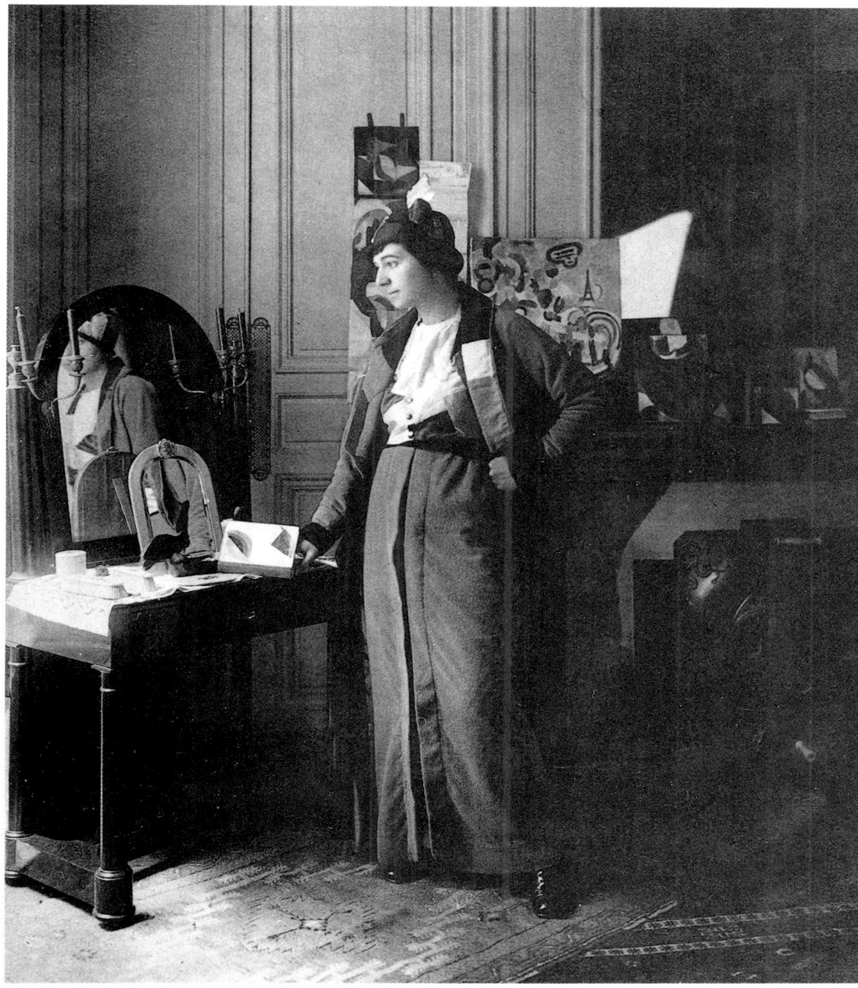

known dance-hall near to the famous restaurant Closerie des Lilas on the avenue de l'Observatoire, to which the Delaunays and their friends repaired every Thursday. It was the haunt of students and shop girls (as it appears in the lively second act of Puccini's opera *La Rondine*), but artists and poets had also taken it up in order to dance the new foxtrot and the tango, which had been introduced to Paris in 1910. Sonia was particularly carried away by the swirling figures of the dancers; in her vision they became swirling colours. For their visits to this popular establishment, Sonia created her first 'simultaneous dresses', made out of squares and triangles of taffeta, tulle, flannelette, moiré, corded silk – anything that came to hand and all mixed together. There is a

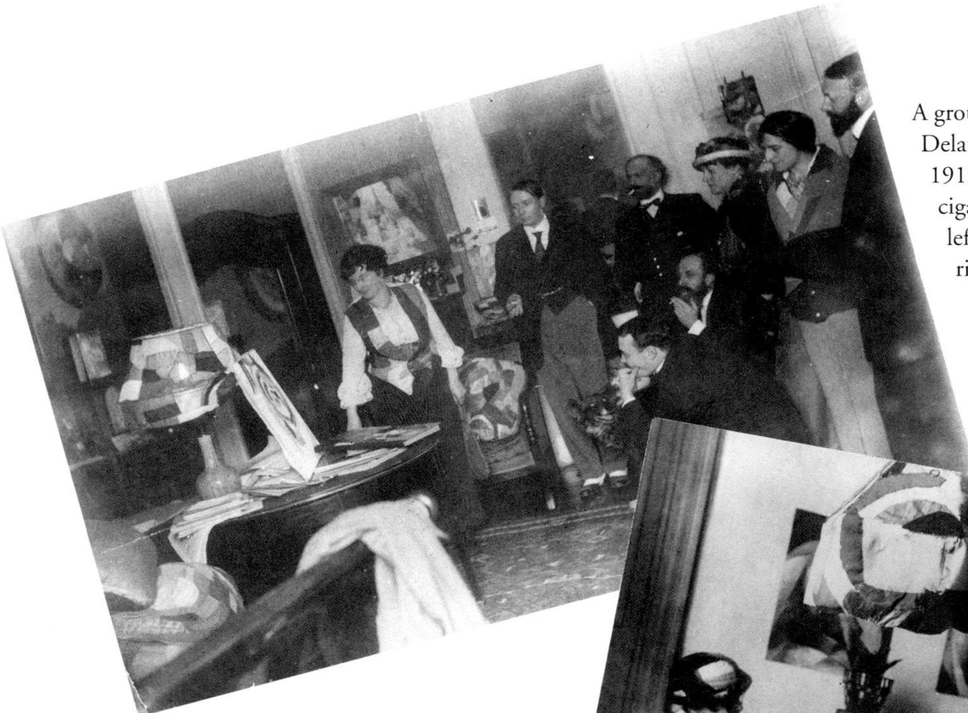

A group of friends in the Delaunays' apartment around 1913. Robert, with slick hair and cigarette, is second from the left, Sonia second from the right.

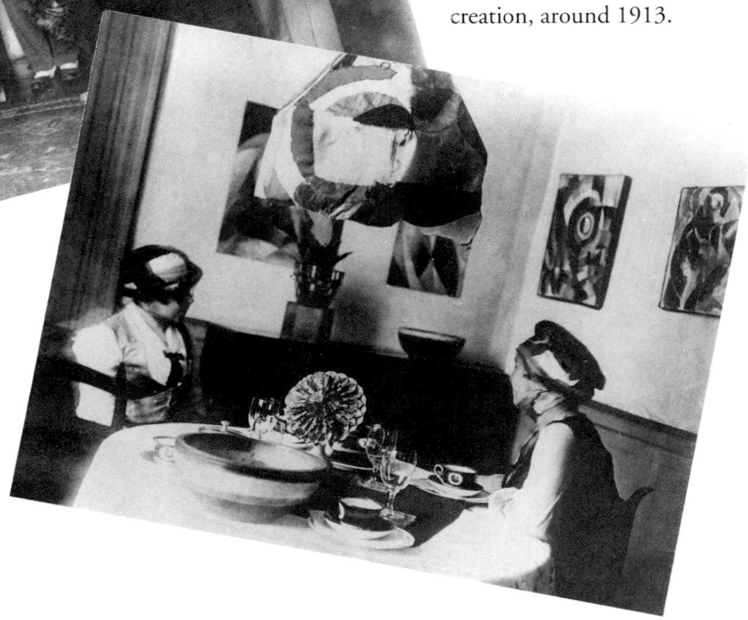

Sonia with a friend (Mme Zarrago) seated beneath a lampshade of her own creation, around 1913.

photograph of her wearing one of these dresses, which closely resembles the patchwork quilt she had made for Charles's bed. Their friend, the poet Apollinaire, wrote of her admiringly, in a violet-coloured suit 'with a wide belt of violet and green, and under the jacket a blouse divided into various zones of lively, pale or shaded colours. It combined old rose, orange-red, dark blue, scarlet, etc.'

Robert wore a red coat with blue collar, a green jacket, sky-blue waistcoat, a tiny red tie, black pants, red socks, black-and-yellow shoes. Sonia was not interested in the fashions of the day; nor was she out to create a new fashion. She simply wanted to brighten the art of clothing by re-using materials in various colour contexts.

She painted four versions of the Bal Bullier (all during 1912 and 1913), using mattress ticking because she could not afford canvas. The most famous

Right, the famous 'simultaneous dress' Sonia wore to the Bal Bullier; and an oil study for Sonia's first major painting, *Bal Bullier*, 1913. (See also colour plate 11.)

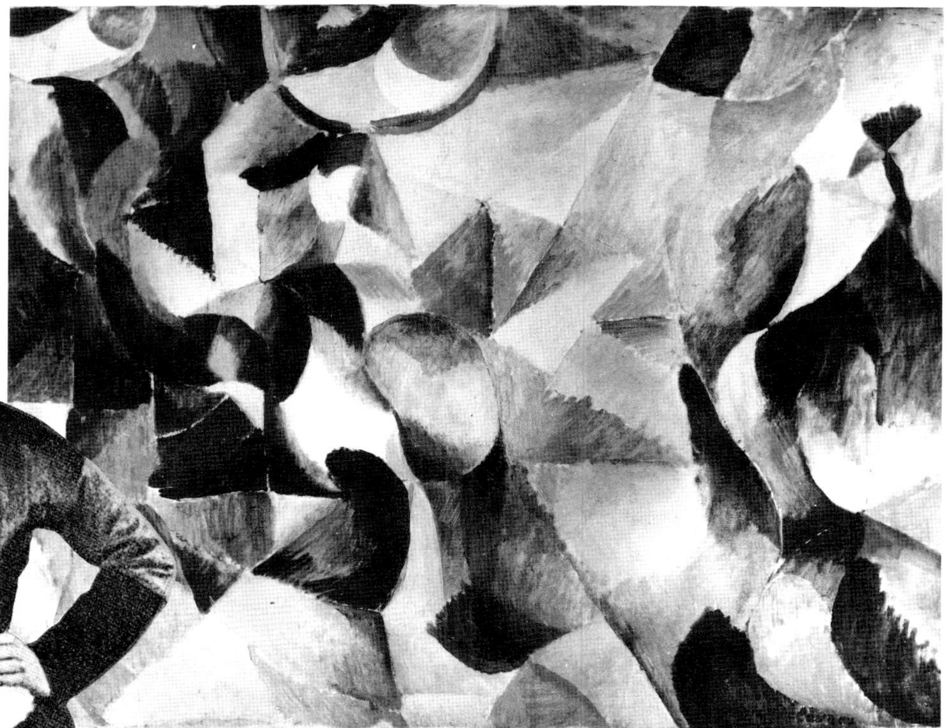

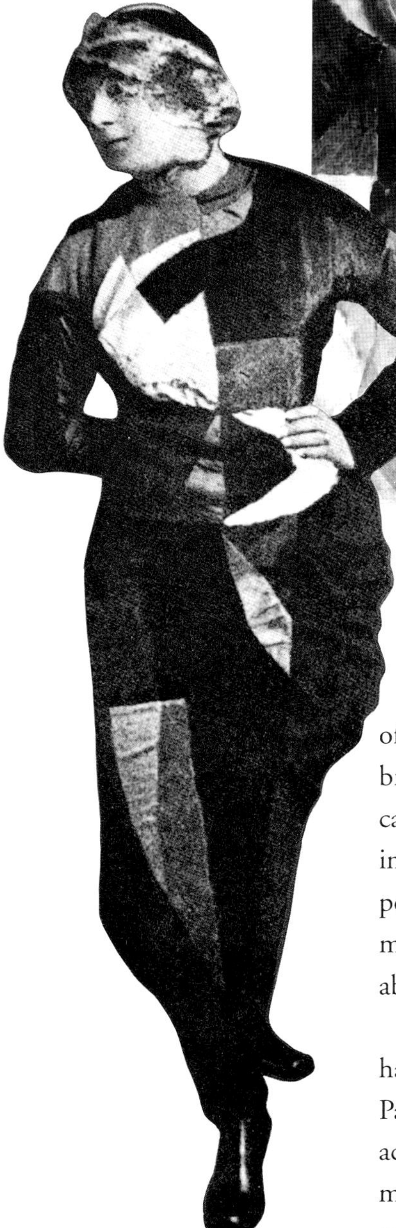

of the four is 3.90 metres wide, a kind of triptych in which she succeeded in breaking with the convention of portraying such scenes as if the dancers were caught in a frozen, immobile instant. Instead, her painting in itself gives the impression of movement – confusing, swirling, chaotic, even *noisy* in its juxtaposition of bright swaths of contrasting colours. Although one can just about make out the shapes of dancers, the painting can also be regarded as an abstract work.

Anyone standing in front of this supremely kinetic painting would have felt that Sonia had come a long way in the eight years since her arrival in Paris. It was difficult to find any direct relationship between this worldly and accomplished work and a painting of 1907 such as the *Philomène*. Then she may have been speaking the language of Gauguin, Van Gogh, even Matisse; now she had found her own.

CHAPTER 5

THE AVANT GARDE

Among the many talented people who became part of the Delaunays' inner circle, two were particularly important to them: Apollinaire and Cendrars. Oddly enough, both were foreigners who used pseudonyms. Wilhelm (or Guillaume) Apollinaire Albert Kostrowicki, born in Rome in 1880 of a Polish adventuress and an Italian army officer, was a poet of some standing when Robert Delaunay, not long before he met Sonia, first made his acquaintance. Apollinaire was an extremely versatile, gifted writer, and in the years before the war he contributed to and edited many short-lived reviews devoted to the new literature and art. Guided by his interests and his talents, he was in the very vortex of modern art, acquainted with all the leading explorers like Picasso, André Salmon, Max Jacob and Alfred Jarry. His introduction to the art of his times took place in 1904, when he met Derain and Vlaminck where they were working together in the outskirts of Paris; and in the next year appeared his first notices of Picasso. In his great poem of 1918, *La Jolie rousse*, he enunciated the fundamental view and aim of the avant-garde:

You whose mouths are made in the image of God's
Mouths which are order itself
Be indulgent when you compare
Us who seek adventure everywhere
To those who were the ideal of order

We are not your enemies
We want to offer you vast and strange domains
Where the blossoms of mystery are to be gathered
Where there are new fires of colours never seen
A thousand imponderable phantasms
Which we have to make real . . .

Apollinaire wrote art criticism for the newspaper *L'Intransigeant*, and his first public comments about Robert's work were far from warm; he wrote of this 'heresiarch of Cubism' (he himself published a collection of stories in 1910 under the title *L'Hérésiarque & Cie.*), whose paintings unfortunately seemed 'to recall an earthquake'. But only two years later, in his review of the Salon des Indépendants in 1912 (where both Robert and Sonia exhibited new works), he bowed to Robert's talent when choosing his huge *Ville de Paris* as the most important work in the exhibition. It was, he wrote, 'more than an artistic manifestation. This painting marks the advent of a conception of art lost since the great Italian painters.'

From that time on, the relationship between the two men, both keen to articulate their artistic ideals, became very close. Indeed, it was in the latter part of that year, 1912, that the *Mona Lisa* was stolen from the Louvre, and Apollinaire, who was sensationally accused of being involved in the theft, underwent a trial. After he was cleared of the charge, he took refuge in the Delaunays' studio in order to avoid harassment at his own address. Sonia and Robert had been in Villerville when the news of his arrest broke, and Robert jumped onto the first train to see what he could do.

According to Sonia, certain people who were called to give testimony at Apollinaire's trial behaved shabbily. In particular she cites Picasso, who was expected to give favourable evidence and instead claimed not to have known Apollinaire personally. It was a 'craven' action that she claimed never to forgive Picasso. Apollinaire seems to have been much less offended by whatever it was that Picasso had or had not said or done. In 1913, when the journal *Les Soirées de Paris* was re-launched with Apollinaire as its editor, its headquarters at 260 boulevard Raspail became a sort of club where Picasso, along with his friend Salmon and other cronies, would foregather from time to time. For the 1918 edition of Apollinaire's collection *Calligrammes*, a portrait of the poet by Picasso was used as frontispiece; and when Apollinaire married Jacqueline

Kolb on 2 May 1918, Picasso was one of two witnesses and gave the couple a Cubist watercolour of a guitarist as a present. By the same token, Apollinaire was a witness when Picasso married the dancer Olga Kokhlova at the *mairie* of the 7th Arrondissement two months later on 12 July.

Sonia, too, seems to have overcome the strong antipathy towards Picasso that she expressed in 1912. At any rate, she notes in her journal, without voicing any special displeasure, every time she runs into him. She records seeing him in January 1935 at an exhibition called *Artistes des Temps Présents*, where he, Matisse and a number of the leading painters of the day (including Robert) were showing recent work. In March of the same year she went to an exhibition of his 'papiers collés' and found that those works had 'aged well'. Again, on 20 January 1936, she went to a show at Paul Rosenberg's gallery of works by Matisse, Braque and Picasso. She thought Picasso's still-life was very good; Braque's too. 'If the qualities of each were joined, it would make a very good picture indeed.' Such was her thought as she left and saw Picasso driving off in his car. He waved to her.

But after viewing another show at Rosenberg's gallery in November 1936, in which works by Matisse, Léger, Braque, Utrillo, Rouault and of course Picasso were included, she felt they were 'all like old pictures in the museums'. Whereas a Van Gogh, which was being photographed in a private part of the gallery, was, she thought, 'magnificent – like life and youth'.

In February 1945, before the armistice but in liberated Paris, she saw Picasso and Paul Eluard come into a restaurant on the boulevard Saint-Germain where she was just finishing her lunch. 'Picasso recognized me, and we spoke for a moment . . . When I first saw them I wasn't sure, Picasso's eyes weren't piercing, they have become light.' Eluard seemed to her older than Picasso, 'who is grey, almost white, whereas the other is entirely white.' In 1946, she remarks on the colour of Picasso's hair again. On turning into the rue Miromesnil from the Métro, she meets Picasso with 'his hair all white', on his arm a young girl of twenty with flowing light blond hair; 'We said hello, he said he was happy to see me, was almost affectionate.'

At these later meetings, she seems to be in slight awe of Picasso, almost proud and flattered to be recognized by him, even though she could write at the same time that he was 'démodé by modern art'. If she was in some insignificant way jealous of Picasso's precocious and continued success, she would not have been alone.

7 The 'Cubist' bed cover Sonia designed in 1911 for Charles's crib. (Musée National d'Art Moderne, Paris)

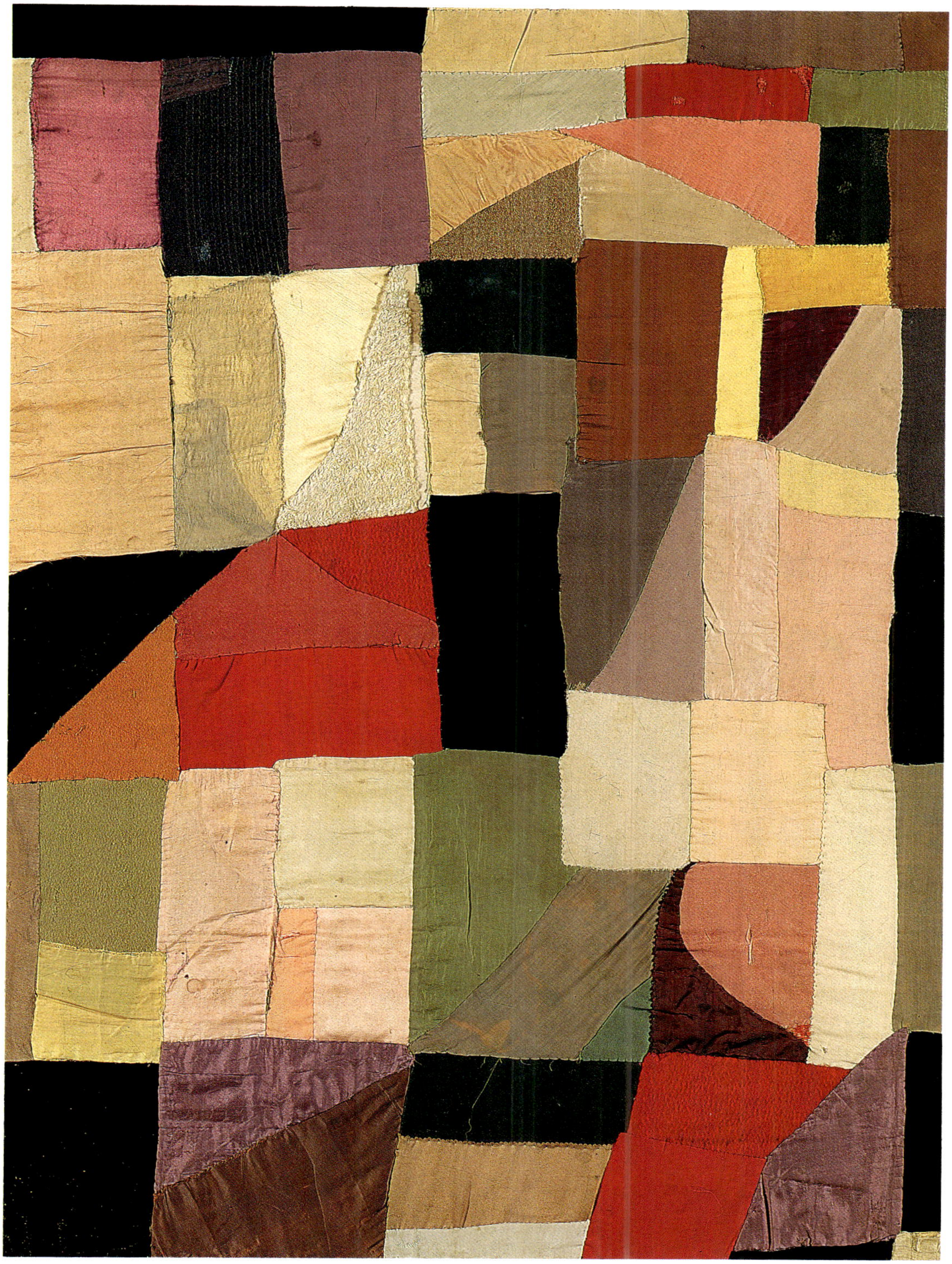

8 A toy box decorated by Sonia for her son in 1911.

9 Below, end papers of Sonia's binding for Blaise Cendrars' poem *Pâques à New York*, 1912.

10 Opposite, cover designed by Sonia of fabrics in 1912 for a book by the Italian writer Ricciotto Canudo, who frequented the avant garde circles in Paris.

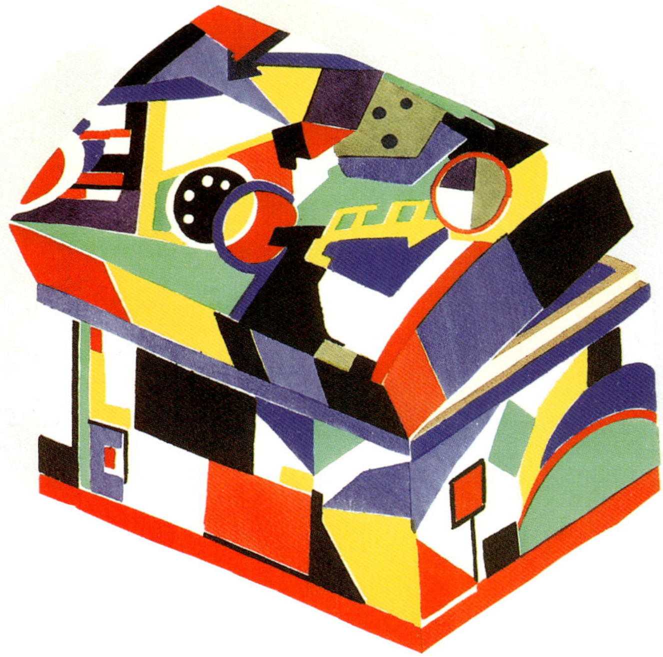

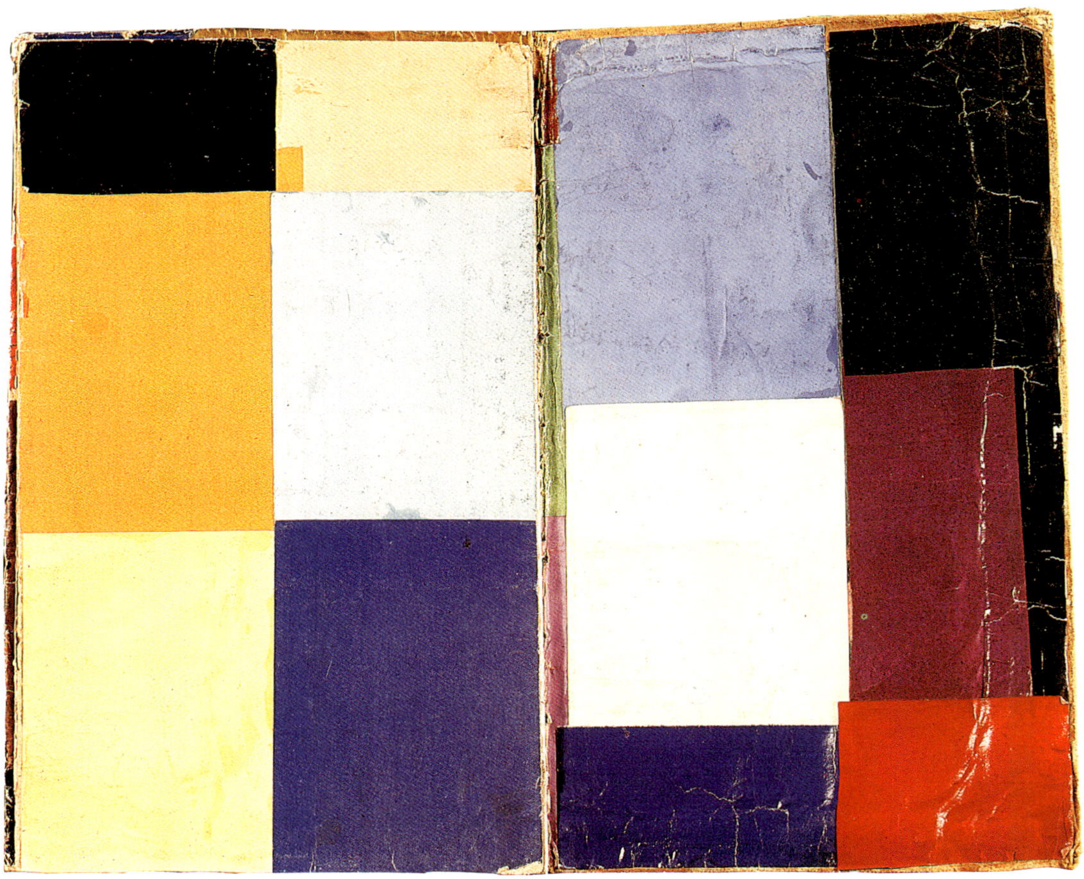

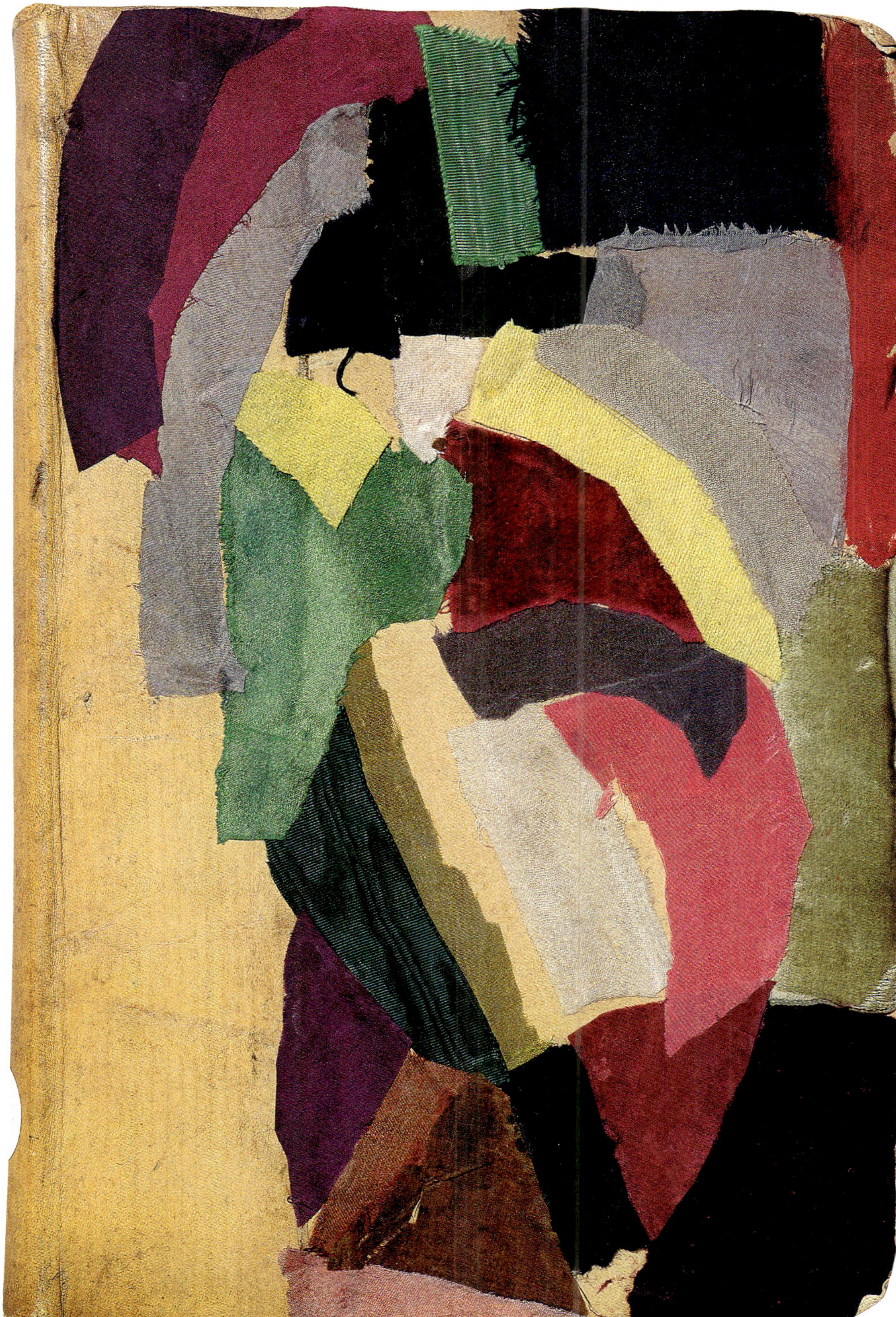

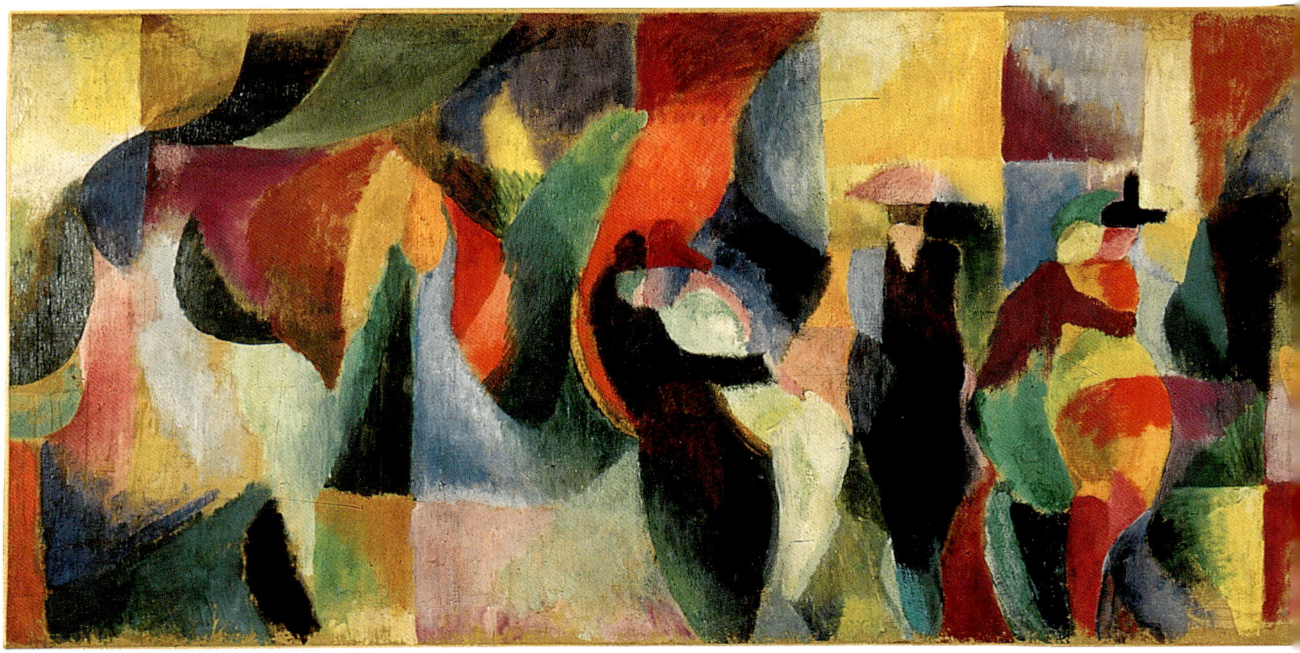

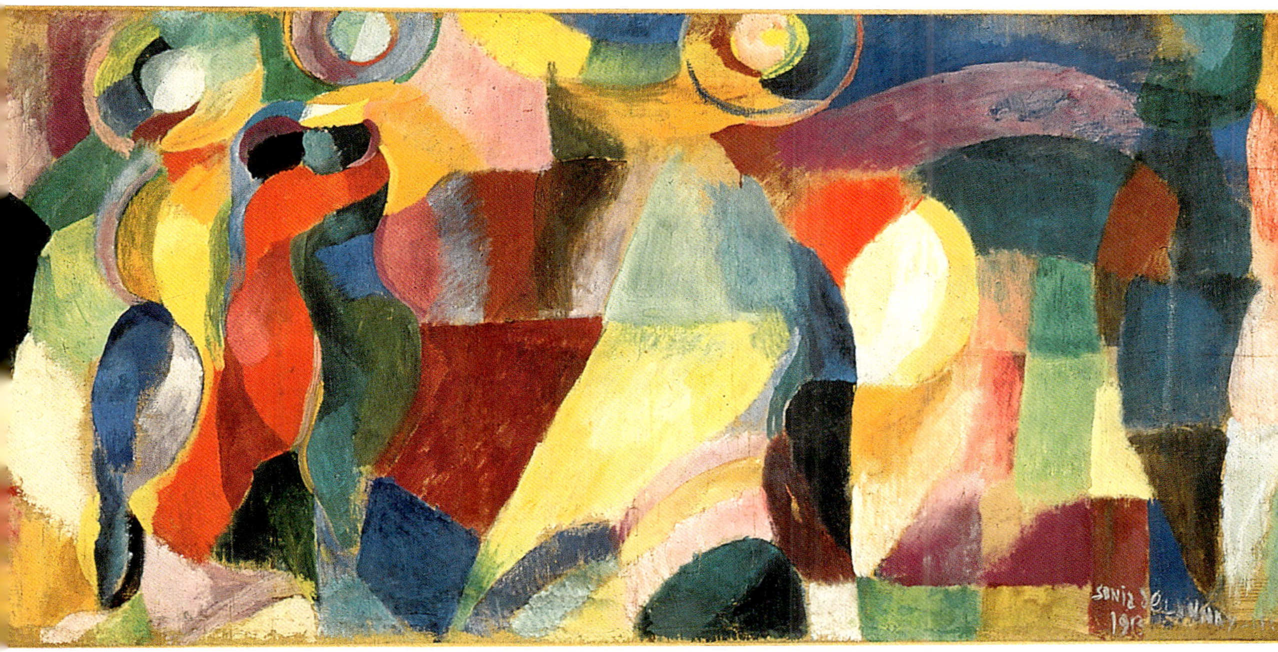

11 The masterpiece of Sonia's early period: *Bal Bullier*, oil on mattress ticking, 1913. She painted four versions in all of this subject; this is the largest and most fully integrated – a prime example of Orphic Cubism.

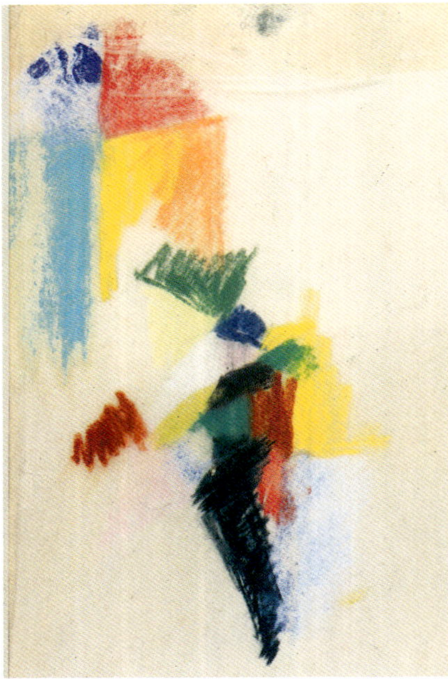

12 Project for a 'simultaneous dress', 1914.

13 Below, one of various paintings called 'Electric Prism' done by Sonia in 1914 before the departure for Spain. (Musée National d'Art Moderne, Paris)

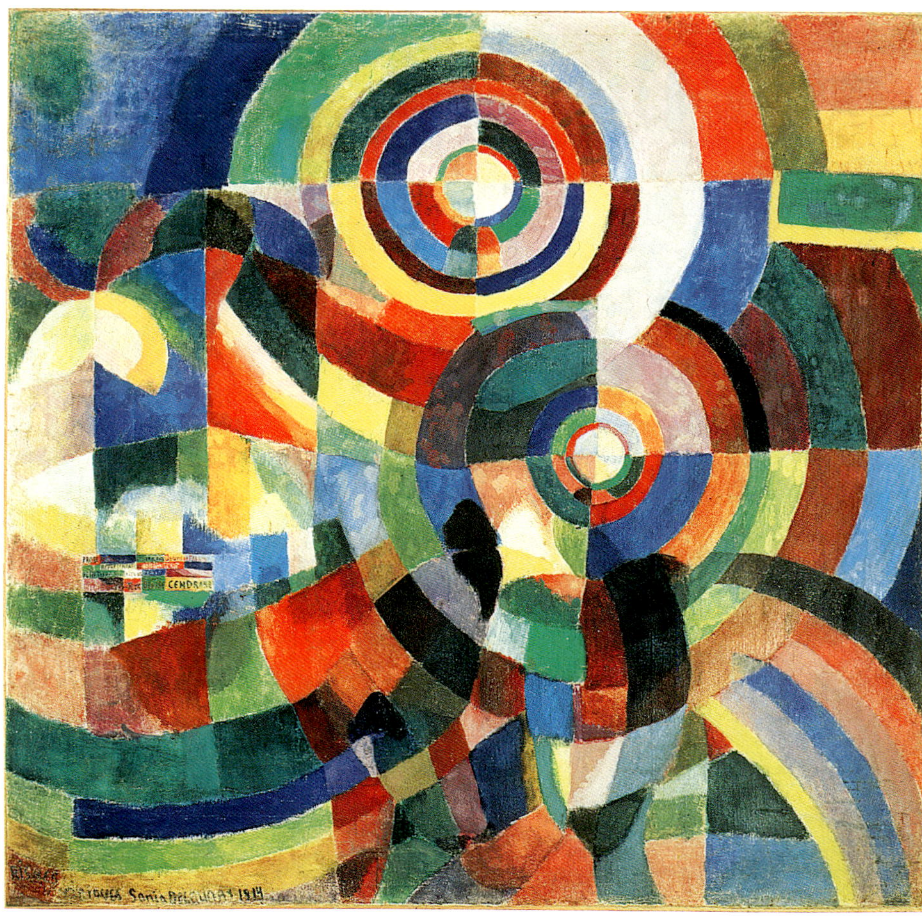

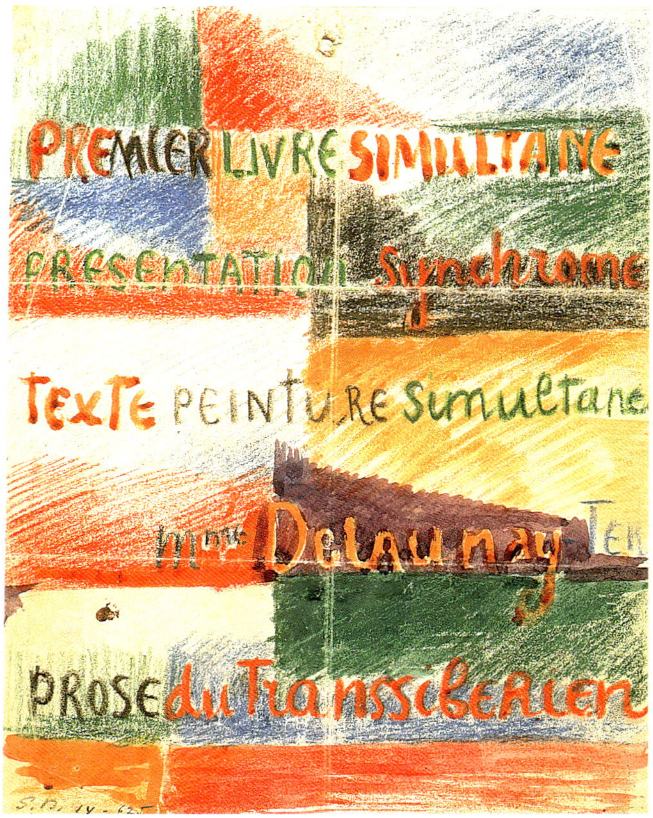

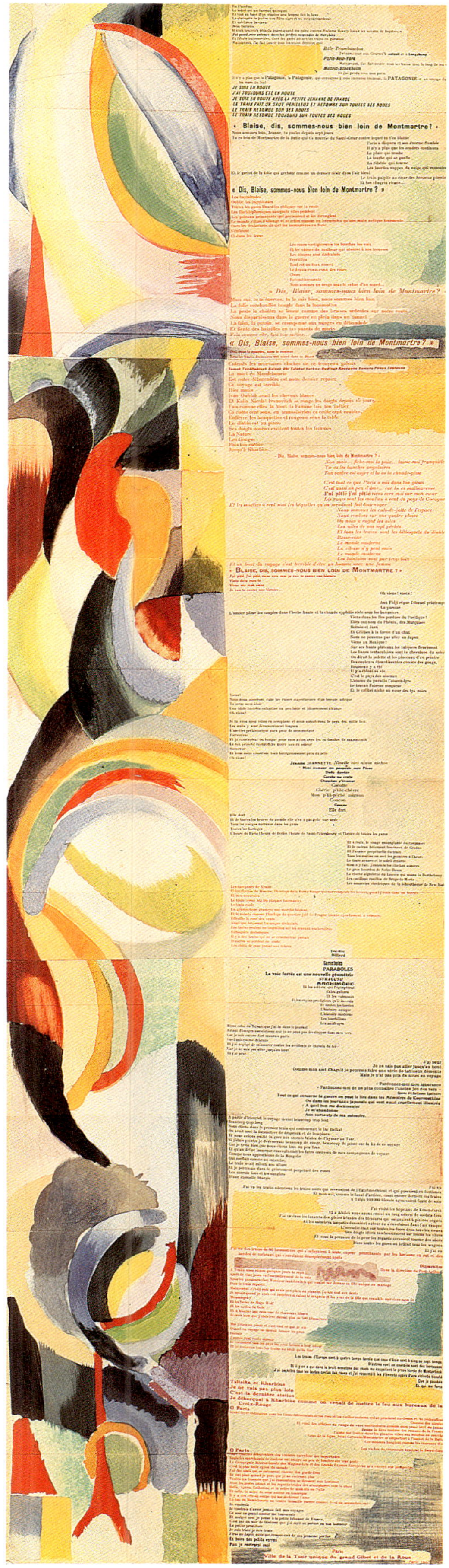

14,15 Above, unfolding publicity design for *La Prose du Transsibérien et de la Petite Jeanne de France*, Sonia's collaboration with Cendrars in 1913 (watercolour and pencil on paper); and right, the 'simultaneous book' (folded-out poem with decorations) itself.

16 *Liqueur*, gouache publicity project, 1916.

17 Below left, poster design for a gas cooker 'Le Rêve', collage, 1922.

18 Below, poster design for the watchmakers Zenith, with text by Cendrars; paper collage, 1914.

19 Bottom, *Chocolat*, publicity project, encaustic on paper, 1919.

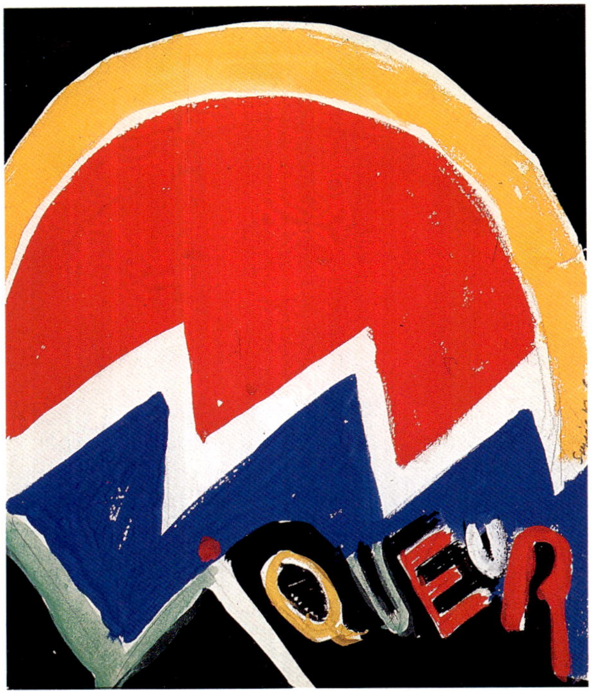

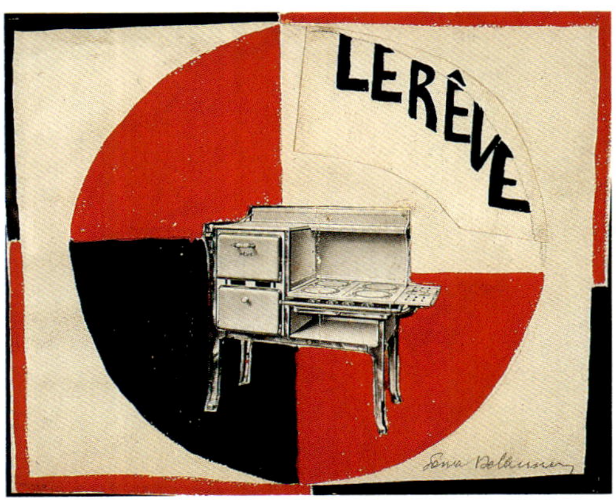

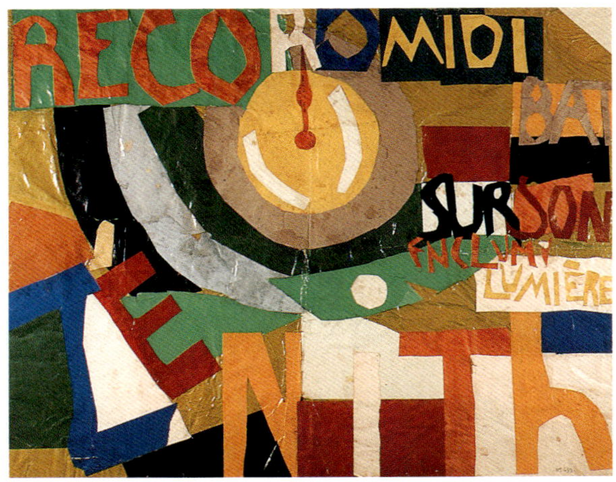

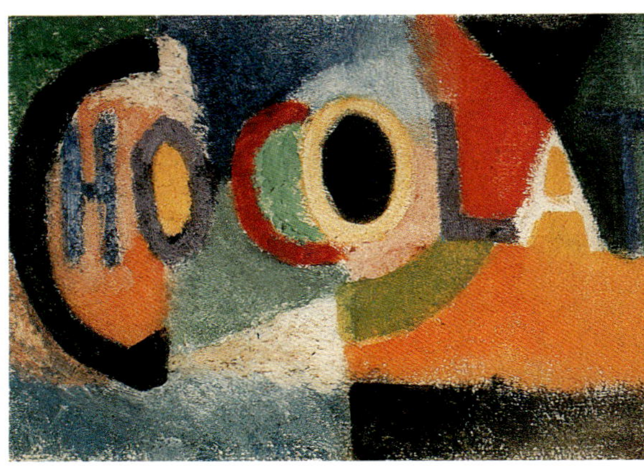

CHAPTER 6

WORKING WITH BLAISE CENDRARS

It was Apollinaire who invented the term 'Orphism' to describe the Delaunays' version of Cubism, and though it was never particularly appropriate or enlightening it is a label which has survived. Apollinaire considered that it described the rhythmic elements in Delaunay's Cubist work and first used it during a trip to Berlin he and Robert took together in January 1913, not long after he had emerged from his hideaway in the rue des Grands-Augustins.

In December 1912 he moved into a new apartment in the boulevard Saint-Germain, and received his friends there on Wednesdays. On one of these occasions, Sonia noticed a delicate blond young man, who turned out to be Blaise Cendrars, recently returned from a trip to the United States. Born in Switzerland and given the name Frédéric Louis Sauser, Cendrars was an inveterate traveller to foreign places; he was settled for the time being in Paris and had recently written a poem called *Pâques à New York*. When she learned that he lived only a few houses away from them, Sonia invited him to call. The day after they met, he brought them a small book – his *Pâques*.

This work, dated 'New York April 1912', is a long poem (207 verses) of freely rhyming couplets, which comprises in effect a personal address to Christ on the day of Easter, and all that that is meant to signify. It is not surprising that the name of Walt Whitman has been invoked to describe Cendrars' style, for the *Pâques* has a good deal of Whitman's long arching

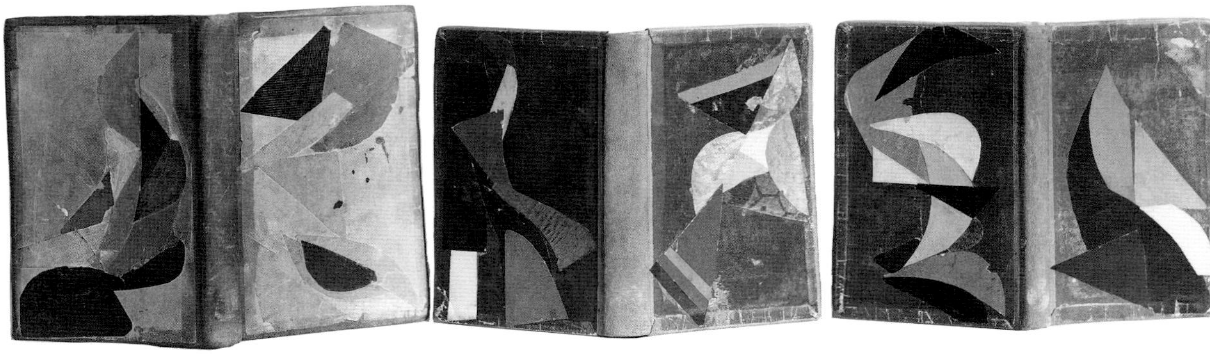

Collage bookbindings made by Sonia in 1913 for works by Jules Romains and Rimbaud.

phrases, lyrical egotism and breadth of allusion. The New York setting is realistic, grim, even painful, with its references to poor Jews and Chinamen and prostitutes, as well as to its destitute narrator/author; but it also carries the emotional religious weight of a wary sceptic straining to understand the miracle.

With her usual gusto when anything original and unexpected was concerned, Sonia read the first few lines, which gave off, as she says, 'a fresh breath of air', and rushed off to a shop in nearby rue Dauphine where she bought all the ingredients for a binding that she imagined for the booklet. Onto a piece of chamois she pasted down pieces of paper; and for the inside of the binding she did the same with large squares of coloured paper. For her it was 'a plastic response to the beauty of the poem.'

From that first day, Cendrars became one of their best friends – a dedicated person who lived poetry in the way that she and Robert lived painting. He became such a constant presence in their lives that Apollinaire even showed signs of jealousy, though in fact Cendrars seems to have been much more Sonia's friend, just as Apollinaire was Robert's.

Soon after this relationship began, Cendrars brought Sonia a work of his called *La Prose du Transsibérien et de La Petite Jehanne de France*, another long poem showing a different aspect of his talent. Here the verses are not rhymed and vary erratically in length; in fact, the poem is an exercise in fragmented thoughts, incidents and references – elements which make one think less of *Leaves of Grass* and more of *The Waste Land*.

The framework of this ambitious poem, in one sense a hymn to trains, is indeed a journey on the Transsiberian Express, as it came to be called, from

Moscow to the port of Harbin on the Pacific coast. Starting from a quick impressionistic description of Moscow ('the Kremlin like an immense Tartar gateau/Encrusted with gold'), Cendrars proceeds to offer bits of autobiography ('I spent my childhood in the hanging gardens of Babylon/I've also attended the races at Auteuil and Longchamp/Paris–New York') and descriptions of what can be seen from the train windows, all intertwined with glancing references to his encyclopaedic knowledge of the world's places and products – from Fiji to Hugo Wolf to the Land of Cockayne, 'Pforzheim jewellery' and 'bottle openers from Sheffield'. His travelling companion is the young Jeanne, known only from her recurring line: 'Tell me, Blaise, are we very far from Montmartre?' Yes, they are very far indeed from Montmartre and farther every day, advancing their watches as they go: 'The train goes forward, the sun goes back.' The poem is steeped in nostalgia for Paris and towards the end for the prostitute back there in Montmartre, Jehanne of the title.

Sonia's great friend, the poet Blaise Cendrars.

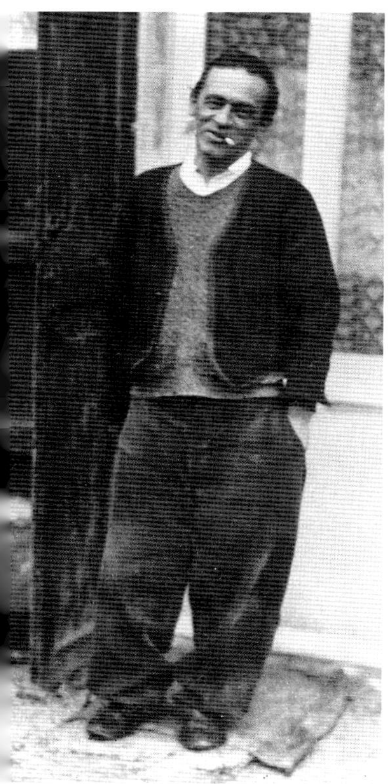

This dense, detailed outpouring of an adventurous man's mind evoked in Sonia the desire to create something which would be in effect a merging of text and design in terms of simultaneous contrast. The means by which this was achieved was to create an accordion type of book, 2 meters long, which could be unfolded and read from top to bottom, shapes and words blending into each other and drenched in bright colours. It was printed in pochoir and sold by subscription, on the basis of a brilliant advertising leaflet Sonia designed, using the name Mme Delaunay-Terk. It finally appeared in November 1913 and created a stir among the intellectual critics, many of whom were derisive of this 'first simultaneous book'. Letters for and against, signed and anonymous, appeared in journals like *Paris-Journal* and *Gil Blas*. Cendrars was even accused of plagiarism. Apollinaire tried to have the last word, in an article he wrote for *Soirées de Paris*: 'Blaise Cendrars and Madame Delaunay-Terck [sic] have made a first attempt at simultaneity of writing and colour contrasts, training the eye to read at a single glance the whole of a poem, as an orchestra conductor reads the superimposed notes in a score with a single look, as one sees with one look the plastic and printed elements of a poster.'

La Prose du Transsibérien no longer seems as revolutionary as it did at the time – just as it is difficult to understand why Stravinsky's *Le Sacre du Printemps* should have caused a near-riot at its first performance in 1913. But

La Prose du Transsibérien is still impressive in its daring inventiveness, its wit and its creative energy.

Though it has become a highly sought-after book by collectors, in its own time it was little more than a *succès de scandale*. The original plan had been to produce 150 copies of the work, but it appears that far fewer were completed. The inspiration for the strange and unique format is said to have come from the fascination of the Delaunays for the Eiffel Tower. The Tower is in fact represented in Sonia's design; it appears in red opposite the final line of Cendrars' poem. Robert calculated that if all the copies originally planned had been printed and bound, they would have equalled the height of the Tower itself if opened out one above the other!

Sonia prepared an oil painting for the large work, and evidently a watercolour sketch in addition. Besides its importance as a demonstration of simultaneous colours, the text is composed in more than ten different type faces, which makes it a rare experiment in typography. Cendrars wrote in the German art journal *Der Sturm*: 'Mme Delaunay has made such a beautiful book of colours that my poem is more soaked in colour than my life. That's what makes me happy.'

Many years later – in 1954 – Cendrars wrote in an article in the journal *Arts*: 'In those days, painters and writers were equal. We lived mixed up together with more or less the same preoccupations. You could even say that

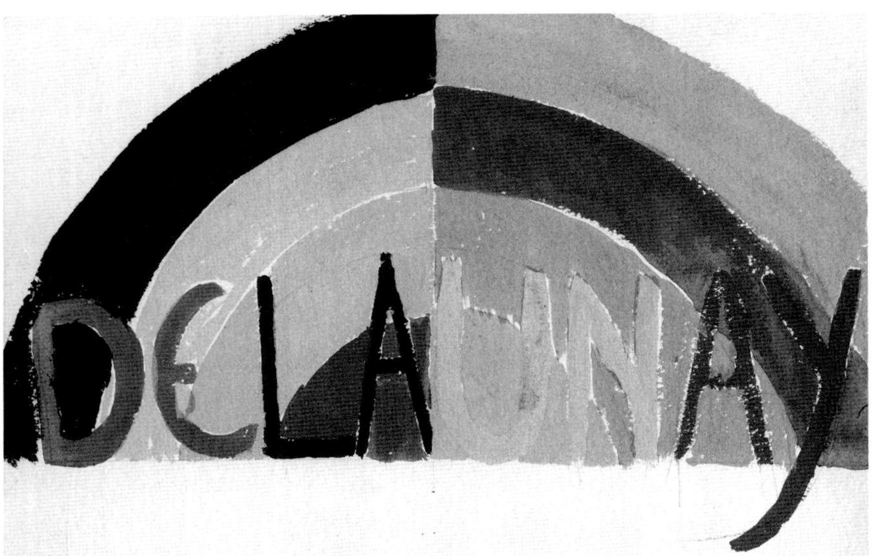

A letterhead designed by Sonia in 1913.

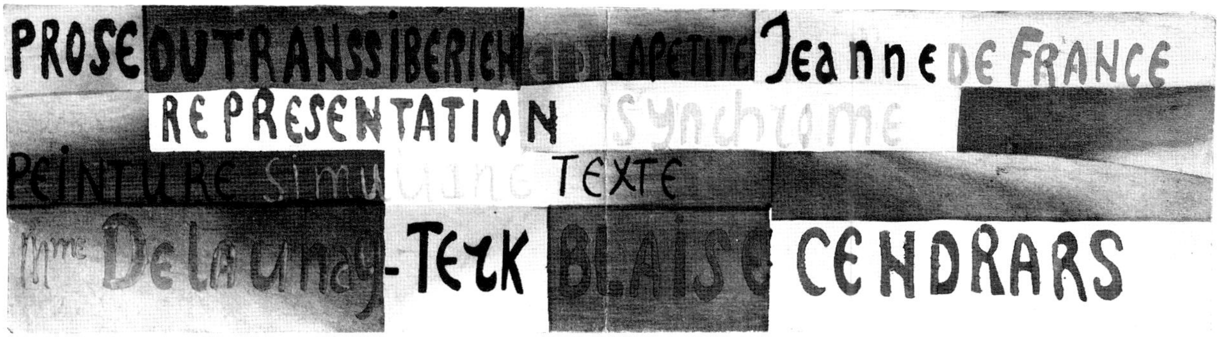

Sonia's arresting advertising leaflet for the fold-out 'simultaneous' book *La Prose du Transsibérien et de La Petite Jehanne de France*, 1913. (See also colour plate 15.)

each writer had his painter. I had Delaunay and Léger, Picasso had Max Jacob, Reverdy had Braque, and Apollinaire had everybody.'

In general, Sonia found that her poet friends were quick to understand how she worked and what she sought to express in her work. As her painting became less and less representational, it was the poets (and not the art critics) who saw that her aim was not to reduce abstract art to an intellectual preference. For her, the abstract and the sensuous had to 'marry', as she puts it. But the self-styled 'abstract artists' did not follow her lead: they tended to cut themselves off from life and its natural rhythms.

At about the same time that Sonia's completely original collaboration with Cendrars was being discussed in Paris, she was exhibiting, along with Robert, at the first *Herbstsalon* (Autumn Salon) in Berlin. Sonia sent four paintings, as well as a good sampling of her work in the applied arts: the cover for Cendrars' *Pâques*, a large toy chest she had painted for Charles, 'simultaneous' dresses, posters, etc. It has often been related that Paul Klee was so impressed by the way Sonia had used squares of colour for the end-papers of her binding of Cendrars' book that it proved an enduring influence on his own work.

Shortly after this *Herbstsalon*, a show was organized by Herwarth Walden at the gallery in Berlin called Der Sturm after the journal of that name, in which the works of both Delaunays were given a room of their own. It was to the catalogue of this exhibition that Apollinaire contributed his poem *Les Fenêtres*, alluding to Robert's series of Cubist paintings of the same title: a variety of views of Paris rooftops framed by a window. Apollinaire later described the poem as deriving from 'a completely new aesthetic'.

Both Sonia and Robert were more highly regarded by German artists and critics than they were by their French counterparts. One of the first friends Sonia made the year she arrived in Paris, Elisabeth Epstein, knew the painter Kandinsky and brought him together with the Delaunays. Kandinsky was the leading force behind the group of painters, including August Macke, Franz Marc and Alexei von Jawlensky, who banded together in Munich under the name of 'Der Blaue Reiter'. Though it is clear in their work that they derived many of their aims from the Fauves, who had been using colour 'as an expressive value in its own right', they became excited about Delaunay's work as well and visited him individually in Paris. In a letter written to Marc in January 1913, Robert enunciated the artistic credo that governed his work until his death: 'I have no artistic belief except in the representation of nature through light.'

At the first joint exhibition of Der Blaue Reiter in 1911 at the Thannhauser Gallery in Munich, he showed five paintings (among them *La Tour, Saint Séverin* and *La Ville de Paris*); and on 20 December, Kandinsky wrote to tell him that the *Saint Séverin* (he painted the nave of that church in several different versions) had been sold, and that there was a potential sale for his 'small' *Ville de Paris.*

In 1912 an article devoted to Robert appeared in the almanac Der Blaue Reiter, published in Munich by Reinhard Piper; and during that year he was visited by Marc, who became enthusiastic about his *Fenêtre* paintings and wrote to Kandinsky that Robert was 'eliminating representation altogether: pure fugues of sound, one might say.' Klee, who had exhibited with the Blaue Reiter painters, also called on Robert in the rue des Grands-Augustins studio; then in January 1913 he translated into German an essay Robert had written, *On Light.*

Until World War I, Delaunay received letters regularly from Macke and Marc, both of whom were to be killed in action. In spite of all these activities and ferment and the interrelations among these various artists, it must be remembered that none of them was well-known or even recognized, except by a handful of forward-looking critics (such as Apollinaire), in their own lifetimes. It was the rump of the established nineteenth-century Salon painters, many of whom in both Germany and France survived into the 1920s, who were still the market leaders.

CHAPTER 7

INTO WORLD WAR I

According to Sonia, Robert had a wild temper and engaged in quarrels which she calls 'epic'. It might have been his 'eruptive violence' which won her over to him in the first place. Once they were married, however, she sought to smoothe away his sharp edges and made herself the moderator who could prevent his falling out with all their friends. She has no hesitation or evident regrets in saying that, from the day they lived together, she put herself in the background and never appeared in the foreground until the 1950s (he died in October 1941). As she saw it, Robert had the brilliance, the nonchalance of genius; she was deeper.

Early on in their life together she recognized that their temperaments were opposed; but they needed to react together to the conditions of life and to communicate their emotions to one another. Though they often went their own ways in their art, there were many things they absorbed and learned together. For example, walking arm in arm they experienced for the first time the electric lamplights that replaced the gas ones on the boulevard Saint-Michel in 1913. Robert became extraordinarily excited when he saw the halo which their bulbs produced; to him it resembled the halo he sometimes saw around the moon. This made such an impression on them both that Sonia began to paint her abstract *Electric Prisms* and Robert his *Disks, moon and sun.* In Sonia's case, she made any number of sketches for the prism paintings, many of them done on the spot with coloured crayons on lined paper. She was putting down what she saw passing on the sidewalks, but she was more interested in the movements of colours than in the mere night-time comings and goings of people in the Latin Quarter. At the same time she made very rapid sketches that indicated the varied effects of artificial lighting. Gradually she merged these two forms of notation, expunging anything that could be read as figurative, so that she ended up with a brilliantly coloured composition of curved stripes and circles with prismatic qualities – oil paintings which bear a distinct family resemblance to Robert's major painting of 1914, *Hommage à Blériot*, his tribute to the French aviator who in 1909 was the first man to fly in his own machine across the English Channel.

Both of them were also influenced in different ways by what they saw every day all over Paris. Robert began to include fragments of public advertising placards in his paintings, and continued to work on numerous versions of the Eiffel Tower, that incarnation of modernity. In 1912, he was stimulated by a photograph in a newspaper to paint his Rugby picture, *L'Equipe de Cardiff*, into which he introduced various symbols of contemporary life: an airplane, the Eiffel Tower, a ferris wheel, billboards. As for Sonia, she actually sketched out a number of poster designs for a firm called Zenith (with words provided by Cendrars). She may well have been struck by the posters of Capiello for Zenith watches which had appeared in 1912, and no doubt dreamt of seeing her new simultaneous posters succeed Capiello's, or even the ones Chéret created for Dubonnet, on the walls of Paris. As it turned out, her designs were not taken up.

Those pre-war years were heady ones for the young Delaunays. They appeared to accomplish miracles of work: not only *La Prose du Transsibérien*, but those endless sketches for Sonia's *Electric Prisms* and other paintings entitled *Tango-Magic City* and *Simultaneous Solar Prism*; and patient hours in preparing Robert's huge *Hommage à Blériot*, complete with the whirling of propellors. Though they lived, talked and dreamt art, they had a wide and vivid social life. Except in the most rigid bourgeois circles, they were social lions, members of the energetic, sparkling milieu of modern experimental artists and writers. Their outsized paintings were shown in the Salon des Indépendants. The critics paid attention to them, either with praise or disdain.

It was in 1913, too, that the famous Armory Show opened in New York and introduced most American art lovers to their first shock of European modernity. Robert had been invited to exhibit, presumably through the

Prisme électrique,
oil on canvas, 1913.

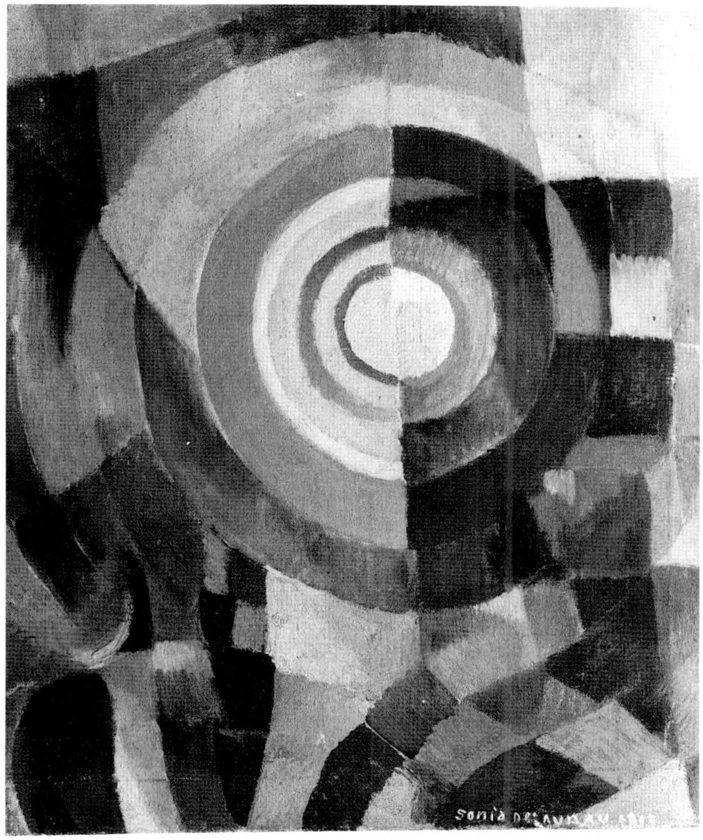

efforts of the American painter, Samuel Halpert, himself an exhibitor, who was an admirer of the Delaunays and had been a friend of Robert's since the early days in Brittany. After a committee from New York called on him in Paris, Robert shipped over three of his paintings, including the important *Ville de Paris* that had made a splash at the Salon des Indépendants the year before. For a variety of reasons of ill-will, and perhaps because of its dimensions – 2.67 by 4.06 m. (9 x 13 ft) – the organizers refused at the last minute to show it. Halpert wrote to Robert about the incident on 18 February 1913, and pointed out that the organizers had also managed to infuriate other contributors, who had consequently withdrawn their works. (Indeed, all the Italian Futurists had elected not to be represented.) 'I never thought for a moment that the picture would not be hung,' wrote Halpert. 'It is really disgusting to invite a canvas and then not hang it.' And he implied that there was some malicious motive behind it.

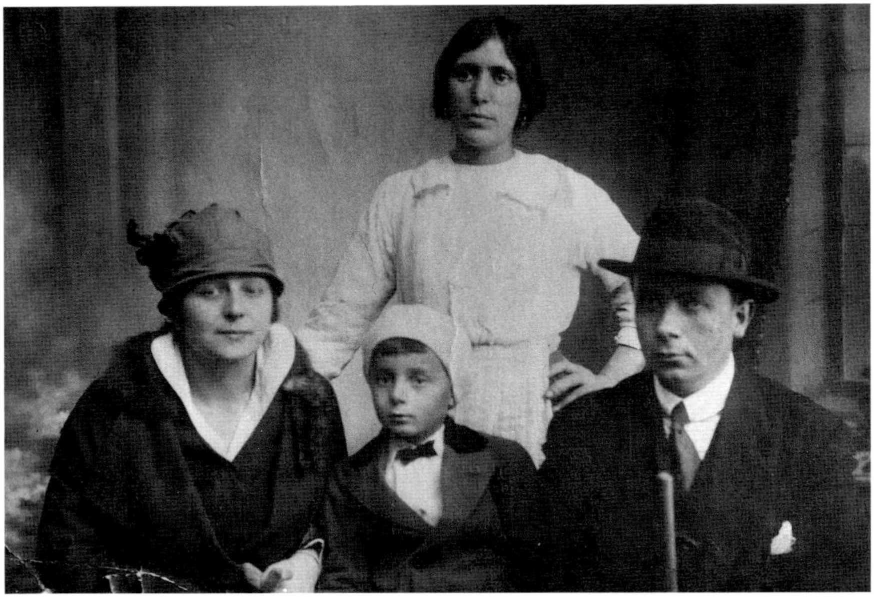

Sonia, Charles and Robert (with a servant, Béatrice) in Vigo, Spain, 1916.

The affair so enraged Delaunay that he instructed Halpert to see to it that none of his paintings was exhibited, but by then it was too late. The committee insisted on including the other two pictures (*Route de Laon* and *Les Fenêtres sur la ville*) while the show was on in New York; when it travelled to Boston and Chicago, however, Delaunay succeeded in withdrawing all three of his works. What is interesting and indicative of the lack of esteem for her work is that Sonia was not even invited to show any of her paintings.

During the summers, they rented villas in the country or used one belonging to the Damours who had brought Robert up; there they would entertain their band of friends, listen to Apollinaire or Cendrars recite their poems, and – above all – paint or make bookbindings or collages or anything at hand that could be decorated. In the spring of 1913 they were in Louveciennes, in the outskirts of Paris, renting a pretty house with the sister of Paul Poiret, the leading couturier of the day, and another couple. Children and nursemaids were included in the vacation. Even during the time they were there, however, the Thursday visits to the Bal Bullier were not suspended. Louveciennes was close enough for them to drive into Paris and back again the same evening.

Another visitor to Louveciennes in 1913 was Georges Yakulov, who had made a reputation as a theatre set designer in Russia. During that summer he worked on a painting called *Composition* which the critic Michel Hoog sees as related to Robert's *Fenêtre* paintings and Sonia's *Solar Prisms,* all of them done in the same period.

The next year they were persuaded by a friend who was the wife of the head of the French Railways to visit Spain. She had three children of her own, and had convinced Sonia that the change of air, the sunshine and bathing in the sea would be good for Charles, who was two and a half years old. They started out in Madrid, where they shared an apartment with this friend, who was Robert's blond model for the painting he began there, *Femme nue lisant* (Nude Woman Reading). By misfortune, Charles caught typhoid fever from one of the servants, and Sonia found herself looking after both of them. Sonia

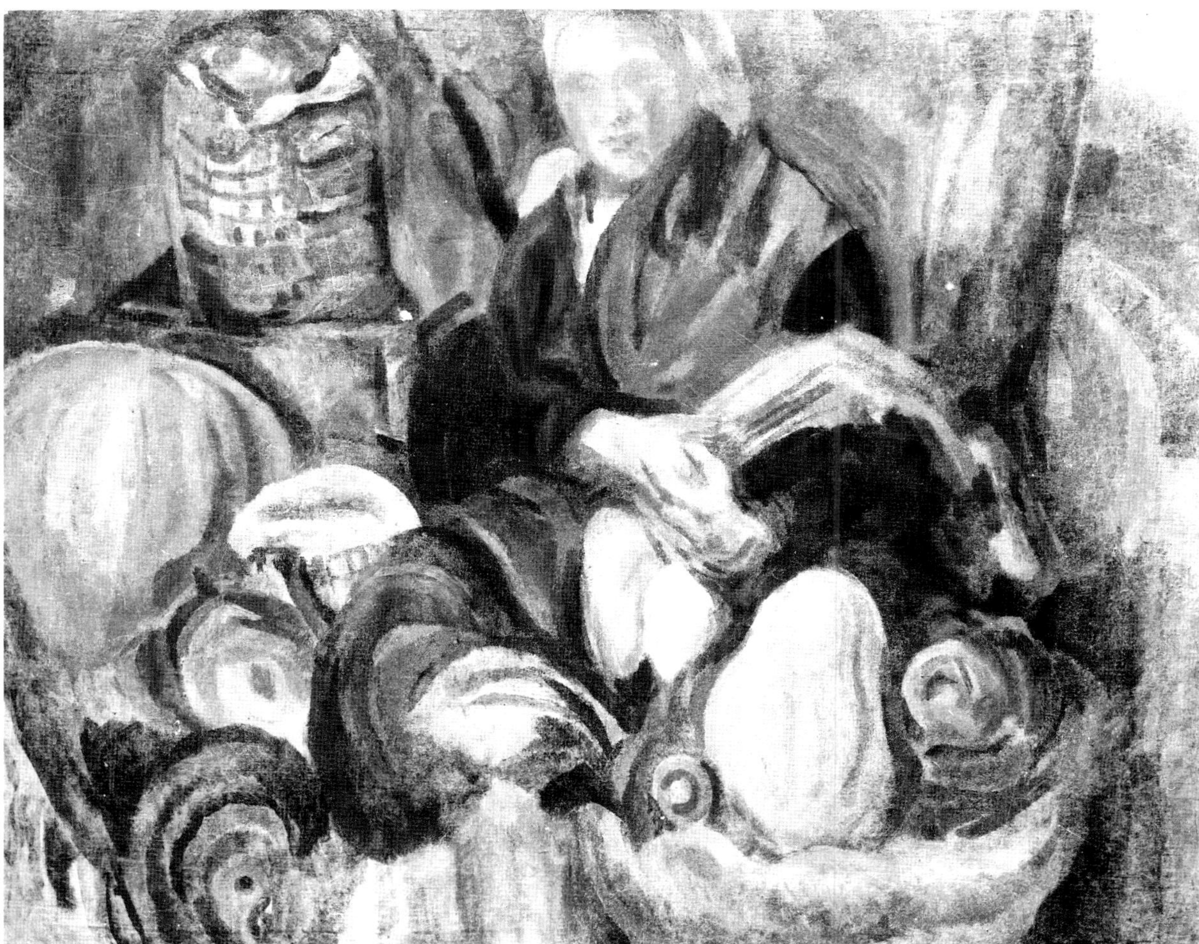

Market, a study from nature, encaustic on canvas, Portugal, 1916.

says that, although Robert was a devoted father, he had no talent for dealing with children; therefore, once the boy was out of danger, she and Robert went to the seaside Basque town of Fuenterrabia, in order to be alone together and rest. It was there in early August that they heard of Germany's declaration of war against France.

As in the case of most people in those circumstances, drastic changes took place in their lives. Since Robert had been officially declared physically ineligible for military service a few years earlier, he was not faced with the threat of mobilization. It seemed to them both that they might well remain in Spain and sit out the war at a distance from the action. Sonia returned briefly to Paris in order to make arrangements for their absence from the studio; but when she returned to Fuenterrabia, she found that Robert had suddenly become blocked in his work. He was suffering from the excessive heat and simply could not paint there. By good fortune they were led by Sam Halpert and another friend, the Portuguese artist Edouardo Vianna, to a village on the north coast of Portugal called Vila da Condo.

The moment they arrived, Sonia fell in love with the place, which was isolated and beautiful. She became drunk with the colours and began to paint at once, as Robert and Vianna did. They could paint peacefully there from morning to night.

It was living in the Iberian peninsula that opened their eyes to an entirely different light. As Sonia writes about it, she notes that all painters have studied light, but light placed against objects – a completely descriptive light – whereas she and Robert attacked the very origin of light, the sun and the moon themselves. The prism of colours they worked out from these sources was 'like a bomb' in the history of painting. What they learned from their experiences was that colour has a dynamic power, a life of its own, which always changes under the influence of other colours that act on it. That was where simultaneous contrast had finally led them.

Sonia wrote later of the Iberian episode that it was six years of happiness. She found that 'the light was not intense, but it made all the colours more exciting . . . giving the impression that one was in a country of dreams.' During the Portuguese visit they painted the local women who looked after them, the plants and flowers in their garden, the still-lifes composed of ducks and vegetables, which reminded Sonia of the Ukraine and which they ate afterwards. She had also become interested in Flamenco singers while in

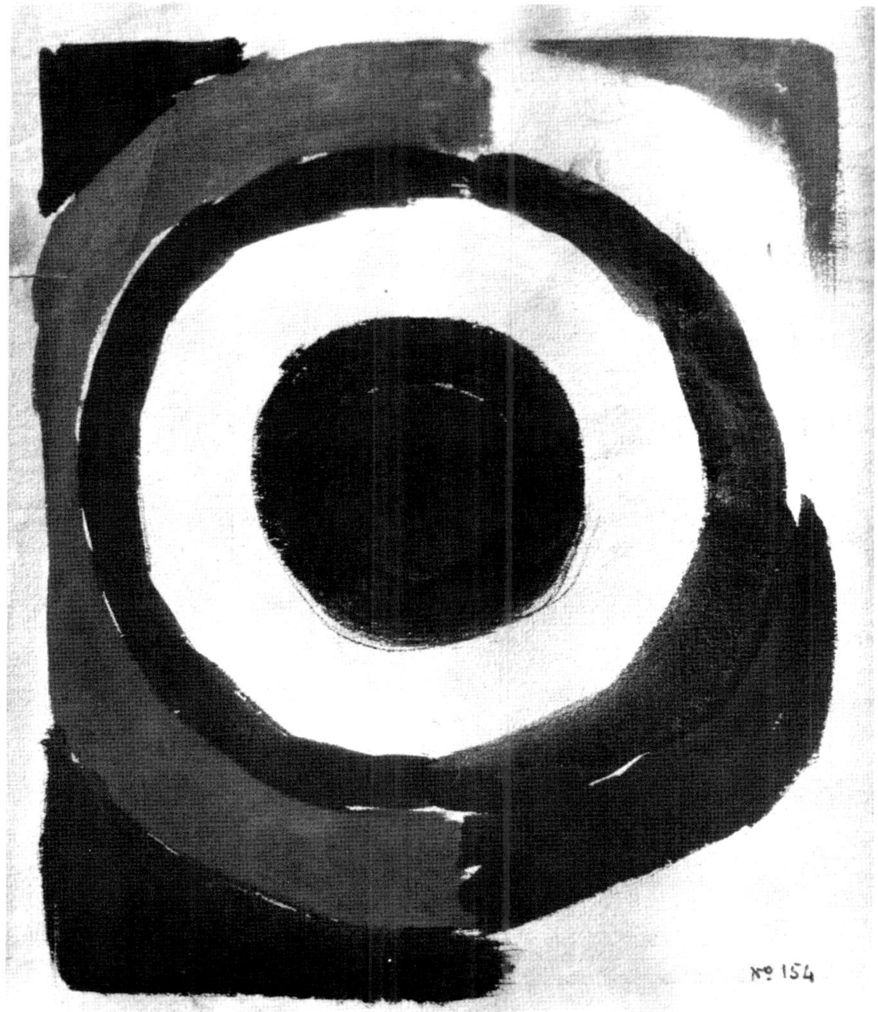

Disk, painted in Portugal in 1916, encaustic on paper.

Madrid, and continued in Portugal to do various versions of this subject, which are like the *Bal Bullier* in spirit. They show that she had by no means divorced herself entirely from the figurative, but as in the earlier painting, she created a sense of movement and music in terms of colour contrasts, circles and prisms. There are two versions of this subject, and in both there are two figures, on the left side a woman with smooth black hair and a rose over her ear and a mustachioed man with a guitar on the right. Even though the elements are quite similar, the later, larger painting (1915-16) is much less realistic and distinct, the figures and the guitar all seem to merge into one

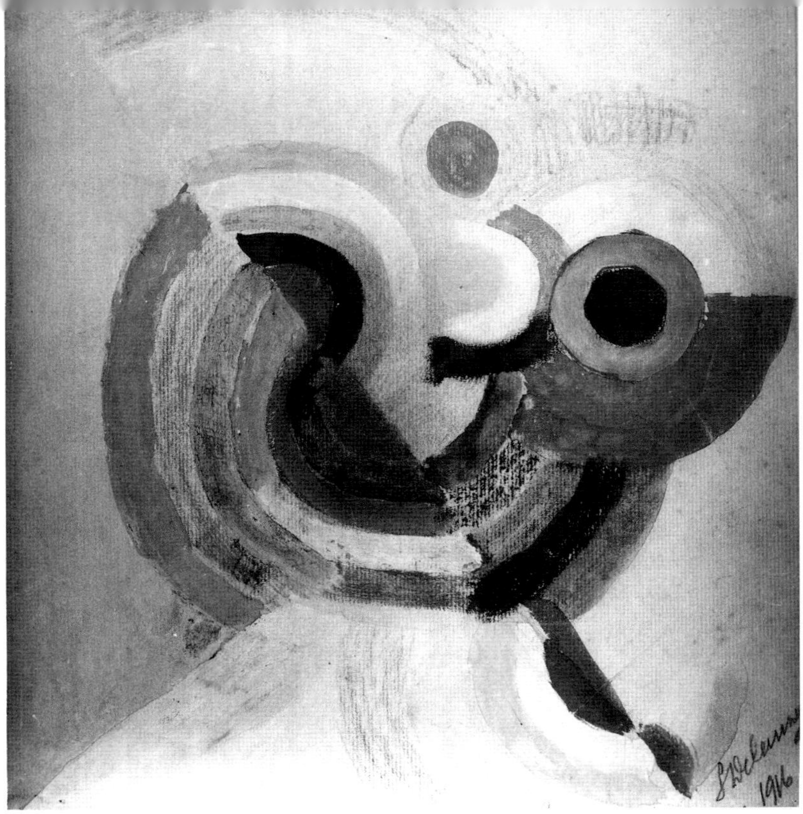

Two paintings called *Dancer*: above, watercolour and pencil, 1916; right, watercolour, 1917 (signed Sonia Delaunay-Terk).

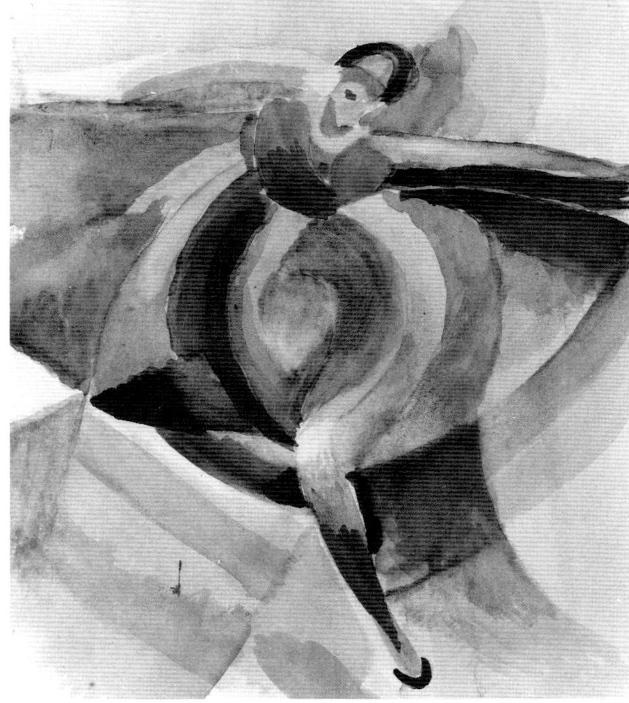

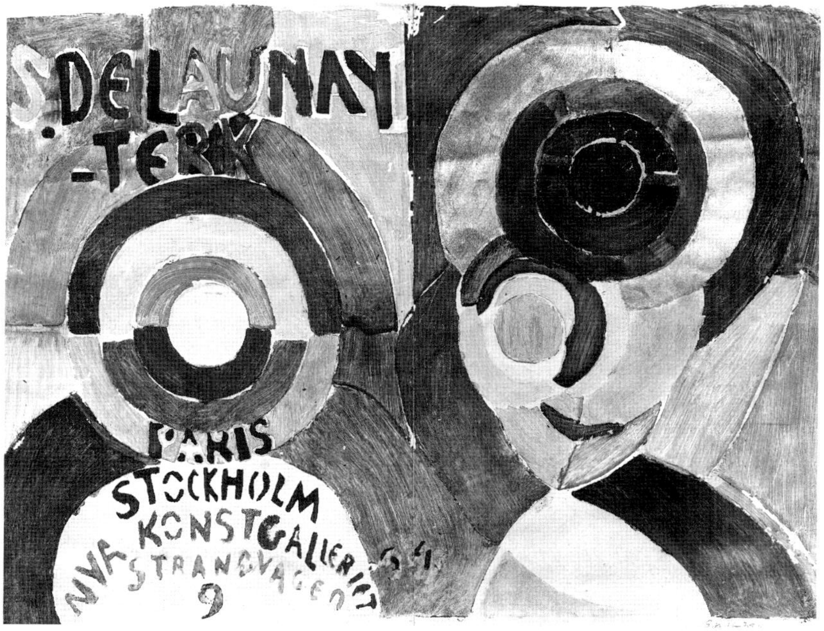

The 'self-portrait' cover Sonia devised in 1916 for the catalogue of the exhibition of her work in Stockholm.

Below, objects decorated by Sonia in Madrid, 1918.

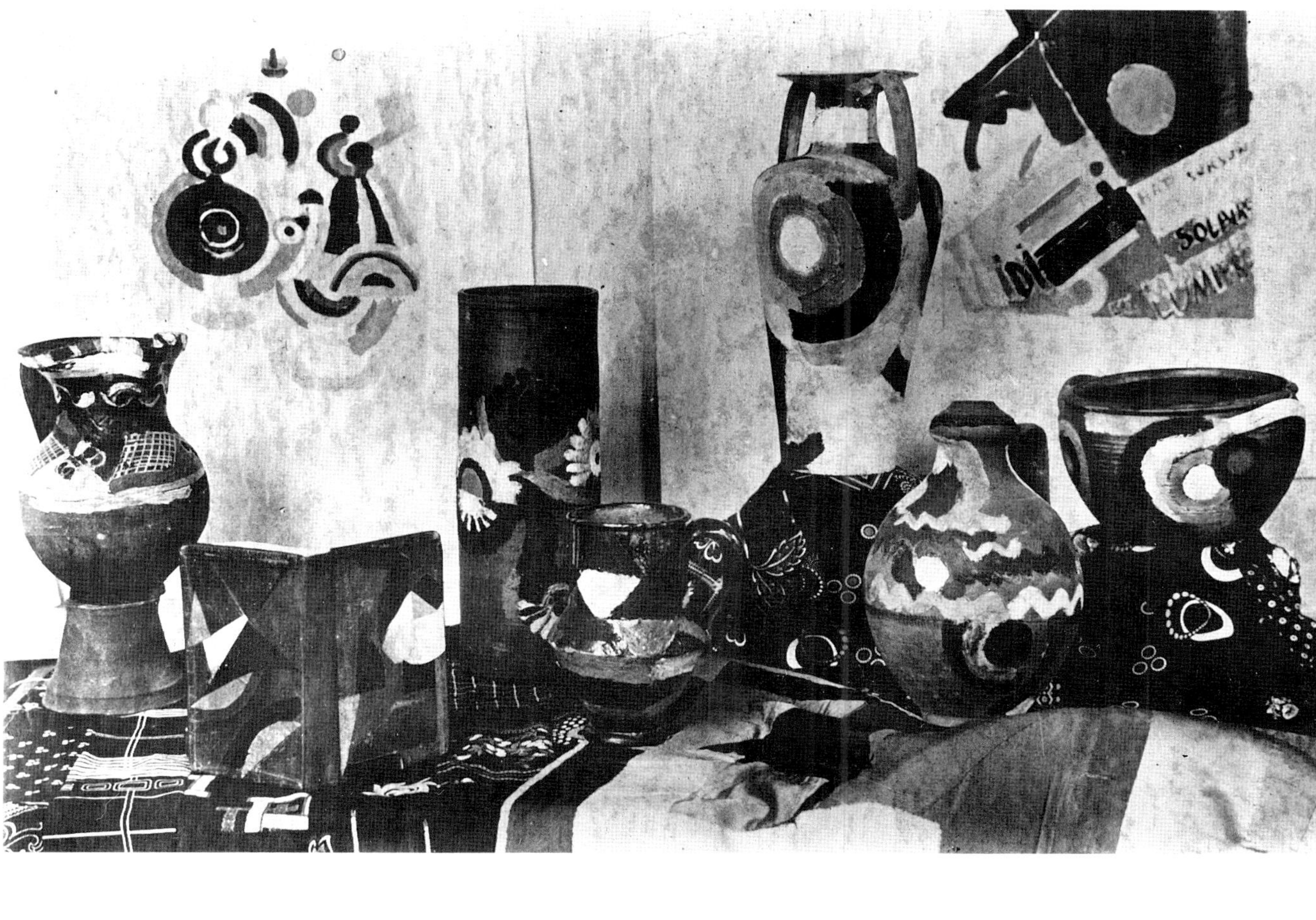

swirl of bright and sombre colours. In the top right corner of the larger version appears the lettering 'CHANTEUR FLAMENCO'.

In writing of this painting – *Le grand flamenco*, as she calls it – Sonia relates that she was seeking the rhythm of music in it. She worked long and hard at it, because she wanted to come out with a picture as beautiful as a Veronese. 'That wasn't easy,' she admits.

Robert returned to Madrid for a little while in 1915, when Portugal officially joined the Allies in their war against Germany, and while he was gone Sonia had a bizarre and rather ludicrous experience. As she describes it, some of the local people considered her an oddity, for she wore a one-piece bathing suit, which 'the women in black', as she calls them, had never seen before and which obviously shocked them. Then some over-zealous person watched her through a telescope as she sat on the front steps of her house painting disks onto a canvas, and in an access of spy-hunting reported to the authorities that this was her means of passing messages to enemy submarines at sea. It was a charge she would have had little difficulty laughing down.

When Robert returned, they went to another village on the north coast of Portugal, Valença do Minho, where they spent some nine months before deciding to make Spain their centre of activity. In an unfinished Jesuit convent in Minho they were able to work on large-format projects. Her most important painting of that period was *The Market at Minho* (1915), which, apart from some preliminary sketches, exists in a large and a medium-sized version. This is a mature, rich work, combining figurative and abstract elements, a complex composition of warm, vibrant colours, representing the animated activity of a market-place, with stalls and vendors, vegetables, fruit, even a bull, all engaged in a brilliant, constantly moving scene.

In 1916 she was invited by an old Italian friend, Arturo Ciacelli, now married to a Swede and owner of an art gallery in Stockholm since 1914, to exhibit some of her works there. This gave her an interesting opportunity to design the catalogue cover. What she provided was a self-portrait, in the manner of the woman in the smaller *Flamenco Singer*, which is in fact an exercise in her prisms, giving the merest impression of a head and face: a simultaneous hat, a huge eye, a sketchy smile, all arranged in a composition of circles that joins with those on the back, where the lettering appears ('S.Delaunay-Terk, Paris, Stockholm, Nya Konstgalleriet' and the address in varying colours).

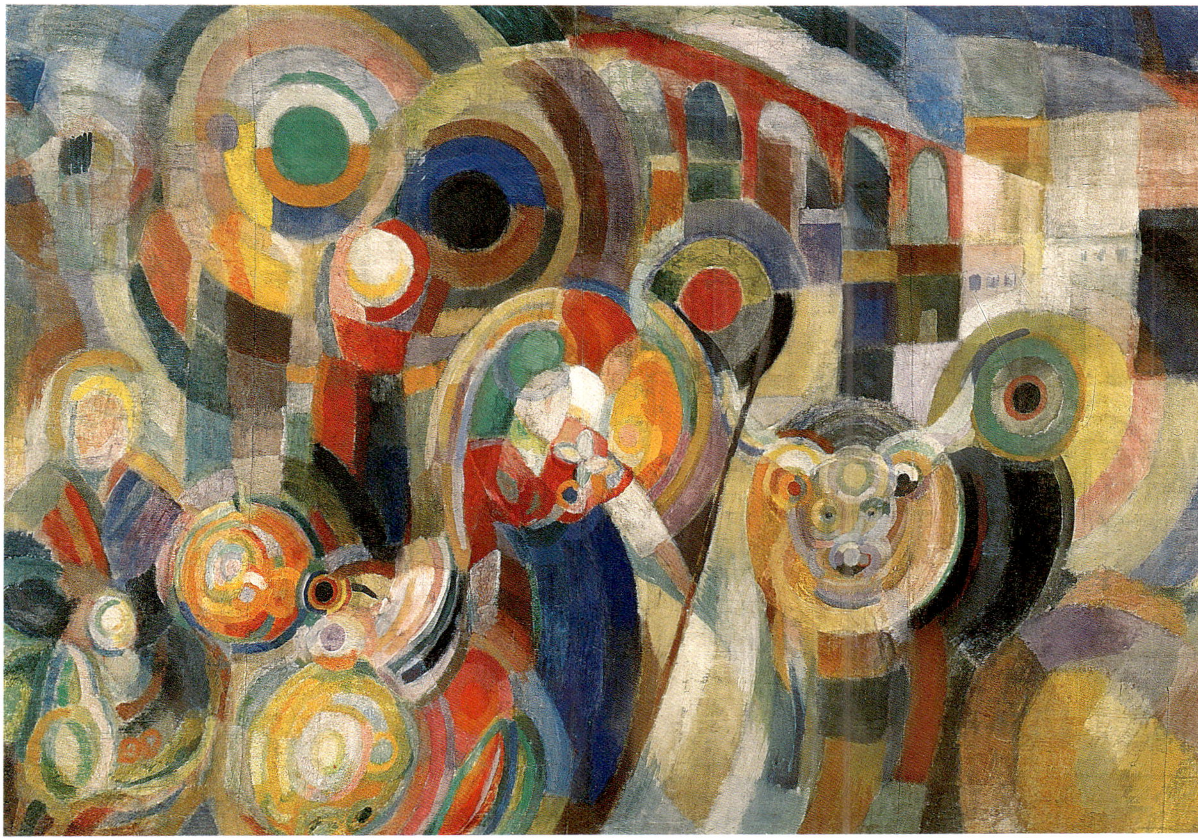

20 *The Market at Minho*, encaustic on canvas, 1915.
This is a subject, done in the style of *Bal Bullier*,
which Sonia worked on repeatedly during the stay in Portugal.

21 Self-portrait, painted in Madrid in 1916.

22 Below, *Chanteur flamenco*, one of various treatments of this subject; encaustic on canvas, 1916.

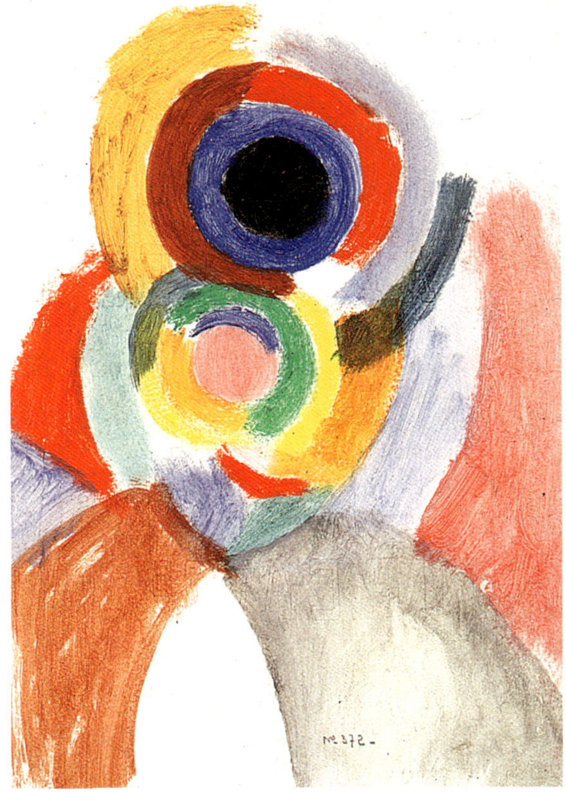

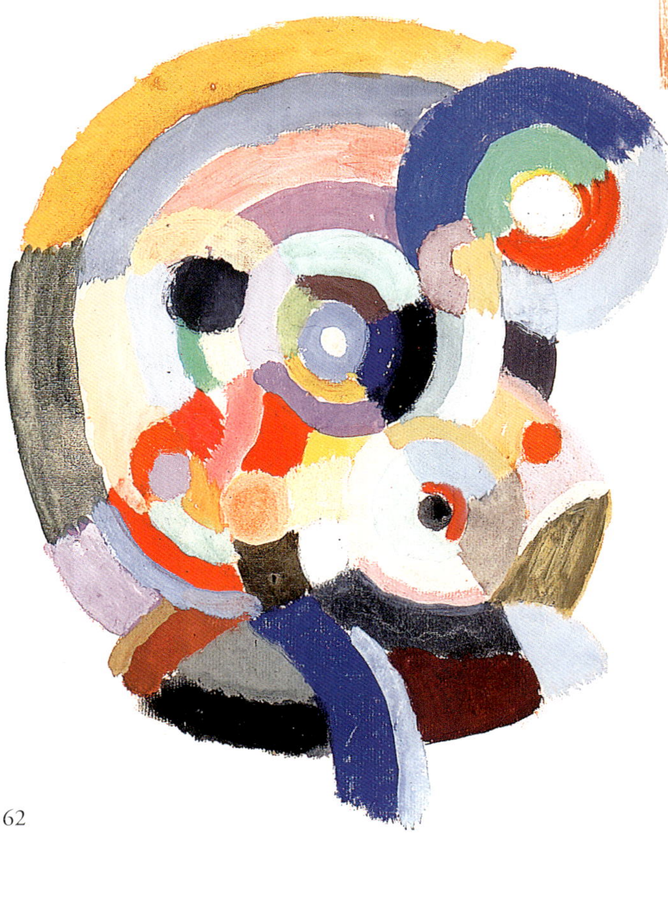

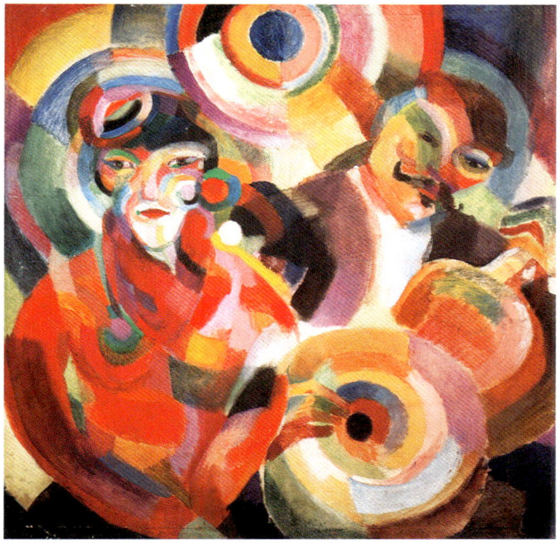

23, 24 Two full-scale paintings of Flamenco singers done by Sonia in 1916. The one below, which she referred to as 'the large Flamenco', has the same elements as the other but has evolved into a less representational picture.

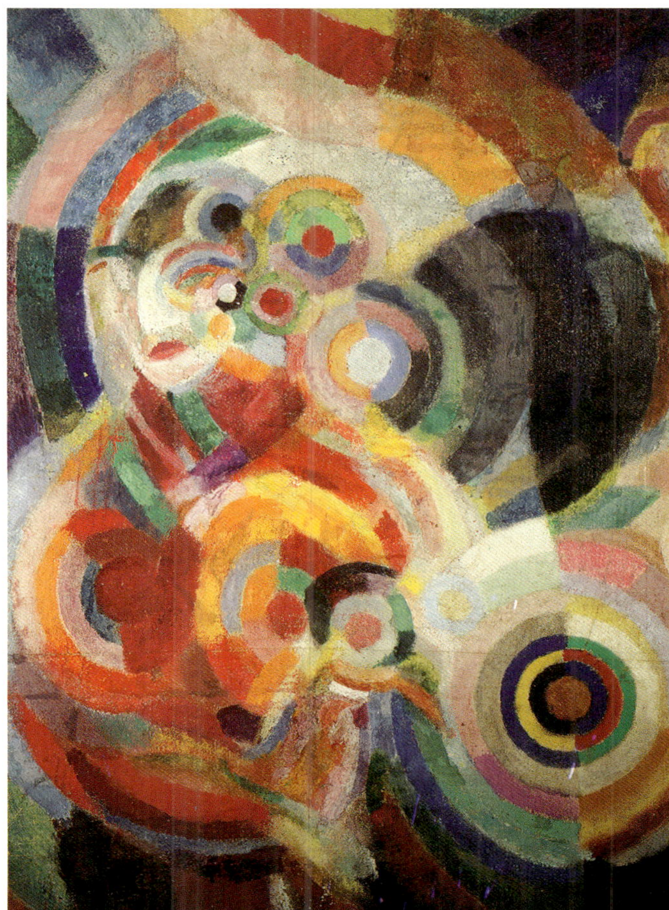

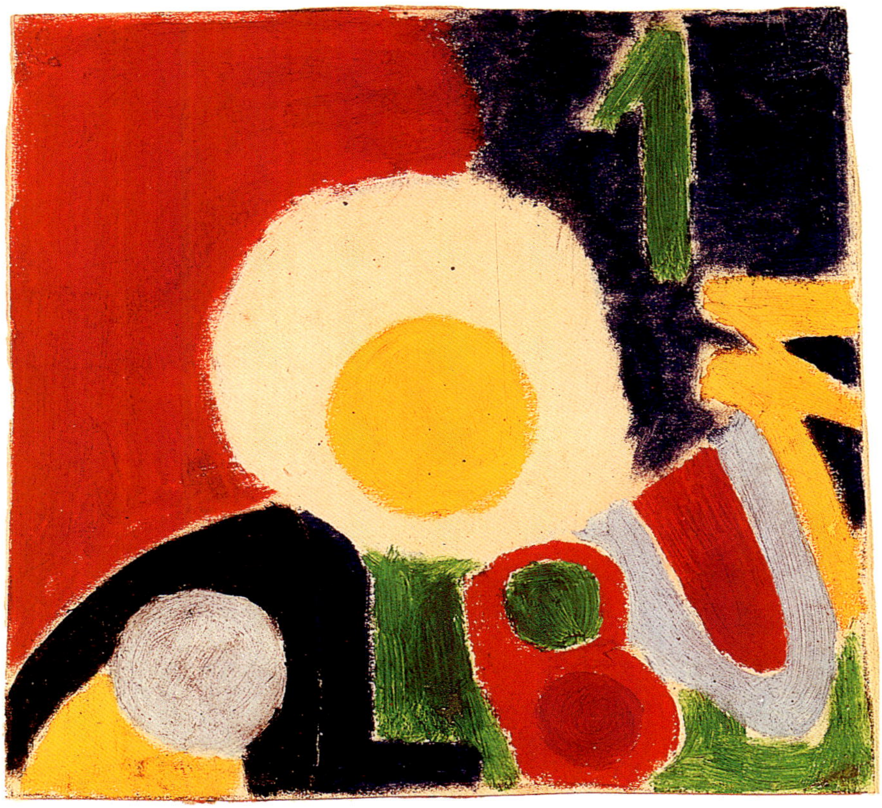

25 Sketch for a journal 'Album No. 1'; encaustic on paper, 1916.

26 Below, *Disk*, gouache on paper, 1915.

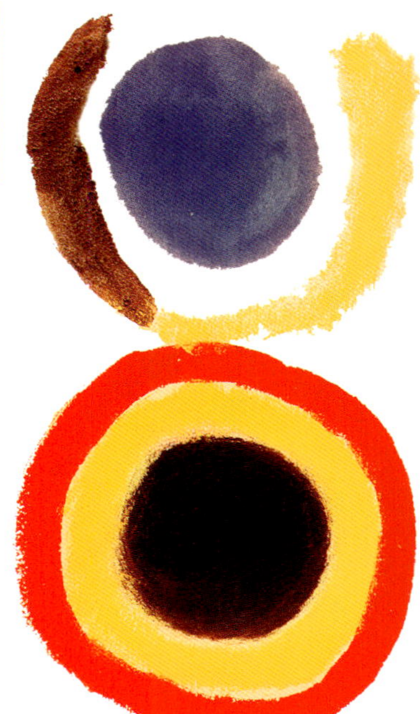

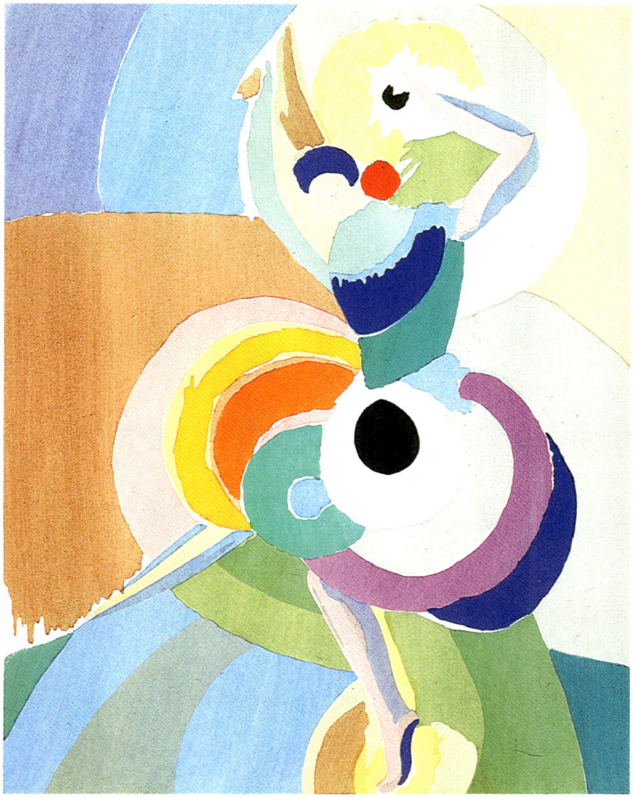

27 *Danseuse flamenco*, 1916.

28 Below left, Portuguese toys, 1916.

29 Below, a sketch for a new night club in Madrid, the Petit Casino, with the dancer Gaby, 1917.

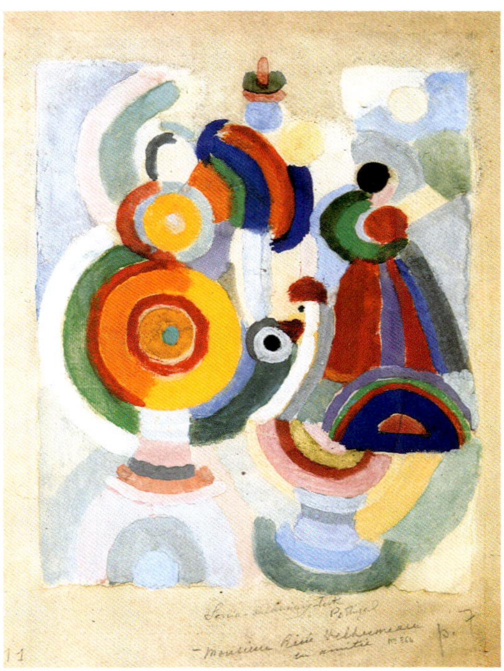

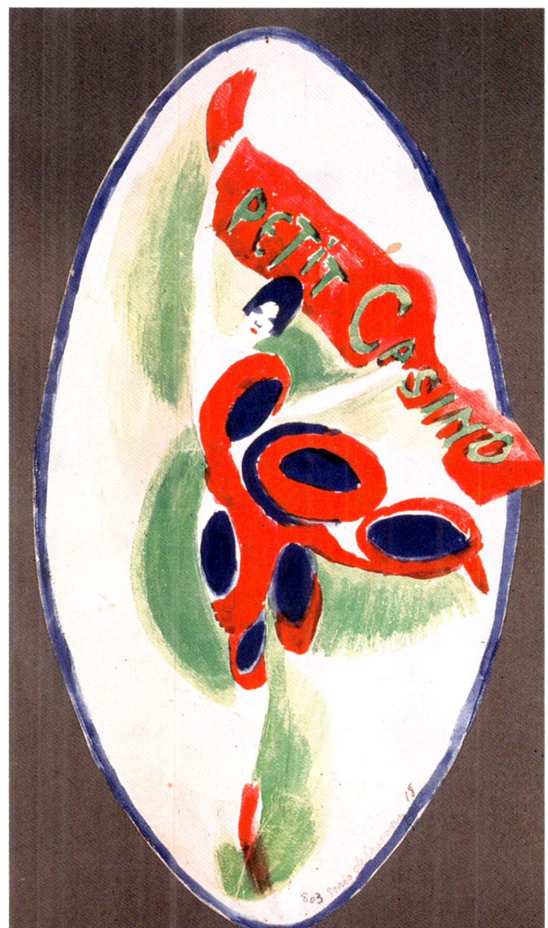

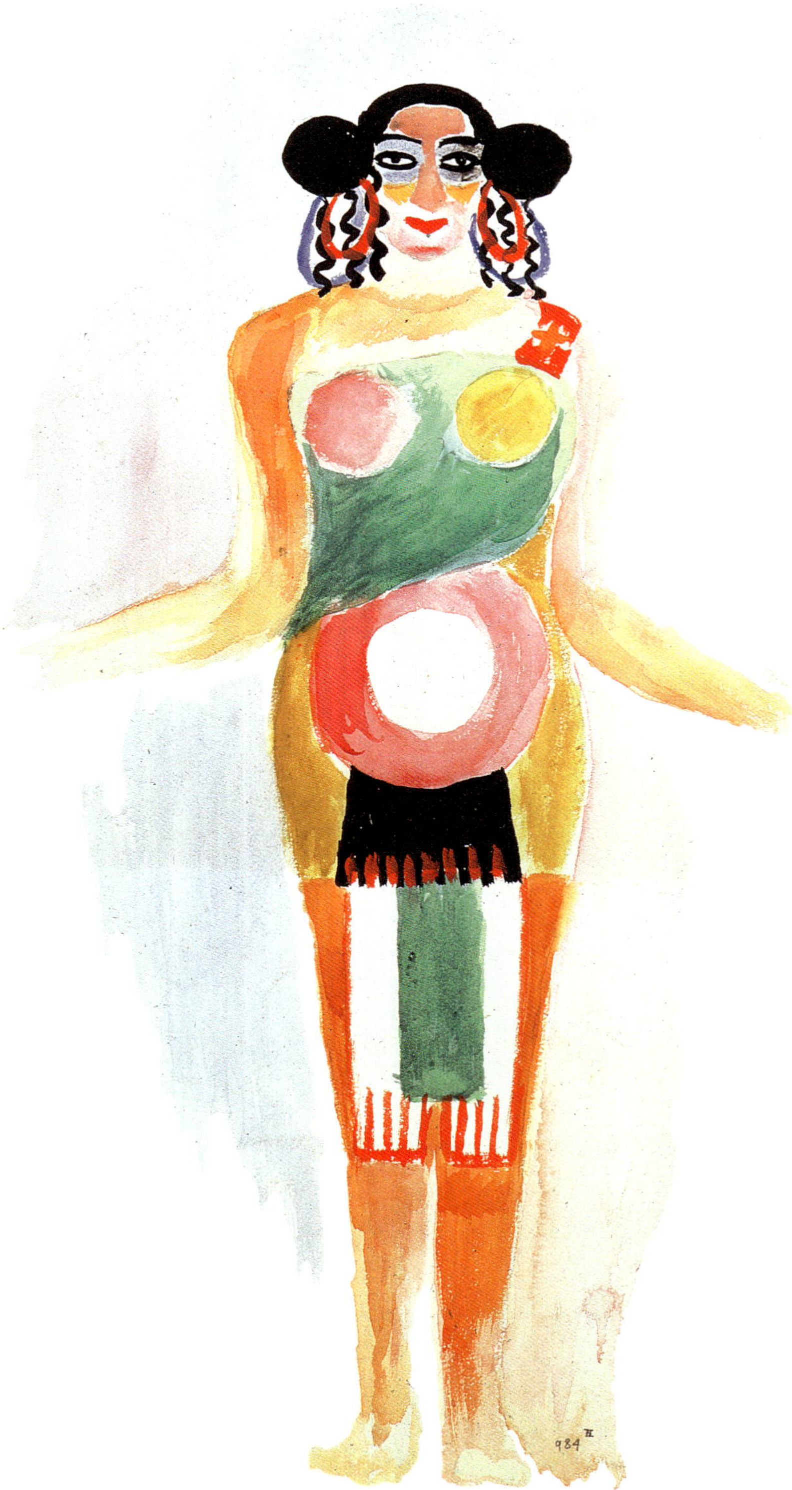

30 Costume design for a production of the opera *Aida* in Madrid, 1917.

31-33 Opposite, sketch of Cleopatra as a mummy, and scarf designs for the Diaghilev ballet, *Cléopâtre*, 1918.

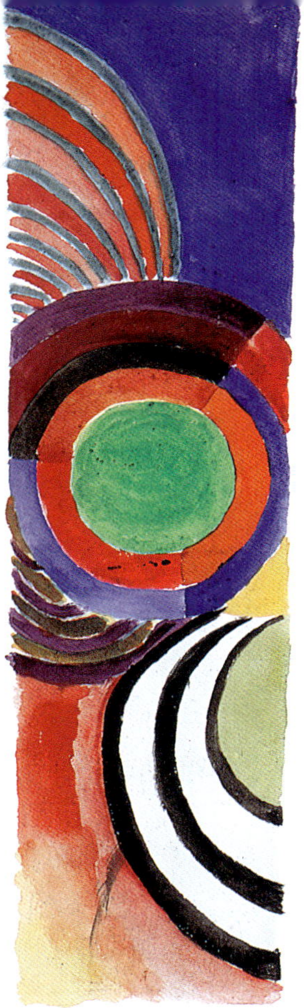

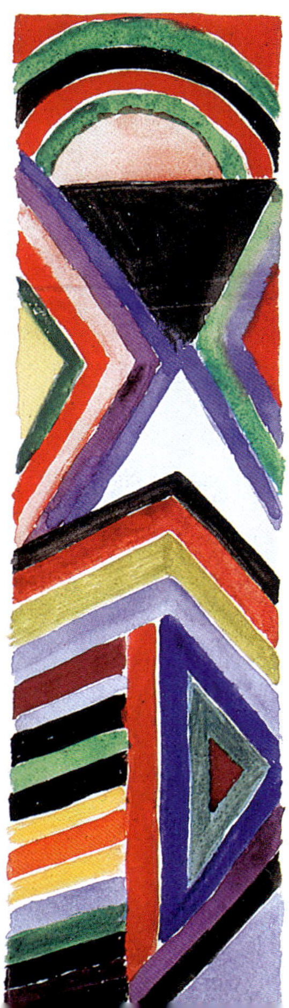

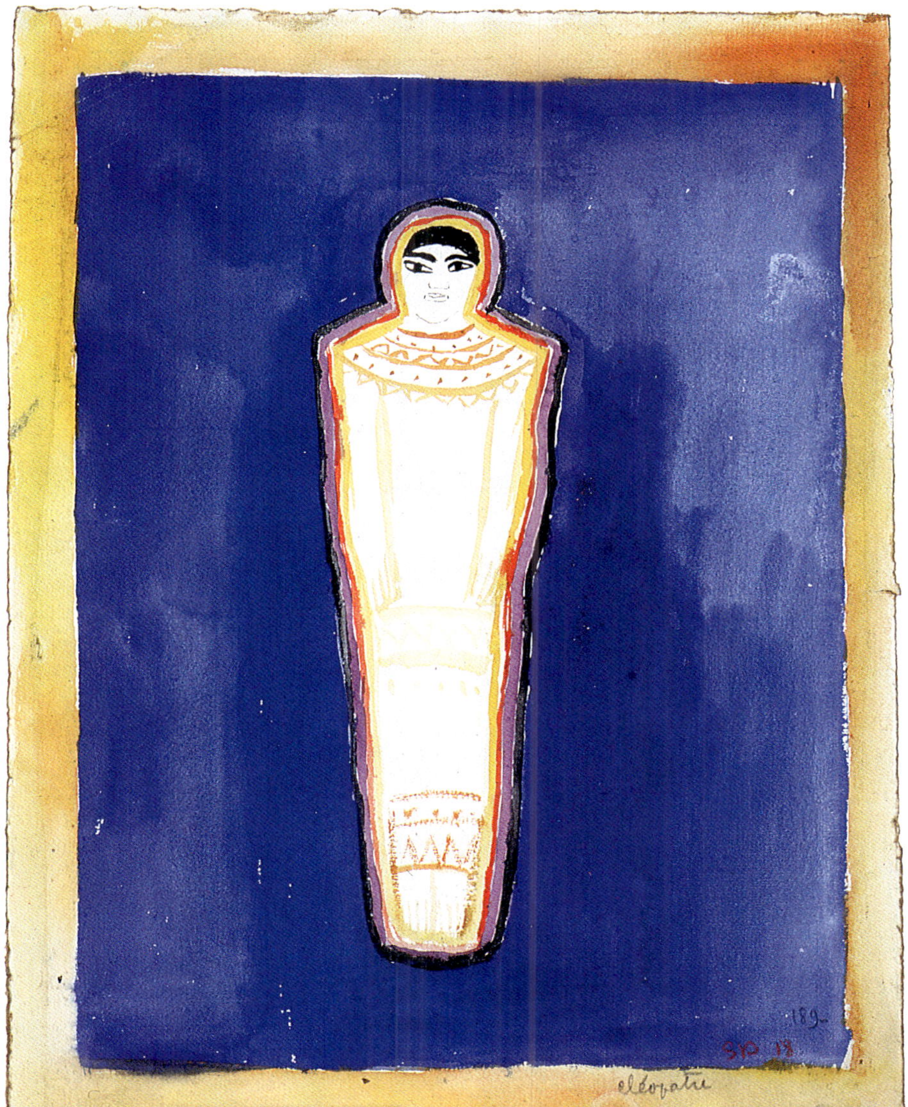

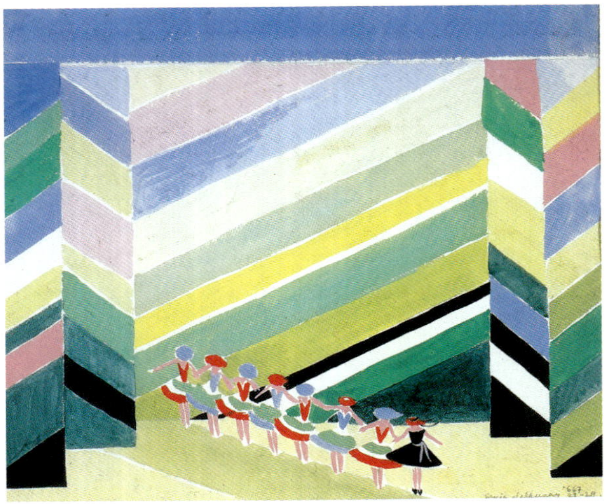

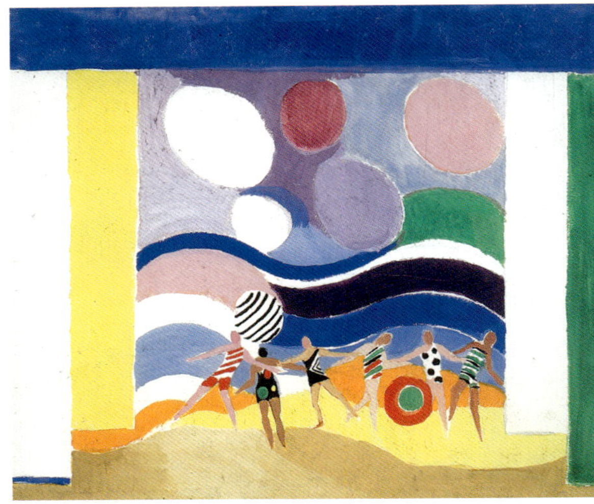

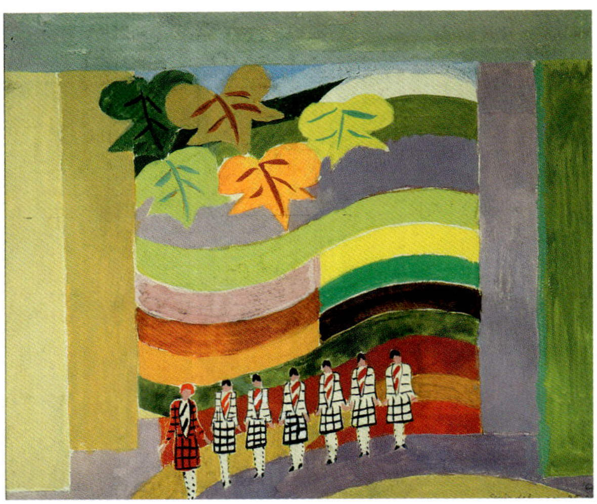

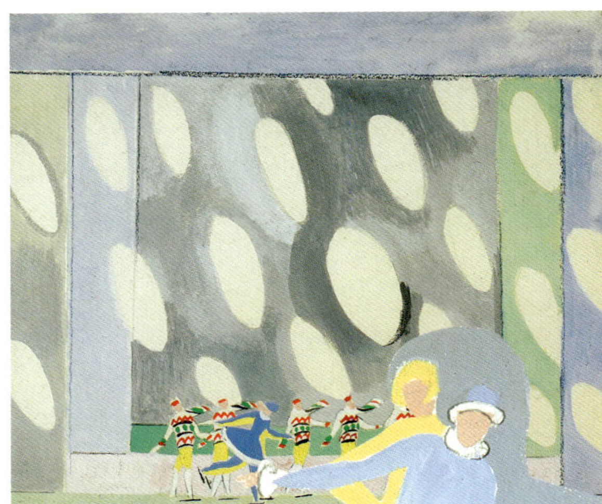

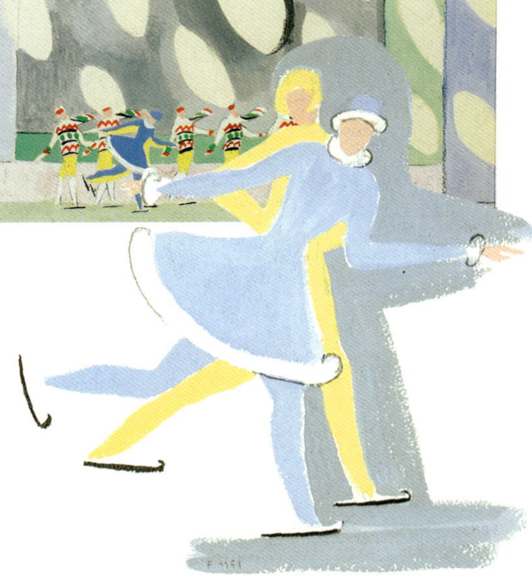

34-38 Four stage designs prepared by Sonia for a ballet planned by Massine, *The Four Seasons*, but never executed; and ice skater costumes suggested for the same ballet, 1928-29.

CHAPTER 8

THE YEARS IN MADRID

WHEN THE RUSSIAN REVOLUTION broke out on 25 October 1917, the Delaunays, who were in Barcelona, may have cried with joy, as Sonia recalled, but in fact it placed them personally in a most difficult situation, because it meant the end of the support she had been receiving up to then from her devoted relatives in St Petersburg.

Sonia recognized that they (or more precisely, she) would have to make their living through some form of applied art. Neither she nor Robert was naive enough to think they could live off their paintings. They saw, for one thing, that they would have to make Madrid their hub; and, as it happened, the great entrepreneur of the Ballets Russes, Serge Diaghilev, was himself in Spain at that time, surrounded by his Russian dancers and hangers-on. They would go together with him in the evenings to listen to the marvellous flamenco artists, who had already excited Sonia's enthusiasm. Nijinsky was there too, and seems to have become infatuated with Sonia. Fascinated by the art of the Delaunays, he proposed creating a ballet together. 'It will be a *mariage à trois*,' he would say in a way that she confesses to having found pleasing.

Diaghilev commissioned Robert to do the sets and Sonia the costumes for a production of the ballet *Cléopâtre*, which had been created in London in 1909, drawn from a novel by Théophile Gautier. Among the dancers who appeared in the 1909 staging were Nijinsky as the young soldier, Karsavina as the young slave, and the part of Cleopatra was mimed by Ida Rubinstein. It

Tchernicheva in the costume Sonia designed for her role in the ballet *Cléopâtre*, 1918; and below, a watercolour painting of the costume she designed for Massine.

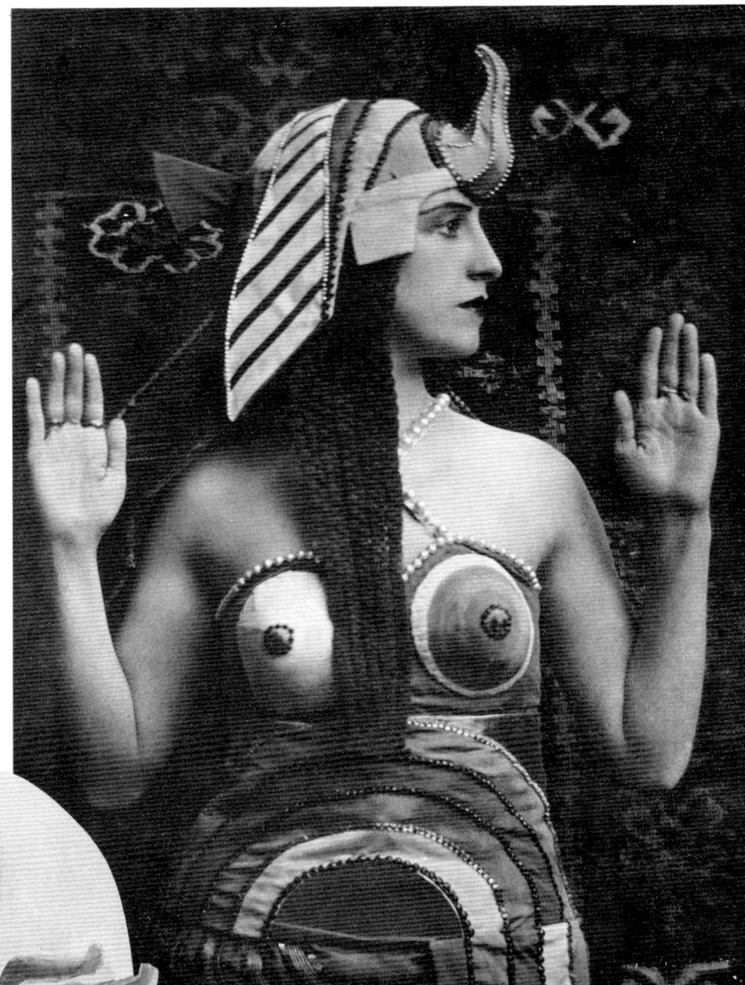

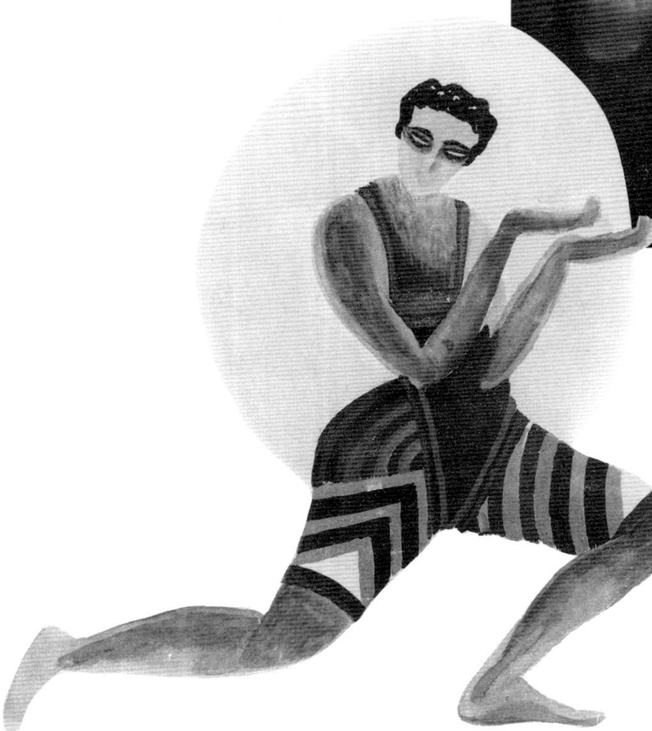

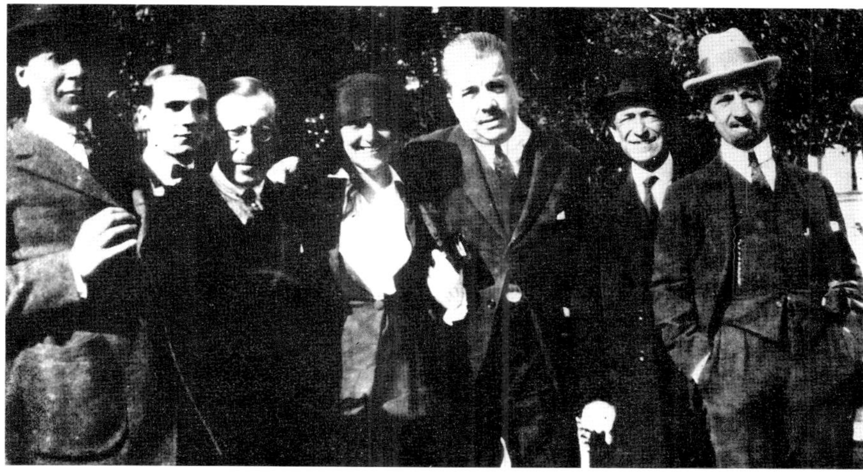

A group of Diaghilev's friends in Madrid, 1919: Robert Delaunay, Boris Kochno, Igor Stravinsky, Sonia, Diaghilev, Manuel de Falla and Barocchi (the first husband of the dancer Lydia Lopokova).

was now being re-worked by Mikhael Fokine, and the reason the Delaunays became involved was that the costumes and sets originally created by Bakst had been destroyed in a fire during a tour of South America. Appearing in the new production were Léonide Massine and Lubov Tchernicheva.

Sonia visualized her Cleopatra as a mummy in the course of being unwrapped. She devised a series of completely different scarves to stand for the mummy's wrapping cloths. Then, once the mummy was stripped of these, the queen's costume consisted of mirror disks and concentric circles, such as Sonia remembered seeing on a sarcophagus in the Louvre. The ballet opened in London, and Diaghilev sent a telegram to say that it had been well received, including Sonia's 'simultaneous gown' for Cleopatra.

Diaghilev was sufficiently pleased with what they had produced to propose that they join his company and participate in the creation of new ballets.

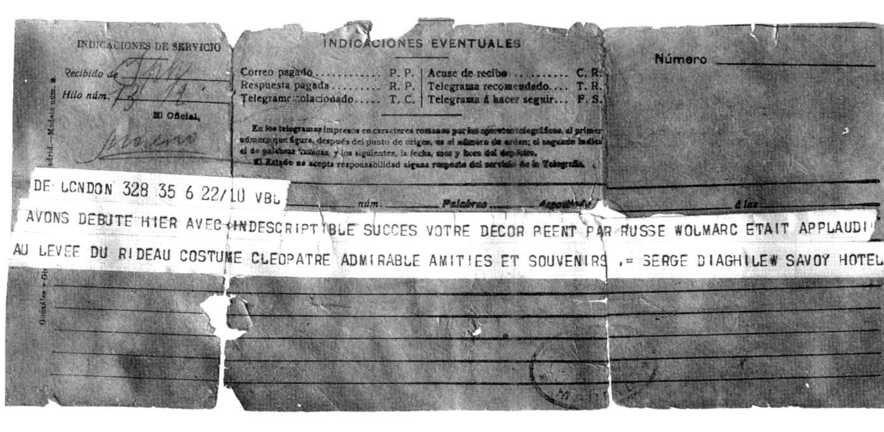

INDICACIONES DE SERVICIO

Recibido de

Hilo núm.

El Oficial,

INDICACIONES EVENTUALES

Correo pagado........... P. P. | Acuse de recibo.......... C. R.
Respuesta pagada......... R. P. | Telegrama recomendado.... T. R.
Telegrama colacionado..... T. C. | Telegrama á hacer seguir... F. S.

Número

DE LCNDON 328 35 6 22/10 VBL

AVONS DEBUTE HIER AVEC INDESCRIPTIBLE SUCCES VOTRE DECOR PEENT PAR RUSSE WOLMARC ETAIT APPLAUDI AU LEVEE DU RIDEAU COSTUME CLEOPATRE ADMIRABLE AMITIES ET SOUVENIRS .= SERGE DIAGHILEW SAVOY HOTEL

Diaghilev's wire to the Delaunays in Madrid, calling the opening of *Cléopâtre* an 'indescribable success'.

One of his motives in making this offer was his desire to rid himself of the two Russian artists Mikhael Larionov and Natalya Gontcharova, who had been doing sets and costumes for him, but who had somehow displeased him. Sonia and Robert, having no wish to be so closely identified with Diaghilev or to lead the gypsy life that went along with working for his company, turned him down.

It may have been the Cleopatra costumes that led to Sonia's next commission – to design the costumes for a production of the opera *Aida* to be mounted at the Liceo in Barcelona. It was the soprano Aga Lahovska who persuaded her, with the argument that the opera was so well known that it needed to be re-dressed in order for audiences to want to listen to it again.

Following the *Aida*, she was asked to decorate a new night club, the *Petit Casino*, which was being launched in a remodelled theatre, and to design a costume for its star, Gaby. Society in Madrid was not slow to become aware of the Delaunays. In due course – 'out of amusement', Sonia writes – she agreed to create clothes for the aristocracy: a tunic, a raffia hat, a parasol, four of each for the four daughters of the Marquis d'Urquijo.

Amusement was not going to pay the bills, so Sonia decided to expand her activities and opened a shop offering interior decoration. This had become a possibility ever since Diaghilev introduced her to the Marquis de Valdeiglesas, who was director of the journal *La Epoca* and well-placed to sing her praises. From 'Casa Sonia', she set out to make drastic changes in the houses of rich people and historic palaces: white became prevalent, she recommended simple materials and decorated screens, side tables, lamps. She was also designing clothes for the Madrid women who could afford them, and appears to have made a successful start in this field. Before long, she also presided over a typical Delaunay salon, to which such artists as the composer Manuel de Falla made their calls. It was there that Diaghilev and de Falla were brought together; eventually, out of that meeting emerged the popular ballet *The Three-Cornered Hat*, with sets by Picasso.

Sonia felt that she was not 'wasting her time' with her efforts in design and fashion: in fact, she called it 'noble work, as much as a still-life or a self-portrait.' In effect, she was being paid for what she thoroughly enjoyed doing and had been doing for years as a sideline to her painting. But now the financial situation was such that she virtually gave up painting between the years 1918 and 1935.

A somewhat official-looking pose of Sonia in Madrid, 1919.

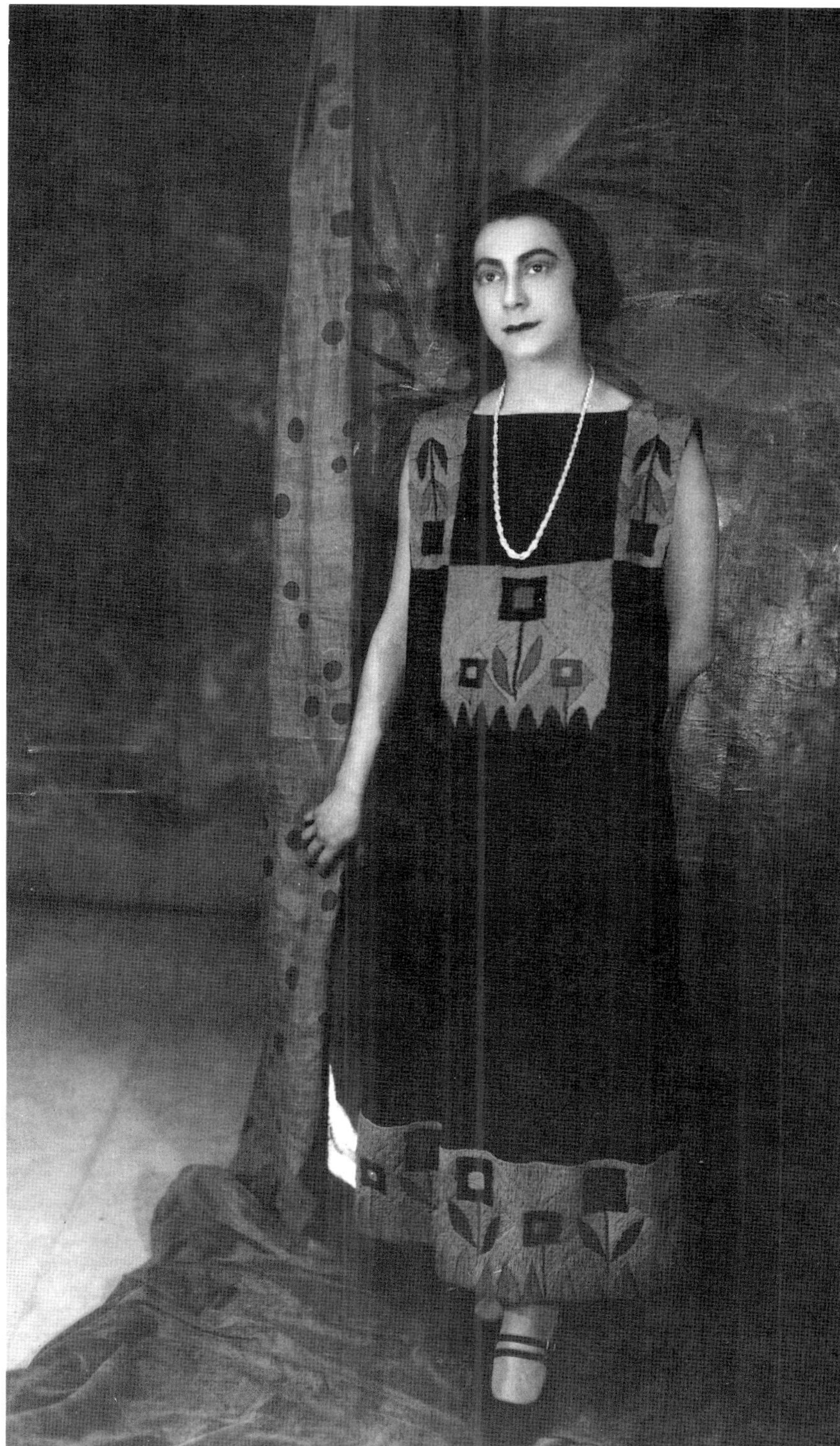

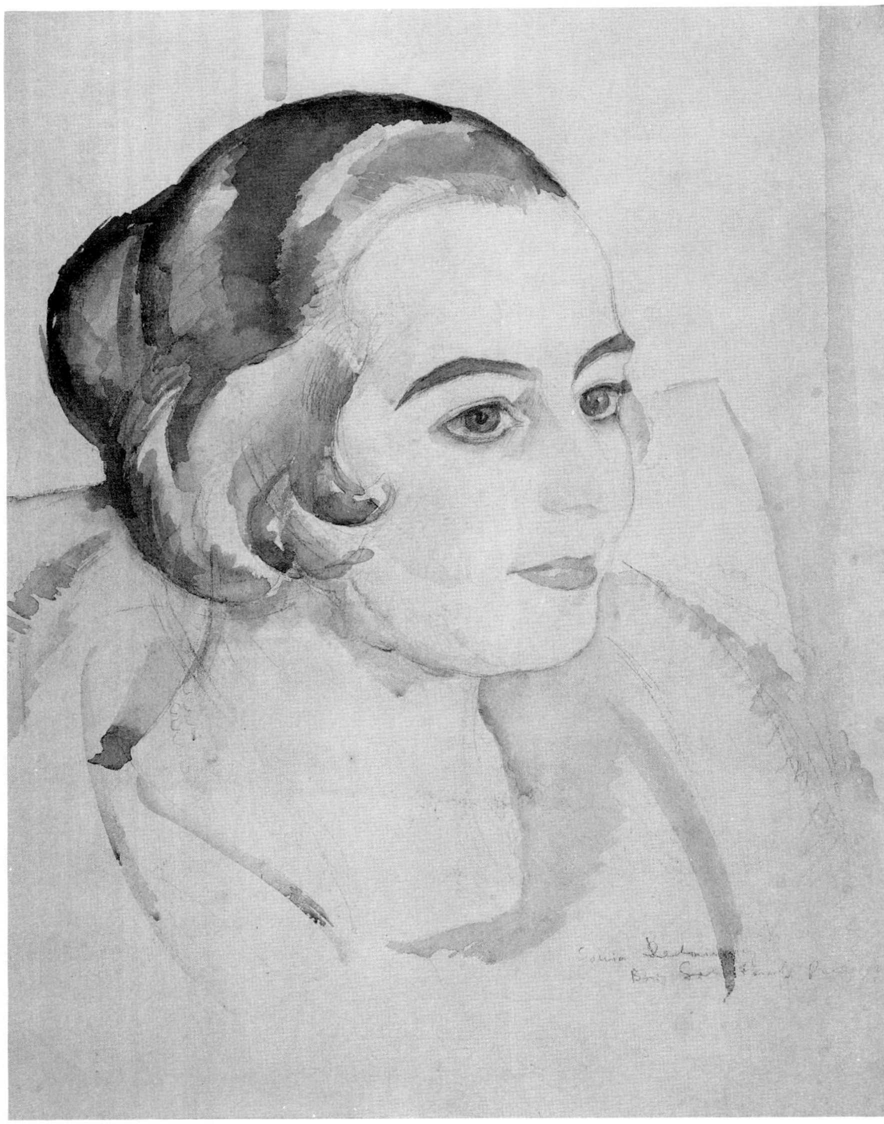

A watercolour portrait of Sonia by Boris Solotareff, 1921.
(The Metropolitan Museum of Art, Gift of Gregoire Tarnopol, 1967 [67.144.2])

CHAPTER 9

BACK TO PARIS: DESIGNING FABRICS

EVEN THOUGH they were ensconced in Madrid and felt entirely at home there after five years, Sonia kept up with news from Paris. Once she heard 'the voice' of Tristan Tzara, the leading Dada propagandist, she began to feel drawn back to Paris. His prophetic Manifesto of 1918, which reached them in Madrid, matched their own ideas: 'We were no longer crying alone in the wilderness.'

Paris was coming back to life. The Dadaist call convinced them that the moment for repatriation was near. Diaghilev, a joint exhibition in a Bilbao gallery, Spanish friends and her activities in 'Casa Sonia' had been holding them back.

But now, in 1921, the time had come. Early in 1919, soon after the Armistice, Robert had visited Paris to sound out the atmosphere, to meet with old friends, and to revive relationships which their long absence had broken, or at least attenuated. In July 1920, and then again in December of the same year, Sonia in turn went to Paris in order to see what possibilities existed there for her in the fashion business,and found the prospects good. Some time between the beginning of October and 2 November the whole household travelled to France.

Once returned, Sonia knew that she had to follow the commercial prospects, and considered setting up an atelier like 'Casa Sonia' in Nice. But her backers let her down at the last minute: they considered her 'too modern' and she was not prepared to compromise, having always done what she wanted. The Delaunays remained in Paris.

At the beginning, some of the people they had known formerly snubbed them – perhaps because they had not endured the war in Paris. But the powerful Diaghilev came to their rescue, and made it clear that he had no time for their detractors. Before long, they were installed in an apartment at 19 boulevard Malesherbes, not far from the Madeleine. And before long, Sonia completely redecorated it with furniture she designed herself – most of it now in the Musée des Arts Décoratifs in Paris. It became, as their Left Bank studio had been, a centre for avant-garde writers and artists, famous for its 'Sundays'. They had lost the inimitable Apollinaire, injured during the war and a casualty of the 'flu epidemic of 1919, and Cendrars had lost an arm in action. But there were hordes of new people – Dadaists and Surrealists: not only Tzara, the Rumanian with his monocle and dandyism, but Philippe Soupault and André Breton. Among the painters and sculptors were Albert Gleizes, Hans Arp (who had introduced them originally to his friend Tzara), André Lhote and Marc Chagall. The novelists included Joseph Delteil and the austere Henry de Montherlant, who could hardly have felt at home in that bohemian milieu. At first, having seen a large painting of disks by Léger at the Salon d'Automne, Sonia and Robert were furious with him for copying their

A typical party of friends at the restaurant Voltaire, in 1928 or 1929. Robert Delaunay is at the left, Sonia at the right: among the others are Mondrian, Sophie Taeuber, Arp, the photographer Florence Henry, Metzinger and Léger.

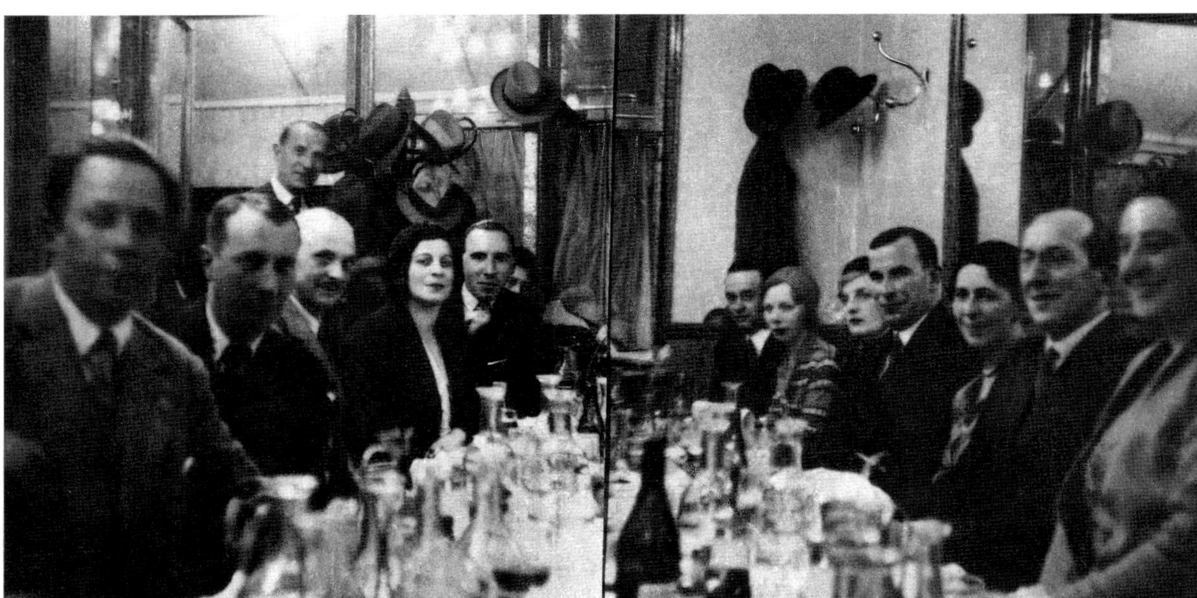

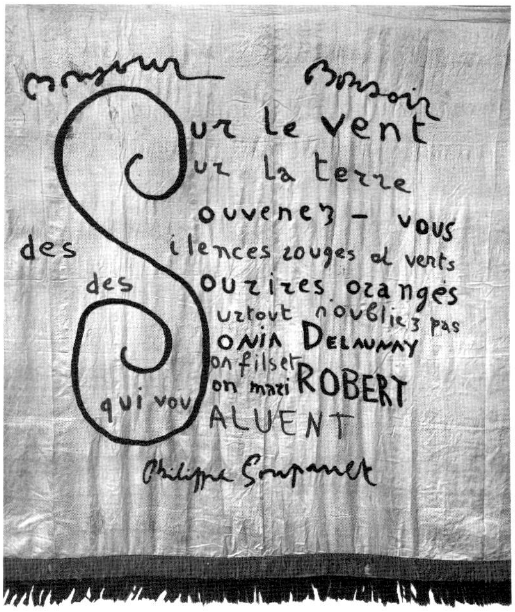

Decorations in the boulevard Malesherbes apartment around 1922: above, a curtain embroidered with a poem by Philippe Soupault; right, a door painted by the Russian poet Mayakovsky.

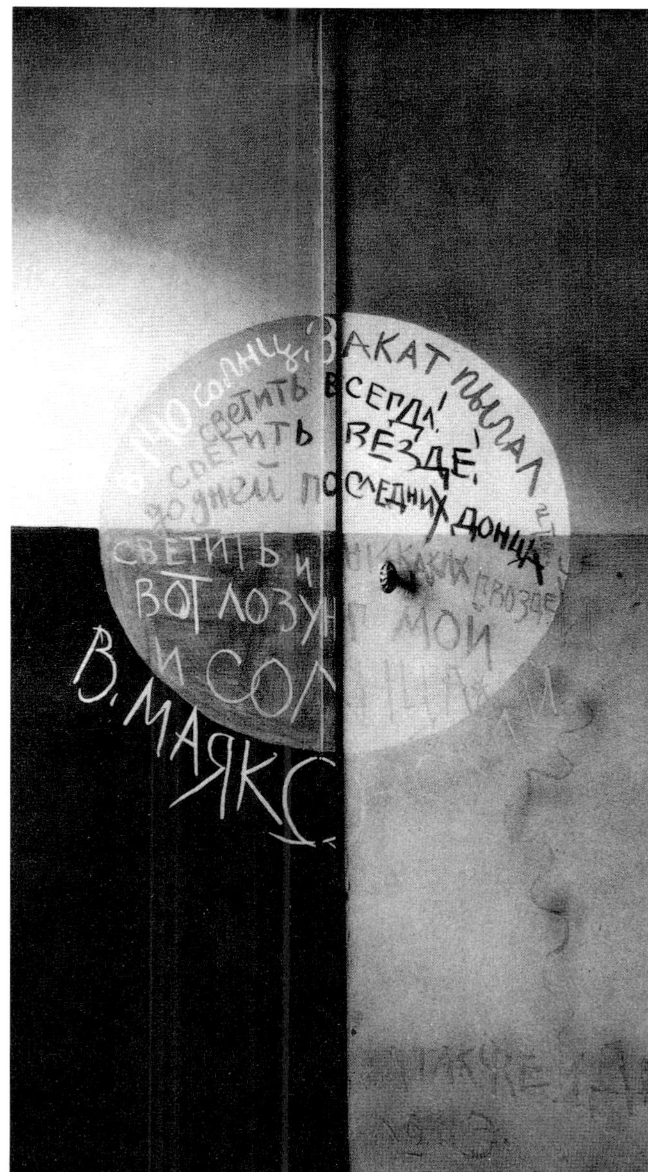

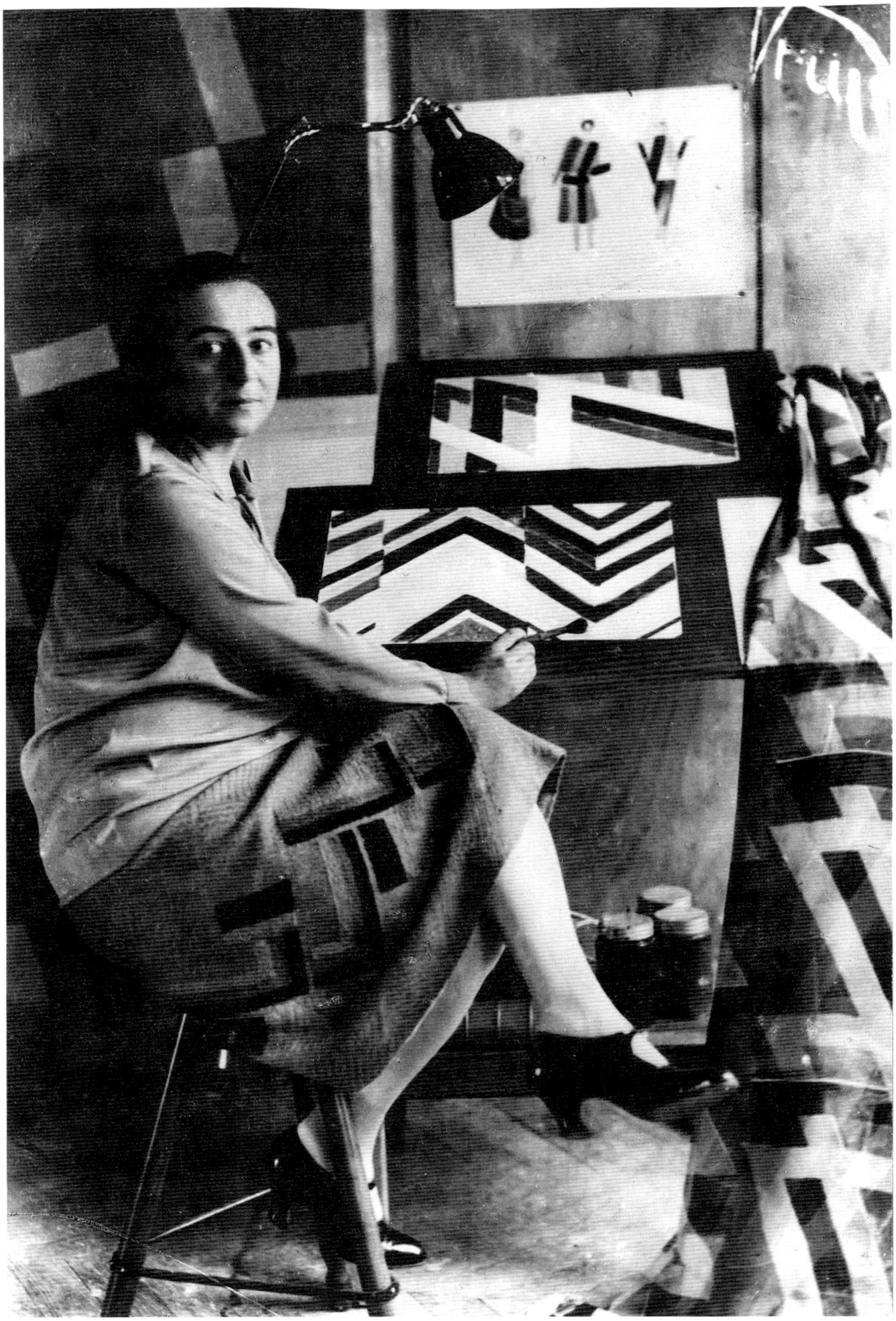

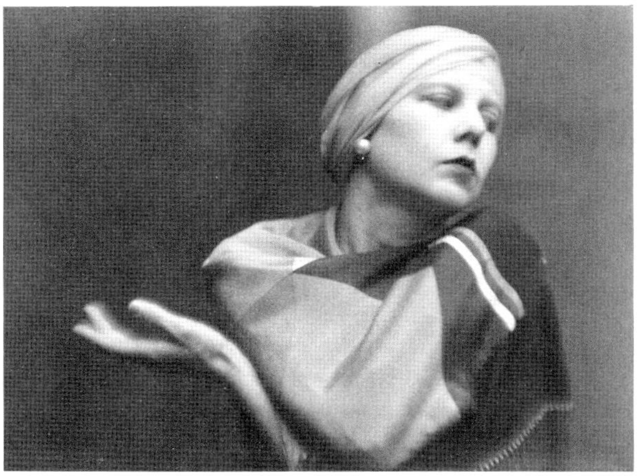

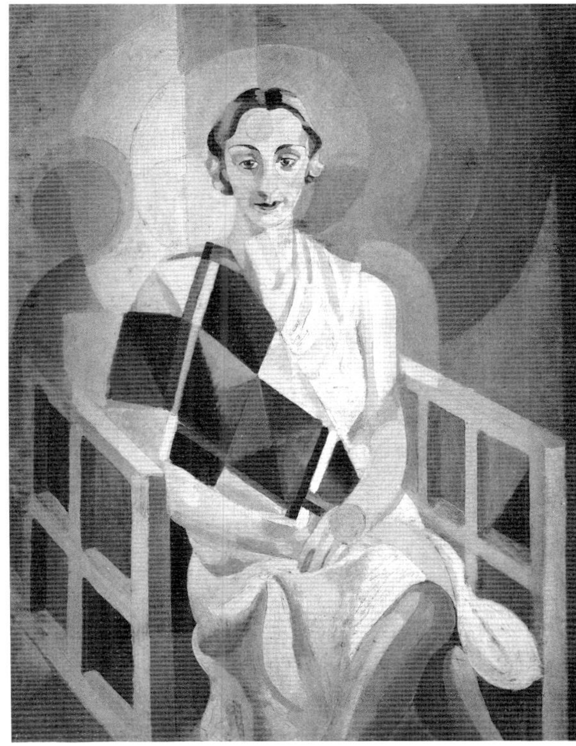

Above, model wearing a scarf designed by Sonia, and Mme Jacques Heim, in Robert's portrait of 1926, wearing another of Sonia's geometric creations.

Left, Sonia in 1923, deeply engaged in her new-found business of fabric design.

style; but later he too was accepted into 'the Delaunay band'. And that band, as Sonia wrote later, 'always moved about together, like a Rugby team' – at least before the schism that took place between the Dadaists (led by Tzara) and the Surrealists (led by Breton).The apartment was a laboratory, a casserole in which the innovative ideas of the moment and of the future were always on the boil. 'We were attracted by everything which bore a spark of originality, we shared our table with the avant-garde of the avant-gardes.'

In 1923, the young Surrealist poet René Crevel described the Delaunay atmosphere: 'After five minutes in Sonia Delaunay's home, who has not been surprised to find in himself more conviction, more hope, even happiness?' Sonia was following ideas she had advanced even before the war for an art without 'hierarchical prejudice', an art of life. Her principles were already being taken up during the 1920s by the Bauhaus in Weimar, where Klee was a teacher, and the Vkutemas in Moscow. Crevel describes her embroidering a verse by Soupault onto a curtain, while the door of the large salon was being decorated with a poem by Mayakovsky and the composer Georges Auric was drawing the key of G. Crevel was attracted by what seemed to him the Delaunays' worldliness and the air of success about them, and he felt that they were exactly the family he wished he had. In dedicating one of his early poems to them he wrote: 'To Robert and Sonia Delaunay of whom I would like to have been father or son, but of whom I am only the friend, but the true friend, the real friend.'

Sonia's attachment to Tzara lasted more than forty years and encompassed a most fruitful collaboration. It was they who launched the famous 'poem-dresses', and in July 1923 Sonia designed the costumes for Tzara's play, *Coeur à Gaz*, when it was produced as part of an experimental evening at the Théâtre Michel in Paris. The music was provided by Auric and Crevel played one of the parts in what Tzara characteristically described as 'the only and most important swindle of the century in three acts'. The evening produced a

Right, the pavilion in which Sonia exhibited her 'simultaneous' designs at the Paris International Exposition of Decorative Arts in 1925.

A model in 1925 sporting a beach outfit designed by Sonia; and that notorious icon of the 1920s, Nancy Cunard, in a typical Sonia Delaunay coat.

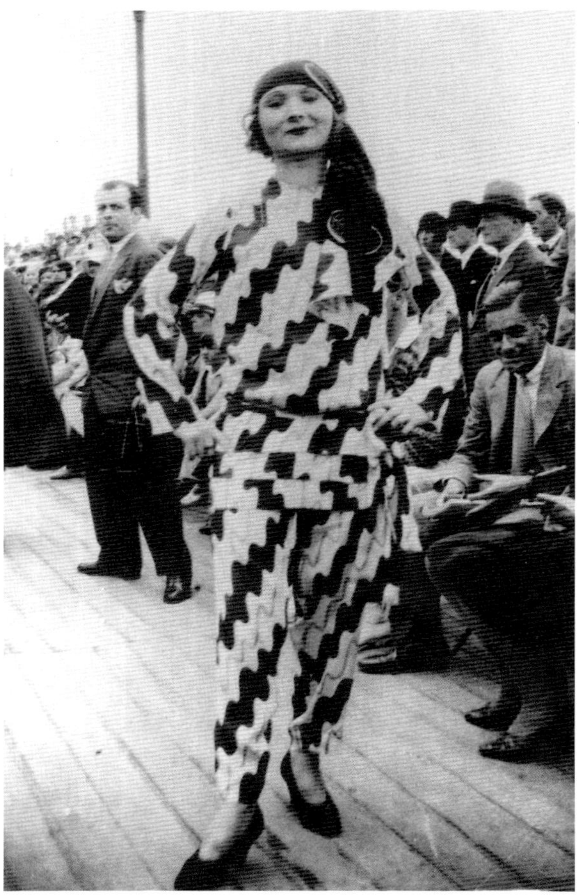

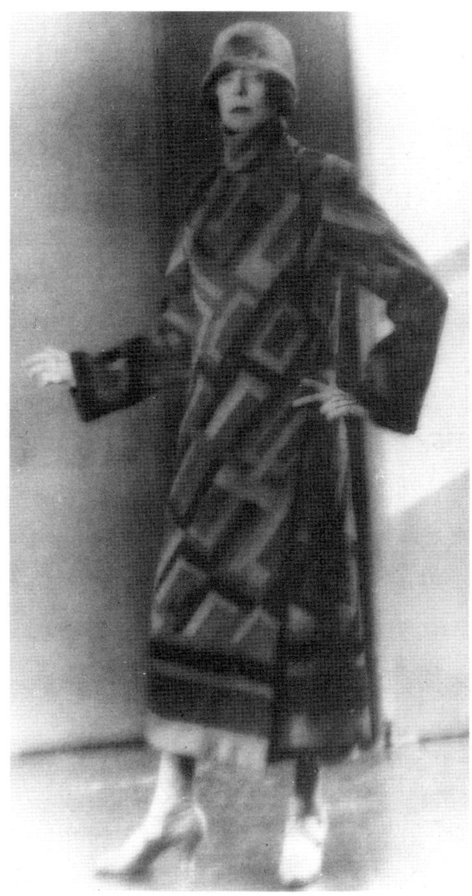

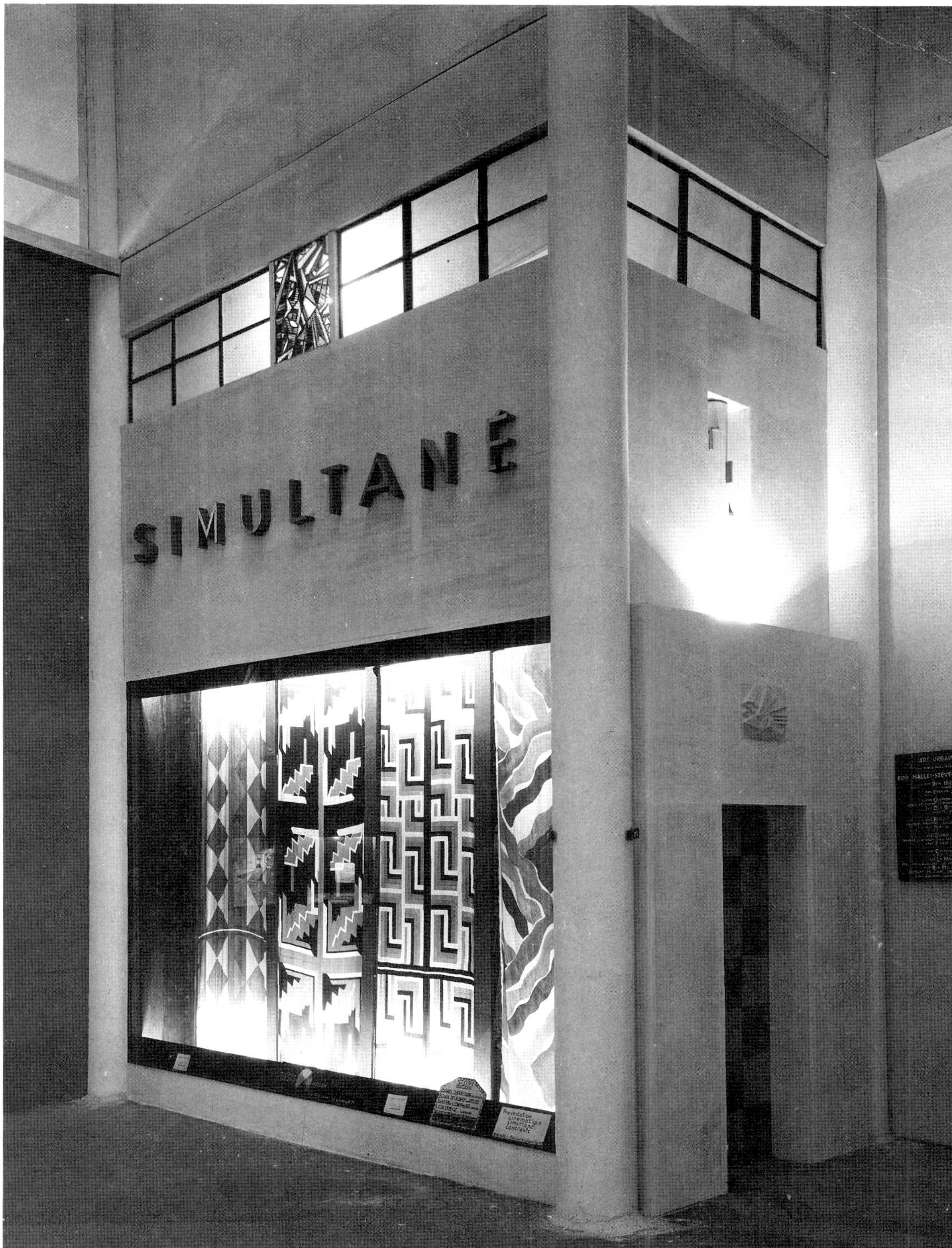
SIMULTANÉ

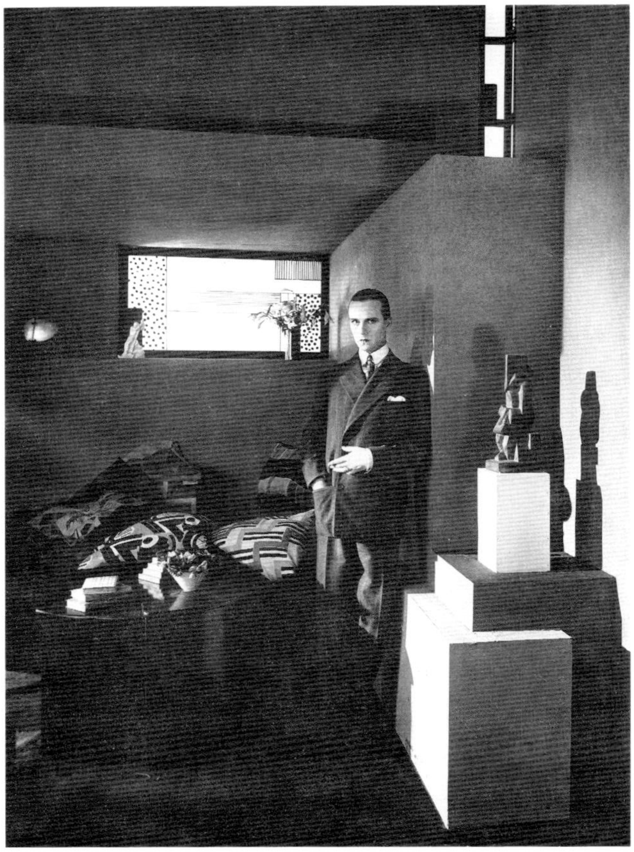

A still from the 1926 film *Vertige*, directed by Marcel L'Herbier; Sonia designed the costumes for the film, but also provided decorative elements, such as the cushions on the divan.

series of riots between two factions vying for control of the Surrealist movement, and even the police were called in to play their traditional part. It seemed to provide a great deal of amusement and enjoyment for the spectators.

Whereas Sonia was expanding her activities almost daily and was, as always, full of plans and enthusiasms, Robert was going through a distinctly thin period. There were very few paintings in the early Twenties; his main interest seemed to be in portraits of the people they had attracted to them: Soupault, Breton, Aragon, Mayakovsky, Tzara. 'All the heads that gravitated around him,' as Sonia put it. He gradually went back to painting, and produced a second series of Eiffel Tower pictures as well as a number of colourful abstracts, or non-figurative paintings as he preferred to call them, which are difficult sometimes to distinguish from Sonia's work.There is a sense in which his best and most original work was behind him, though he continued to paint until his death.

By 1923, the Delaunays were in relatively easy circumstances. The sale of the Rousseau *Snake Charmer* in 1922 certainly solved their short-term financial problems. And Sonia had quickly started operating a fashion house out of the boulevard Malesherbes address, designing clothes for well-known actresses, both for their personal use and as costumes on stage. Even the reigning star of Hollywood, Gloria Swanson, is known to have bought at least one of her dresses from Sonia. Most of the materials she used in the making of these clothes were her own designs, and in fact it was these fabric designs which became the basis of her improving fortunes.

When she first opened (on the same floor as the apartment) her boutique, her fashion studio, her fabric house – for it was all of those – she did not anticipate that things would go so well, that it would become a *business*. She had professed to dislike the trappings of business, and here she was with a registered office, headed stationery, publicity leaflets, display windows.

Her involvement in fabrics began when she provided more than fifty designs to a silk manufacturer in Lyons as early as 1923. In 1924 she founded her own company with four directors, among them the prominent couturier Jacques Heim. In Paris there were many opportunities for Sonia to exhibit her creations at various celebrations, charity balls, annual artistic gatherings. But her greatest success came in 1925, at the Exposition Internationale des Arts Décoratifs, for which she designed and decorated a 'simultaneous boutique'

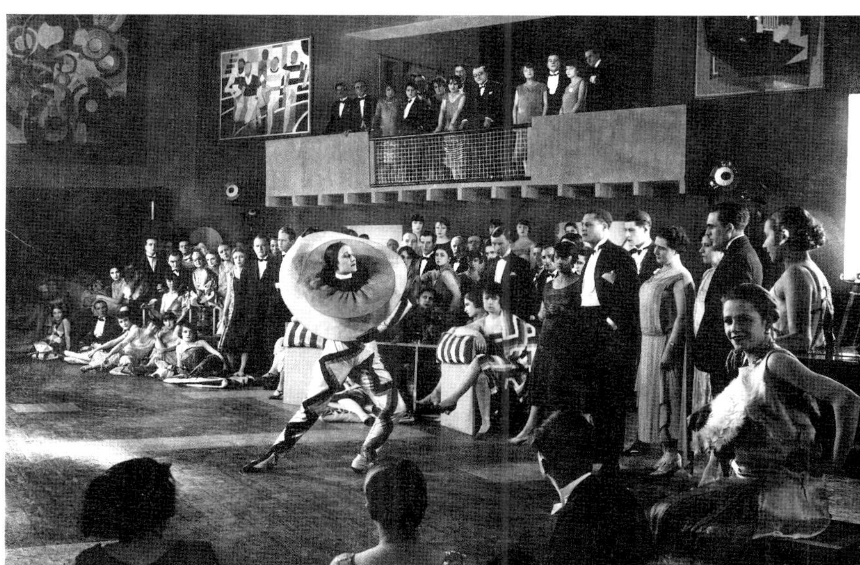

A scene from the film *Le p'tit Parigot* (1926), with costumes by Sonia, and paintings on the walls by Robert.

with the help of Heim. At their stand, which was situated on the Alexandre III Bridge, mannequins showed her various creations, among them a group of fur coats in her geometric style.

At this juncture the fabric manufacturers were seriously courting Sonia and wanted only geometric designs. It was in 1925 that a long-lasting and profitable collaboration with the Dutch department store of Metz & Co. began. During some thirty years this company bought about 200 of her designs for fashion and home decoration. Her output up to the 1930 world Depression was prodigious, and her work became known in London at Liberty's and in certain department stores in New York. She was designing not only fabrics of enormous and apparently unlimited variety, but carpets and panels and handbags, a constant stream of fabric and fashion drawings in gouache, and also costumes for two films in 1926: *Vertige*, directed by Marcel L'Herbier, and *Le p'tit Parigot*. She had become so well known for her fabrics and clothing that she was invited to the Sorbonne to give a lecture on 'The Influence of Painting on the Art of Clothing' during a conference organized by what she calls 'the group of philosophical and scientific studies'. She spoke about the current liberation from academic couture, the changes in social behaviour which had led to greater freedom in women's clothes, the intimate relationship between the designer of fabrics and the *couturier*, the attraction and attractiveness of geometric forms in fabrics – and she introduced the revolutionary idea of *prêt-à-porter* (ready-to-wear), which seems to have originated as a suggestion of Robert's.

Her fabric designs constitute one of the most impressive contributions to twentieth-century decorative arts. They sum up most of the trends of the first half of the century, and at the same time they have never become 'dated'; even today they are admired, not as historical objects but as designs for any age. These designs, with their bright colours reminiscent of Orphism and 'simultaneous contrast', their combination of sumptuousness and artistic rigour, attest to the outcome of a whole movement which had preoccupied art since 1910: Cubism, Futurism, Russian Suprematism, Neo-Plasticism and De Stijl in painting and sculpture; the architectural ideas and aims of Auguste Perret, Adolf Loos, Walter Gropius, Marcel Breuer (whose wife was one of her customers); and even the work of Paul Poiret in fashion. As Dorival puts it, in her creations Sonia was 'the incarnation of her times'.

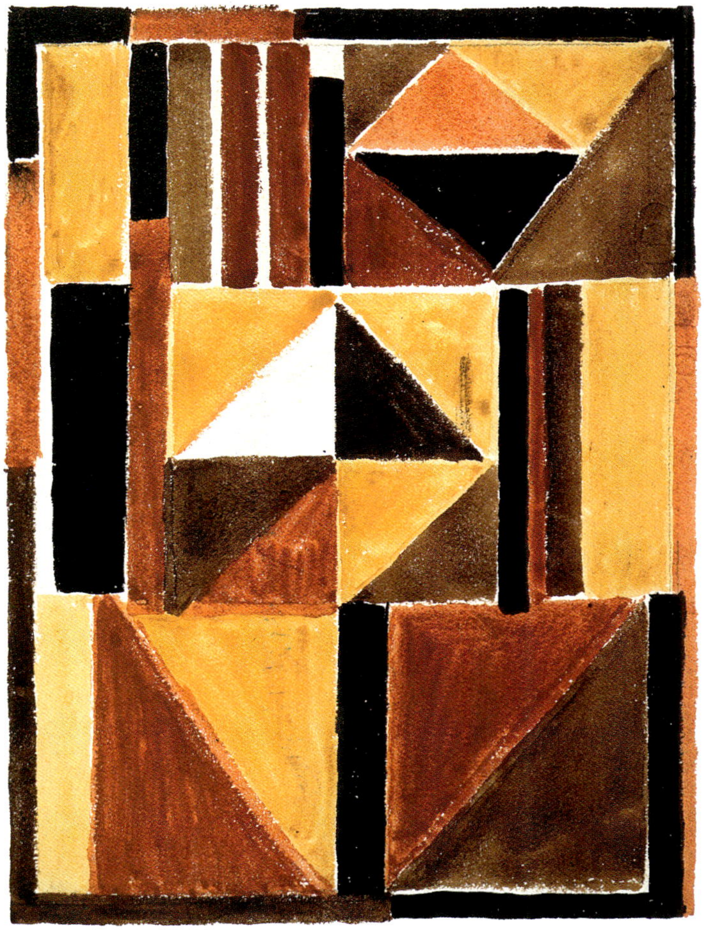

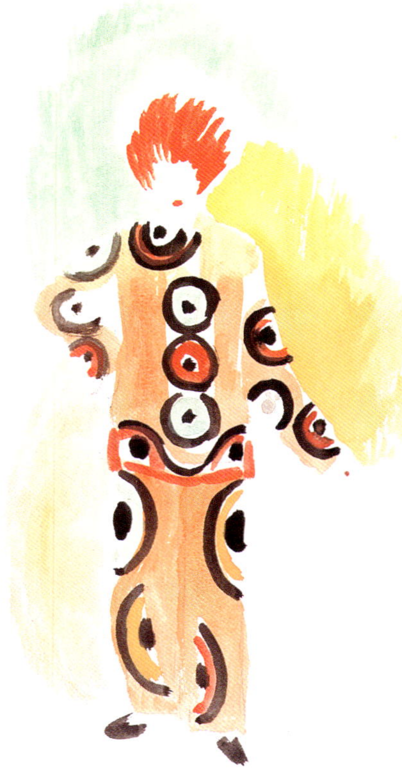

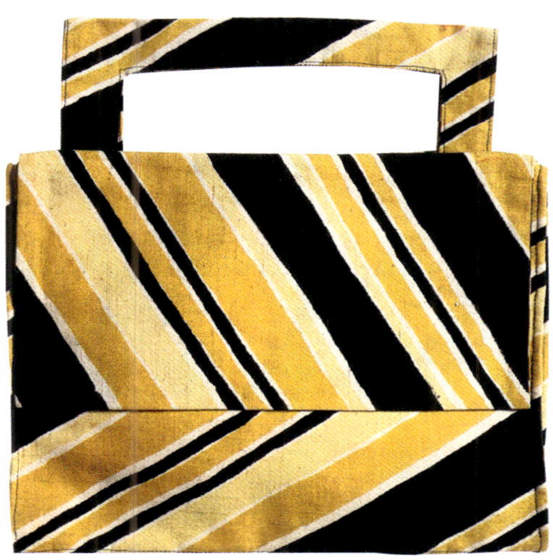

39 *Harlequin*, a rug designed by Sonia in 1924.

40 Pyjamas designed for Tristan Tzara, 1923.

41 A striped handbag, designed in 1925.

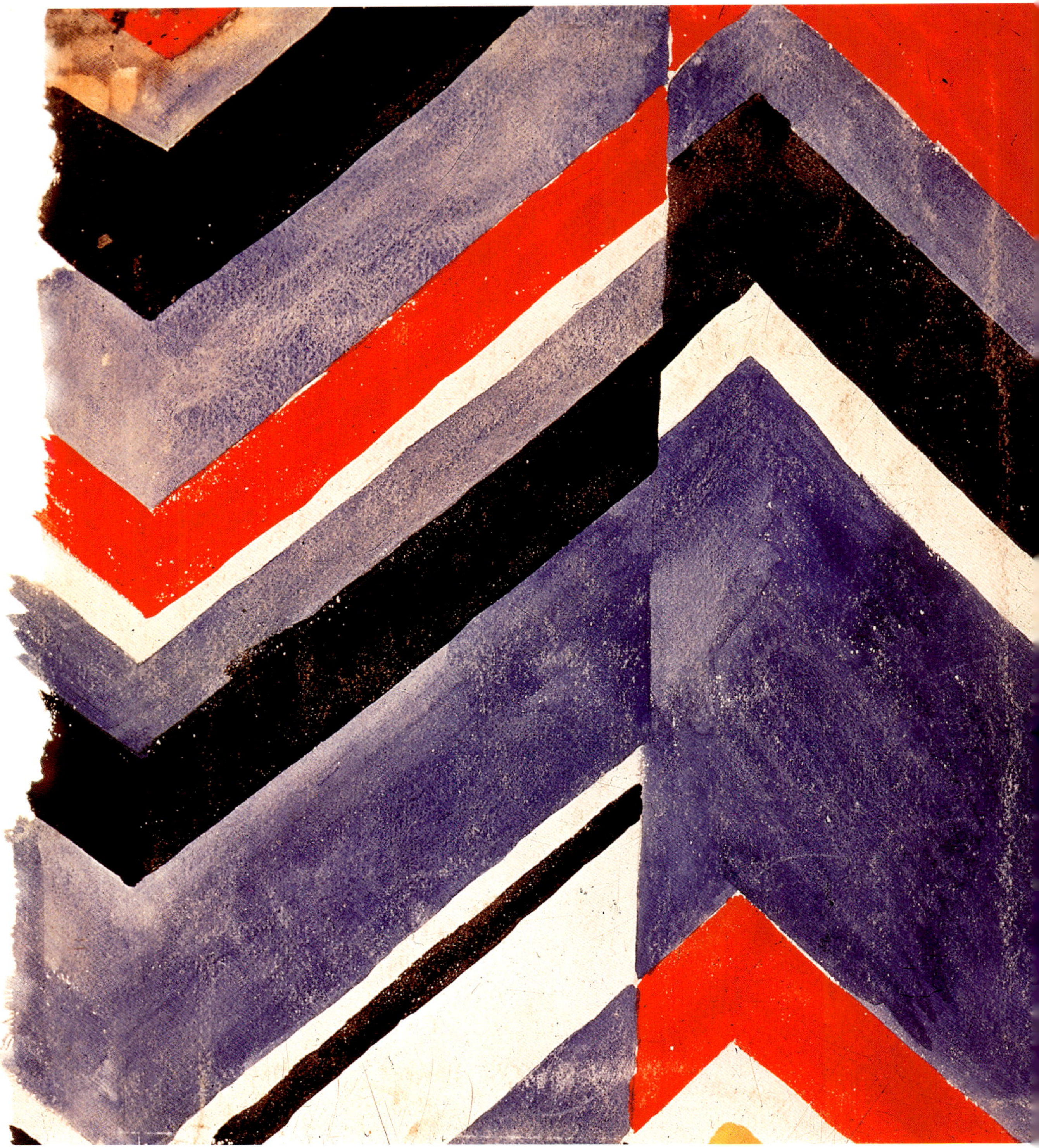

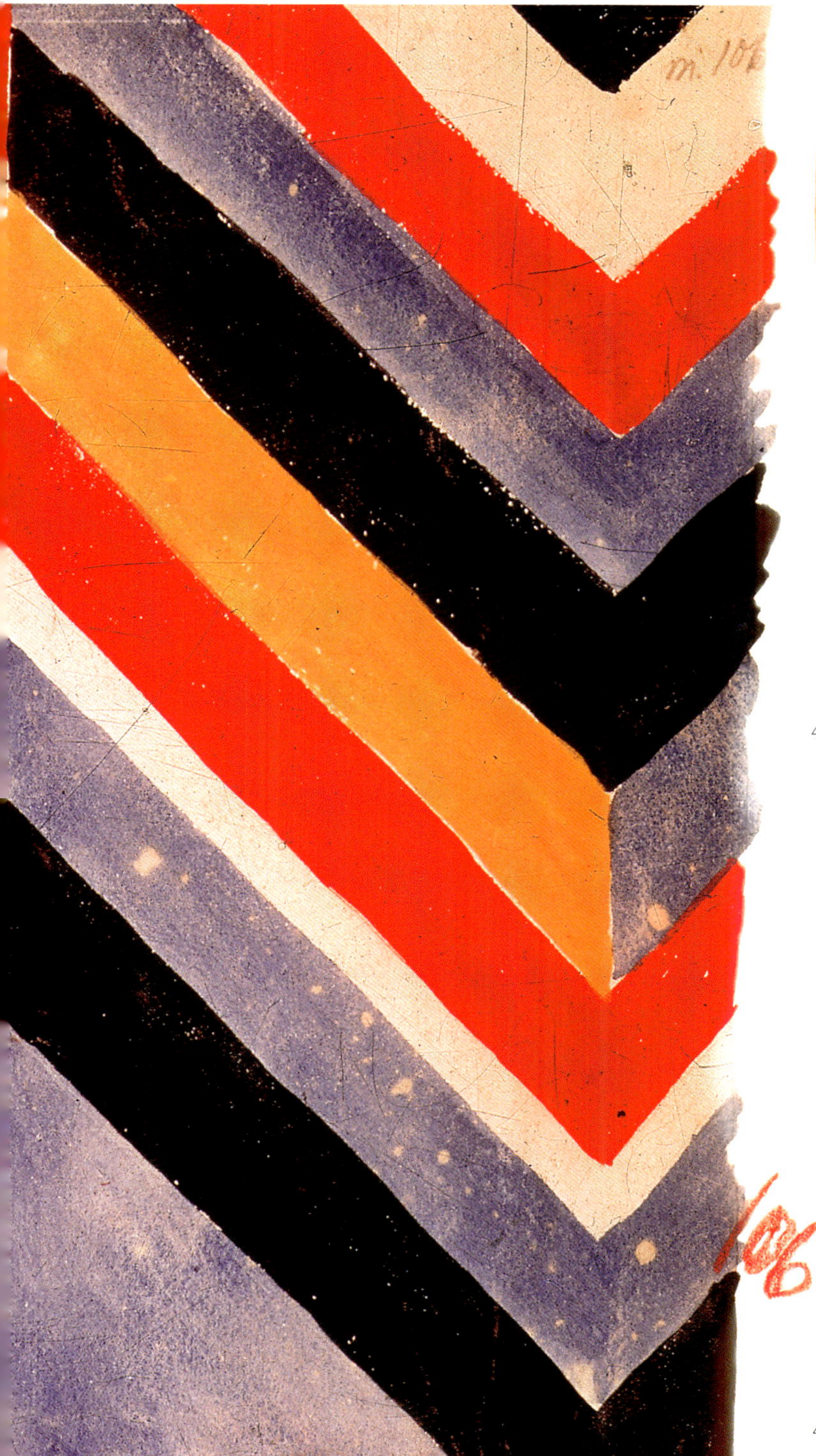

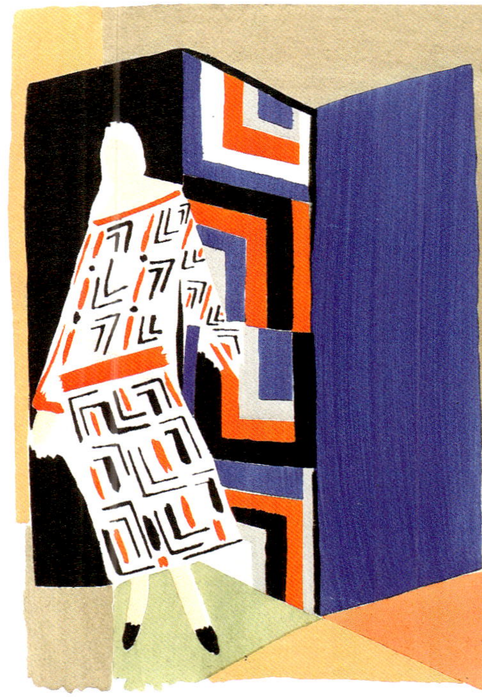

43 Dress for a woman sketched in front of a screen designed by Sonia, Indian ink, 1924-25.

42 Fabric design No. 6, 1923. (This was one of Sonia's favourite designs.)

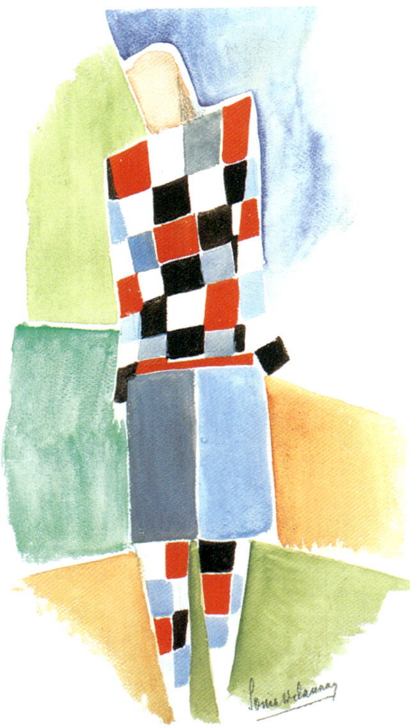

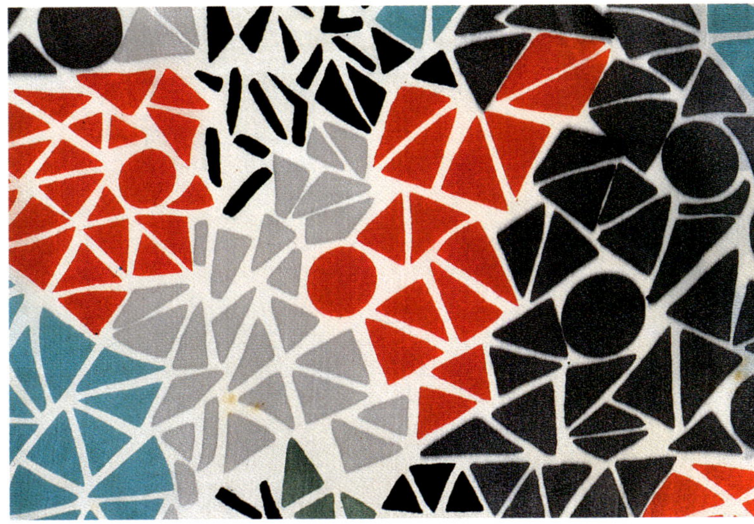

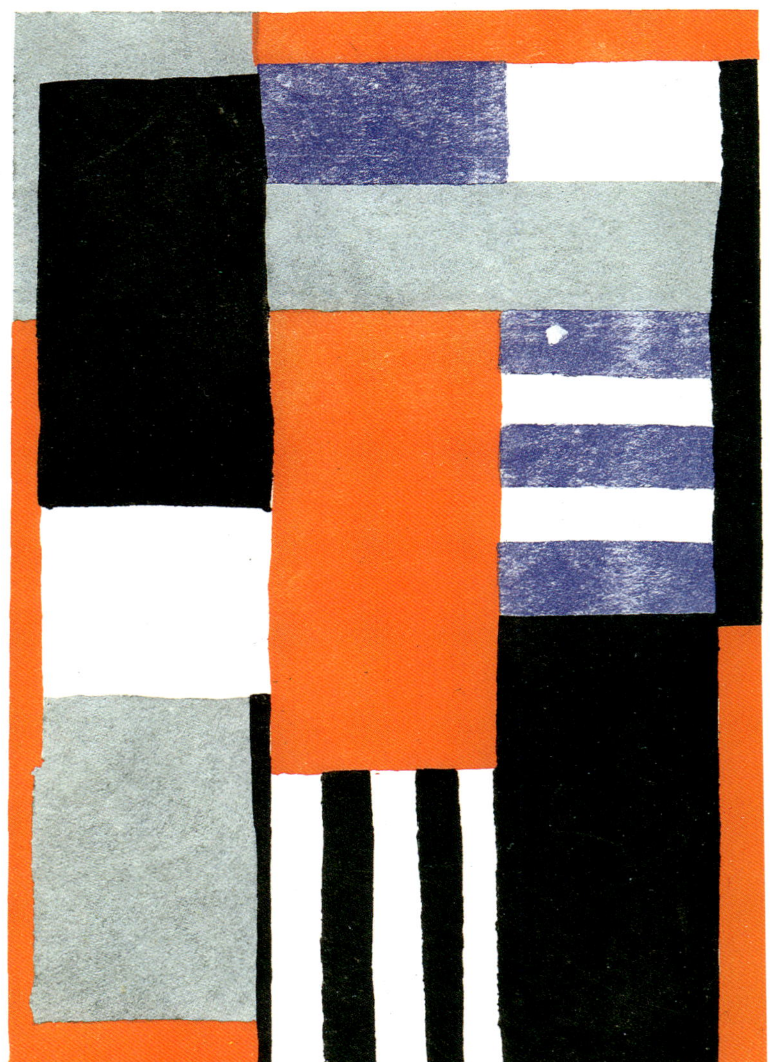

44 A man's outfit, 1925, for *Adam*, a magazine of men's fashion.

45 A silk design of 1925.

46 Blue, red and black rug of 1925.

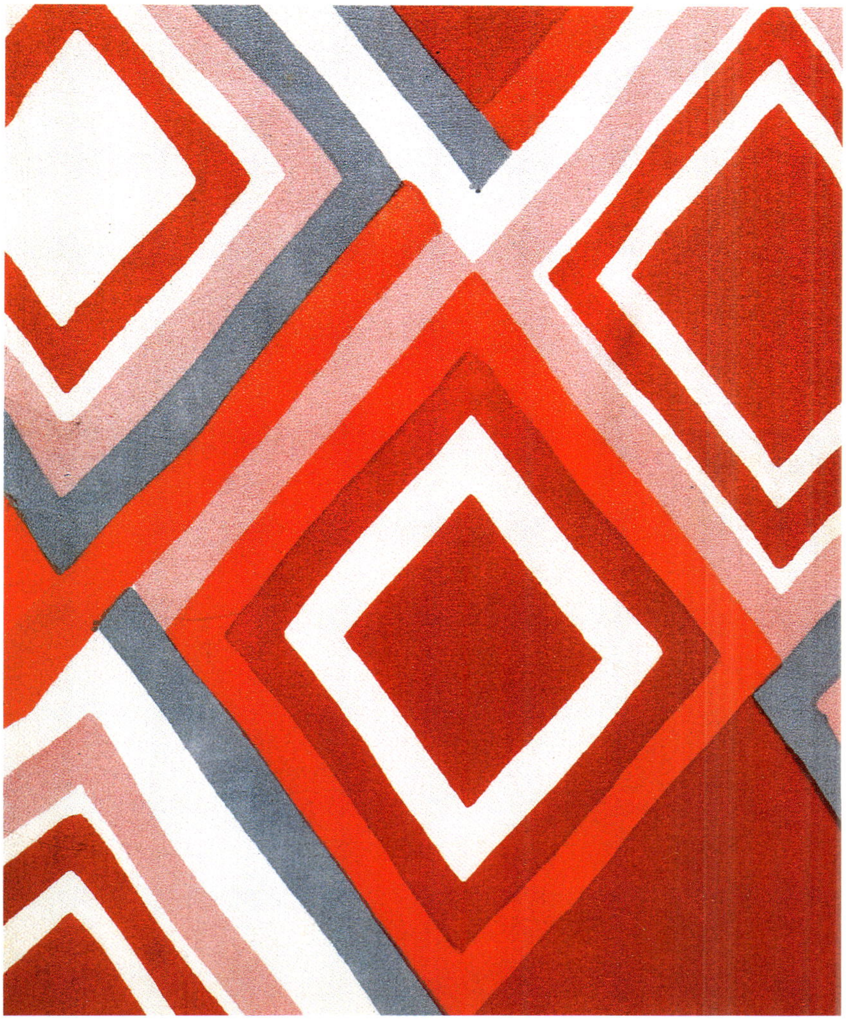

47 Chequerboard fabric pattern, 1925.

48 A gouache sketch of a skier's outfit, 1925.

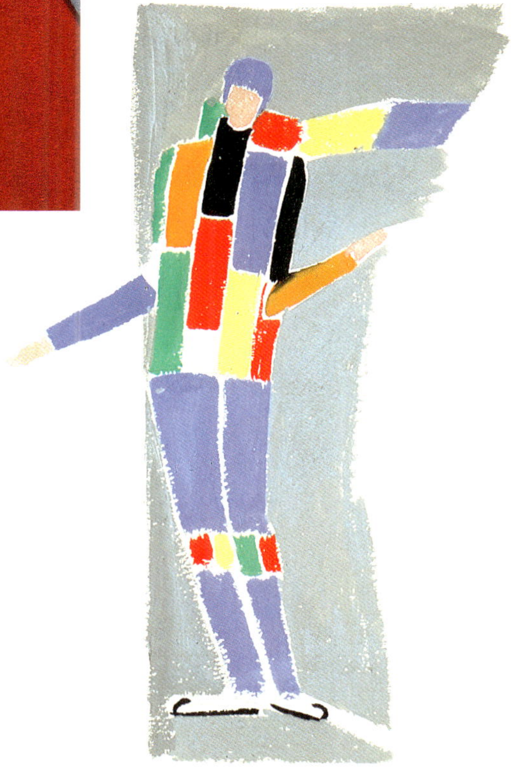

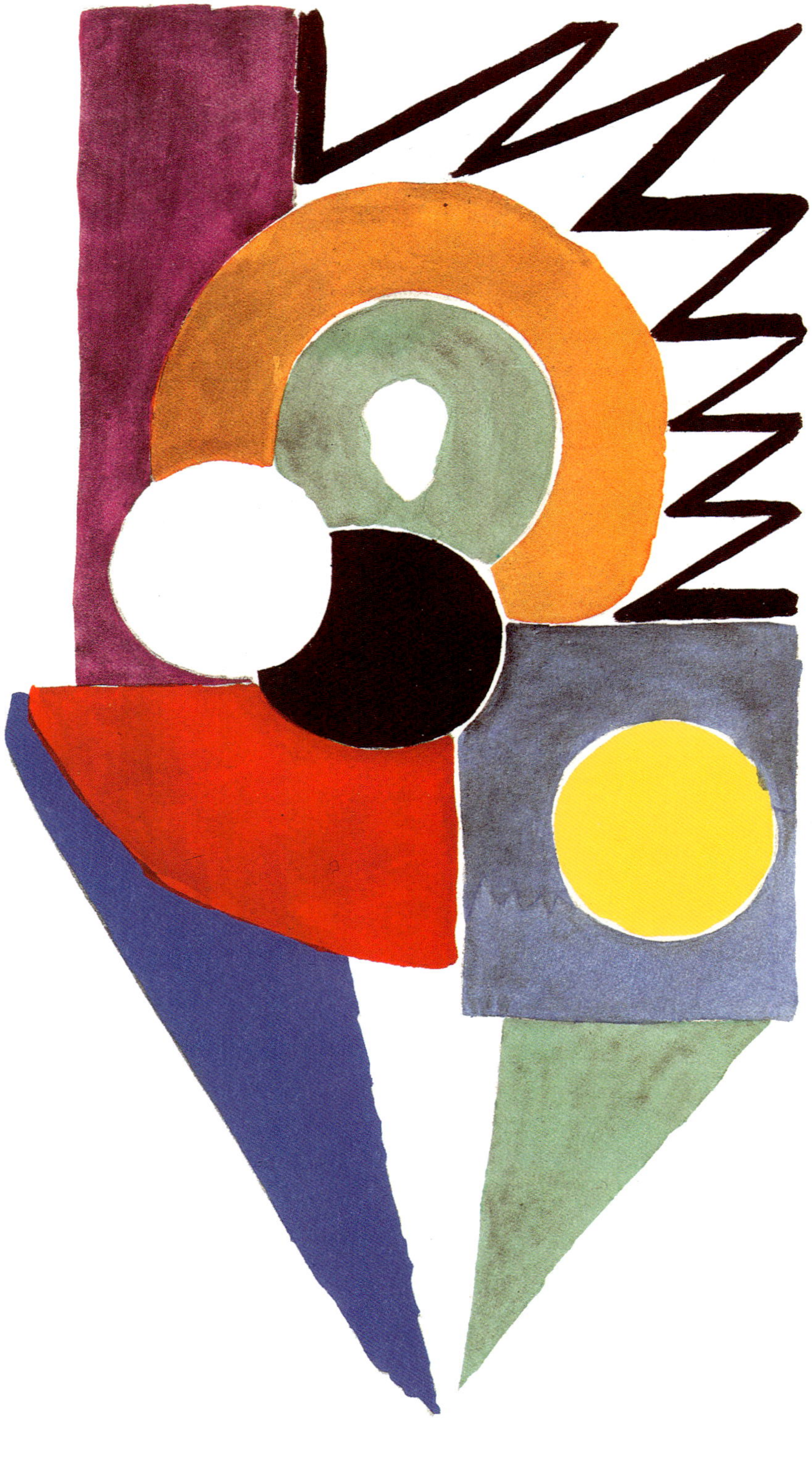

49 Opposite, *Danseuse électrique*, dance costume sketch, watercolour on paper, 1923.

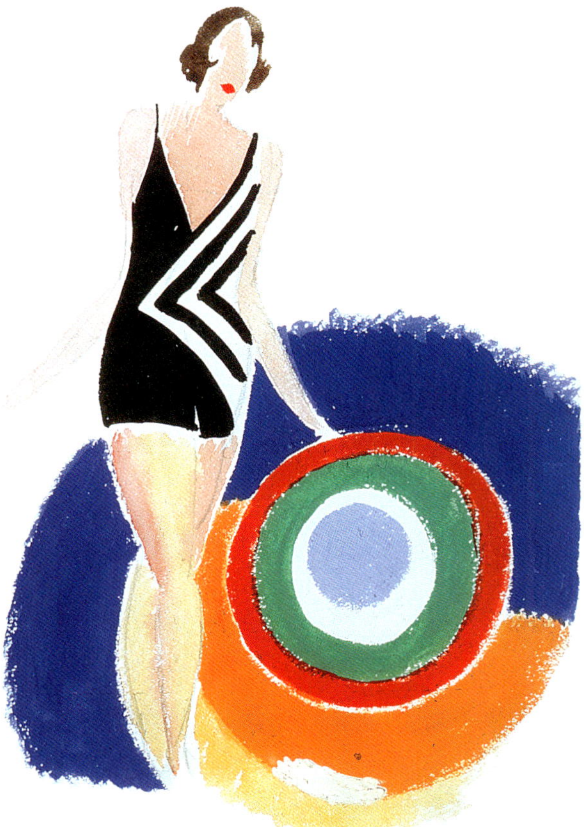

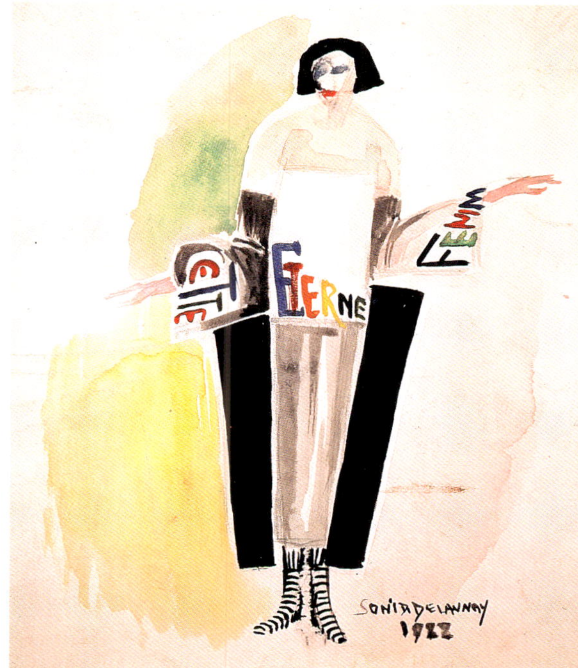

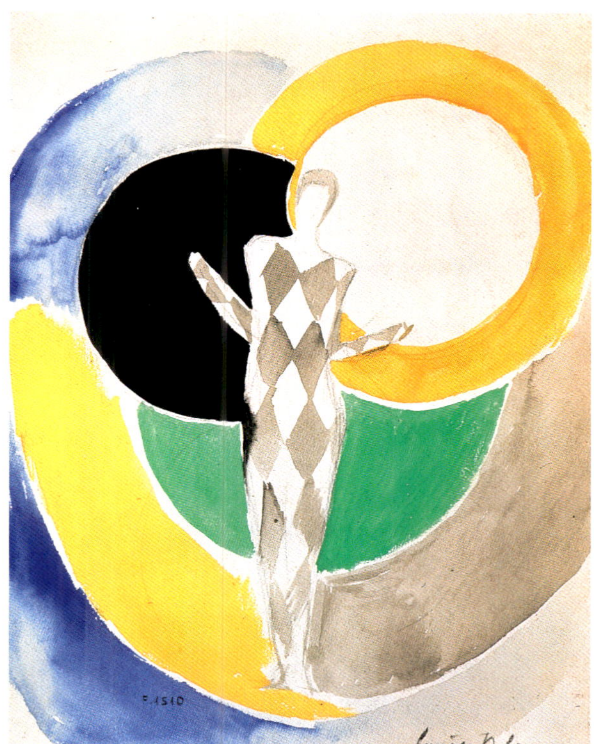

50 Woman in beach wear, 1928.

51 *CETTE FEMME ETERNELLE*, a suggestion by Tzara for one of Sonia's 'poem dresses', 1922.

52 *Pierrot* design, gouache, 1930.

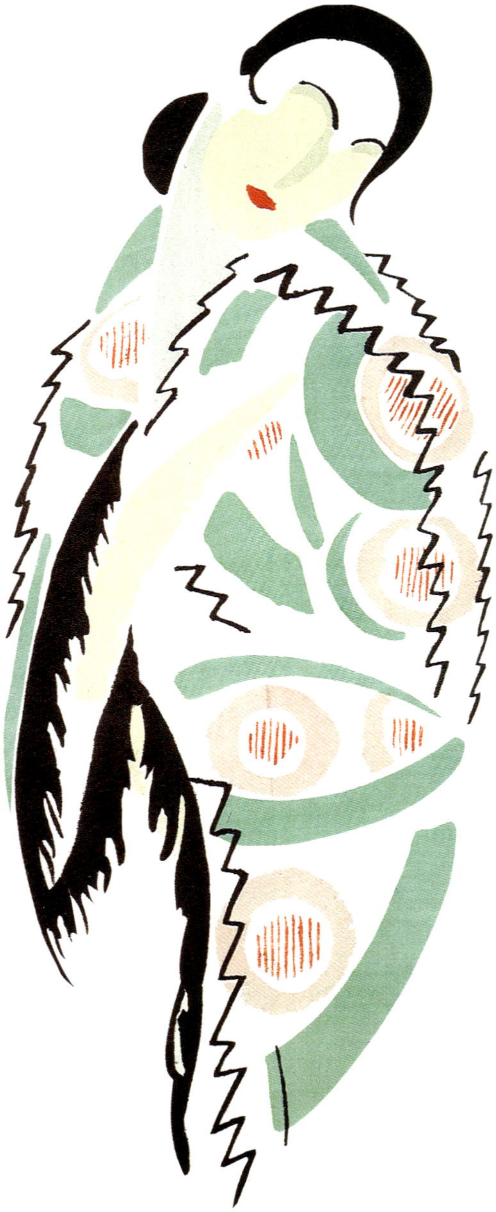

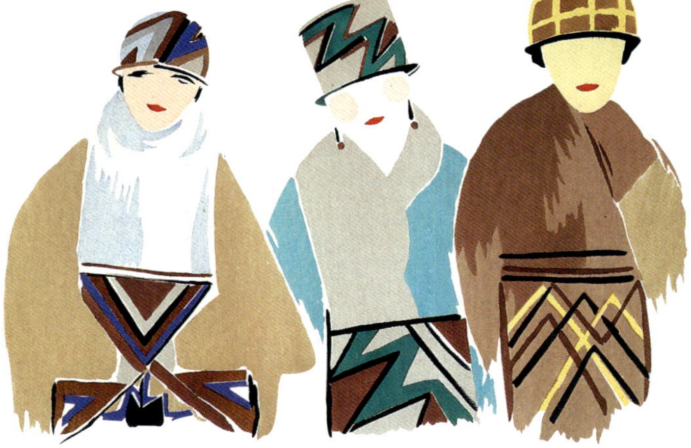

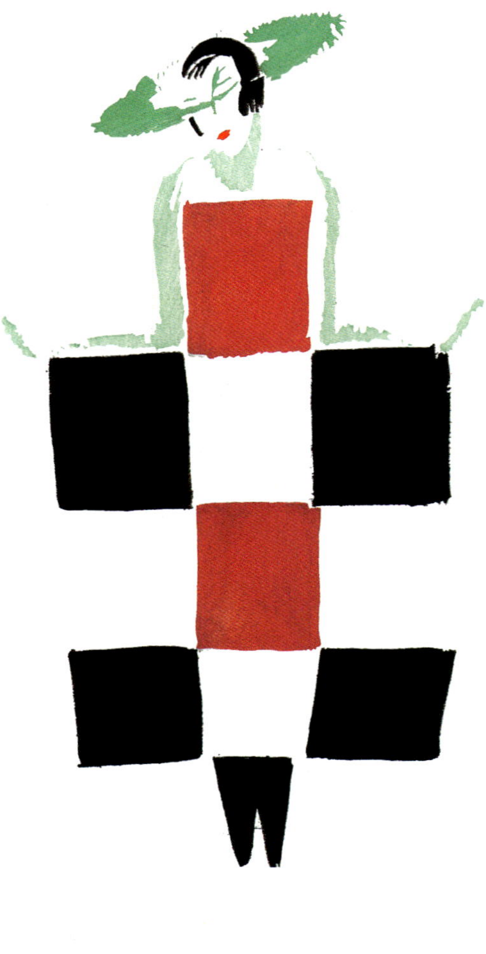

53 Spanish shawl, 1922.

54 Designs by Sonia of hats for women, 1923.

55 Cube design of a woman's costume for Carnival in Rio de Janeiro, 1926.

CHAPTER 10

'YEARS OF LIBERATION': HARD TIMES

THE GREAT DEPRESSION brought a halt to this sustained commercial success: the market for luxury goods grew weak, lucrative orders from the United States were drying up, the whole business world was in deep disorder. Sonia was hard put to know how to keep her workers occupied and, even more, how to pay them. She claims that what she and Robert decided to do in this crisis came to her in a flash, while they were sitting outside of La Rotonde across from the Dôme brasserie on the boulevard du Montparnasse. Sitting in the *terrasse* of the Dôme was a man smoking his pipe in the sun; it turned out to be the Belgian artist Georges Vantongerloo, whom they knew well and who gave every appearance of being completely at peace with himself and his idleness. It struck her that she and Robert, too, could sit and daydream in the sun; they could simply turn their backs on her business operations and return to the life they had led before. It sounds naive and thoroughly impractical, but it is more or less what they set out to do.

She later called the period from 1930 to 1940 her 'years of liberation', but that can only have meant liberation from the exigencies of running a business, for economic realities forced her to continue to provide fabric designs and to undertake orders for clothes from rich women, though it was now on a much more informal basis and brought in far less money.

First she closed down the business; then in 1935 they moved from the comparative luxury of boulevard Malesherbes back to the Left Bank and a studio apartment at 16 rue Saint-Simon, where she lived until she died. Robert clung to the independence of the studio in the rue des Grands-Augustins, and indeed lived there when he was absorbed by his work. They started out these years of liberation with a stroke of luck, provided by an extremely rich shipowner, Jean Delhumeau, who bought one of Robert's paintings, *Le Soleil, la Lune et la Tour Eiffel.* This was the beginning of Delhumeau's collection, and in due course he also bought the *Hommage à Blériot* for 50,000 francs. Indeed, he became a friend of the Delaunays, and invited them to visit his summer home on the Ile d'Yeu. Along with Arp and his wife Sophie, they went to spend a week there, then visited Carnac, where they had a happy reunion with Tzara.

Before long, she found that her life was still, as she writes, 'complicated, divided, fragmented' between the personal orders she continued to receive from couturiers, particularly Jacques Heim, the publication of articles in magazines, projects for window displays and posters, meetings with architects, engineers, potential backers. And all the while she had to cope with Robert's haphazard attitudes, keeping track of and dating his paintings for future reference and exhibitions, sales, gifts to museums, etc. One fortunate result of all these preoccupations was her resumption of a long-abandoned youthful habit of keeping a journal. From 1933 she made an entry each day, sometimes only practical notes of expenditures, orders, telephone calls received and made, furniture purchases, but also records of conversations and events.

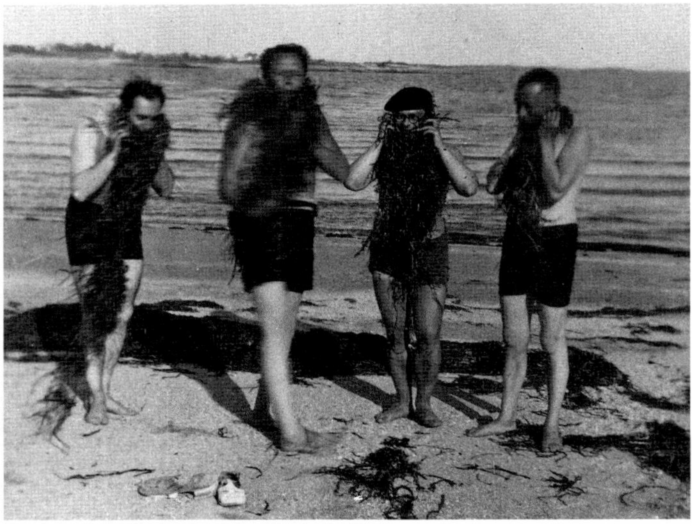

On the beach at Carnac in Brittany, around 1930: Robert Delaunay, Tristan Tzara, Jean Arp and an unidentified friend on the left.

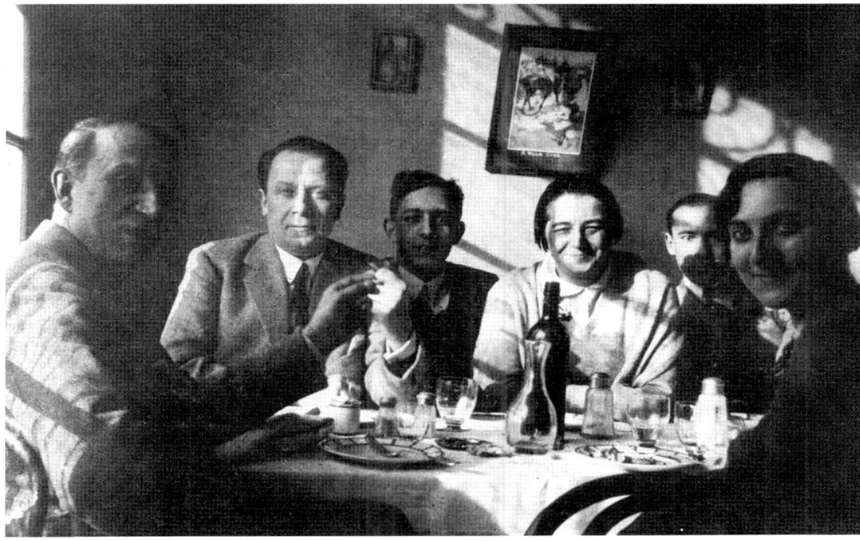

Robert (second from left) and Sonia (third from right) with friends around the lunch table at Nesle-la-Vallé.

The journals of the Thirties show that not only the Delaunays but their whole band were confronted with intense financial problems. As soon as a cheque in payment for a design or a dress was received, Robert would be sent off to pay the overdue electricity or telephone bill. Jacques Heim was very slow in paying for the work Sonia did for him; she was constantly having to send reminders and copies of unpaid invoices to him and other customers. To help eke out their earnings, she took on a few students – Elisabeth 'Ella' Wharton, Philippa Brooks, Marcelle Debouchy – who paid 300 francs per month for three lessons a week. Eventually, they became assistants of a sort, part of their training being to make copies for the record of Sonia's many fabric designs. (Her numbering of them had by 1933 reached the 1200s).

Sonia also did a bit of interior decorating when an opportunity arose, and tried to supplement their income by providing accessories for her customers: scarves, gloves, handkerchiefs and handbags, as well as ties for presents. There were fewer of the rich American women she had counted on in the Twenties. Those who still called on her began to complain about prices as the value of their dollars kept falling. In June 1934, for instance, a Mrs Corday was on the verge of ordering an entire wardrobe for the season in Palm Beach, but cancelled at the last minute because of the disadvantageous exchange. Yet Sonia wrote in her journal on 7 September 1934: 'If one does it well and it is not too expensive, one could work all the time at couture.' She

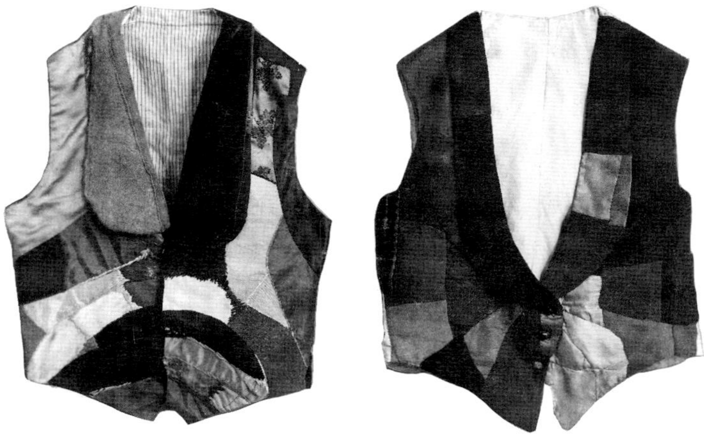

Two waistcoats created by Sonia for Tzara and Crevel.

had a couple of faithful French customers, among them Marie Cuttoli, who became a beloved personal friend.

As manager of the family's accounts, Sonia had to record every sale of paintings as it occurred: a little canvas of Robert's (*Sacré Coeur*) and a small sketch from life (*Quai du Louvre*) sold for 700 francs, Solomon Guggenheim bought one of the Eiffel Tower pictures in April 1934, M. Delhumeau was thinking of buying a couple of pictures (one of Sonia's, two of Robert's), a picture was sold by Robert to the dealer Bing on 18 May 1934 (2,500 francs), etc. But what these records make particularly vivid are the frustrations of an artist who is not unknown but not yet widely collected. People were prone to telephone to say that they knew of a possible client for Robert's paintings or Sonia's fabrics; then the client might not turn up at the appointed time or might suddenly decide to leave Paris. Those who came generally expressed great enthusiasm, asked for prices, went away to think and sometimes said the prices were too high or else said nothing at all.

In September 1934, Sonia was in negotations with a Mr Schweizer of Zürich, who wished to commission Robert to do a portrait of the President of the Zürich Chamber of Commerce. He wanted a French painter, the portrait could be 'modern', and price was no object. Sonia showed the man various portraits Robert had done, and without much fuss they agreed on a fee of 125,000 francs, with 10,000 in advance and the rest on completion. Sonia thought, 'It all has the air of a joke or of a madman or maybe *real*.' But nothing more was heard of it.

There were many opportunities for Robert to show his paintings and Sonia her designs. In December 1933, she was preparing for exhibition at the Salon des Indépendants Robert's Rugby football painting, *Equipe de Cardiff,* and her own *Bal Bullier,* among others; and early in the next year she was working on the project of a painting for the Tuileries exhibition. Working on this led her to jot down some thoughts: 'In the matter of colours everything is a question of number. This conception of colour is a new point of departure in perception itself. Up to the present it was all daubing, this is the basis of a new visual science, whose discovery is personal through our sensitivity, but whose development could be made by generations of people, who will create a new language.'

She came back to this subject in April 1934, while working on the same painting: 'There's a clarification in painting taking place at the moment. Colour becomes number, these relationships create the rhythms of an art far from the Impressionists. The same thing in life in everything that happens at the moment. But few people understand it and, as Gleizes says, one could die before it's understood. But what importance does incomprehension signify when faced with conviction? For example, the great revolutionaries. They're the martyrs of the modern age and it's always they who prove to be right in the future.'

She sought to clarify this idea of colour and number in a piece she wrote much later, an autobiographical résumé for her retrospective at the Musée National d'Art Moderne in 1967-68. In speaking of the fabric designs she had made in 1923, she said that for her 'they were and remain ranges

Furniture designed by Sonia originally for the boulevard Malesherbes apartment.

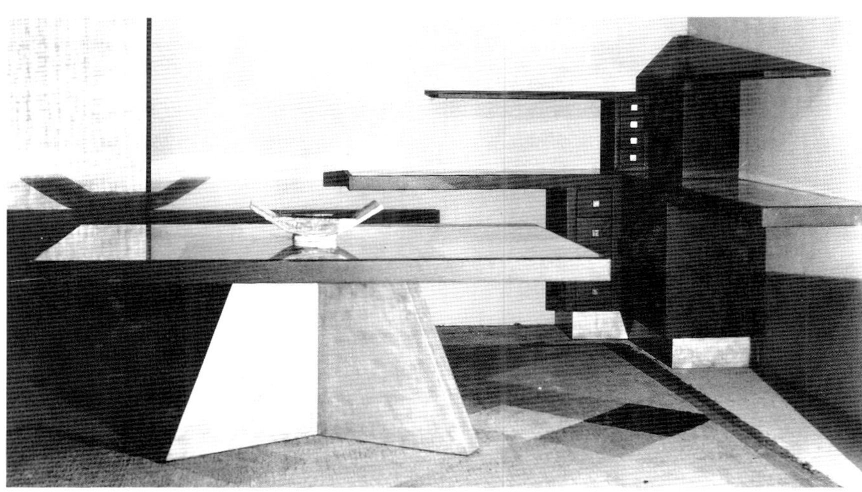

of colours, and based on the purified conception of our painting . . . My research was purely pictural and in plastic terms a discovery which served both of us in our painting. Rhythm is based on numbers, for colour can be measured by the number of vibrations. It is an entirely new concept which opens up limitless horizons for painting and can be used by anyone who will feel and understand it.'

In January 1935, Robert participated in the show called Artistes des Temps Présents, and in February they both took part in an exhibition *Artistes d'Aujourd'hui* at the Petit Palais, where Robert had a big success, especially with his *Ville de Paris.* In March he was given a one-man show in the Galerie Art et Décoration, owned by Albert Lévy. The fledgling Museum of Modern Art in New York mounted an important exhibition in 1936, called *Cubism and Abstract Art.* Six works by Robert were included: three from the Museum's own collection (a 1927 lithograph of a 1909 painting *Saint Séverin,* a 1909-10 ink drawing of a tower with a ferris wheel and a 1910 ink drawing of the Eiffel Tower), the others an oval-shaped *Fenêtre* of 1912 lent by the Léonce Rosenberg Gallery in Paris, a circular oil painting of around 1913 called *Disks* – 'Composition simultanée; les disques soleils' – lent by Delaunay, and a privately owned *Rhythm without End* of 1935. Although the show was intended to be a more or less comprehensive *tour d'horizon* of Cubist and post-Cubist art, Sonia's name appears nowhere in the characteristically knowledgeable introduction by Alfred H. Barr, Jr.

But exhibiting pictures, and having them enthusiastically reviewed, did not necessarily lead to profitable sales. Their combined income was so inadequate that Robert was receiving unemployment insurance from the State. An inspector came to see her about this in November 1934, and in order to support Robert's claim to be unemployed in his profession, she showed the man published reviews of Robert's shows and a list of the museums that owned his paintings. The inspector came a second time for more details, but said encouragingly that, since the monthly payments had not at that point been stopped, chances were good that they would continue.

In February 1935, the Delaunays decided to appeal for work to their friend Jean Cassou, who was employed at the Louvre. Sonia typed out a letter from Robert to Cassou, asking if there was any work he might do for the State. Cassou responded overnight, telling them to go to the Hôtel de Ville for an interview with a M. Darras. On 5 February, Sonia went with Robert to see,

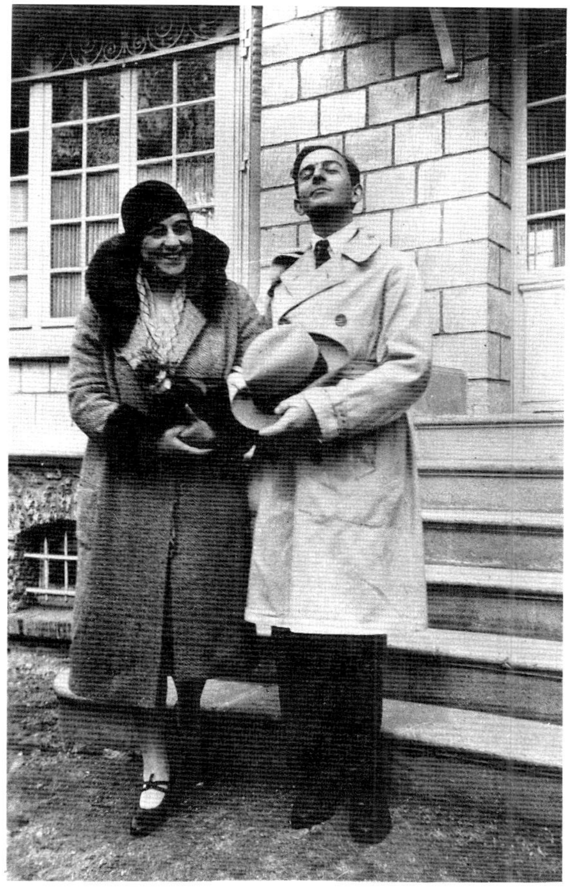

Sonia and her twenty-year-old son Charles, around 1932.

first of all, a M. Bourgeois. After Robert explained his circumstances, Bourgeois said he would speak with Darras, who was the Director of Beaux-Arts, and another man whose name was Contenot to see if they could work out a commission or a purchase for a museum of one of Robert's paintings. Bourgeois did not think the city of Paris could come up with more than 10,000 francs, but this would perhaps be supplemented by the State. He wanted to discuss it with Cassou and promised to write within two or three days. By 22 February they were informed that the Beaux-Arts declined to buy a picture. This was in some respects ironic for the decision was taken only a few days before Robert's *Ville de Paris* was so widely acclaimed at the Petit Palais exhibition.

Sonia's energy and fortitude enabled her to take these frustrations and hardships in her stride. At the age of fifty, she enjoyed a dependable constitution. She had put on weight (she was always fond of bonbons) and began to look matronly though energetic. Her only physical disability was chronic asthma, for which she was treated by two intelligent doctors, Viard and Allendy, who were to appear under different circumstances in her life during World War II. She makes almost no complaints about her personal travails in her journals; her days were so busy and so full of often futile activities that she had little leisure to ponder the difficulties she faced. She was meeting with representatives of Macy's, New York, and Marshall Field in Chicago, showing them her fabric designs but not being particularly successful in getting them to place orders. There were running legal disputes with dealers and customers; she wrote an astounding number of letters every morning. And all the while she and Robert were keeping up with artist friends, going to their studios to see their newest work: Naum Gabo, his brother Antoine Pevsner, Kandinsky ('a painter of value, but older than the group of abstract artists'), Giacometti, Moholy-Nagy, Chagall, Mondrian. Because Charles had become interested in jazz and popular music, she also found time to go with him to concerts at the Salle Pleyel. Her comment on a musician by the name of Johnson was that he was 'more constructive, more purely abstract than Duke Ellington, but less brilliant.' She heard Coleman Hawkins on 23 February 1935, and after a Louis Armstrong concert she decided that his was 'absolutely abstract music'. She was never particularly astute about music and mentions it only rarely; for Charles's sake, she made an effort to understand and appreciate the jazz to which he eventually devoted his life.

Almost every day there were gatherings at lunch and dinner with friends at a number of habitual bistrots. And every night, whatever had gone before, they would all meet at the Closerie des Lilas to end off the evening. In spite of the deepening economic crisis, in spite of ominous political events, there was no despair among the Delaunays' familiars. There was a feeling that prosperity might be just around the corner (as the politicians said); and in the Delaunays' case, it was usually the owner of the Metz store, Hugo de Leeuw, or someone like Delhumeau, who appeared at just the right moment to bail them out. They were also in frequent contact with a German woman called Hilla von Rebay, who looked after the interests in Europe of the Solomon Guggenheim Foundation and was active in keeping the Delaunays and the powerful Mr Guggenheim in touch.

CHAPTER 11

THE INTERNATIONAL EXPOSITION OF 1937

In 1933 Sonia wrote in her journal of 'a suspicion of a deep friendship' with an architect who wanted to work with her on large projects of mural art and light animation. Identifying this man only as 'A...', she writes that the experience revealed to her how 'starved' she was for 'spiritual exchanges with others', implying at the same time that she had to resist his amorous approaches in order to protect her 'interior life', to which no one until then had had access and which she hid behind a wall of good humour and optimism.

The person she refers to so discreetly may have been Adolphe Audoul, who, in concert with another well-known architect, Robert Mallet-Stevens, obtained a commission for Sonia and Robert to collaborate in the decorations for a grand exhibition, backed by the Popular Front government of Léon Blum, to be mounted in 1937.

The *Exposition Internationale des Arts et Techniques dans la vie moderne* was a prime example of the French illusion in the late 1930s that all was, or soon could be, normal again. It was a valiant and optimistic attempt on the part of French government and commercial interests to restore some of the confidence France and the rest of the world had lost in the throes of the grinding economic depression. But this would-be morale booster was mounted in a dangerous and anxious time: Spain was engaged in a savage civil war, unemployment and labour militancy were endemic in France, Hitler's Germany was building up its armed forces at a hectic pace, the political universe was radically polarized and uneasy alliances were being formed with little conviction. It could not be said that the prospects of peace and prosperity were bright.

The 1937 Exposition devoured almost two years of the Delaunays' lives. The first mention of it in the journals is on 26 December 1934, when Sonia noted that she was doing 'fabric designs and projects for the 1937 exposition.' By January 1936 she was consulting a lawyer, Etienne Caen, about the contract terms being offered.

The Delaunays' contribution to the artistic side of the exposition was not universally popular; the more conventional and commercially successful artists of the period were far from sympathetic to their style. Indeed, there were artists and art critics of great influence who simply rejected modern art as a heresy, who regarded anything that smacked of Dadaism, Surrealism or Cubism as anathema – which makes it all the more remarkable that the Delaunays, identified with all three of those movements, should have been chosen to decorate two pavilions in which the French would be vaunting their technological achievements. As it turned out, the most sensational work shown for the first time at this 1937 exposition was nothing by the Delaunays but Picasso's *Guernica*, which was displayed in the Spanish (Republican) pavilion and became the obvious target of venomous criticism.

Sonia and Robert had been asked to participate in the decoration of two temporary exhibition buildings: the Pavillon des Chemins de Fer and the Palais de l'Air, both under the architectural aegis of Audoul, René Hartwig and Jack Gérodias, and both devoted to the advances made in the technology of transport. The preparations and painting were under way in 1936, in a huge garage on the avenue de la Porte de Villiers in the outskirts of Paris, where a team of out-of-work artists had been assembled to take part in the large enterprise. According to Sonia, all was not peaceful in her 'phalanstery', an ironic reference to the ideal socialist community promoted by the nineteenth-century French utopian thinker, Charles Fourier. The group worked under severe difficulties, most of them caused by the conflict between the architects on the one side and the decorators on the other, but their main conflict was with the decorator in charge, Félix Aublet.

As early as January 1936, Sonia was chafing at Aublet's attitudes and the obstacles he put in the way of making decisions: 'At this moment, with all that is being proposed to us as our responsibility, there should be an enormous amount to do. I like very much to create and carry out my commitments, but I don't have enough lust for money. Whereas he does. As always, he has not answered.' This complaint that Aublet was not answering, was not available when needed, becomes a leitmotif in the following months. Letters of protest are written and sent to him, futile telephone calls and expeditions by car are made to his house. In one of many quarrels with him, she told him that she 'did not like weak people who gave up in midstream.' On another occasion, when he was behaving irresponsibly, she said that 'one has to choose between the life of pleasure and the life of work.' And he irritated her so much that she called him 'an extraordinary liar and hypocrite.'

The contract was not agreed and signed until April 1936. Sonia was not part of it; she told Aublet, 'I don't want my name to appear in the contract, because it seems to me that, since my work is not being specifically recompensed, it has no business being there, but I am free to help Robert and to replace him if I want to . . . I am free and mean to remain so.'

The misunderstandings and recriminations became so intense by the beginning of December that Sonia enlisted the help of one of her customers, a Mlle Labeyrie, who knew the Blums. She promised to mention one specific problem to the Premier who was dining with her on the 2nd. Two days later, Sonia noted that whatever had been holding up work on the Pavillon des Chemins de Fer was now resolved and they could begin. Their good friend Marie Cuttoli was also called upon to put their case to Blum, which she did and with good effect.

The frustrations and unrelenting friction Sonia and Robert experienced were only a tiny part of those suffered by the hordes of workers engaged in constructing the Exposition itself. It was an over-ambitious plan, including the demolition of the 1878 Palais de Trocadéro across the Seine from the Eiffel Tower, and the building of a new, distinctly modern one (the Palais de Chaillot) which would house a number of museums. The Exposition was officially opened on 24 May, though many of the pavilions were still being built and decorated even when the crowds began to arrive. The Inspecteur-Général des Beaux-Arts, Albert Laprade, gave his view of its purpose in his introduction to the official guide, 'One sees in it a sort of lively aspiration towards "something else" though still vague, towards the grandiose, the "out-of-scale", towards order, heroism, the ideal, solidarity, social awareness.'

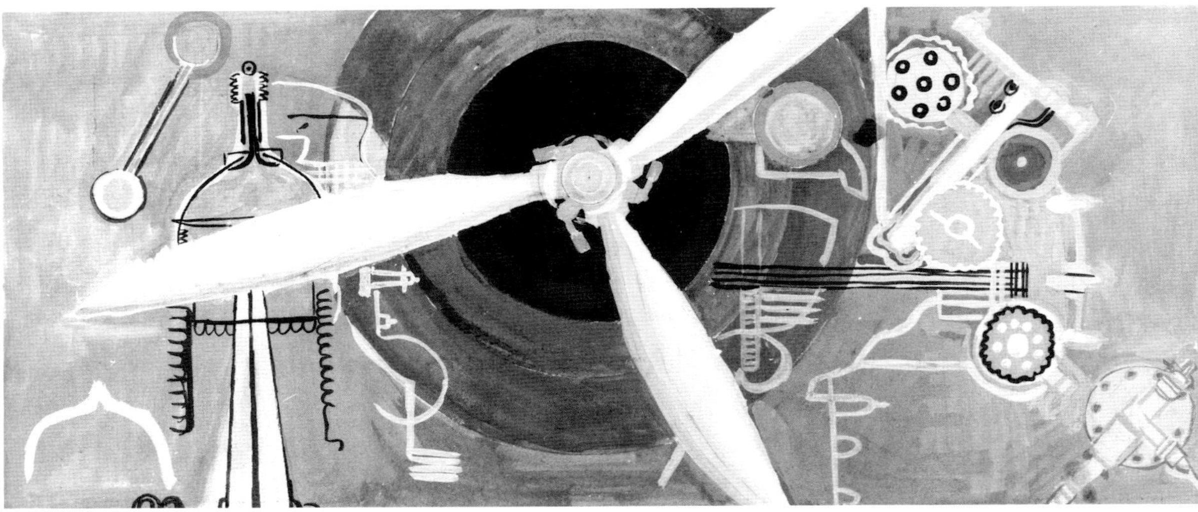

A watercolour sketch of 1936 by Sonia for a panel to be installed in the Palais de l'Air in the 1937 Paris exposition.

The railroad pavilion was housed in the old Gare des Invalides and the Palace of Air nearby in an extraordinary, futuristic, transparent all-metal building in the shape of an airfield hangar on the Esplanade des Invalides. The interior brought to mind, according to one contemporary writer, the rings of Saturn and certain trajectories of air flight. It may have owed something in its basic conception to Pierre Chareau's glass house of 1931 (much maligned at the time); at any rate, like the Chareau house, it was more exciting when lit up at night than it was during the day, and it included in its interior raked walkways which much later inspired the moving treadways which join the various storeys of the Charles de Gaulle airport. Its 'cosmic' decor was credited to the decorator Félix Aublet and the artist Robert Delaunay.

What the Delaunays created for these venues were enormous murals or panels, expressing the spectacular advances in transportation that had taken place so quickly within their own lifetime; indeed, Robert's *Hommage à Blériot* had been devoted to this theme as early as 1914. Now they offered a new, collaborative homage, in their own abstract, highly mobile and colourful style of frenetic circles, squares reflected into infinity and dazzling beams, to the inventors and mechanics who had made those advances possible.

Right, a view of the Palais de l'Air with Sonia's panel at bottom right.

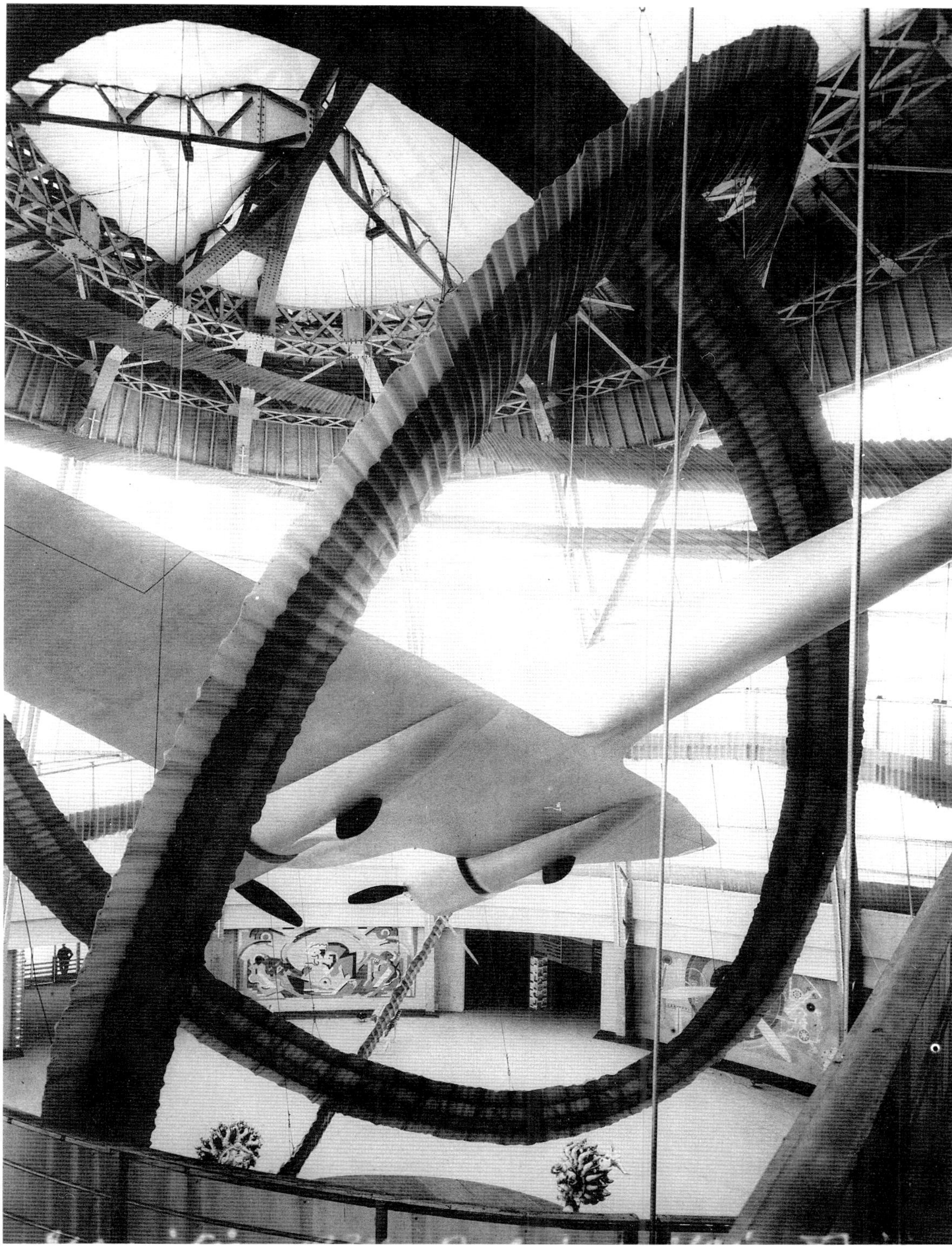

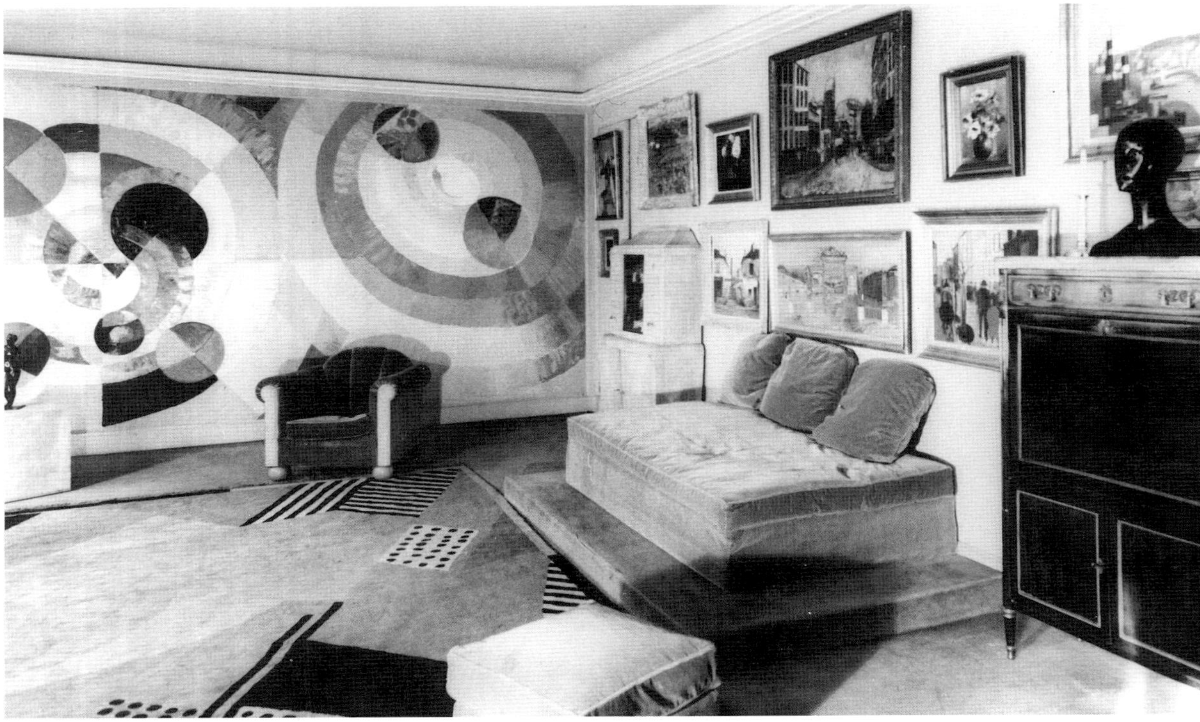

The living-room of the collector Dr Viard, with a rug designed by Sonia and a massive wall painting by Robert.

A reporter wrote at the time, 'These immense panels of Robert and Sonia Delaunay constitute the decoration most suitable to aerodynamic constructs, racing cars, planes meant to dash up into the sky. The abstract character of their art symbolizes the advance of a technique increasingly removed from mankind and nature. But its dynamism affirms faith in a progress that transcends man's being crushed by the machine.'

And of Sonia's specific contribution, Louis Cheronnet wrote in literary flight that she 'leads us amid memories of travel in sun-filled regions full of lightning in the style of Rimbaud.' Her most successful and colourful work was for the railroad pavilion, where she painted *Voyages lointains* (Distant Journeys) and *Portugal.* These no longer exist, and can only be judged from gouache sketches and black-and-white photographs; but the exhibition judges awarded Sonia a gold medal. (Robert had to be content with a 'diplôme d'honneur'.)

One happy result of the Exposition was an improvement in the Delaunays' finances. In September 1937 they went on a short motoring tour in the South of France, calling on friends in Saint-Raphael, Antibes and

Grasse, and returning to Paris by way of Aix, Tarascon and Avignon. They were home again on 2 October, and problems related to the Exposition immediately re-emerged. Consequences of the Exposition persisted like constant echoes. There were first of all questions that arose over payments to the artists who had helped them – which was Robert's responsibility. Then, once the Exposition was closed to the public on 25 November, no one was clear about the ownership of the actual works Robert and Sonia had created for the two pavilions, and what was to become of them. This was something no one seems to have taken into consideration at an earlier stage. At first it appeared that the art works might actually be the property of the Ministry of Commerce, but at the beginning of 1938 they were finally advised that their paintings and panels belonged to them so long as they did not form part of the walls to the extent that they could not be lifted away. In February they received official confirmation of this, but they would be charged for taking the works down and delivering them into safekeeping. There is no doubt the artists wanted to retrieve as much as they could of their work, particularly as there was talk of some of the decorations being used in the French pavilions being planned for the New York and San Francisco World Fairs of 1939. It had also been suggested that the whole Palais de l'Air be moved intact to a new location in Paris and made a permanent exhibition.

Reading the details of these and other rumours and reports that were daily events makes one realize how much time is wasted or lost in every creative life on plans and projects that never happen or on regrets and litigation concerning things that have gone wrong. Upon receiving advice that demolition of the Exposition was to begin on 10 February 1938, Robert signed cheques on account to the man in charge of the operation for 'the disposition and maintenance' of the works they wanted to save. In the end, their paintings and reliefs went to a storeroom at 80 avenue du Maine, where they remained throughout the War, but there were obviously a number of items which escaped their attention, including Sonia's two paintings for the Pavillon des Chemins de Fer.

It is not surprising, in view of the anxieties caused by their attempts to disentangle this situation, that Sonia should have had a severe asthma attack. She had to go to Dr Viard's clinic (where she found Raoul Dufy consulting the doctor); she was given an injection, and informed that she had emphysema, a distressing ailment of the lungs – though this did not seem to make an

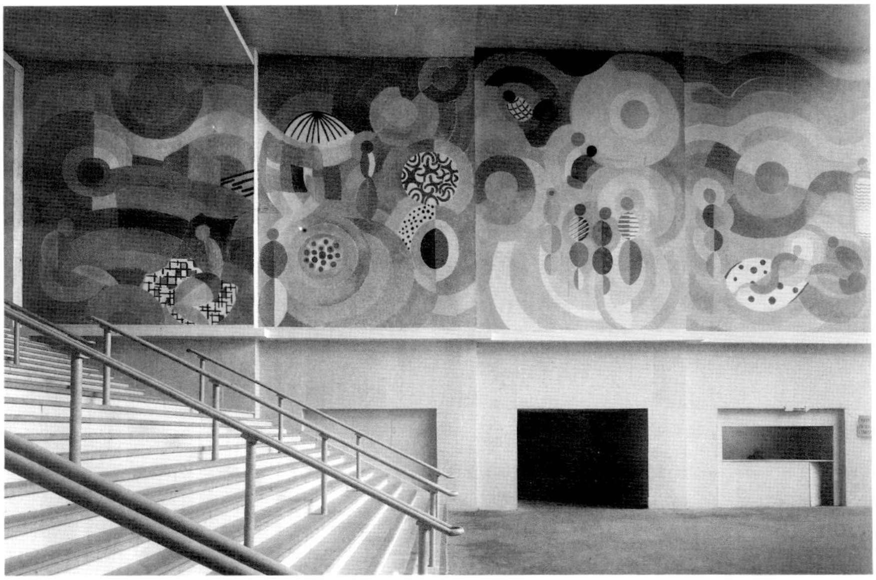

A view of the Pavillon des Chemins de Fer, with Sonia's much-admired *Voyages lointains* at the right.

impression on her. Viard told her in July that she was 'at the end of her tether', and advised her to rest for at least two weeks. Typically, she paid no attention and went on without any change in her way of life.

On 5 December 1937, Sonia and Robert received a telephone call to warn them that his mother was very sick and probably dying. She was now living in the Hôtel de Paris at 149 rue Legendre in the Batignolles area and for many years had been in touch with Robert only rarely and spasmodically. From time to time she had been visited by Charles, who seems to have been fond of her. Sonia and Robert went at once to the hotel, and in her bedroom, as Sonia noted without comment in her journal, Berthe Delaunay (Mme de Rose), feeble and on the point of death, asked Sonia to forgive her for all the misery she had caused her.

She was buried, as she had wished, in Versailles on 8 December. Among the people who attended, Sonia makes special mention of Mme Damour, Robert's aunt. Evidently a rift had developed between Robert and his uncle; at the funeral Mme Damour was very affectionate and promised to see whether she could reconcile the two men; but nothing more came of this.

Another reminder of the past took place the next week – on 14 December. This was a meeting of the committee of the 'Amis de Rousseau' in the house of Mme Paul Guillaume. The Mayor of the town of Laval, some

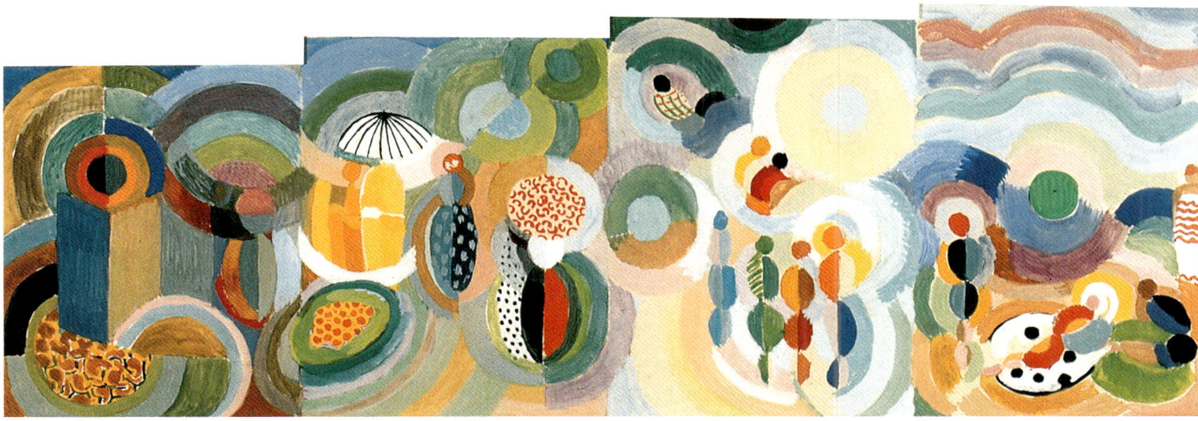

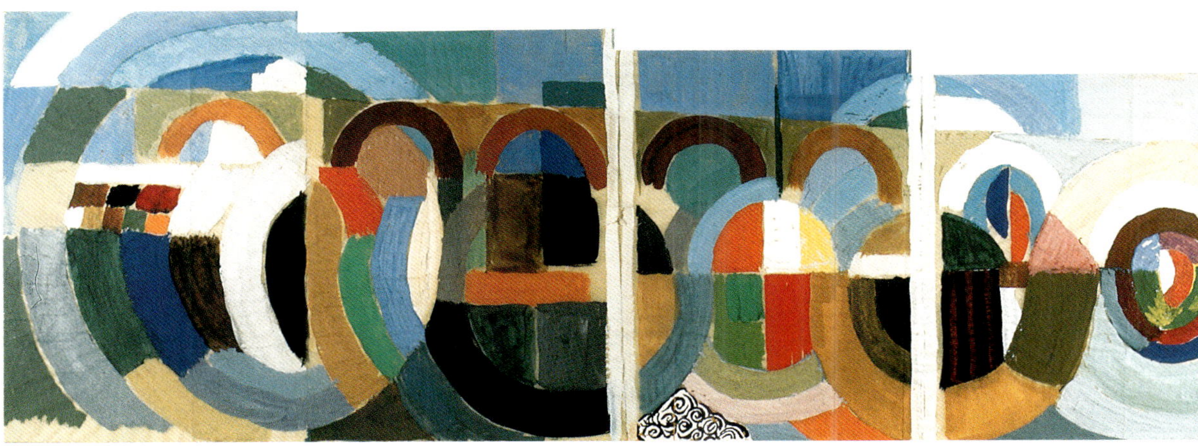

56, 57 Two gouache sketches for *Voyages lointaines*, Sonia's panel in the Pavillon des Chemins de Fer at the Paris Exposition of 1937.

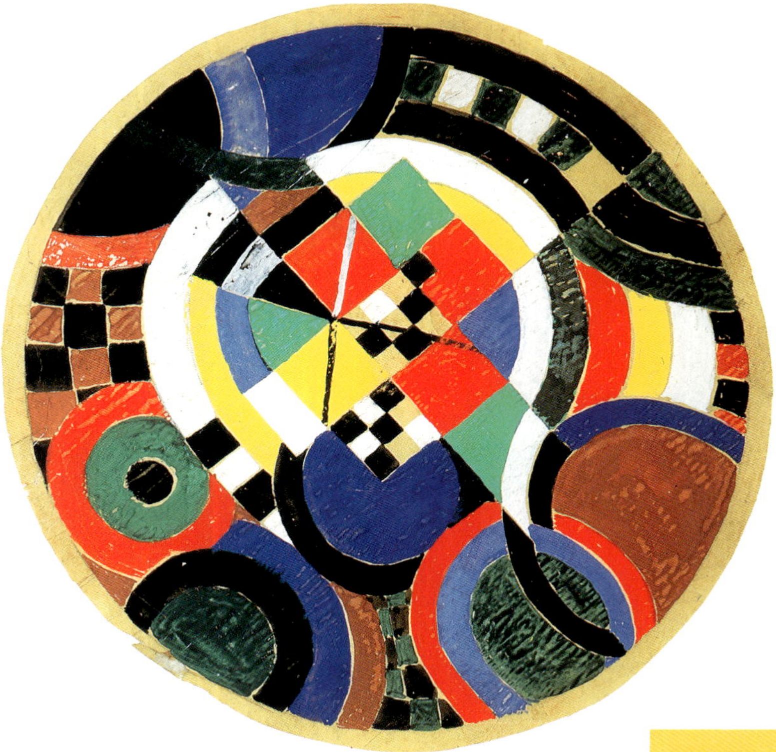

58 Ceiling design for the Paris Exposition of 1937; never executed.

59 One of Sonia's designs for decorative panels to be installed in the Palais de l'Air at the Paris Exposition of 1937.

60 Above right, Matisse (with beard) photographed against two of Sonia's panels in the huge garage where the work was carried out for the 1937 Exposition.

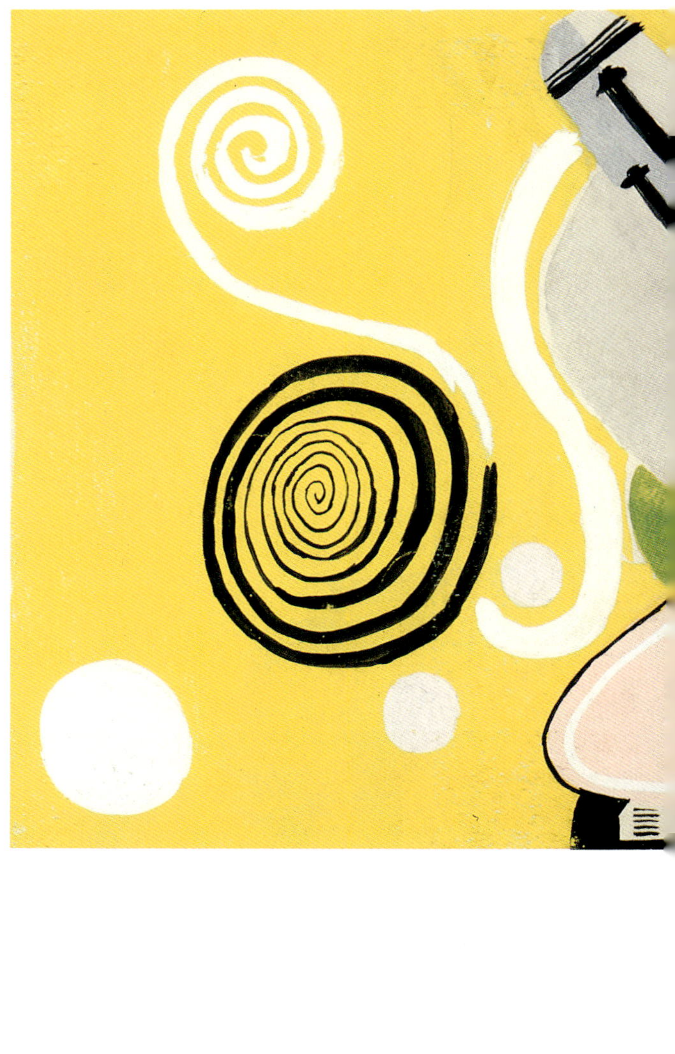

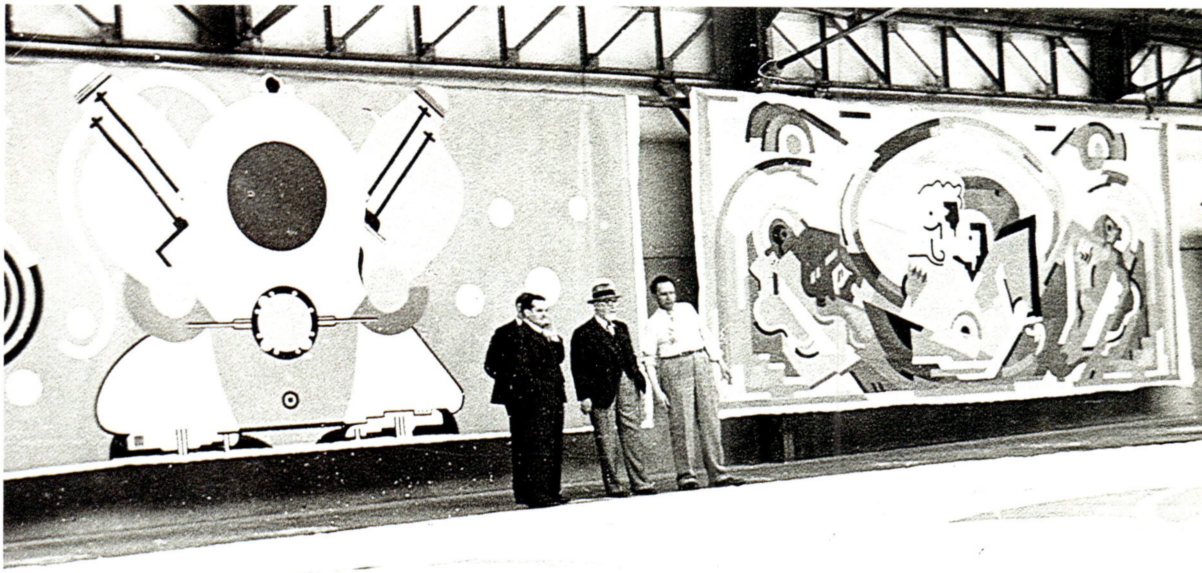

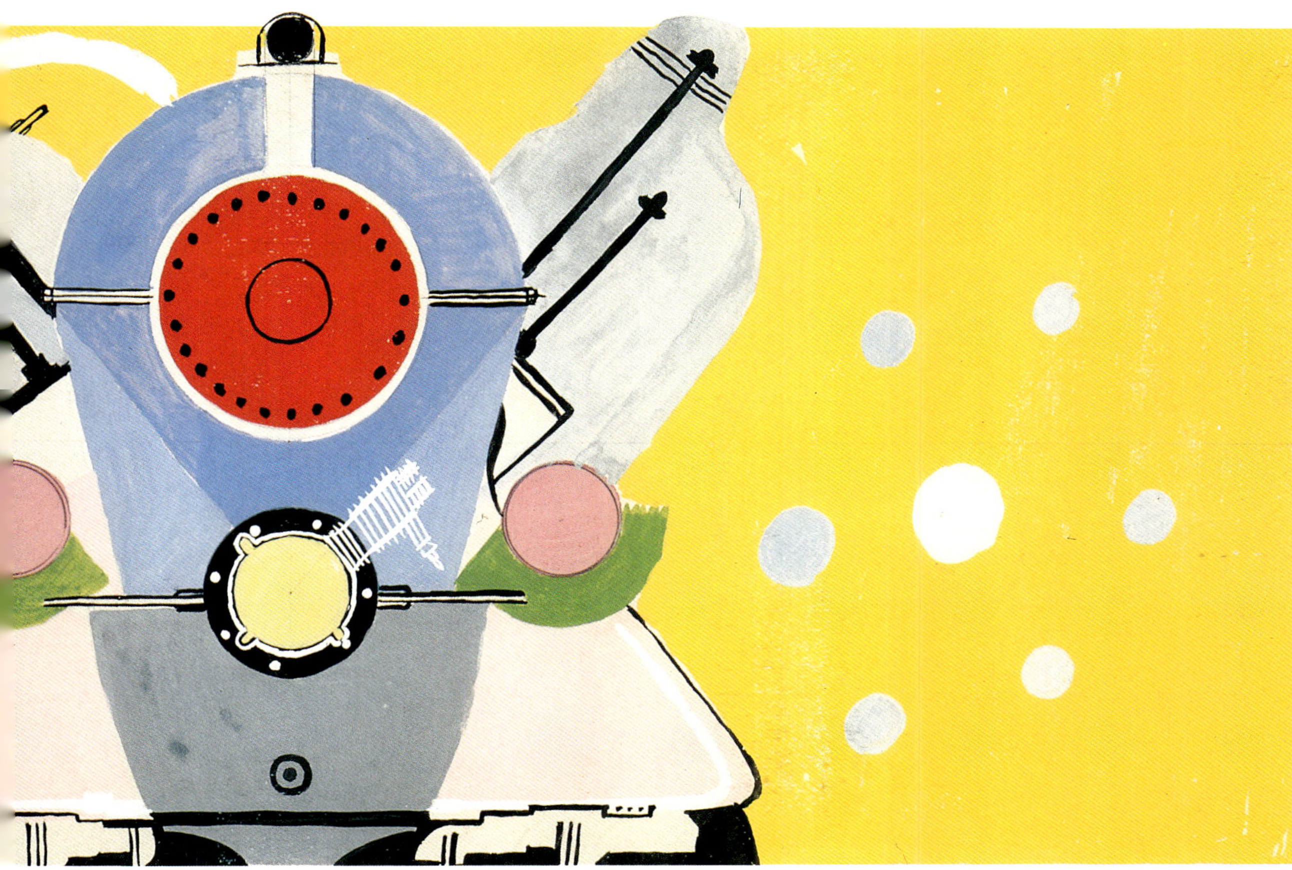

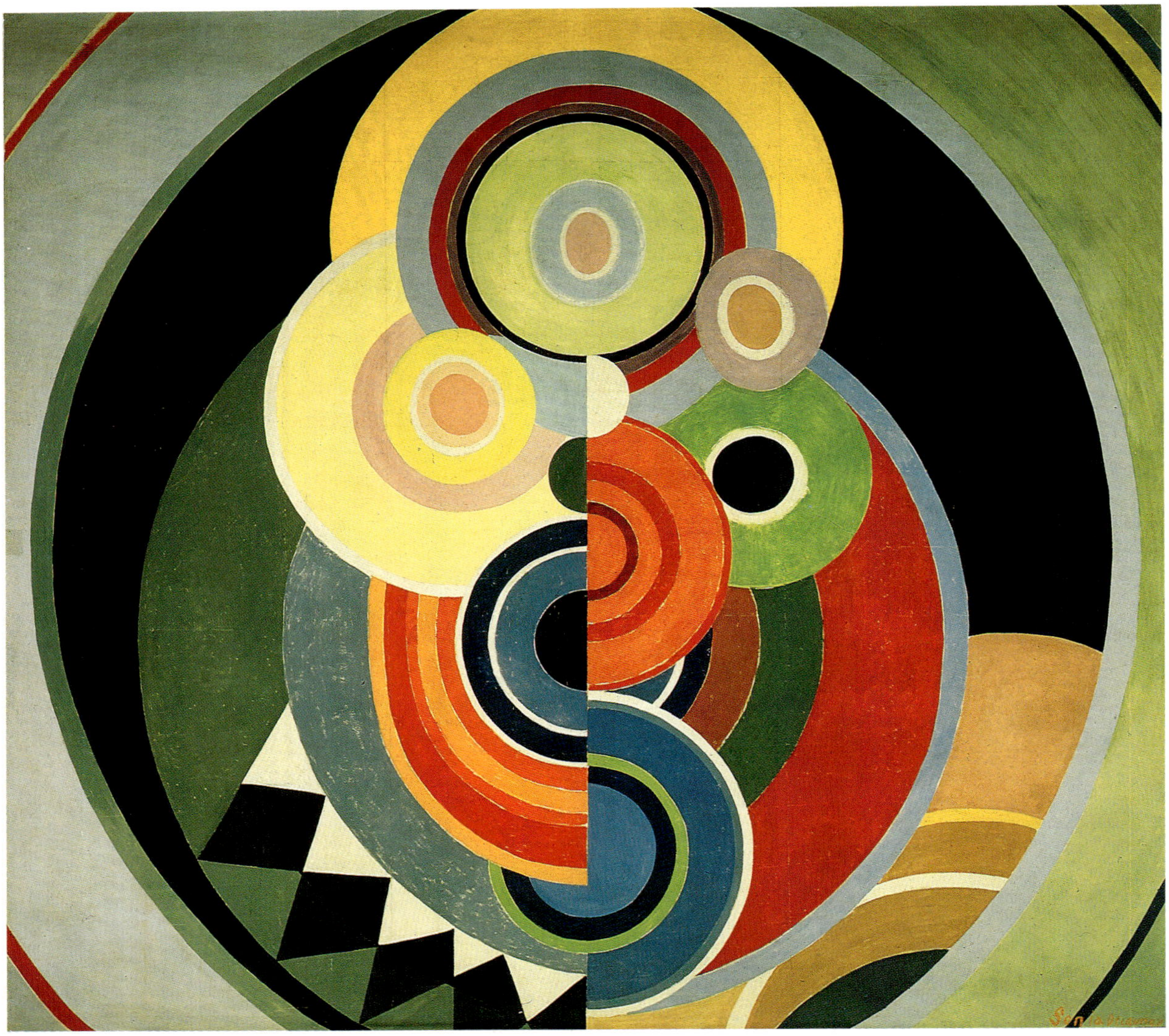

61 *Composition*, gouache on paper; the monumental version painted by Sonia for exhibition at the Salon des Tuileries, 1938.

280 km. south of Paris, where *le Douanier* had been born, was there to discuss a plan to place a commemorative plaque on the facade of the Rousseau house, and also to establish a grave in perpetuity with a monument. Uhde, who had first brought Rousseau to Sonia's attention, was there as a founding member of the committee; she records that she left the meeting with him. The next time she ran into him was in January, when she and Robert went to one of their favourite restaurants, Chez Georges in the rue Mazarine; they dined all three together. As for Rousseau, it is interesting that Robert possessed some of the artist's writings. He was telephoned by a woman from the Commercial Section of the United States Embassy who wanted to know the price of these manuscripts. Sonia wrote: 'Robert answered that he had not considered selling them and would have to think about it.' Later, she was to be grateful that Robert had not been tempted to part with them.

Even though things had become a bit easier for them, and Robert had even bought a new car in December 1937, they paid a visit together in February to an official called M. Huisman to see about the possibilities of a commission for Robert. According to Huisman, one might have thought of a painting or decorative work for one of the Embassies, but he knew there were none that needed anything at that time. He also mentioned the postal and

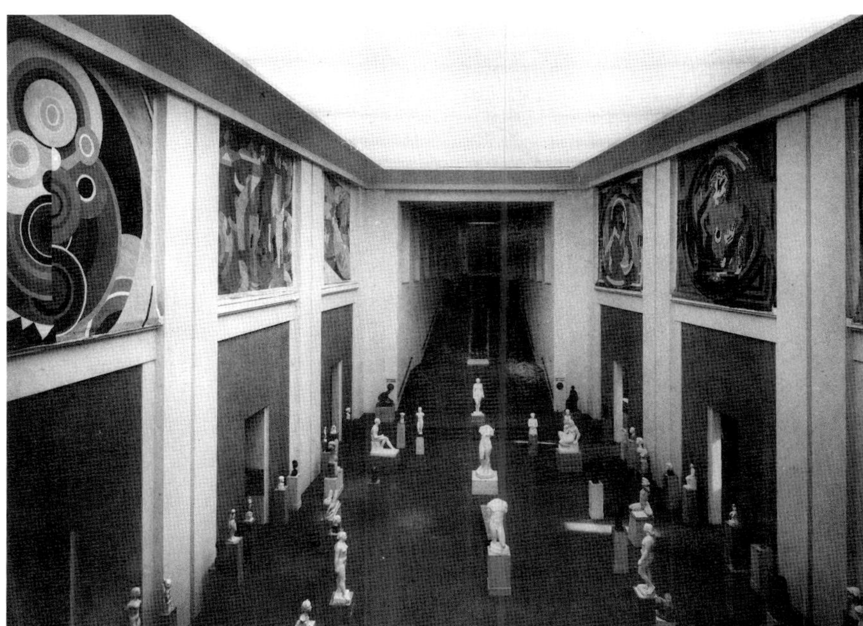

A view of the 1938 Salon des Tuileries, at which Sonia exhibited the painting opposite.

telephone service (PTT), but that was not in his bailiwick. He suggested other people whom they might see, but again this is a project that simply faded away.

It was not until later in the year that Mr Guggenheim came with Hilla von Rebay to see Robert's paintings. Rebay had laid the groundwork beforehand, and they showed the collector Robert's *La Ville* of 1911, *Le Soleil* and one of the *Fenêtres*. What he settled on was *La Ville*, for which he paid 60,000 francs. Robert also showed the last three pictures he had painted, and Rebay was most impressed by them. Robert put a price of 30,000 francs each on them – or a combined price of 75,000 francs for all three.

Guggenheim, who made the somewhat specious but flattering pronouncement that France was the greatest democracy in the world, also asked after Charles, whose drawings he had seen and admired. In these years, when Charles was in his twenties, he showed a decided talent for drawing; some of his work was actually exhibited in a gallery. But his interest in music was greater, and finally won out.

It may have been as a result of the sale to Guggenheim that Sonia began to look for a house in the country. They already owned a tract of hunting land ('un terrain de chasse') in Nesles, which they had bought by some means through the offices of M. Delhumeau, and could perhaps cash that in if they found a new place. Towards the end of August they drove down again to the South in the new car, going as far as Saint-Tropez and stopping on the return trip in Grenoble to visit André Farcy, the curator of the Museum there, who was one of Robert's earliest admirers in the museum world and one of his greatest supporters. The Farcys were extremely anxious about war, which they were expecting from moment to moment. But Sonia, as soon as they were in Paris again, started an exhaustive search for a property in the area just south of Versailles. She records every agency she consulted and every property she went to look at. With the same tenacity she brought to all her activities, she was dauntless and determined in this quest. The search went on for several months, and it was not until early 1939 that she decided on a 'ferme au bois' in the village of Gambais that was among the first she had been shown. One of its irrelevant features was that it was a neighbour to the house once inhabited by Landru, the famous bluebeard of the Twenties.

The Sudetenland crisis came to the boil in mid-September, while she was in the midst of her house-hunting. On 13 September Charles, who now had a new apartment in the rue Chaptal near Pigalle, stayed overnight with

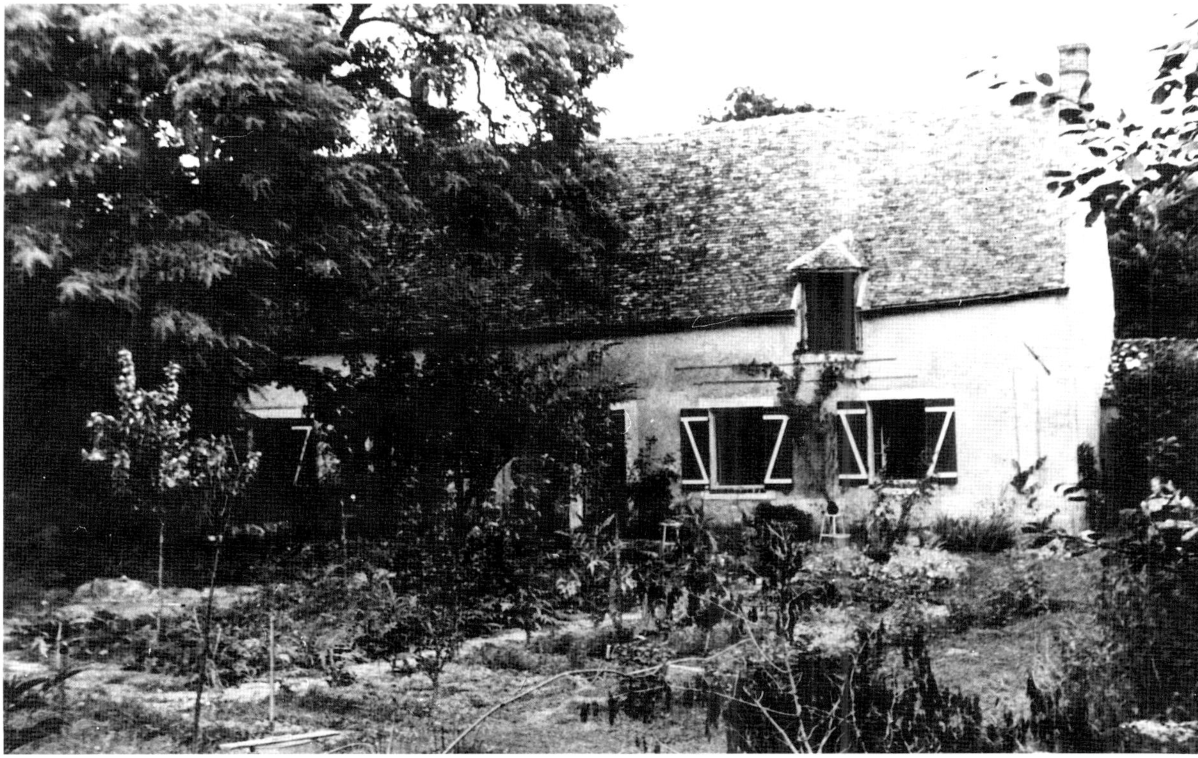

The country house at Gambais. Both Sonia and Robert are buried there.

Sonia in case he should be called up. Nothing had happened by the next day, though she was informed that one of Robert's Portuguese paintings, La *Femme au Potiron* (Woman with pumpkin), had been sold at the Petit Palais for 1,500 francs. It was not until 24 September, when Sonia and Robert were out driving together looking at properties in the forest of Gambais, that they saw the mobilization order and decided to return to Paris.

Charles had been mobilized that morning and sent to a camp a little way outside Paris. Sonia and Robert drove straight away to visit him there and to see whether there was anything he needed. In a day or two, in fact, he was transferred to a location in Paris, and by the 6th of October he was demobilized.

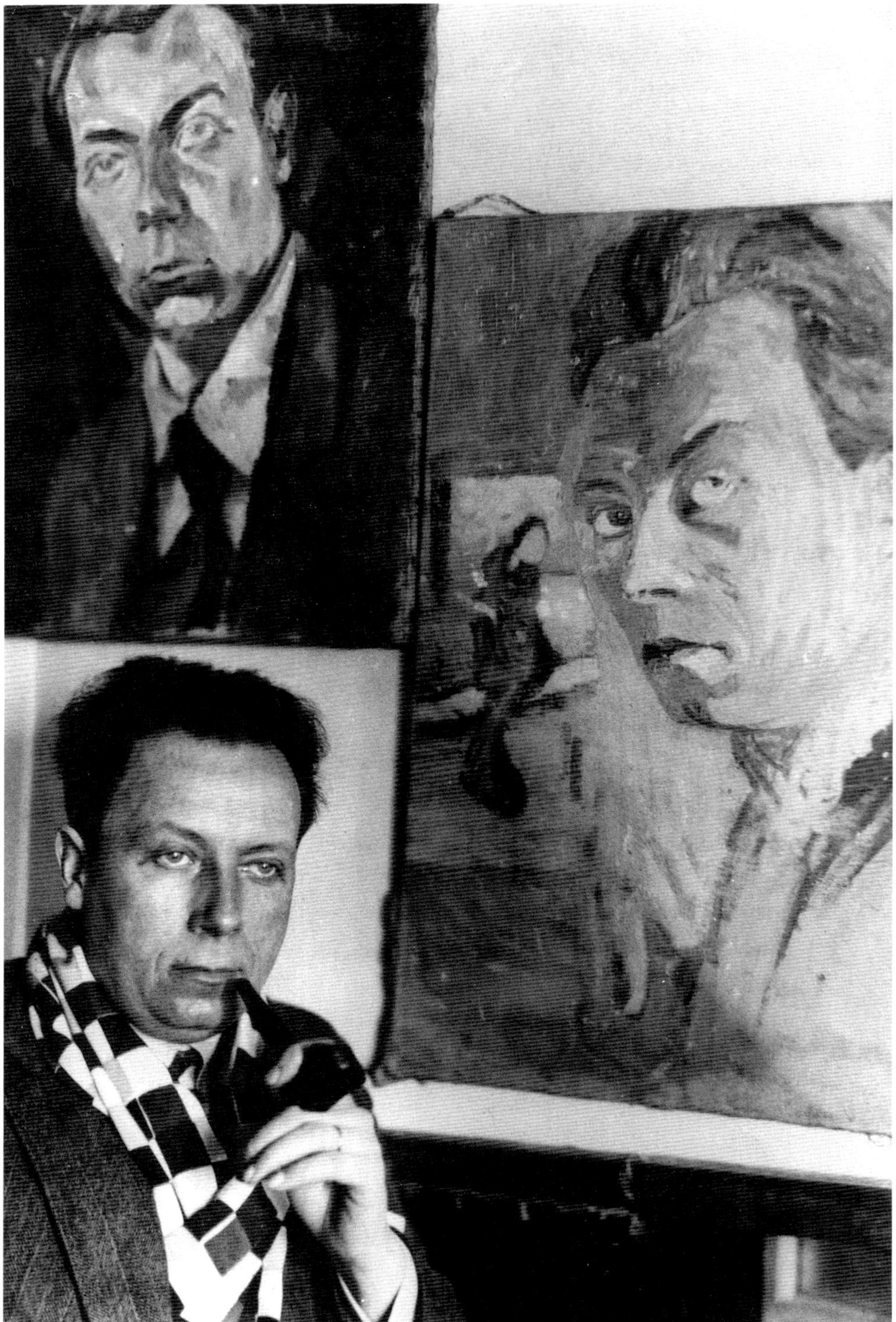

CHAPTER 12

LIFE AFTER ROBERT

THEIR SUCCESS at the 1937 Exposition (even though Sonia claimed their pavilions were 'sabotaged' and only a small portion of the potential public saw their work) led to a variety of offers. Gleizes, who had an entire room at the Salon d'Automne, invited Sonia and Robert to show some of their works that year. In 1938, Othon Friesz invited them, along with Jacques Villon and André Lhote, to paint large panels for the Salon des Tuileries. The place of honour at the Salon was awarded to Matisse's sketch for the famous *La Danse* that he painted for the Barnes Foundation in Merion, Pennsylvania.

In 1939, there was an exhibition at the Galerie Charpentier, inspired by Robert, of all the non-objective artists. Called the 'Salon des Réalités nouvelles', this marked the effective end of the Surrealists' brouhaha; they were no longer able to lay down the law in artistic matters.

During this year when World War II broke out, Sonia was painting at the top of her bent, now definitively devoted to the abstract and developing the sophisticated techniques in oil and gouache which enabled her now and for the rest of her life to paint those forceful, compelling designs in undiluted colours.

Robert Delaunay photographed in the late 1930s in front of two of his self-portraits.

Robert knew by 1938 that his life was threatened by cancer, but he did not spare himself or slow down his rhythm of activity. In fact, he instituted his 'Thursdays' when a group of young disciples would meet at the rue Saint-

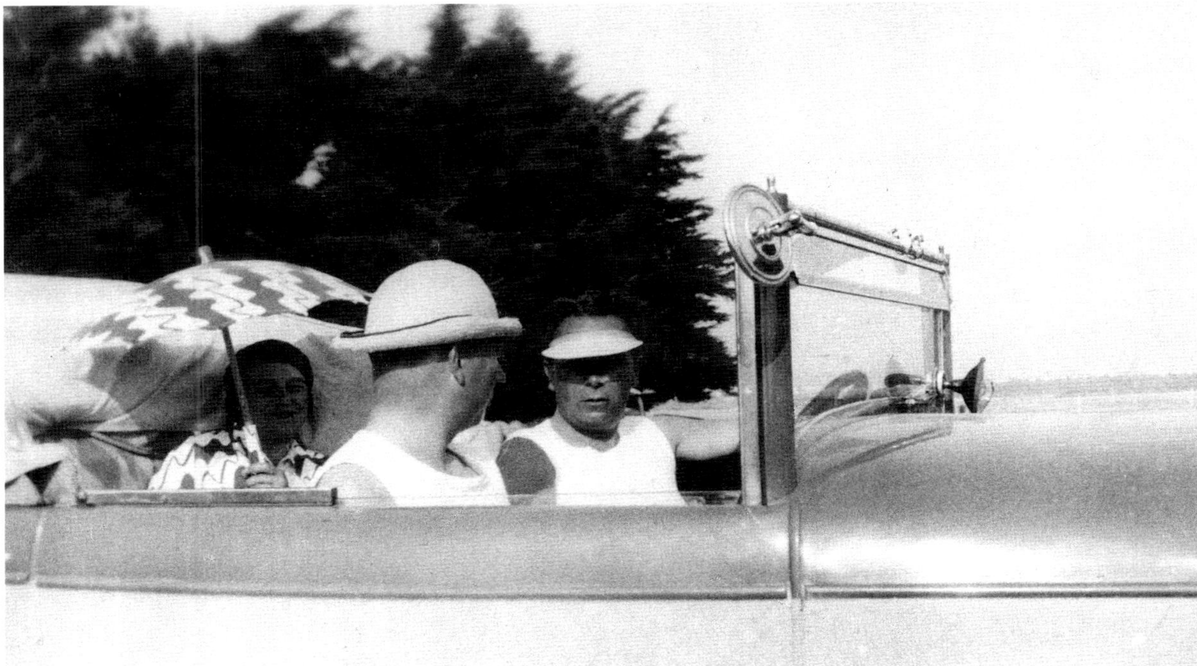

Sonia motoring, around 1938, with Arp and Robert (at the wheel). She is wearing a dress of her own design with matching parasol.

Simon studio to hear him discourse on painting. And he was working on future 'Salons des Réalités nouvelles' which did not take place because of the war.

During the early days of the war, the Phony War which they called in Paris 'la drôle de guerre', their friend Marie Cuttoli suggested that, for safety's sake, Sonia and Robert leave Paris for the Auvergne. They did as she advised, setting out with a car full of suitcases and the cat of the moment, Moumoune. But Robert did not care for the area, and so they went on to the Midi, where they caught up with other artist-friends who were already there: Alberto Magnelli with his wife Suzy, Hans and Sophie Arp, and others. The Delaunays found an apartment in Mougins, which they filled with a multitude of rolled-up paintings Robert had brought with them from Paris. Magnelli remembered that the first time he and his wife came to see the Delaunays, they had to walk over paintings which covered the floors.

Robert was determined to behave as if he were not facing death. He said that he still had so much to express, so much to do. In mid-October 1941, they took an excursion to Châtel-Guyon, where he collapsed. He was taken to Clermont-Ferrand and was operated on there; then moved to a clinic in Montpellier, where their friends the Delteils and the Allendys were living. By now Robert was not always conscious of what was going on; Sonia simply smiled at him, as she had done before in the darkest of hours, like the crisis of 1929.

During the afternoon of 24 October he seemed to be quite normal again. Only when the priest came to visit did he perhaps understand that he was on the verge of death. After the priest left, Sonia asked Robert what had taken place and he answered, with extraordinary clarity of spirit considering his condition, 'I told him he was boring me.'

Later he said, 'Life's no good if there are lies . . .' And she told him that, as far as she was concerned, she hated lies and had always tried to avoid them. When she sat down in a chair near the fireplace he called out,'You're so far away from me there, why do you leave me alone?' She changed her seat and sat close to him, her hands in his. Later she wanted to read the newspaper, but being fearful of tiring him she did not read out in a loud voice as she usually did. 'You keep everything to yourself!' he said. So she read to him an article on Russia. All through the late afternoon and evening, he was rapidly sinking, though he still wanted to talk about this and that.

Sonia kept vigil with the night nurse from 9 until his last breath at 2 a.m. It was 25 October, eight days after they had set out for Châtel-Guyon, when he died, having, as she wrote, 'lived his marvellous dream right to the end.'

Delteil, with his American wife Caroline and his sister, and the Allendys came to see the body. Charles was not able to arrive from Paris until the 28th. In her journal, she copied out the following affidavit that had been required by the civil authorities:

' *To the Mayor of Montpellier*
'Cimitière St Lazare, Montpellier
'Delaunay, Robert husband of Sarah Stern
'age 56 years plaque 1540 Section SI
'Numéro 34, du 4ème rang
'Montpellier 27 Octobre 1941'.

Though Robert's death was not unexpected, it left Sonia feeling both deserted and uprooted. While she was still in the Montpellier clinic talking to the nurses, showing them photographs of paintings and of herself and Robert in their youth, she was occupied and insulated from grief. Even the next morning, when she visited the morgue to sit with the body for a little while (it was too cold to stay longer), Robert was still a presence. Her friends came for the burial, and Charles too was at her side. Robert was buried in the St Lazare cemetery on a glacial, windy day. She put two dahlias on the coffin, one dark red, the other striped white. The coffin was to be transferred later, after the war, to Gambais.

Two days later, she was in Mougins gathering together all Robert's papers and documents with a view to preparing a tribute to him and his work, while it was all still fresh in her mind. She would handle the technical side, Delteil would write about Robert as a man and poet. As far back as 1926, they had collaborated in a book called *ALLO! PARIS!* for which Robert had created ten lithographs. When Charles pointed out that the wartime shortage of paper would make publication of a book about Robert unlikely, Sonia was not to be deterred. If paper could be bought in advance, she would buy it. Her preoccupation was to keep Robert's memory alive; in a sense, that was a means of keeping herself from dissolving.

Sonia had a way of talking about her marriage with Robert as if it were a perfect match. And yet she gives away, from time to time, the minor ways in which he could irritate her – his bad temper, his messiness, his obsession with expensive touring cars, his lack of paternal sensitivity. In 1943 she witnessed an acrimonious dispute between a couple she knew, and afterwards wrote in her journal, 'People really spoil their lives – If they could see death closer at hand, if they knew what it was like when one of the two disappears – they would be more sensible. I was always thinking about that, but not Robert, and he spoiled a lot of our life together.' But three years later, when she re-read a bundle of letters he had written to her, she was gratified to rediscover how much love he expressed for her in the letters, because, 'having suffered so much, I've had moments of doubt. Apart from the perpetual arguments and money, I've had a beautiful life.'

It is hard to know how she felt about the years when she gave up painting in order to support the family. It was as if he considered that *he* was the artist and could not be expected to engage in menial activities for the purpose of earning money. Indeed, there is no evidence that he spent much of his time at all thinking of ways to earn money.

There are good reasons to believe that he was unfaithful to Sonia on occasion, but the physical side of their relationship does not appear to have meant a great deal to her after the first few years. What he offered her, and what she evidently needed, was his intellectualism, his unswerving dedication to his painting and his vision. She was, in fact, his greatest admirer, his most fervent supporter; although she was by no means a doormat to be walked over, she was practical, realistic, and when it was a question of holding the family together she recognized that she was better fitted for the role than he was.

But in those early days after his death, it was natural that she should remember the best of him and be most anxious to preserve him. She felt his loss deeply; on the 14th of June 1942 she wrote in her journal that she experienced his disappearance that day – over six months after the event – more strongly than she had at the end of October. But she was lucky to have found friends in the area, for it would have been virtually impossible to return to Paris and in fact she was homeless again, as she and Robert had been in 1915. The Arps lived in a pretty house in Grasse surrounded by olive trees, and the Magnellis were also in the neighbourhood. She decided to live there as well; and then began the three most taxing years of her life.

Not only was she alone (Charles had had to return to Paris immediately after the funeral); she also had to find the means to support herself during a wartime period of fragile and unreliable communications, sheer danger, constant and besetting uncertainties. At the very outset, she had to see about selling the car to best advantage, withdrawing from the apartment in

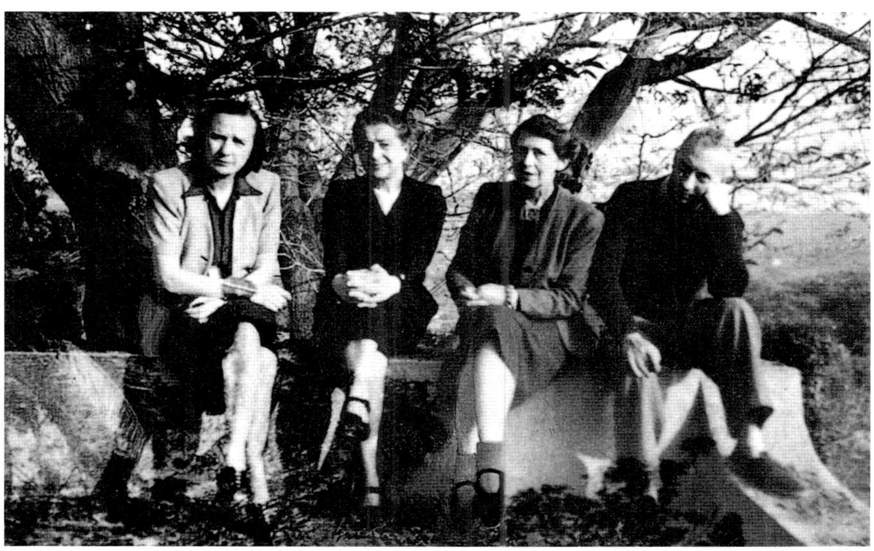

Sonia in Grasse after Robert's death, with Nelly van Doesburg, Sophie Taeuber-Arp and Jean Arp, 1942.

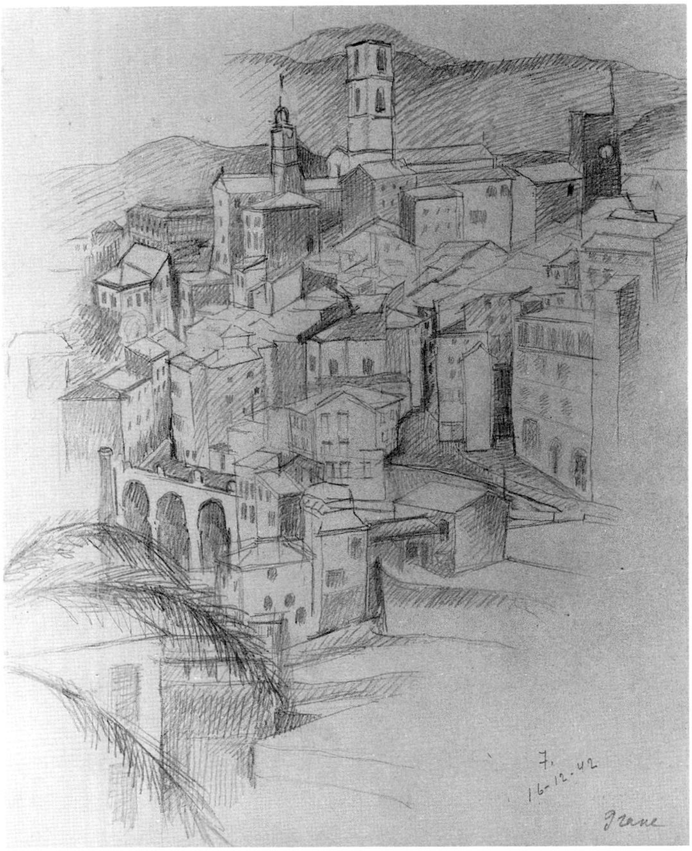

A pencil drawing made by Sonia in December 1942 of a view of Grasse.

Mougins, making sure that her official documents were in order, registering with the police.

Through it all, she had to deal with quantities of luggage: trunks full of rolled-up paintings, suitcases and hampers containing drawings and sketches. In her journals during these years, she was constantly setting down the quantity and contents of the luggage she was transporting from place to place – for she could settle down in one abode for only short periods. In the beginning, it was hotels: the Splendide in Cannes, the Grand Hotel in Grasse (70 francs a day in a room once occupied by André Gide). Then, some time in 1942, the Arps managed to cross over into Switzerland, the country where Sophie Taeuber-Arp had been born, and Sonia lived in and looked after their house in Grasse. This gave her a more secure and comfortable perch than the hotel rooms, but she was dogged by difficulties caused by the owner of the house. Arp had also managed to take with him across the border, at Sonia's request, some of

Robert's paintings, and that led to a voluminous and frustrating correspondence, for Sonia was always anxious to know whether paintings were being sold and money being deposited in banks on her behalf.

It is interesting to learn how many people whom she knew were also spending these war years in southern France. Her close colleague of former years, Jacques Heim, was in Cannes with his wife, presumably conducting his couturier business there. During those few days she spent in Mougins right after Robert's burial, she lunched at a restaurant where she saw Jeanne Léger with her gigolo, joined a bit later by Paul Poiret; she wrote in her journal, 'That band are repugnant.' In December, she ran into the composer Germaine Tailleferre in Grasse. Her Paris doctor, Charles Viard, and his wife Aline were in the area, which was fortunate in view of Sonia's chronic asthma. Uhde, she learned, was hiding somewhere in the Midi under a false name, 'because he had been persecuted by the Nazis, having written against them at the beginning of the war.' Her most intimate friend, Nelly van Doesburg, widow of the De Stijl painter who had died in 1931, was installed near Lyons, and they exchanged letters almost every day. By the same token she wrote to Charles at least five times a week. Indeed, her correspondence was enormous; she made a note everyday of letters written and letters received, as well as every telephone call she made, and every visit to the Préfecture in search of advice or help.

In early December, Arp and Magnelli proposed that she join them in preparing some lithographs together. This appears to have been the first work she did after Robert's death. The amusing aspect of this collaboration, which was published as a book only in 1950 in Switzerland, is that each of them contributed to each of the lithographs rather than producing their own – and this is perfectly clear on examination.

Towards the end of that month she travelled by bus and train to Montpellier to spend Christmas with the Delteils. Even from there she was writing to Dr Schmidt, of the Kunstmuseum in Basel, to discuss the possible sale of a picture to him.

On New Year's Day she went to the cemetery: 'I stayed for quite a while, there wasn't anyone else there, the weather was fine, the quietude did me good – I had done what I wanted to do – I had spent the holidays near him, looking after him as if he were alive, and I saw his look and his smile – so ironic and sad.'

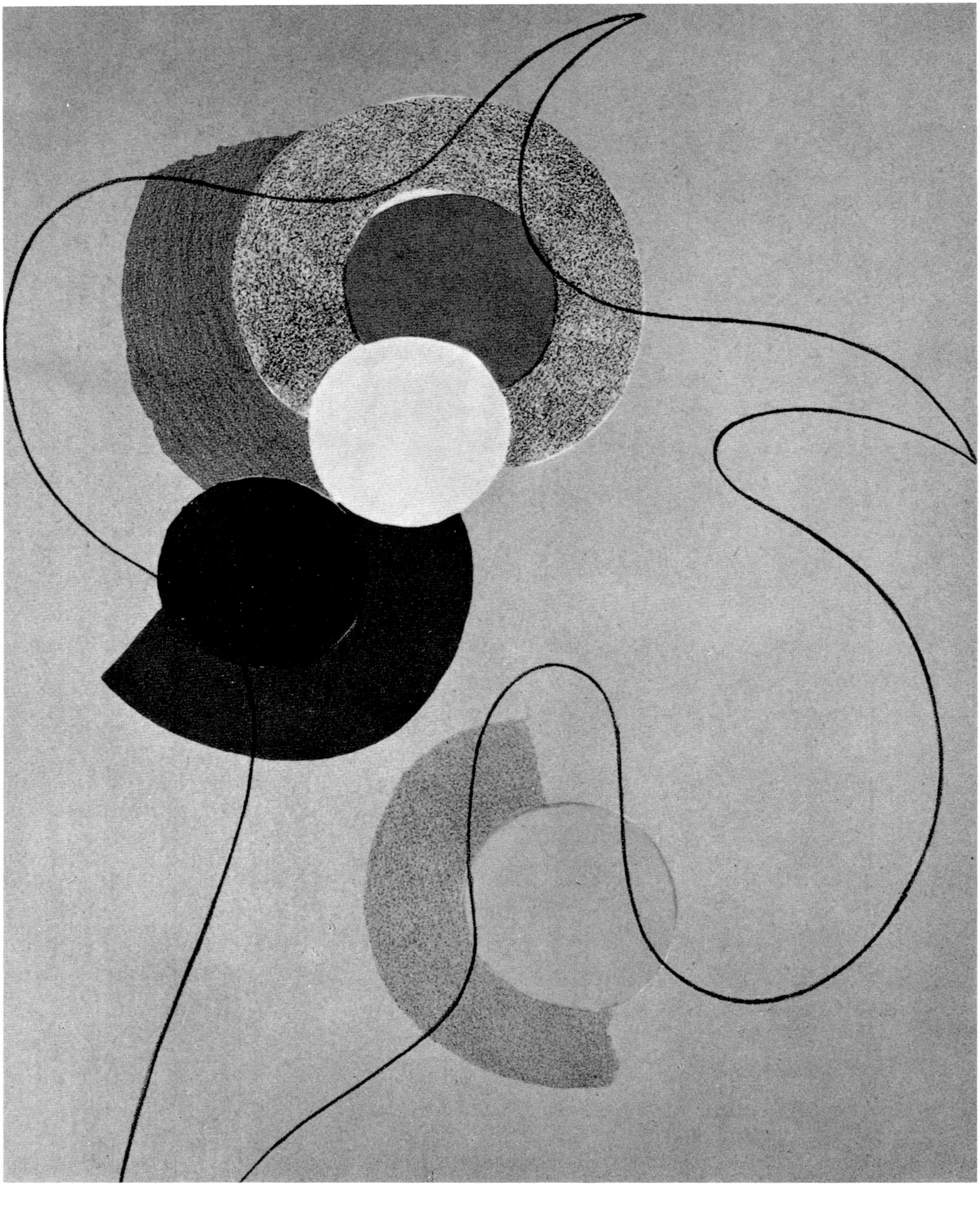

One of the joint lithographs made by Sonia and Arp in 1942.

In mid-January 1942, travelling as always with Moumoune in a basket, she took the tiresome train journey to Lyons, where she was met by Nelly van Doesburg. Her purpose, aside from seeing her dear friend, was in fact to discuss Robert's pictures with the curator of the Grenoble Museum, André Farcy, whom she already knew from earlier contacts in Paris. When they met, she told Farcy that she and Charles intended to sell pictures only to museums and not privately. Farcy expressed interest and asked for the price of one of Robert's *Fenêtre* paintings. During the course of the conversation, the name of the sculptor Ossip Zadkine came up; she was told that the authorities had confiscated all his sculpture. And Farcy asked Sonia whether she too had run into any problems through being Jewish. She suddenly awakened to the danger that she might be stripped of all her property for racial reasons and that the paintings might therefore be forfeited.

On the way back to Grasse from Grenoble on 28 January, she wrote in her journal that Farcy was 'a proper bastard [*salaud*]', but her intuition was more acute than his and she had seen through his game. Once returned, she went to see her Paris lawyer Etienne Caen (presumably Jewish), who was now practising in Nice, and told him about the incident in Grenoble. Caen's mother, whom Sonia had learned to know, said she was quite right to be anxious about the situation, that they were all living 'at a time when anything could be done under the pretext of race', and that one could not be too careful. The situation would be a bit better, these friends suggested, if Charles were made the sole heir, rather than heir to one-quarter of the estate. Sonia also thought of sending to Switzerland some of the cases she had with her, in order to ward off the danger she had felt with Farcy in Grenoble. She was able to do that later in the year when Arp went off to Switzerland.

In March 1942, Mme Caen went to Paris for two weeks and encountered terrifying problems there. At the same time, her husband went into hiding in Paris for fear of being taken hostage. 'It is really a disgrace to humanity,' Sonia wrote, 'the things that are going on in France now, one can hardly believe it's true.'

Among the people she got to know in Grasse were a rich couple, Didi and Aurore Chenu, art collectors who owned a villa there and were interested in Robert's work – and hers as well. She found the husband 'truly very refined and cultivated.' They were friends also of the Magnellis, and the six of them, in addition to a daughter of the Chenus (who married during the war) met frequently for lunch or dinner.

On the whole, there was no shortage of social gatherings in the area at that time. Sonia records lunches and dinners in restaurants with friends in Nice and Cannes, and even describes various conversations; on one of these occasions she said, 'We no longer need Anglo-Saxons to dominate us in France, all those people are more barbaric than the Latins. What we need is an era of spirituality like the one in the third and fourth centuries and again in the twelfth and fourteenth.' This is a rare utterance of cultural identity and purpose reported from her own mouth, but it is not at all clear in what way the Anglo-Saxons (which no doubt included the Americans) had been dominating French culture. She retained a certain reflex anti-Americanism most of her life. In 1948, in commenting on her attitude to Communism, she lamented its 'sordid materialism – even worse than that of the Americans.' And a couple of years later, when it was suggested that she ought to go to America to help put Robert across, she was far from enthusiastic about the idea – and indeed never went.

By the end of 1942 Sonia was restless, having had enough of her day-to-day existence in Grasse. 'I haven't enough calmness', she wrote on the 1st of January 1943, 'to plunge into creative work and I believe I won't have it for some time.' All she was doing was some sketches in a small booklet, using 'Crayolor', which she didn't like. She describes a typical day: 'In the morning to the hotel, where I picked up letters from Switzerland and a visiting card. Telephoned from there to the Chenus and when I returned for lunch to the Magnellis. Then read the newspapers I brought back with me. Put the cat out in the garden. Then worked: I have three colour designs in my notebook. Then read Balzac to relax.'

Her problems were mounting. Contact with Switzerland was virtually cut off, which meant that payments she had been receiving from Mme Sacher, a member of a Swiss family whose great fortune derived from pharmaceutics, came to a halt. She was, however, extraordinarily tenacious where money matters were concerned. She would write again and again to Mme Sacher and to Arp (whose wife died early in 1942, asphyxiated by gas in a freak accident), asking whether they could find a way to transfer funds to her, as she was truly in need. The only saving grace was that M. and Mme Chenu were willing to buy a painting from her from time to time; and this would generally tide her over the worst crises. In addition, an occasional sale would be made in Paris – in February 1943, she was informed by the dealer Guyon that he had received 1,500 francs for a watercolour – but these could hardly be counted on.

In 1943, indeed, living conditions were becoming ominous. For the first time she was finding it difficult to buy bread, though she went daily to the local provisioners and had become well-known to all of them. She planned in March to send a letter to 'old Guggenheim' in New York to ask him to send $1,500 to Switzerland. In the event, she addressed her letter to Peggy Guggenheim, saying that the money had to be in Switzerland in three months. The news from Russia was encouraging – Rostov fell in early February, and a few days later Kharkov was taken – but the outlook in her area of the Riviera near the Italian border was not favourable. There were rumours that all Jews would be evacuated from the Alpes-Maritimes. Early in May, she met through anxious friends in Cannes a M. Goldfeld, who thought the authorities would soon be making everybody move from the region: some, he claimed, were already making expensive arrangements to go to the Haute-Savoie.

Nelly van Doesburg came from Lyons for a visit in April, and told her that Farcy was very keen to have a picture of Robert's for Grenoble; the picture he wanted, one of the *Fenêtres* was, however, in Switzerland. Sonia evidently put aside her probably unjustified anxieties about Farcy's intentions, and started at that point to try to make contact with him again. Repeated telephone calls failed, and it was not until July, after her dogged persistence was rewarded, that she was able to travel again to Grenoble (with the cat, of course), and arrange the sale of not only the picture Farcy particularly wanted but also one of the *Formes circulaires*.

Charles had managed to travel south from Paris for a one-day visit on 17 May 1943. She met him in Cannes with a litre bottle of olive oil, three sticks of a shaving cream called Rasoline, some Gillette blades and half a litre of eau de cologne. He had brought with him a sketch by Robert for the *Hommage à Blériot* and a copy of *ALLO! PARIS!*; evidently she thought these might be saleable. A few days later the Paris art dealer Louis Carré was in Cannes; she took her usual bus trip from Grasse to meet him there and to talk over the things that were most on her mind: Robert's pictures and her need for money.

In June she moved back to the Grand Hotel, for conditions in the Arp house had become unbearable. During this summer, she was constantly hearing rumours of a collapse of the Italian army, and warnings of possible bombardment, even an Allied landing. A new fear was engendered – that the

Germans might occupy the southern half of France. And then one morning in September she was awakened at 6.45 a.m. by a gunshot. From her bedroom window, she could watch German occupation troops in action, whereas the night before there had been none in evidence. On the 9th, German troops appeared in the corridors and in front of the hotel. The Italian cars and trucks that had almost invisibly patrolled Grasse were disarmed; and the next day she was told that all civilians had to leave the hotel *in one hour*.

The Germans assigned two Italian soldiers to help her with her suitcases; then one Italian and one German soldier accompanied her with her bags to the Hotel Parc Palace. The next day she had to return to the Grand for additional luggage she had not been able to take with her on the first trip. While there, she was moved by a conversation with a young German sentinel who had served in Russia and had a terrible memory of it.

The whole town was full of Germans, and yet she was able to go through her usual routines unscathed. In October she managed to make a visit to Montpellier to see the Delteils, who seemed to be in less hazard, and to visit Robert's grave on the anniversary of his death. But on 5 November she learned that Charles had been released from prison where he had spent several weeks – having been arrested because of what he called '*relations communes*', which may have been a veiled reference to friends who had been caught resisting the Germans.

By now, there were often planes overhead at night, even some bombing in the distance, and she heard that peasants were being rounded up with hidden arms. Yet she was working again – with renewed vigour; on the 1st of January 1944 she recorded that she had started a large gouache, based on one she had done the March before. And on the 6th she finished 'the second gouache of 1944'. 'I have not painted much,' she wrote, 'but as always observed and reflected a lot, and what I am doing now is the fruit of that. I find that it's a progression on what we were both doing and an evolution in our painting. Also it's less doctrinaire and more human.' And she speaks of drafting a letter to Charles to explain once and for all the attitude she and Robert had towards life and to explain their apparent clumsiness in dealing with material matters. 'We were guided by a single aim, which was our painting, without making concessions to ease along the way.'

62 Abstract composition, lithograph, 1940.

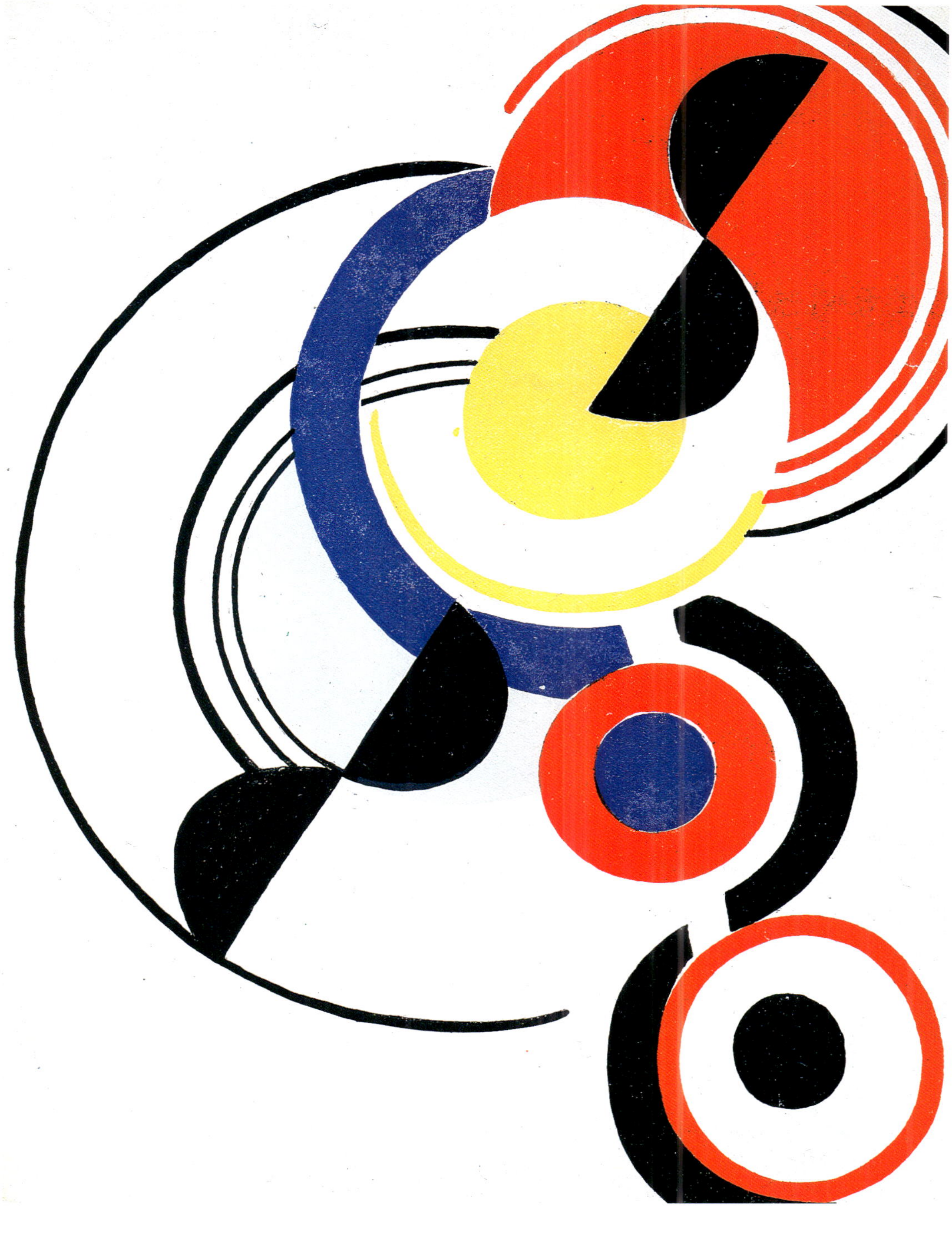

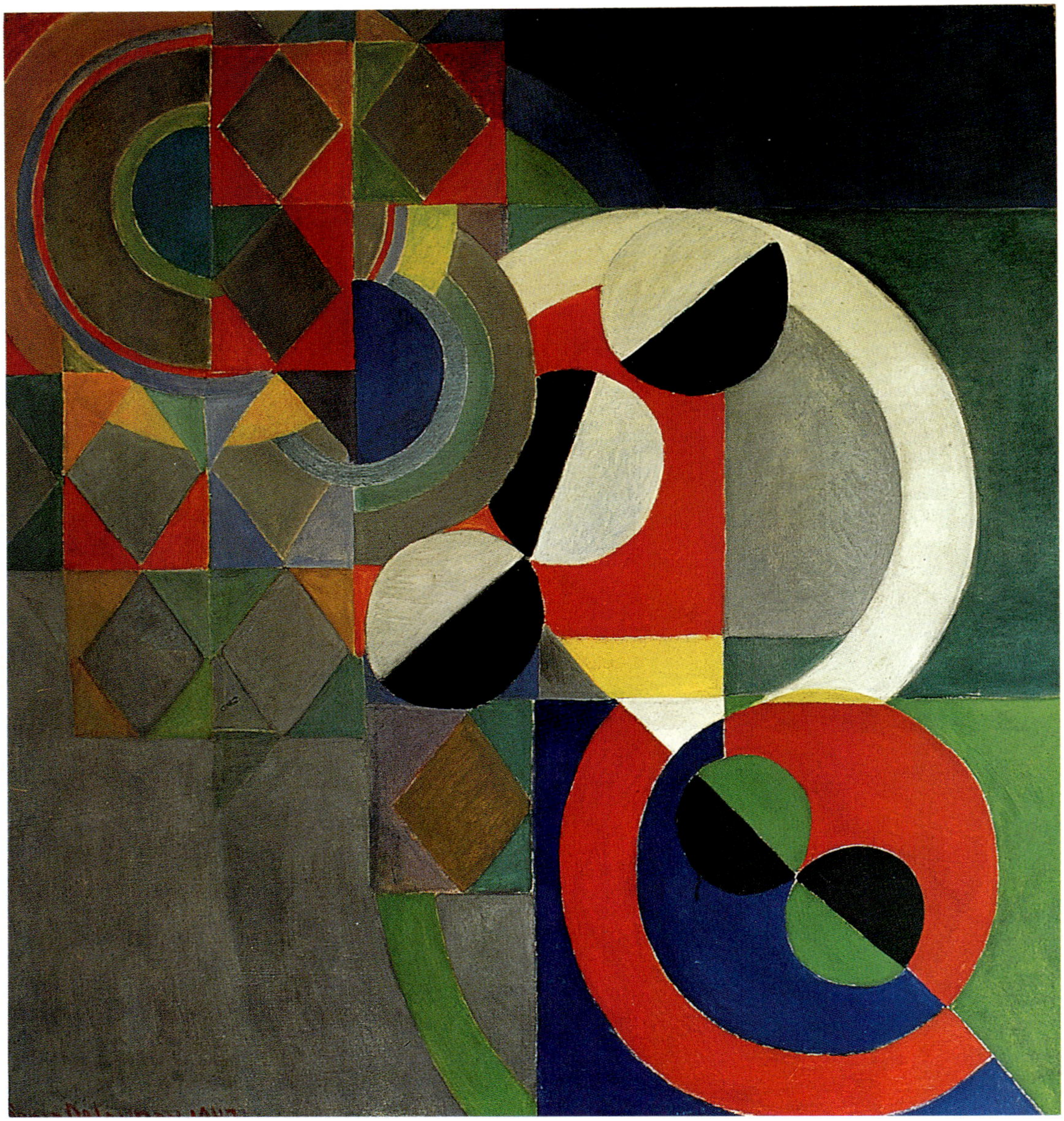

63 *L'Affreux jojo* ('Scallywag'), oil on canvas, 1947.

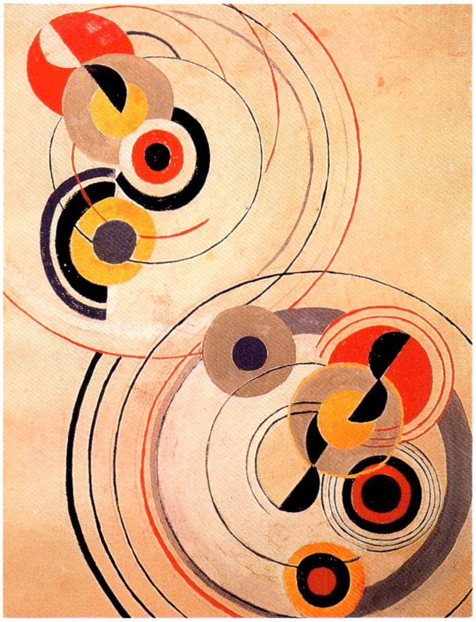

64 *Composition*, project for a book cover, *c.* 1945.

65 *Rhythme couleur*, oil on canvas, 1939. (Musée de Lille).

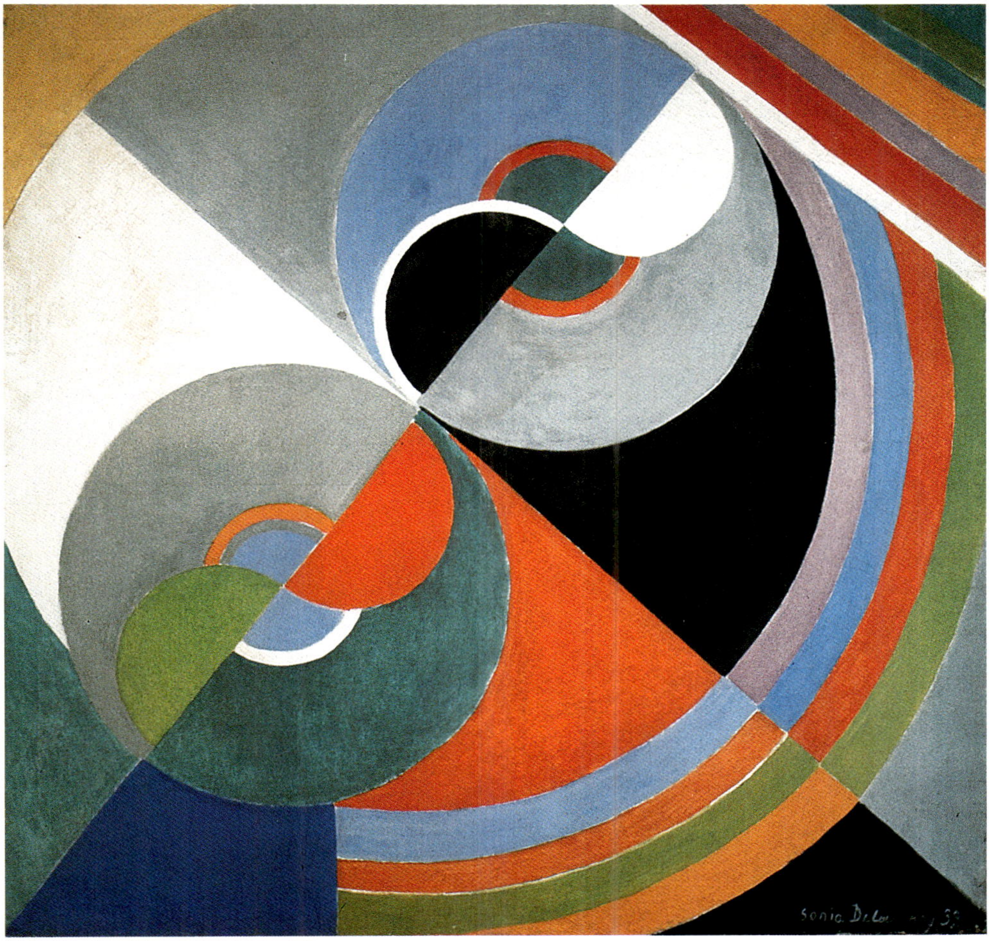

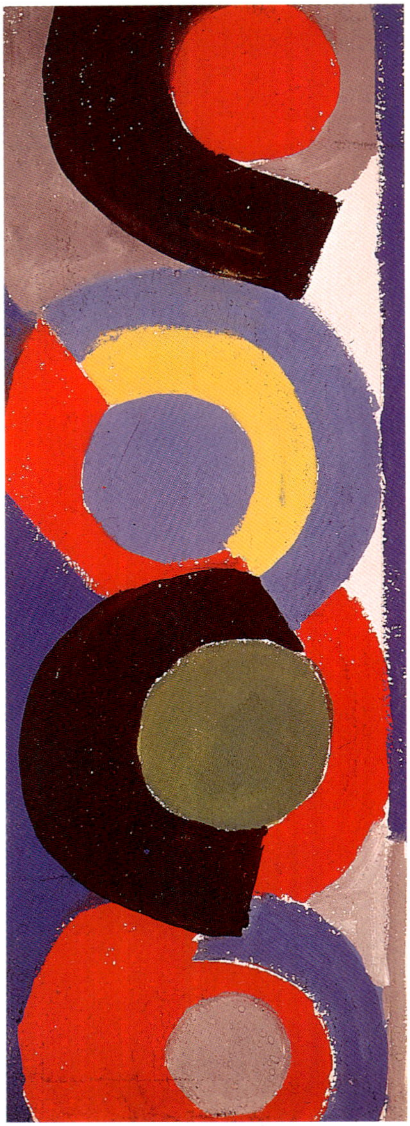

66 *Rhythme coloré*, gouache sketch, 1957.
(By permission of Gimpel Fils, London).

67 *Circus*, gouache on tracing paper on canvas, 1952.

68 Opposite, *Composition. Rhythme*, tapestry, 1955-58.

69 *Cactus*, oil on canvas, 1958.

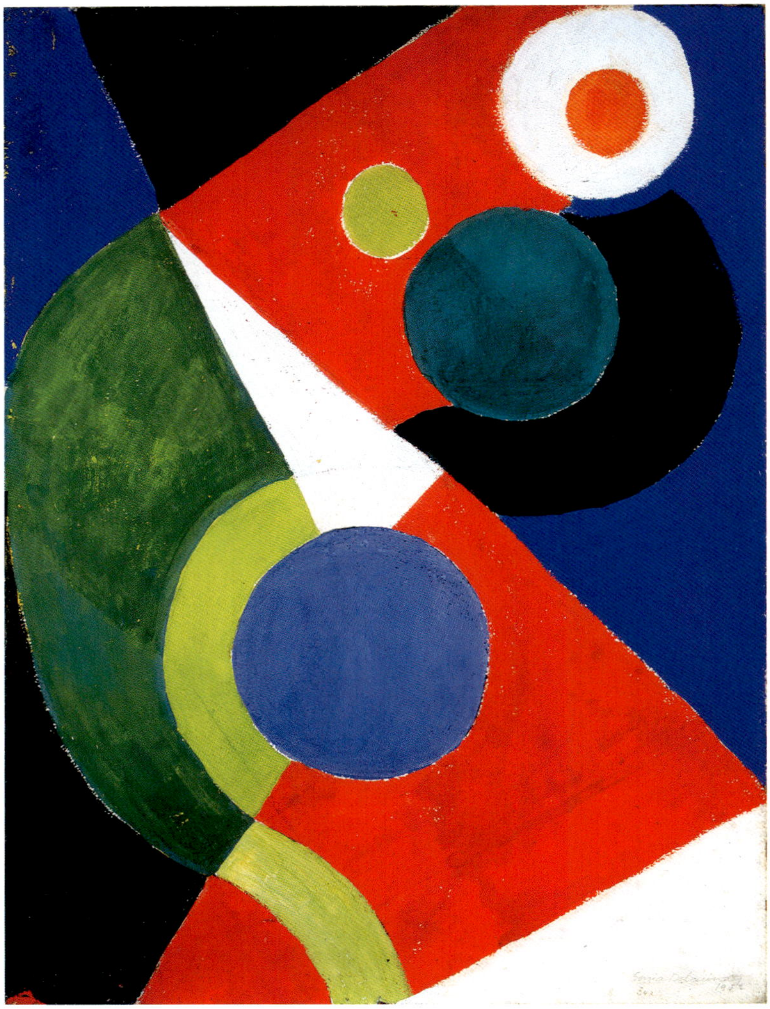

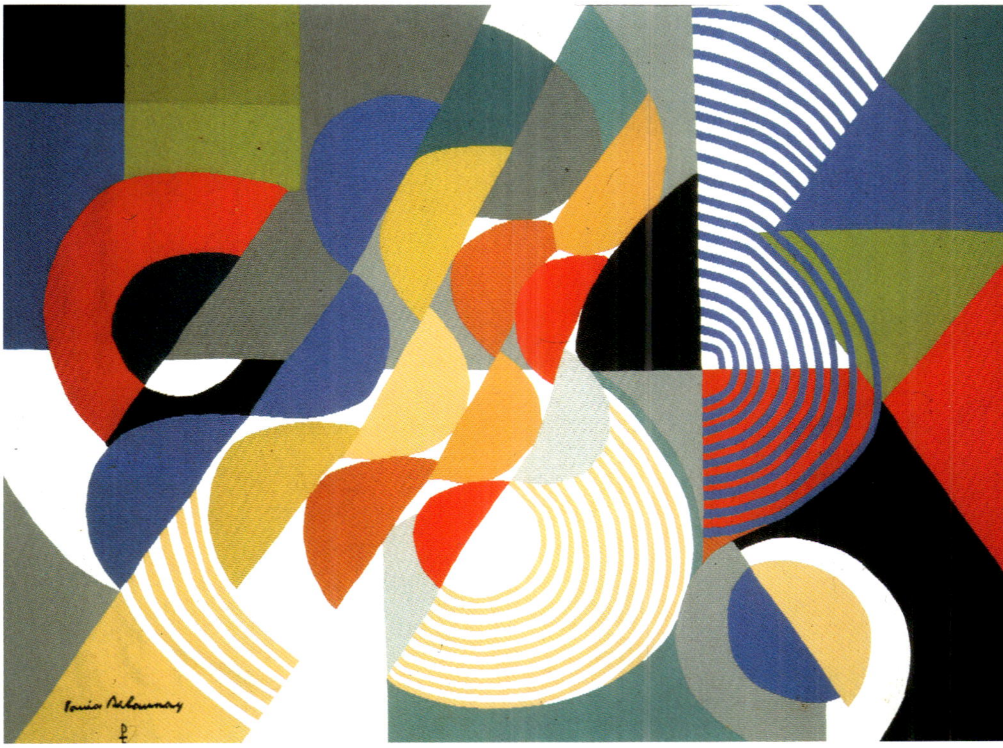

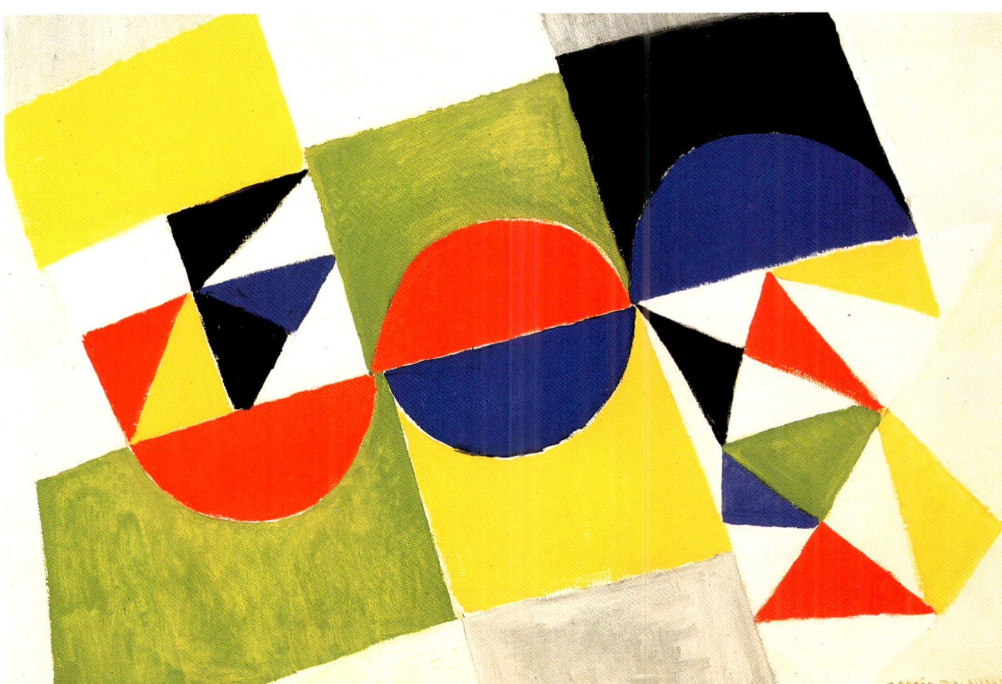
SONIA DELAUNAY

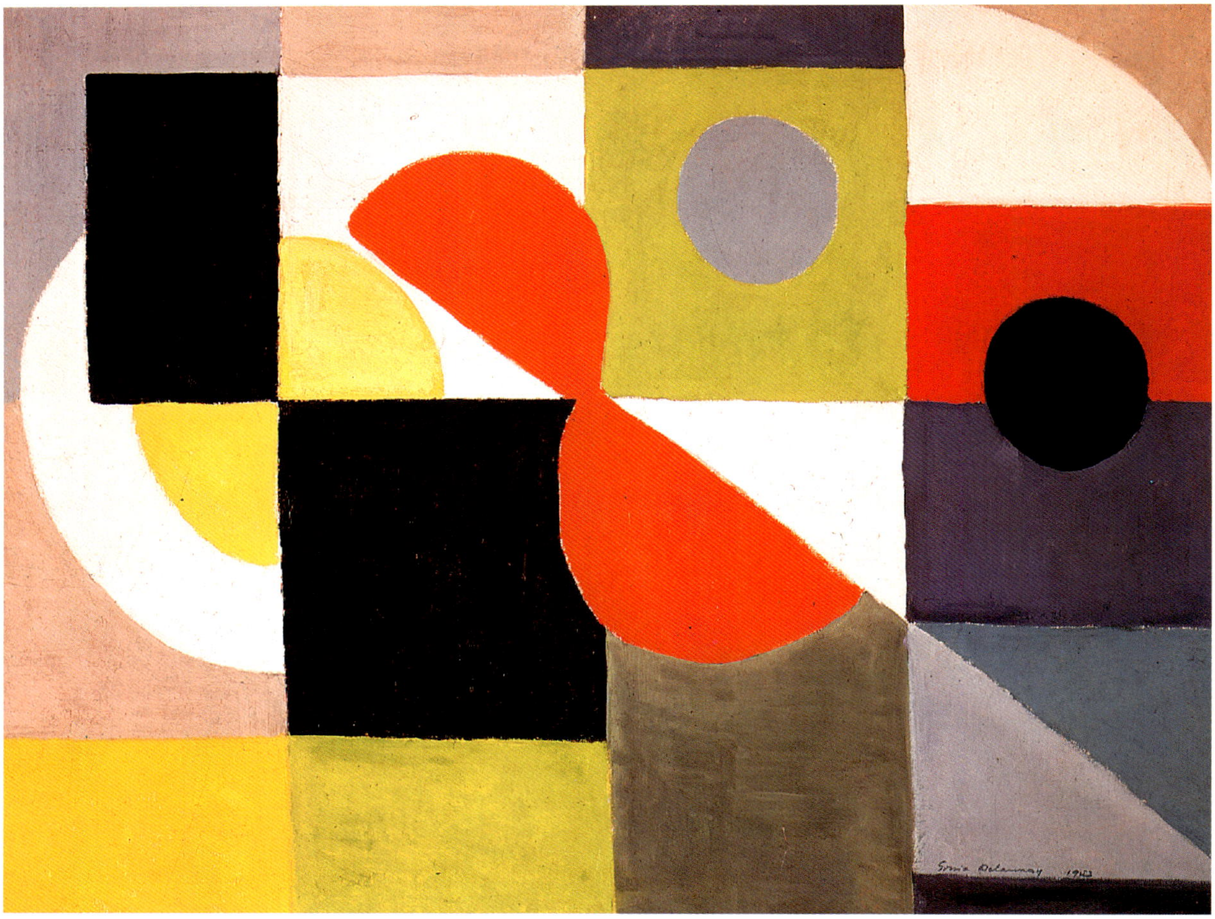

70 *Rhythme coloré* No. 132,
oil on canvas, 1953.

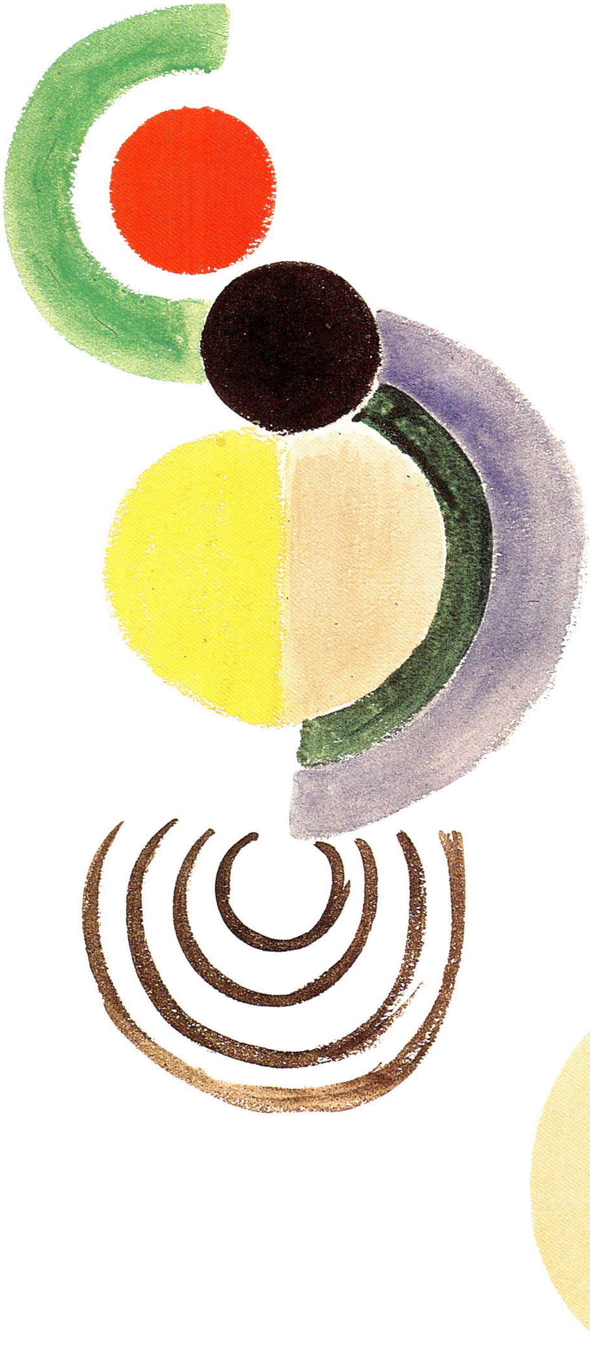

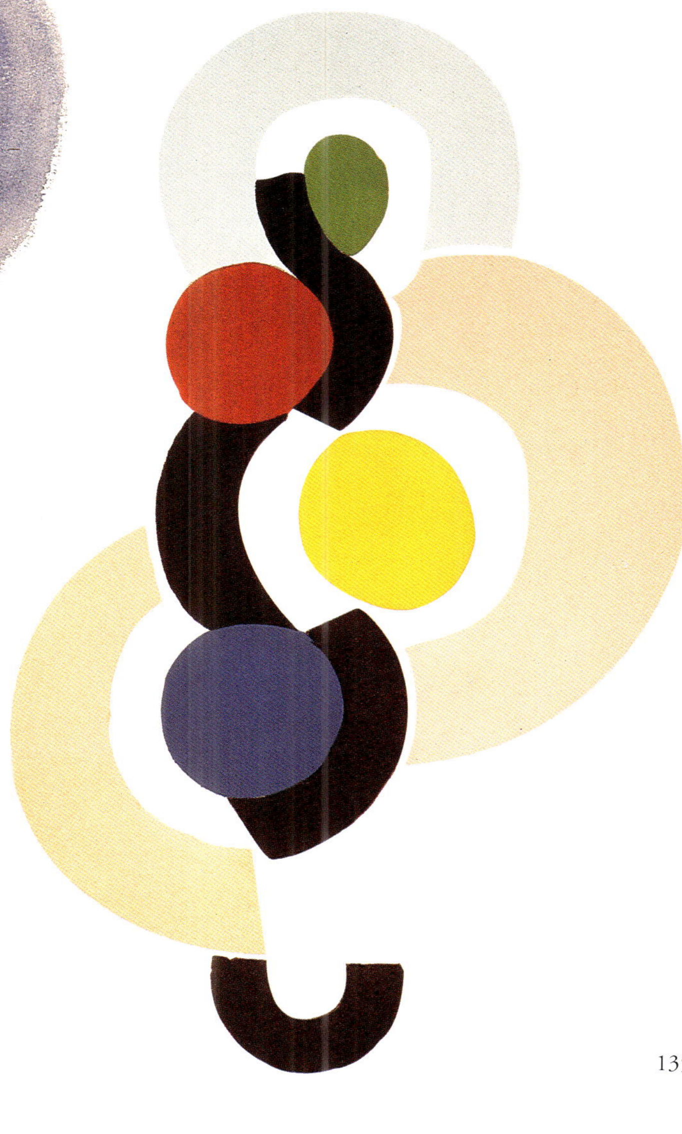

71,72 Two gouache paintings of dancers; the one on top, done in 1925, inspired the paintings by Robert called *Rhythme sans fin*. The other was painted in 1960.

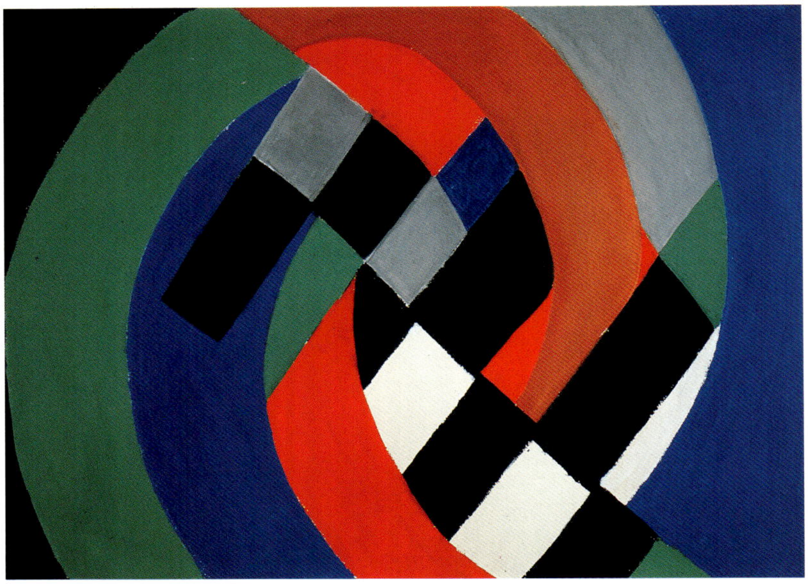

73 Gouache, 1960.

74 *Joker*, gouache, 1961.

75 *Rhythme couleur*, oil on canvas, 1962.

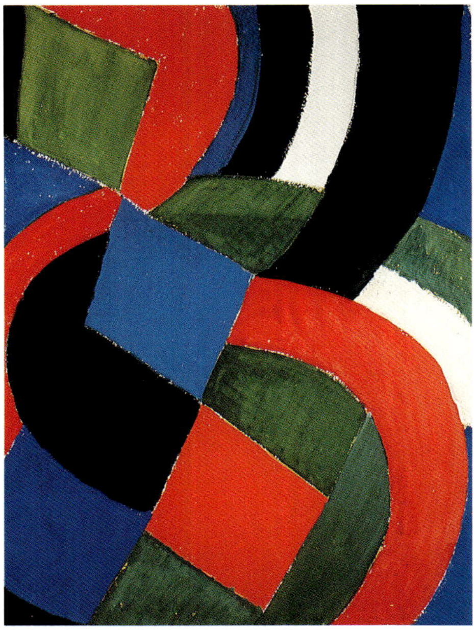

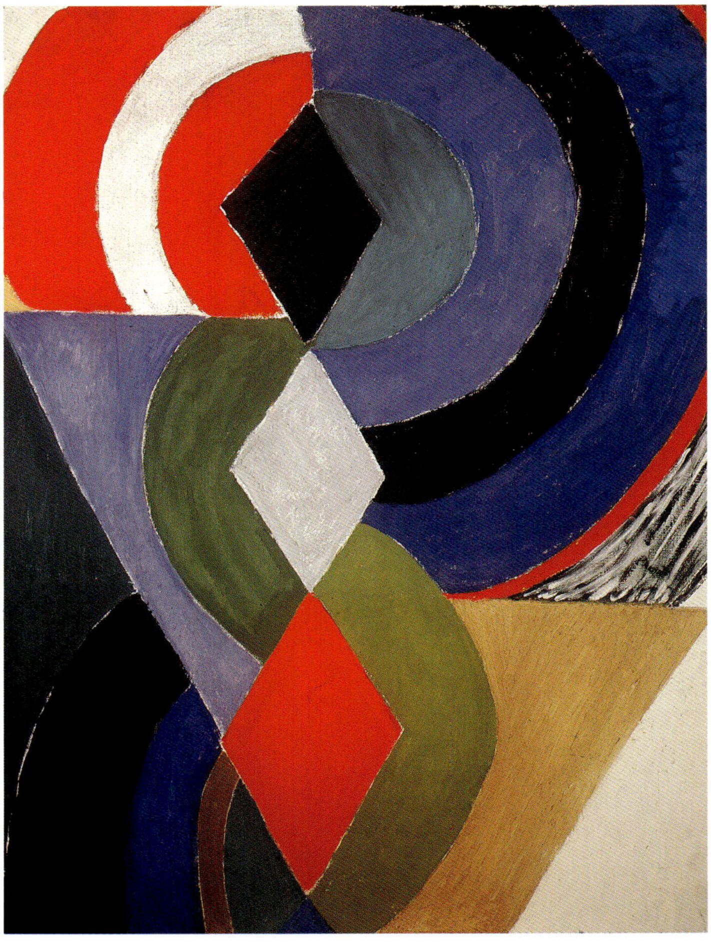

CHAPTER 13

THE LAST STAGES OF THE WAR

In 1944 Sonia was no longer living in a hotel, but in a kind of boarding house, where she shared the kitchen and salon with a number of other people. Though she was working on her gouaches, and enjoying the work, she was also preparing for the worst. Now that there were frequent alerts, planes passing overhead, the sound of bombing in the distance, she made yet another count of the suitcases, trunks, rolls, baskets, etc. that she was storing in the Chenu villa (there were ten pieces), and in addition there were eleven trunks belonging to Arp. In case something should happen to her, she also typed out lists of all Robert's paintings and their location.

In mid-January she asked the Commissaire de Police about the rumoured evacuation: would it be only from the towns on the coast or from the whole Département? The Commissaire was not able to provide an answer. At the end of the month, he went so far as to say that as yet there was no question of evacuating Grasse, but if she wanted to go somewhere else where food might be more readily available, that would obviously be better.

Among her fellow-tenants in the house were an intelligent couple called Weiss, who believed that the Allies would try to take the French line of defence against Italy in order to cut off the German forces. Later there were rumours of the Germans having requested negotiations with the British and Americans in Monte Carlo, because of the Russian successes on the eastern front. In both cases, there was a sorry lack of substance.

Sonia was unnerved, she wrote, by the feeling that she did not have enough money to do what she wanted; and it was especially painful when one had to depend 'on a madman like Arp', who was neither answering her letters nor transferring money to her. She thought of the paintings that were still in the studio in Paris and wondered how they might be used to cover her debts. Only Charles could deal with that, but he seemed not to understand how vital it was. She wrote criticizing his attitude, 'for not realizing what he had "in his hands" . . . and in the end I suggested that he enlist the help of Carré [the dealer], offering him an interest in the paintings there until things became normal again.'

This provoked a 'violent' reply from Charles on 3 February 1944, and she had to write again, restating all her suggestions for ways to pay their debts. She found that he had not managed things at all well. On 8 February, she sent him two manuscripts by *le Douanier* Rousseau, 'L'Orpheline russe' and 'Le Voyage à l'exposition'; the time seemed to have come to sell them.

A Dr René Charry got in touch with her from Toulouse to express an interest in buying Robert's *L'Espagnole.* It had been done with encaustic, and when she examined it now she found it was in bad shape. The wax colours had not adhered well and were crumbling away in some places. They had also

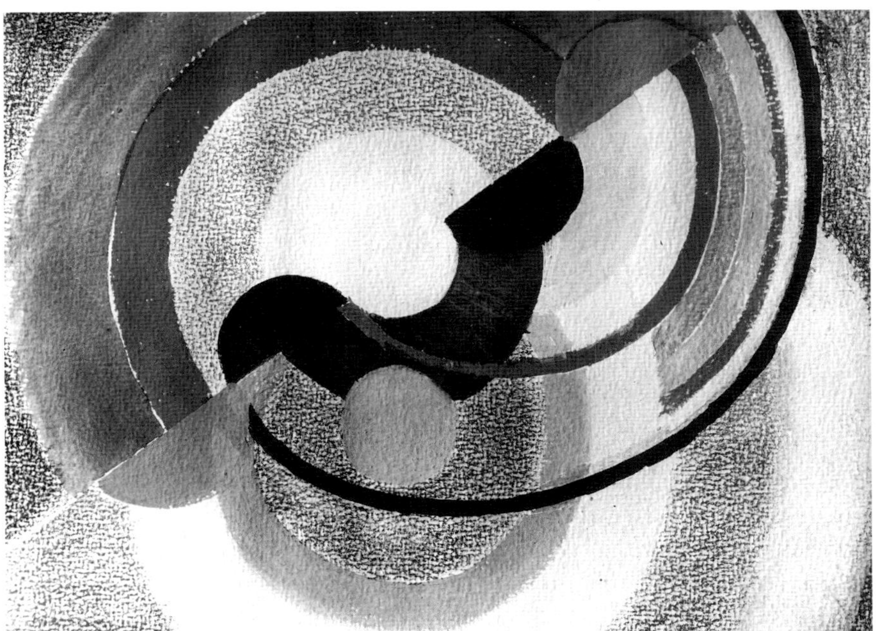

Two paintings in gouache on paper, done by Sonia while in Grasse in 1943 and called *Rhythmes colorés.*

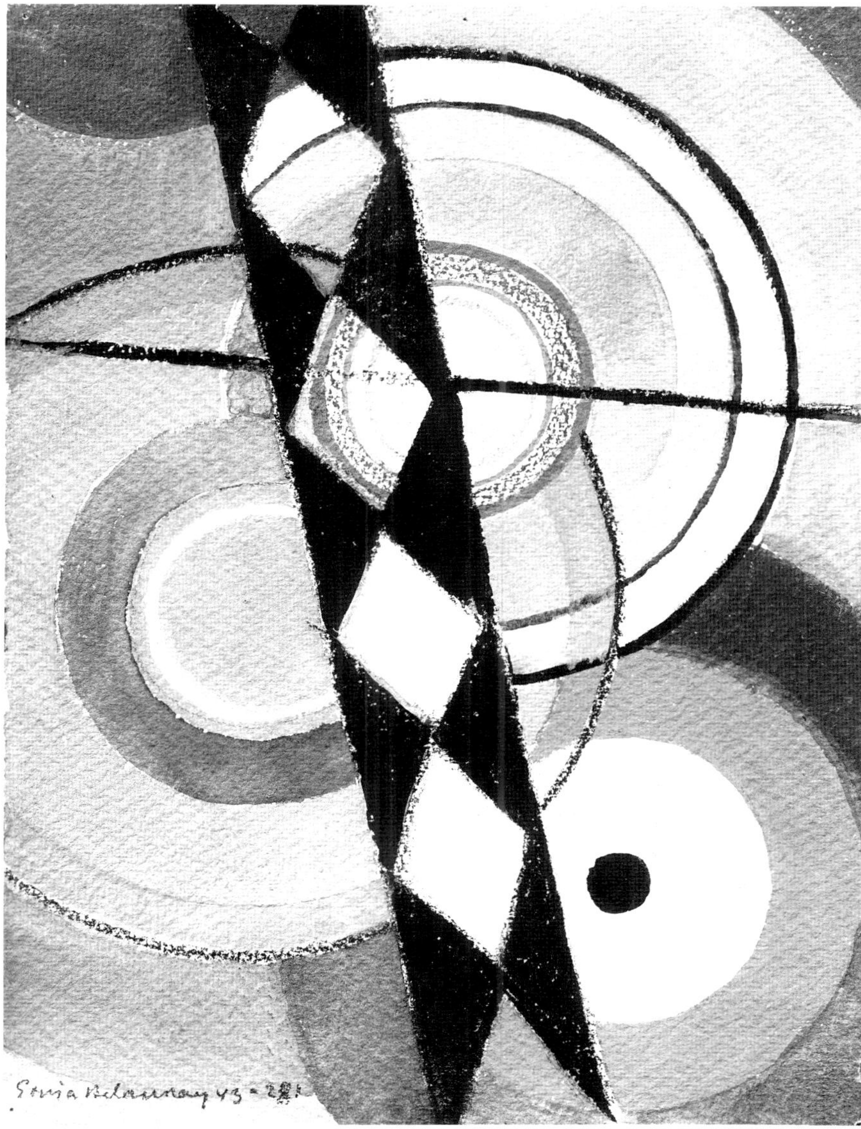

gone dull. Without any hesitation she did what Robert did not like to say he did but did all the same: retouched the painting with gouache.

She remembered that, when he painted that work, he was always asking her advice on what colours to use. 'In the matter of colours, he had absolute confidence in me and always followed my suggestions.'

The bombardment increased during the first few months of 1944 to the point where she was often awakened during the night. On 21 March, when there was an alert that lasted an hour, she stayed on the balcony outside her bedroom from which she could see what was happening in the street. Official cars came past with Germans, and in one she saw a civilian Japanese.

On that same day she received 15,000 francs from Dr Charry in payment for Robert's painting. She started to plan what she would do with the money left over after paying her bills and moving to Toulouse with the Weiss couple, when she received a letter from Charles asking for 5,000 francs in order to avoid having to sell any pictures to Carré. He was convinced the dealer would take advantage of them and not pay enough. This was such a blow to Sonia that, 'in order to overcome my vexation, I began to wash my linens, sweaters and other woollens.'

A few days later, the Commissaire de Police told her that evacuation was imminent because Grasse was only 20 km. from the coast and there were fears of an Allied invasion. The beaches had been mined by the Germans. On 30 March she bought a railroad ticket for Toulouse, intending to depart on 12 April. She was acting not only on the basis of the Commissaire's advice but also because she had begun to hate the type of people living in the house, whose focus was entirely on petty day-to-day matters which seemed to her completely irrelevant in the immediate circumstances.

Charles wrote on the 1st of April that he had found among his things a watercolour by Robert of the towers of Notre Dame, a sketch of 1937 for the Palais des Chemins de Fer, and a small encaustic *Fenêtre*. He had left Paris and was staying in a village called La Palisse in the neighbourhood of Fontainebleau; he was considering going on to Montigny-sur-Loing if things deteriorated still further in Paris.

In a state of uncertainty and changing moods, she cancelled her trip to Toulouse: would she be any better off there? What friends did she have in Toulouse? There was at least some relief in the news from Charles in mid-May that he had obtained 20,000 francs for the Rousseau manuscripts. And at last she decided that the time had definitely come to pull up stakes and travel on to Toulouse.

Events were moving quckly. On 6 June 1944 the radio gave the first news of the Normandy invasion. On 15 August she heard reports of the landings southwest of Cannes. By then, however, she had left the coast on a long, slow and tedious journey by stages to Toulouse. In the station at Cannes, while she was waiting to board the train to Marseilles, she was approached by

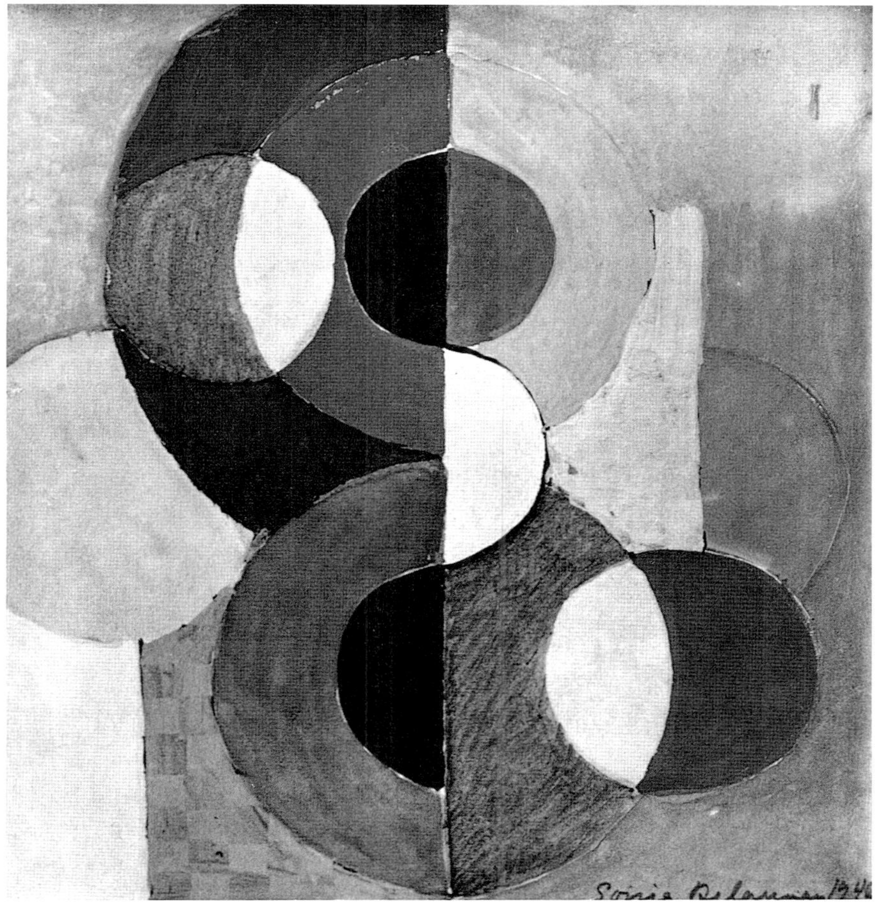

Rhythme couleur, gouache on paper, 1942.

a shady-looking character ('un type louche'), who showed his papers and asked for hers. When she handed him her identification card, he asked her her religion. She answered 'orthodox' and he countered with the suggestion that she was in fact Jewish ('israelite'). She said no, and why did he ask that? He pointed to her maiden name: Stern. With all her strength of character, Sonia refused to be bullied and said he was welcome to telephone the Commissaire de Police in Grasse, where she was very well known, having lived there for three years. The young man let her pass.

The trajectory of her journey took her from Cannes to Marseille, then to Montpellier, Béziers and finally Toulouse three days later. Once there, she found a number of people whom she already knew. She stayed for a while with a couple from Paris, the Brunets, though she eventually came into conflict with them. She also knew Dr Charry, of course; and one of her favourite people, Tristan Tzara, was working for the radio service of Toulouse, along with a group of lively intellectuals. They were a saving grace, because by early September she was writing in her journal that she desperately missed intelligent people and intelligent conversation.

At that time she received a card from Wilhelm Uhde, inviting her to lunch with him on 7 September 1944 at the Café de la Paix at 12.30. When she arrived, she found that the restaurant was closed. But Uhde approached her, and she says that if he had not she wasn't sure she would have recognized him. He had a little white pointed beard and had grown extremely thin and old. It all made a painful impression on her. They had to wait a long time for a table at another restaurant in the Place du Capitole and had a very poor meal. He spoke to her of his exodus, of his work and all he had lost. When he left her she was deeply depressed.

The next day she met the wife of Jean Cassou, who gave her news of Paris, 'of the arrival of de Gaulle, the indescribable enthusiasm. The Parisians

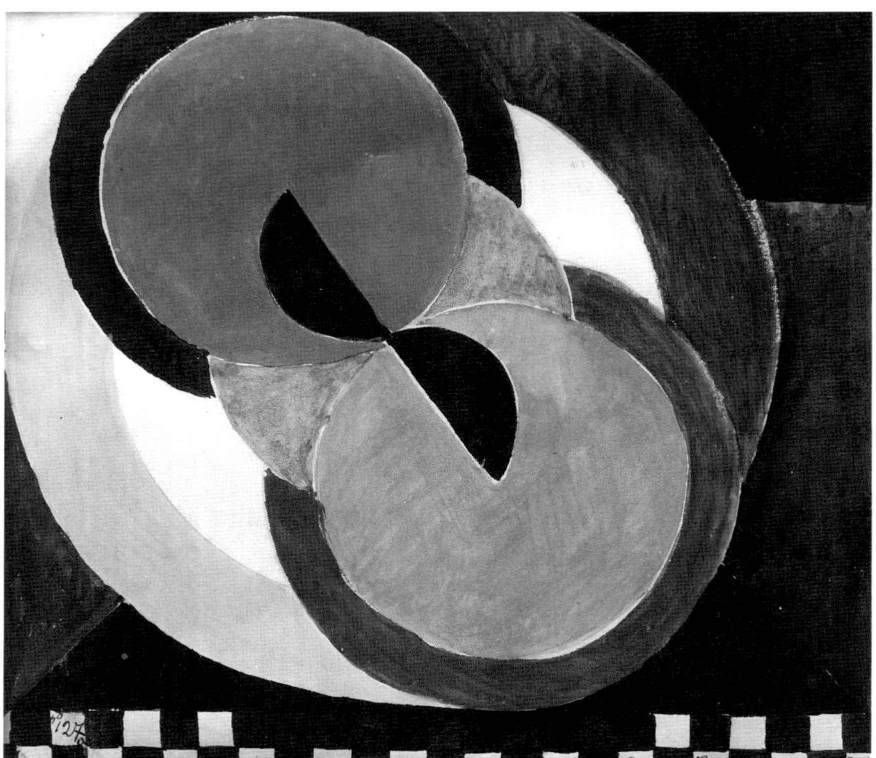

A 1943 watercolour, *Composition*, painted by Sonia in Grasse in 1943.

liberated themselves, before the arrival of the F.F.7 [Free French forces], before the Americans and Britons because of a delay of the latter in relation to the directions given to the Parisians.'

All during this period, she was reading English-language novels such as D. H. Lawrence's *The Rainbow* and *Sons and Lovers*, and the American best seller *Anthony Adverse*. Even earlier, she had found and read a curious American novel called *Mamba's Daughters* by Dubose Hayward, author of the more famous *Porgy*. She was captivated by its picture of Charleston, South Carolina, and the life of the black people in that community.

André Farcy arrived in Toulouse from Grenoble, accompanied by his mistress. In conversation with Sonia, he said that he was 'against the Jewish picture dealers and in general foresaw a movement of anti-semitism in two or three years if they started up again as in '36.' He was the same man, of course, who had alarmed her two years earlier with his remarks about the sculptor Zadkine.

In October she made yet another pilgrimage to Montpellier and Robert's grave, but remained there only three days. On the 27th she was back in Toulouse, and on the 1st of November she started her return to Paris, arriving first in Orléans, where she changed trains. At the Gare de Lyon in Paris, Charles was waiting for her and took her to his apartment in rue Chaptal, because the apartment in the rue Saint-Simon was still occupied by a wartime tenant. It was not until December 1944 that she recovered possession.

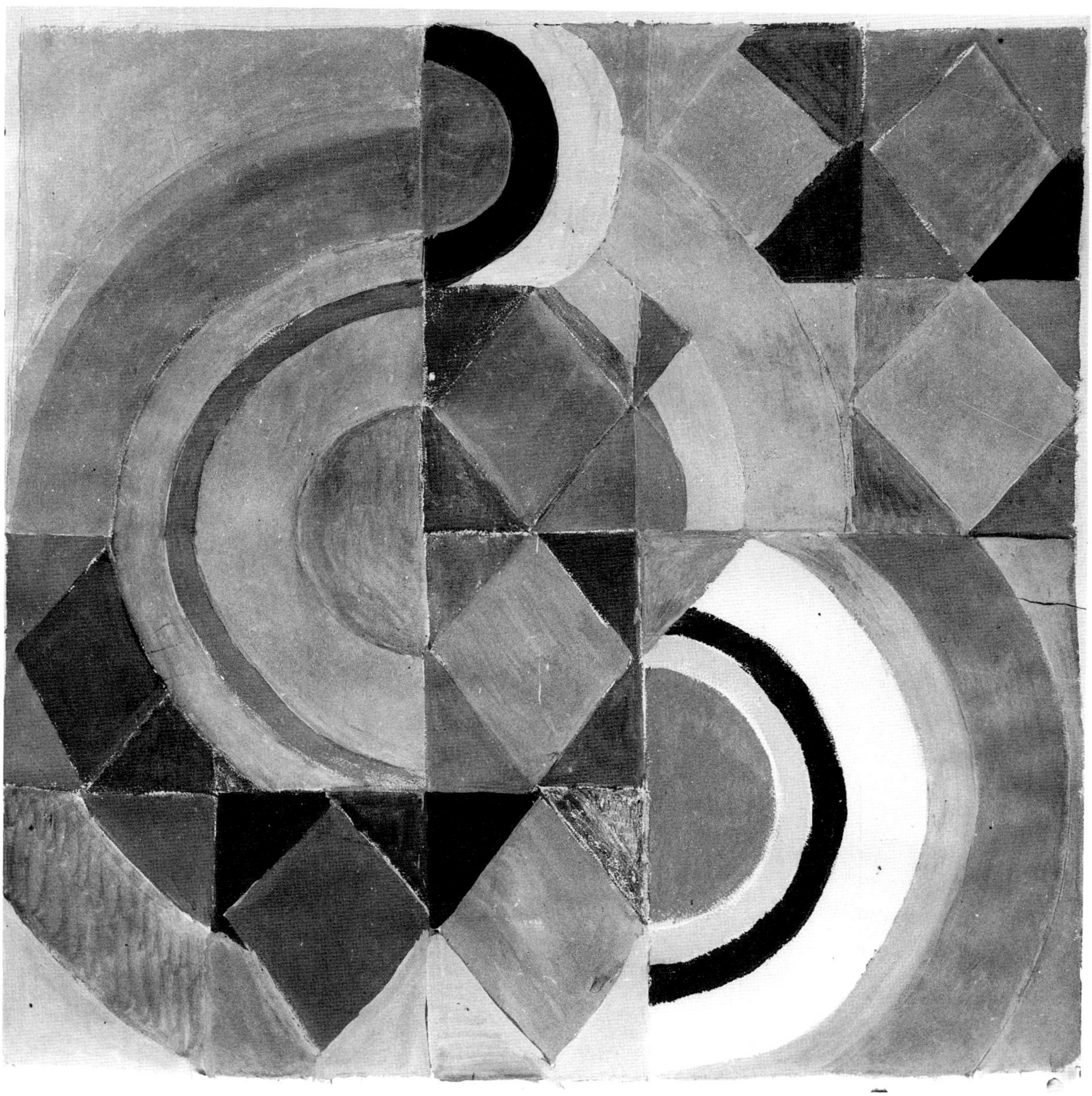

CHAPTER 14

BACK TO PARIS AGAIN: ESTABLISHING ROBERT

THE PARIS SONIA CAME HOME TO was a far different place from the Paris of her heyday. She was almost sixty when she returned, and had already completed two-thirds of her life. The whole cultural climate of Paris had changed. Instead of the light-hearted, cocky anarchy of Dada and the Freudian fantasies of Surrealism, there was the rather dour Existentialism of Jean-Paul Sartre and his band. Instead of the insouciant charm of the film *Sous les Toits de Paris* and the delicious *chansonniers* of the Twenties, there were the mournful laments of Edith Piaf and Juliette Greco. While there was important intellectual activity, the sense of ferment and the release of gaudy bubbles was gone; there were no Scott Fitzgeralds living off champagne and dancing the night away. And most significant of all, Paris was no longer the art centre of the world; New York had taken over that role during the course of the war.

The post-war years in France were also filled with political and economic instability. For the first time, the Communist party was nibbling around the edges of power. The difficulties of reconstructing the shattered economy of the country caused widespread unrest among the workers, and strikes were the order of the day in Paris. This threatening cloud of turmoil and disaffection and conflict was raised only when de Gaulle, the symbol of French heroism, tradition and *gloire*, became head of the Fifth Republic, with a new Constitution. Sonia was a firm admirer of de Gaulle. Like most people

Rhythme coloré, gouache on paper, painted after Sonia was back in post-war Paris.

over sixty, she gradually became much more conservative in her political views; she supported the spokesmen of stability and traditional French values; she was appalled at the student uprisings and their anarchic message in 1968; she became attached to de Gaulle's successor, Georges Pompidou, and particularly to his wife, a highly cultivated, attractive woman who was eventually a close friend of Sonia's. In spite of various protestations of independence and horror of the business world, she inevitably became attached to the establishment, which she and Robert had despised in their youth.

Whatever avant-gardes were floating about in Paris after the end of the war, Sonia was not to become part of them. In due course, she took up again her relations with Nelly van Doesburg, the Magnellis and Arp. At one point, she had the impression that Arp was looking for a second wife, and that 'if I were willing . . . How stupid!' Her dear old friend Tzara too seemed to want to remarry – but Sonia, determined to establish Robert in what she perceived as his rightful place as an artist of the highest rank, clung to her independence. Soon after her return, she wrote: 'My main purpose in life is to see to it that Robert's work is properly valued, something which did not happen during his life. Delteil says that's because he offended too many people.' Accordingly, she kept reminding herself that she must not waste her time in social gestures with people who had nothing spiritual to offer her. There was not enough time, if she was to accomplish all she had in mind on Robert's behalf and to continue her own painting. 'I love life but not people,' she wrote on 1 January 1945; and in 1947, 'I prefer creation to life.'

But before she could embark on her mission, she had to refurnish a way of life for herself in Paris. Obstacles had to be overcome before she could move back at the rue Saint-Simon address. The tenant, a Mme Debray, had left the place a mess, and Sonia considered the owner of the property liable for all the damage and missing objects. There was not much she could do, however, except to get it cleaned out and repainted, and move back in again on 12 January 1945. In retrospect, Grasse began to look attractive to her again: 'Ultimately Grasse is very dear to me, I have nothing but friends there, and I would like to go back for some time.'

Instead, she burrowed her way into the fabric of Paris again, seeing old friends like André and Simone Lhote, and opening negotiations for the re-establishment of Robert's career. While coping rather testily with the problems caused by days without water or electricity, she began her conversations

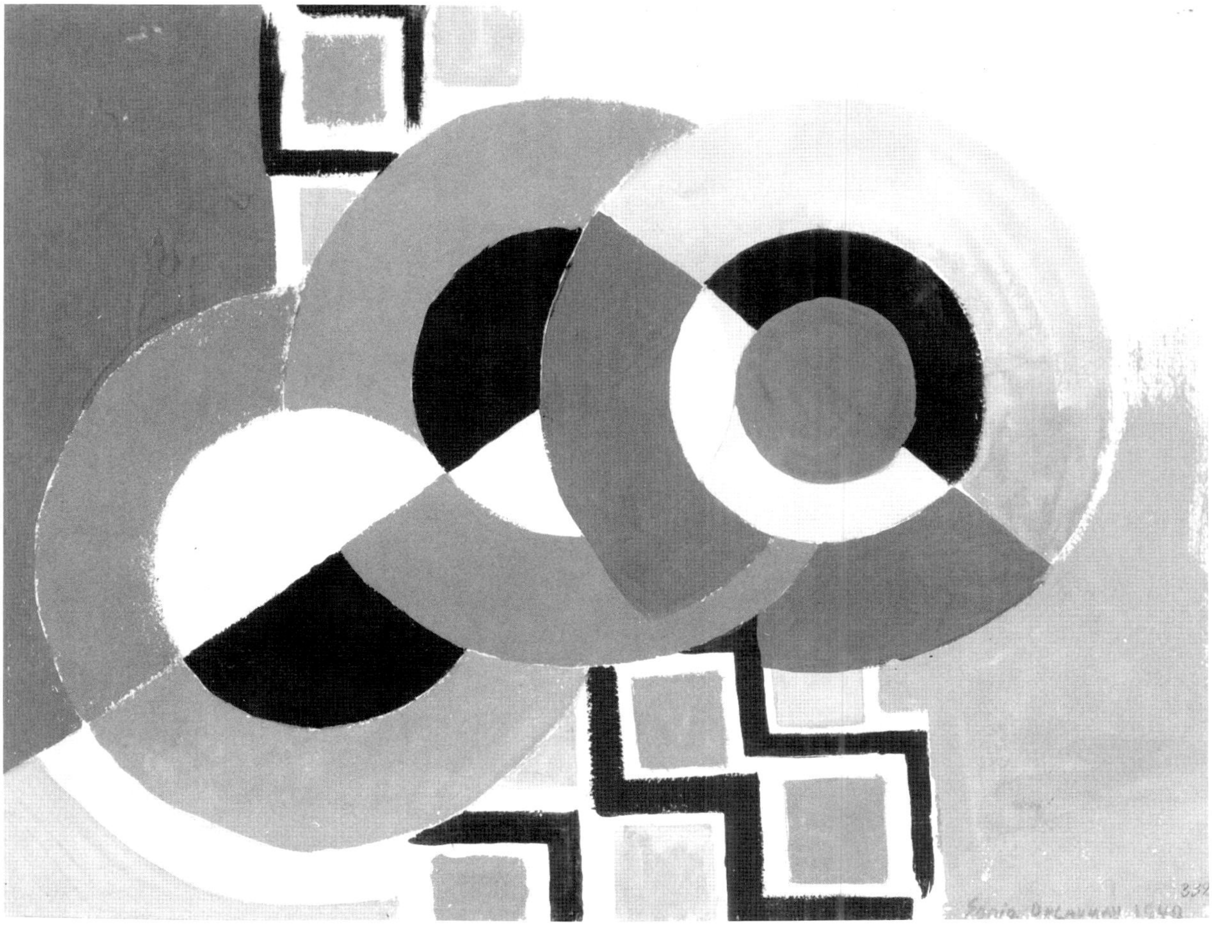

A gouache on paper painted in 1949.

with Carré which were meant to lead to a one-man show. She was also approached by M. Nebelthau of the Galerie Drouin and Nebelthau, who was setting prices of 30,000 and 40,000 francs on Robert's still-lifes. But she was depressed and repelled by the world of dealers, with their intrigues and their 'manipulations des toiles'. Nebelthau was warning her against Carré and Carré accused Nebelthau of having been a wartime collaborator. As she persisted in these distasteful negotiations, she informed Charles that, if her efforts succeeded, he would inherit a great fortune of pictures.

The German forces capitulated in May, and all Sonia could foresee was famine and sickness. She was in a depressed mood even though Charles was enjoying his work with the Paris radio establishment and she had great faith in de Gaulle, whom she saw on 2 April driving through crowds in an open automobile.

She considered making a firm deal for Carré to control all Robert's pictures and to pay her a certain amount of money every year. In the end, this is not what was decided; instead, she and Carré pursued their plan for a large retrospective of Robert's work to take place in Carré's gallery in 1946.

She stated her aim to Carré in November 1946: 'This exhibition has to make clear how Robert's painting evolved and how abstract art grew out of Cubism. It's only because of him that it happened this way.' But its preparation meant a great deal of work for her. While making out lists of Robert's paintings yet again, she remarked that Kandinsky did this himself, which was much simpler – but that was not in Robert's character.

Charles was worrying about money, which she found irritating: 'I can't do more for him than I am already doing – I have to think also about having enough in hand for the immediate future in order not to be forced to sell but to be able to wait for the right moment.' Charles clearly believed that his parents had been feckless, dedicated dreamers with little understanding of the practicalities of life. He could distress Sonia, not so much by what he said as by his critical attitude towards her. 'He criticizes my spiritual side,' she wrote. 'He doesn't know me.' In defending Robert, she said to Charles that, whereas people had taken Robert for mad and a good-for-nothing, he was the only one who had left something real, a palpable heritage from which Charles would profit.

The retrospective was scheduled to open on 17 December. On 29 November, Carré telephoned to ask what artists Robert had frequented in the 1906–10 period and who had influenced him in the Cubist years. As the query was related to preparation of the catalogue, she answered that when she first met him Robert was seeing Metzinger, and when he was in Brittany his companions were Sam Halpert and Max Weber – then Léon Kroll – and he also knew Picasso and Braque. Then Carré put someone else on the phone, and Sonia explained that, 'before the influence of Cézanne, Robert had been influenced by neo-Impressionism, had been brought to it by his mother, who had good taste and did a little neo-Impressionist painting herself . . .' Basically, she considered that Robert was barely influenced at all by the artists he knew; he had done Cubist painting because that was the period for it. He also knew Surrealists but was in no way influenced by them. 'He was a solitary, he did not take part in a group.'

The show was officially opened in Carré's gallery at 10, avenue de Messine, at 3.30 in the afternoon on 17 December. Sonia noted down the people who were there: Mme Kandinsky was among the first and stayed a long while, the Magnellis naturally came, the Vantongerloos, Léger, Villon. The curator of the Zürich Museum told her that they would be buying a painting; and Lhote, at the end, said that the Louvre would buy *La Ville* No. 2 (1910) and the *Femme nue lisant* (1915).

In all, twenty canvases were shown, ranging from a *Saint-Séverin* of 1908–09 to a still-life with red tablecloth of 1937. In the catalogue there were fifteen reproductions, the Apollinaire poem *Les Fenêtres* of 1912 (which ends with the lines 'The window opens like an orange/The beautiful fruit of light'), and an elegant essay by Jean Cassou. Sonia could not have asked for a greater success. Carré said to her, 'Robert Delaunay's work is saved and he will take his place beside Braque, Picasso and the others.' This, of course, would be honey to her ears, even if it happened to be a slight exaggeration.

Along the way to this successful denouement, she noted in her journal that she felt she had not played her cards badly, though a good deal of the success was happening by itself. All the same, 'I could have made mistakes, but I think I have avoided them. I also think the pictures are going to attain very high prices.' Then, when Robert was included in a study of modern artists

One of Sonia's post-war oils on canvas, 1948.

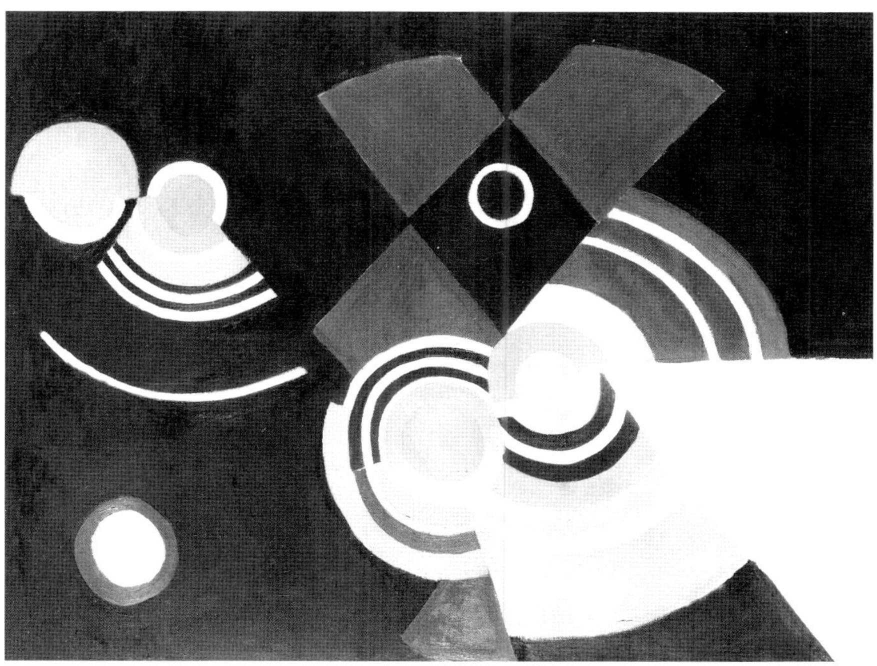

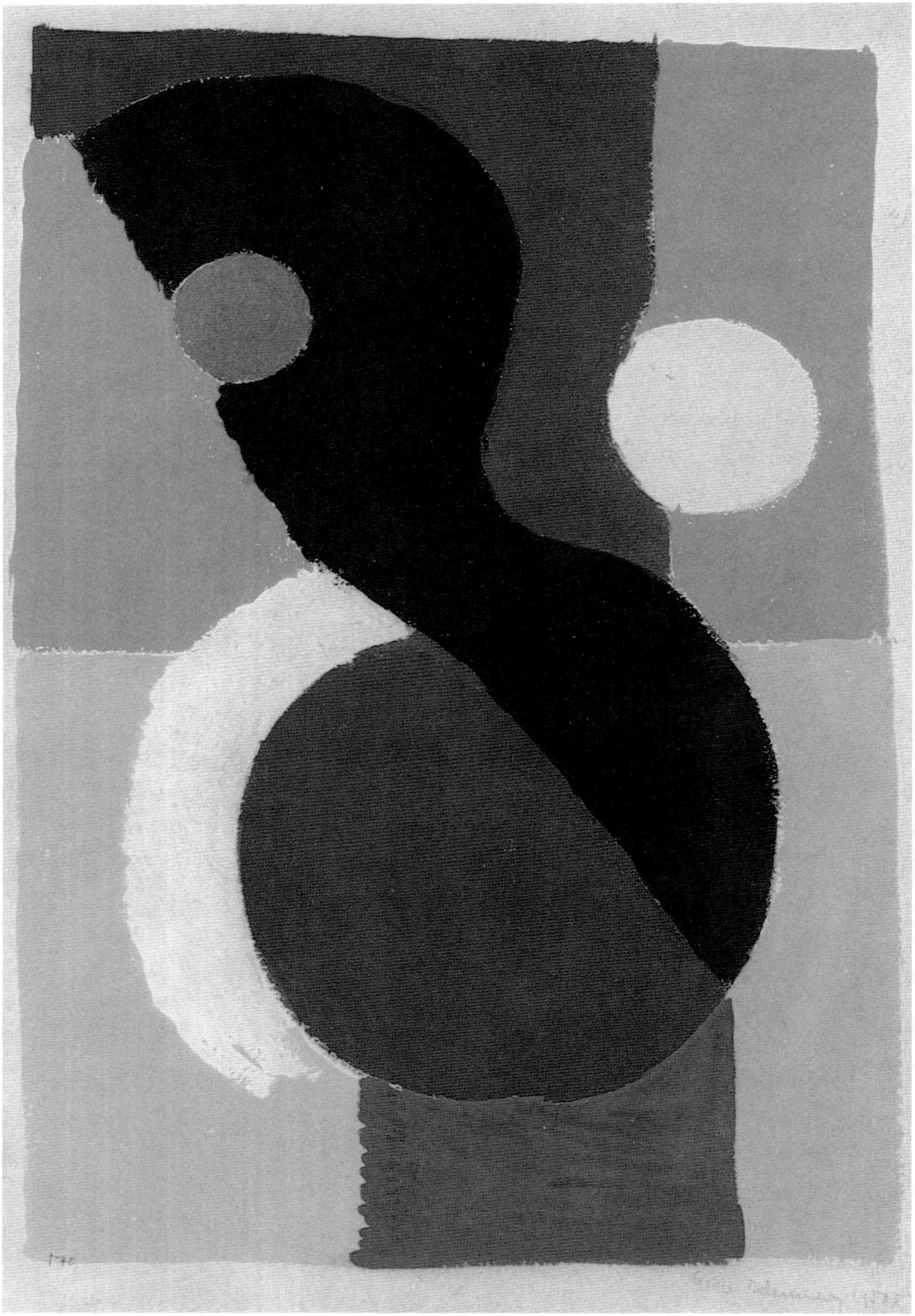

An imposing gouache design of 1950.

published by Skira, her comment was that Robert now had his place and could not be 'dispossessed' from it. He had been ranked among the most important painters of his generation, higher than Gleizes, Lhote, Villon and the like.

Carré continued to make plans for broadening Robert's acceptance and exposure. After the appearance of the Skira book, he was enthusiastic about the possibilities of a large exhibition of Robert's work in the United States; Sonia felt they should wait for the Museum of Modern Art in New York. When Carré wanted her to speak out about the part she had played in Robert's life, not only as his wife but in his work, she responded that she did not like people to speak of her apart from Robert, that they had been not just husband and wife but 'working companions'. After Dr Viard referred to all Robert owed her, especially since his death, she commented that it might be true, 'but I consider our work, our painting, so much a totality for which we both lived that it seems to me what I am doing is only normal.'

In 1946, in addition to preparing for the Carré retrospective, she had helped an old friend, Frédo Sidès, to organize the second Salon of the New Reality – the first of which had had Robert's active support back in 1939. By December 1947, however, she resigned from the Salon committee; its members, she felt, were 'drowning in administrative formulas and forgot the main objective of art and its integrity.' And a few months earlier she noted in her journal the news of Wilhelm Uhde's death. What struck her as worth recording was that she had received some word of him a few days before. No other comment was required; her marriage to Uhde might just as well never have taken place.

Her persistence on Robert's behalf gradually began to bear fruit. She and Carré exercised great patience, holding back while Robert's work appreciated in value, and selling pictures with tactical finesse. Within the next few years, he was represented not only in most of the main museums and galleries in Europe, but the American galleries too began to seek out a Delaunay for their collections of modern painting. Apart from Solomon Guggenheim, who had bought paintings by Delaunay in the Twenties and Thirties, none of the Americans had shown much interest in Robert's work until now.

She kept careful note from then on of exhibitions in which Robert was included. In May 1946, several months before the retrospective, she had commented on a show at the important Galerie Charpentier of a hundred masterpieces of the School of Paris; they included works by Matisse, Rouault, Picasso, Braque, Dufy, Utrillo, and the familiar Rousseau, *The Snake Charmer*, that had once belonged to the Delaunays. A large work of Robert's was placed, to her satisfaction, between Miró and Max Ernst. By the beginning of 1955, she felt entitled to say, 'I have realized for Robert what he dreamed of – to be among the premier painters of his times.'

She resumed contact with the circle of young aspiring artists who had met weekly with Robert during the last years before the war. They included such names as Richard Streiff, Gazier, Birkel, Tessier, Besançon, Simonetti – none of whom is remembered today. It was decided that they would meet once a month. She was kind and helpful to them, and enjoyed the company of young people, but she told them more than once that whereas technique in painting was fine, great paintings were achieved only by artists with a spiritual gift. She did not feel any 'genius' in the group; she described some of them as 'armchair painters'. These younger would-be artists were also keen on theory and intellectual analysis, which is one reason why they had been attracted to Robert in the first place; but for Sonia, who found her instincts more trustworthy than any theories, this approach had always been inimical.

Just after Christmas 1946, when the excitement over the Carré retrospective had died down, Charles, who had recently married Denise Chaput, a young woman about whom Sonia had some doubts, announced that he would be taking his wife on a honeymoon trip, and that they intended to spend the next summer living in Gambais. Sonia, who had been looking forward to being in Gambais herself, was devastated but managed not to let Charles see.

76 The knave of spades designed for a set of playing cards, 1964.

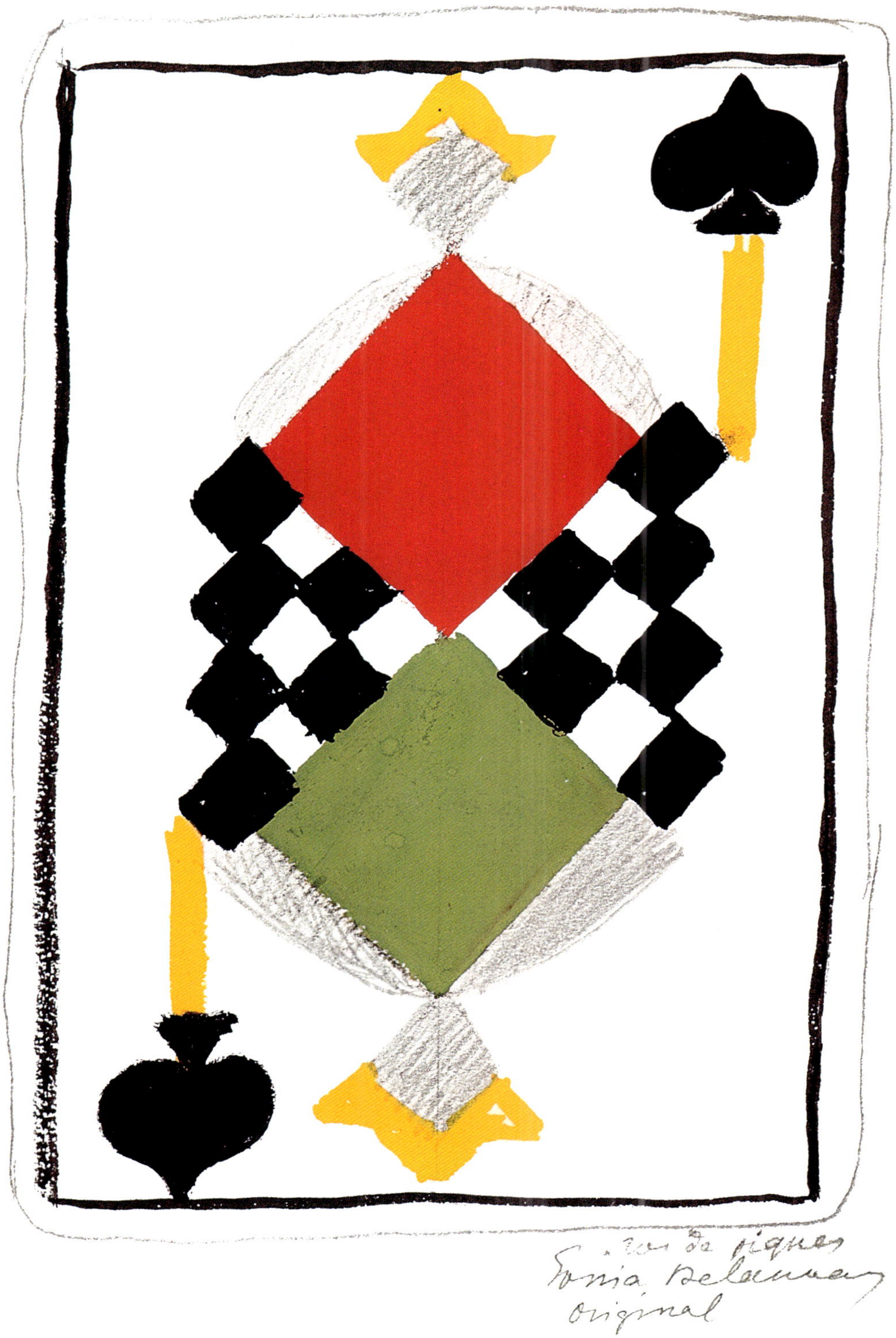
Roi de piques
Sonia Delaunay
Original

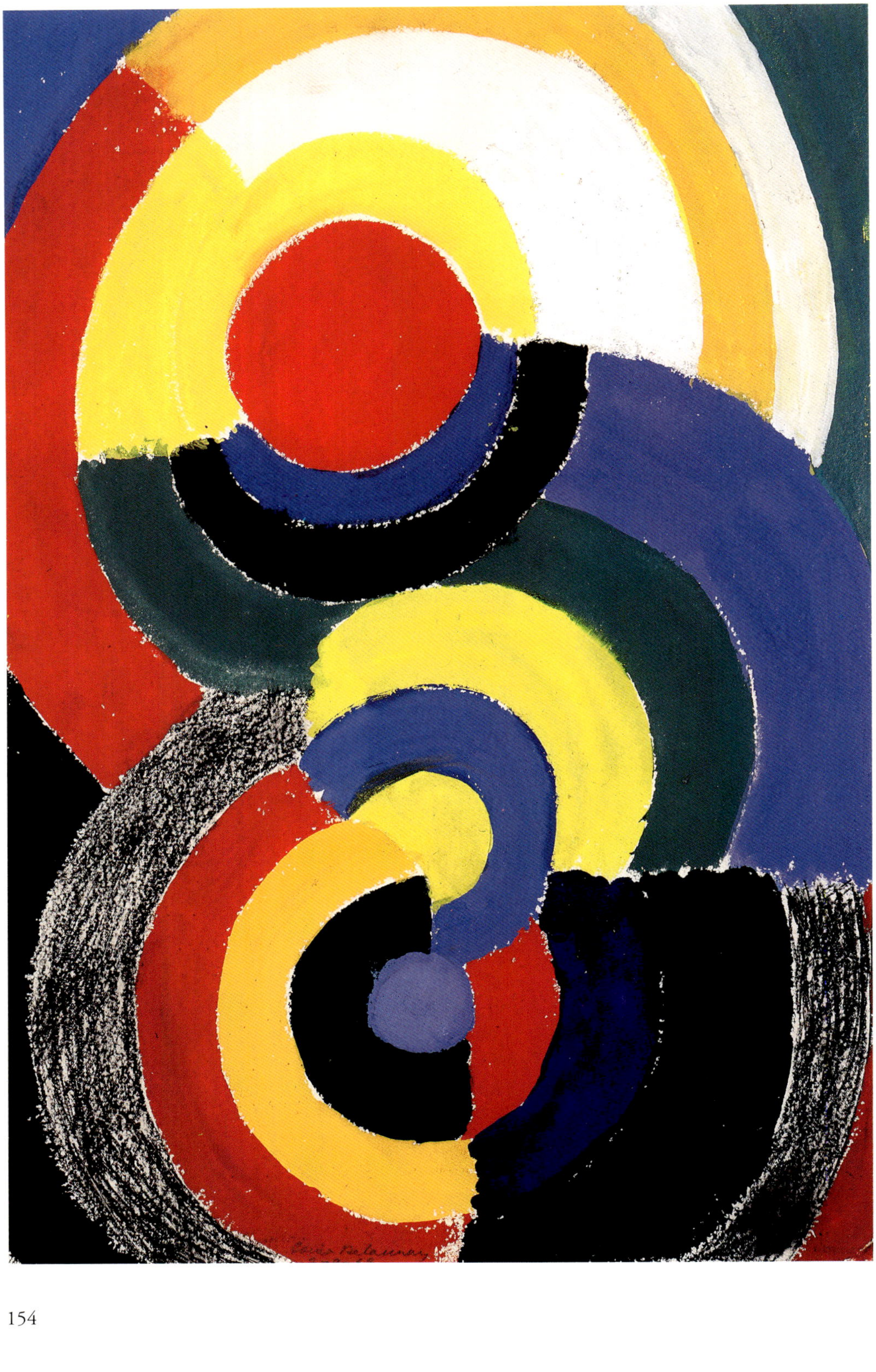

77 *Rencontre*, gouache on paper, 1962.

78,79 Two paintings of 1965 from the series called *Icone*.

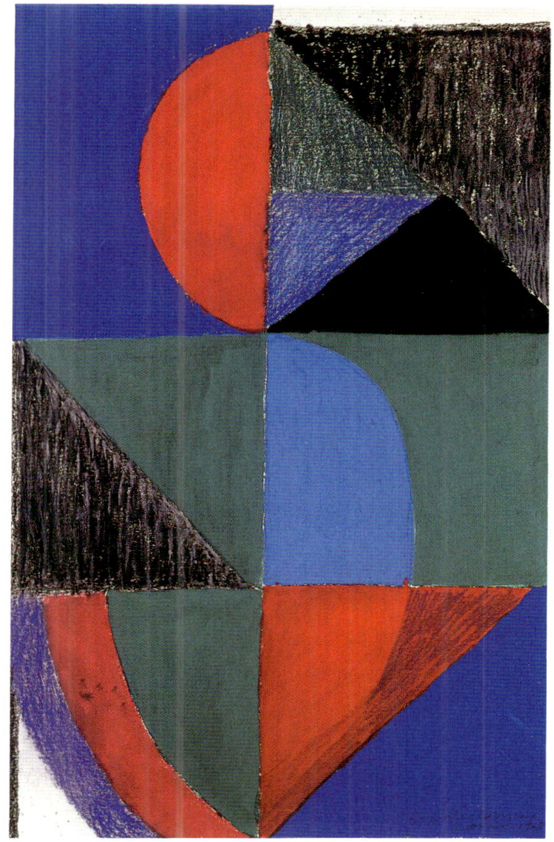

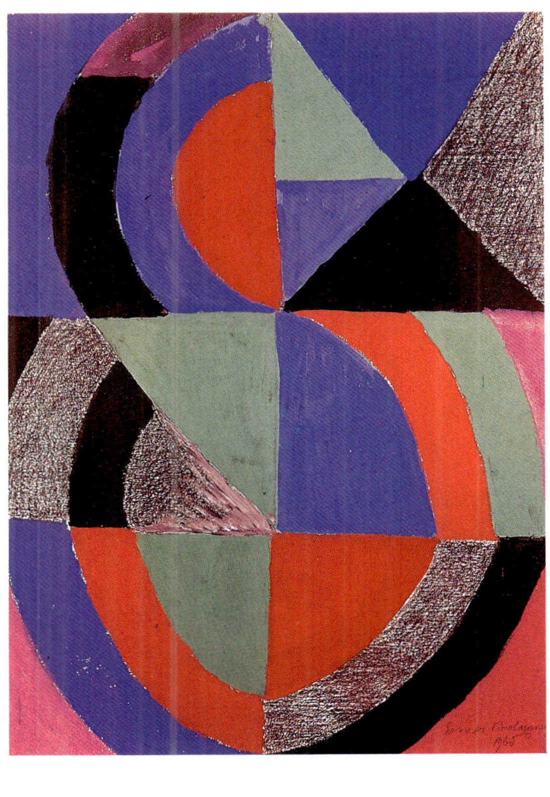

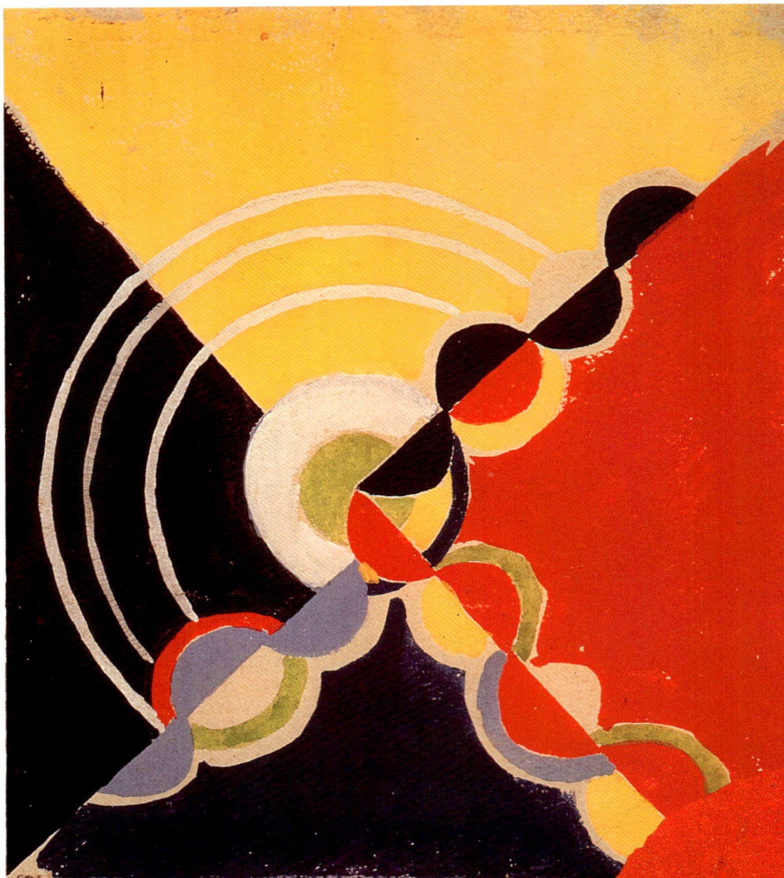

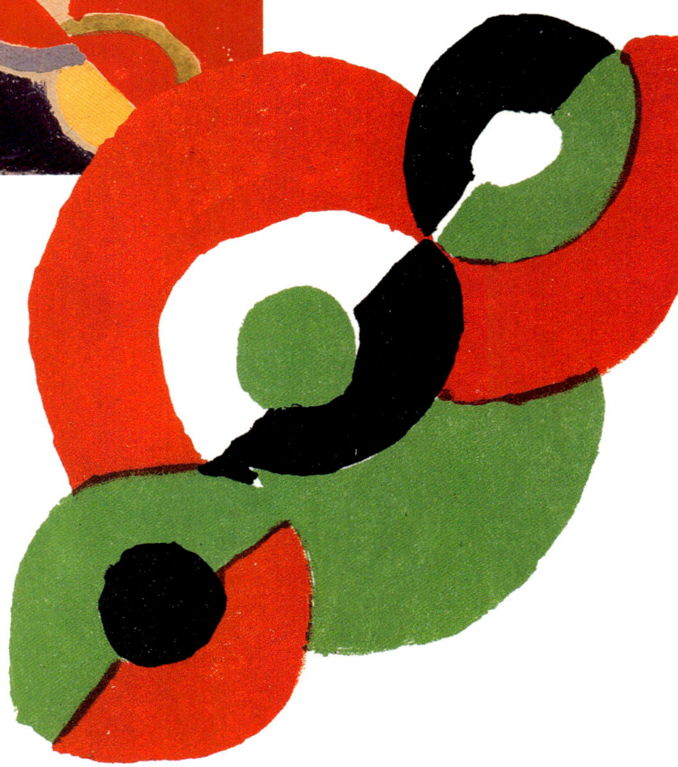

80 Gouache, *c.* 1965.

81 Design in green and red for a poem, 1965.

82 Opposite, *Tryptique*, oil on canvas, 1967.

83 Opposite below left, *Rhythme-couleur*, gouache, 1967.

84 Opposite below right, *Point noir*, gouache, 1965.

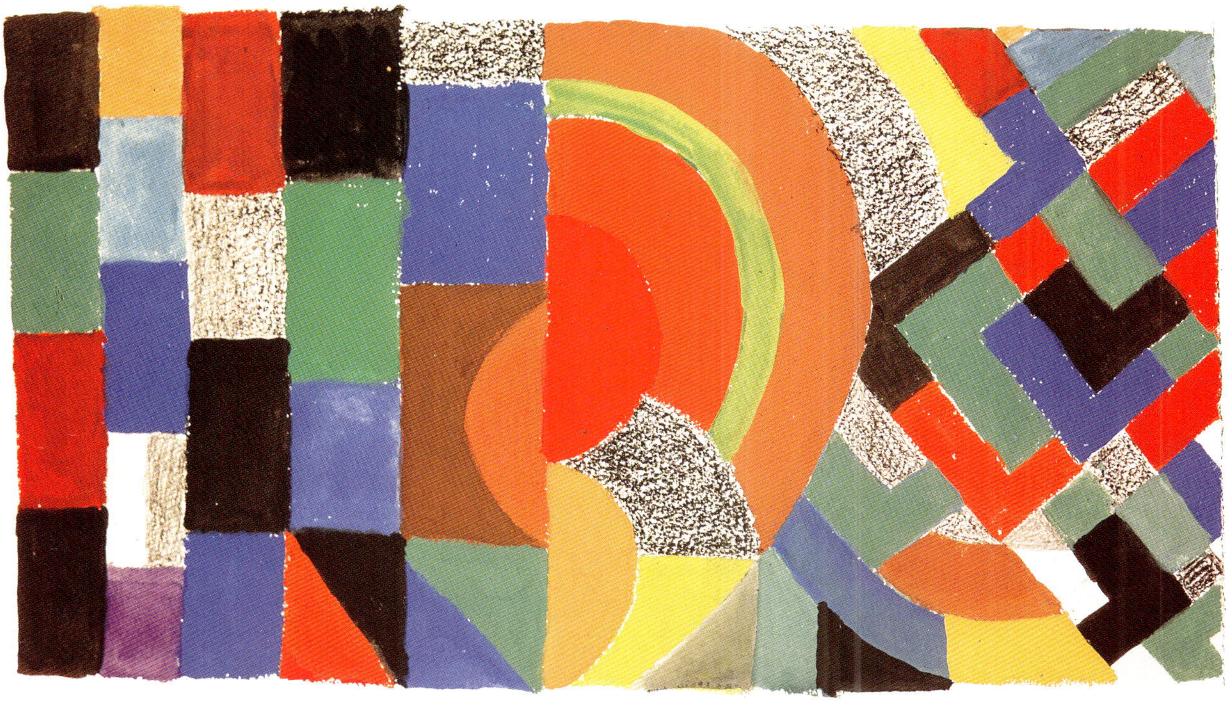

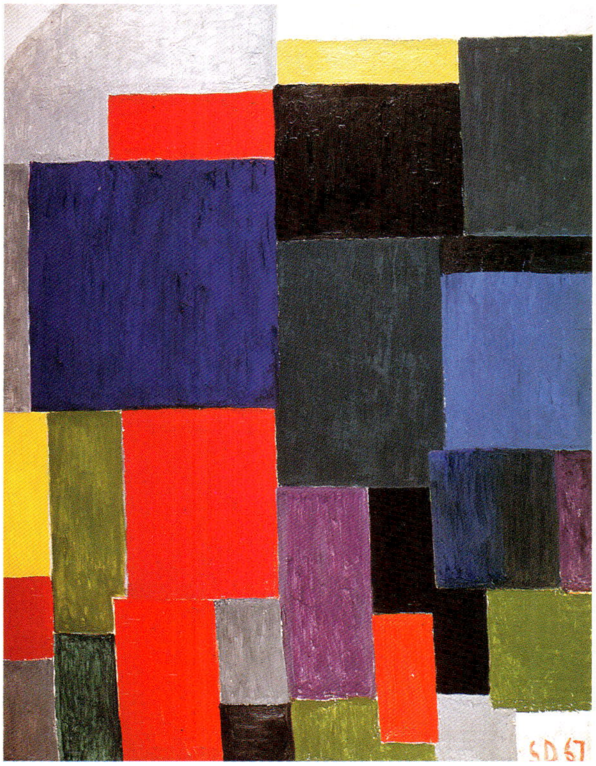

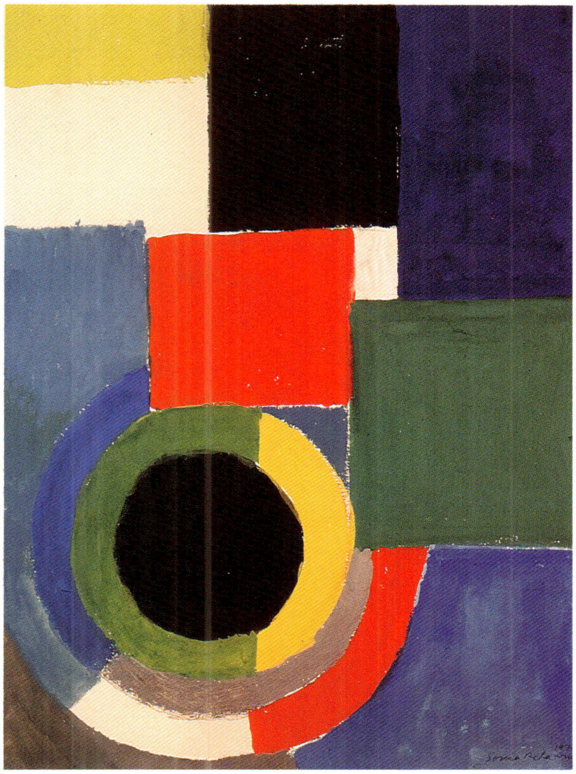

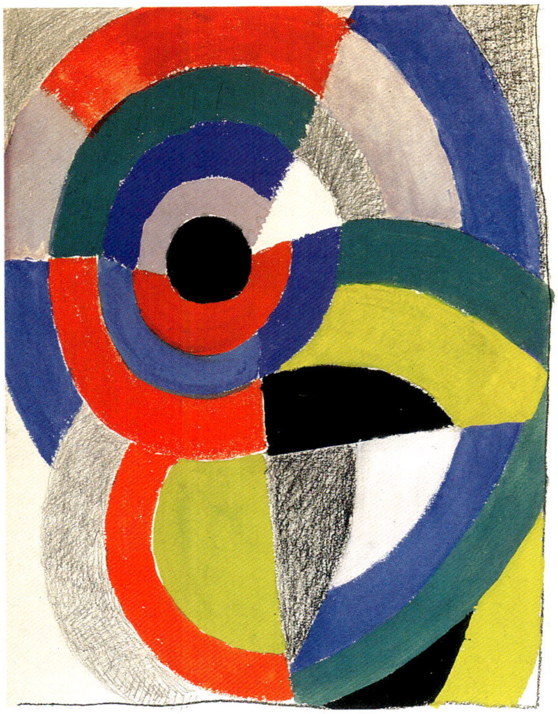

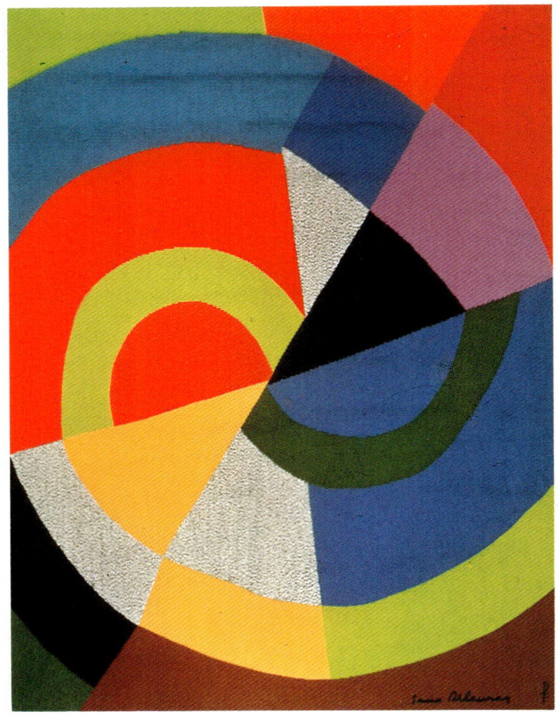

85 Above left, *Bleu*, gouache on paper, 1968.

86 Above right, *Diagonal*, rug, 1970.

87 Right, *Finistère*, gouache on paper, 1968.

88 Opposite, *Rhythme-couleur* No. 1633, oil on canvas, 1969. This is the painting President Pompidou took as a present to President Nixon on an official visit to the White House.

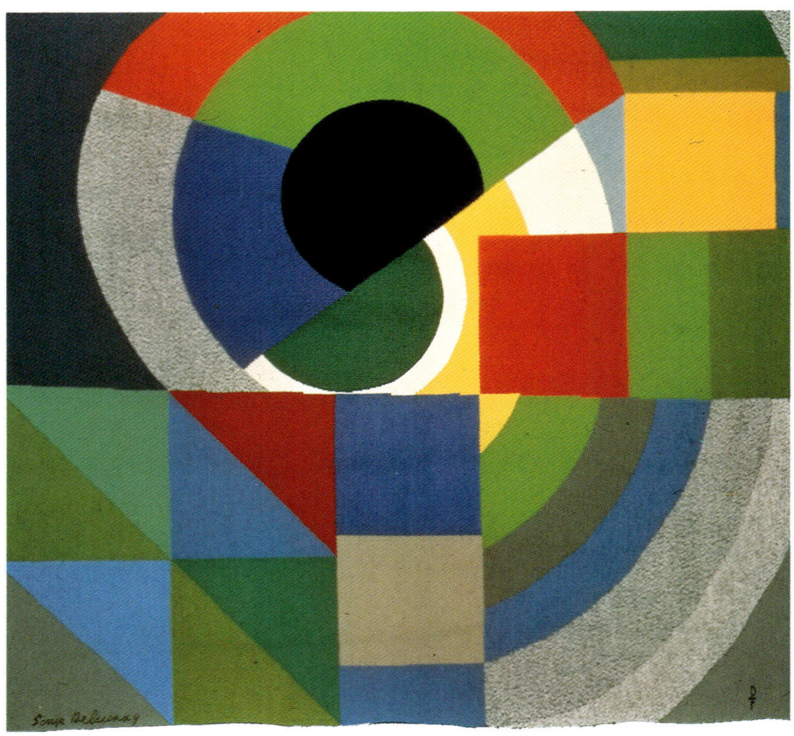

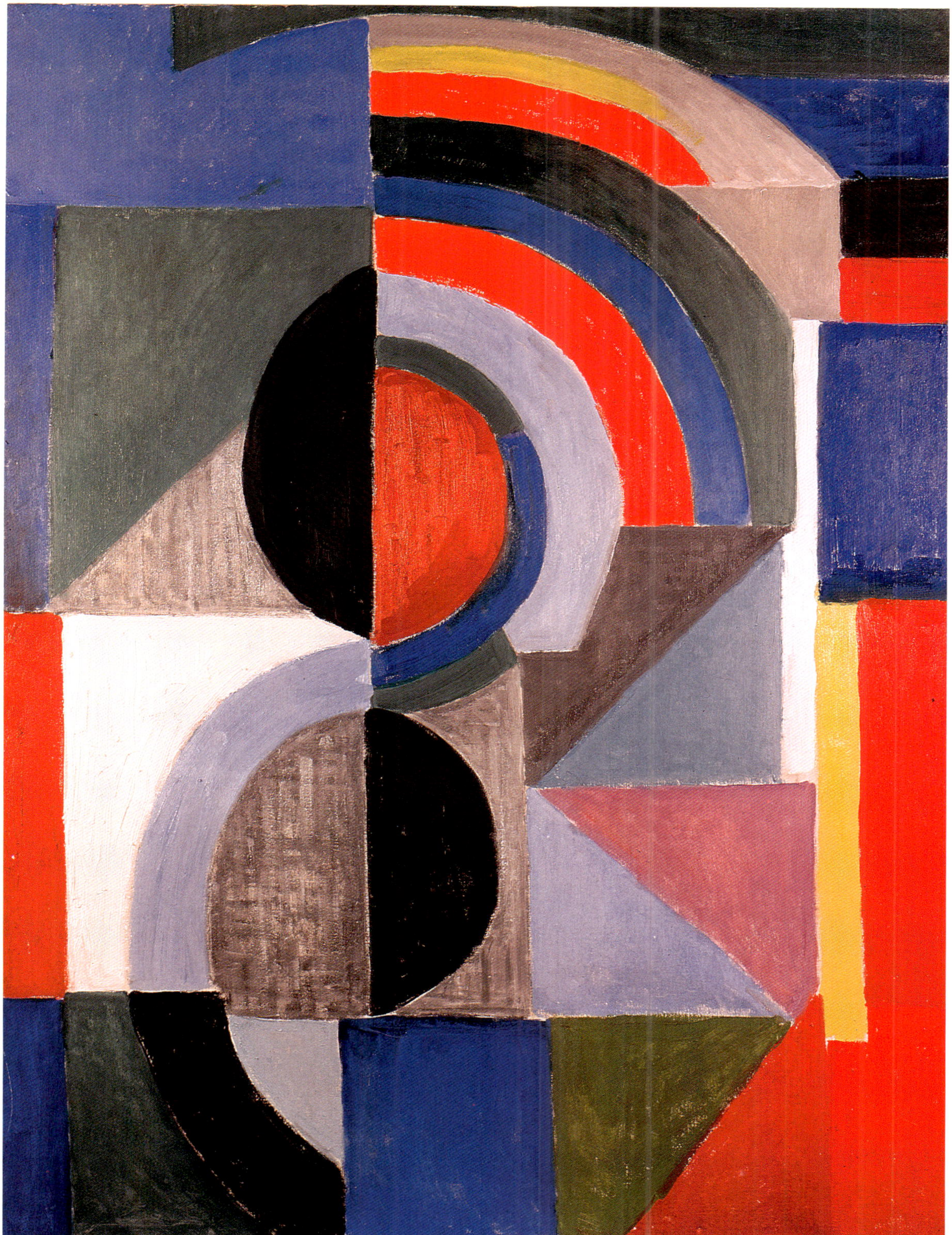

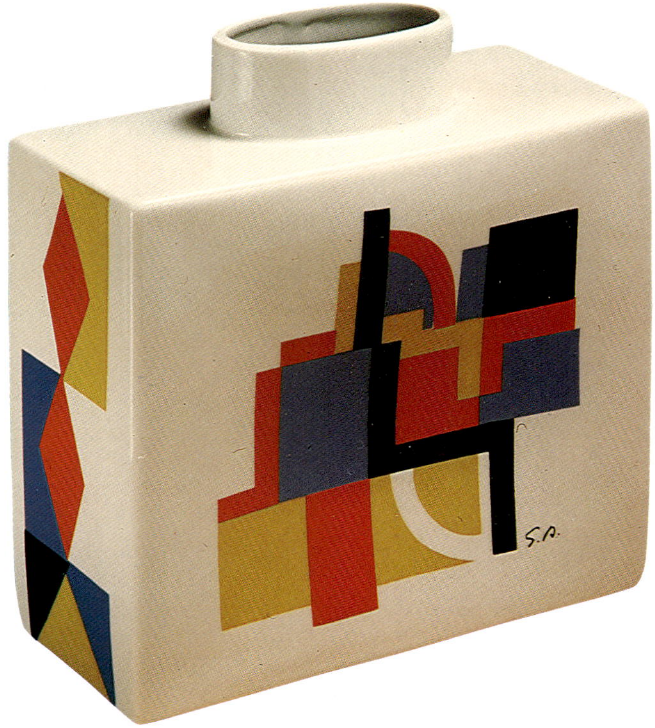

89-91 A dish, a cubic vase and a platter designed by Sonia in 1969.

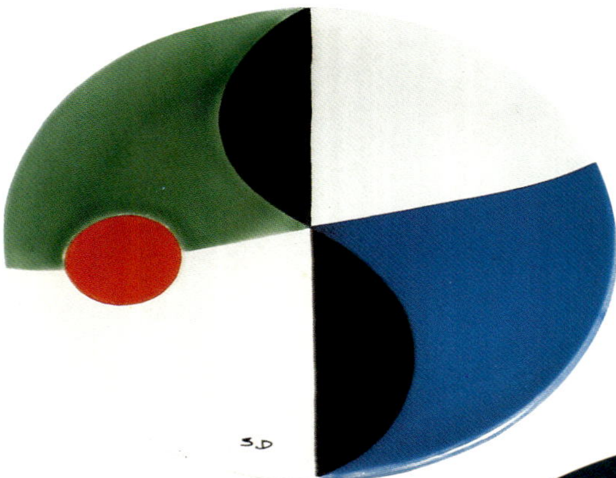

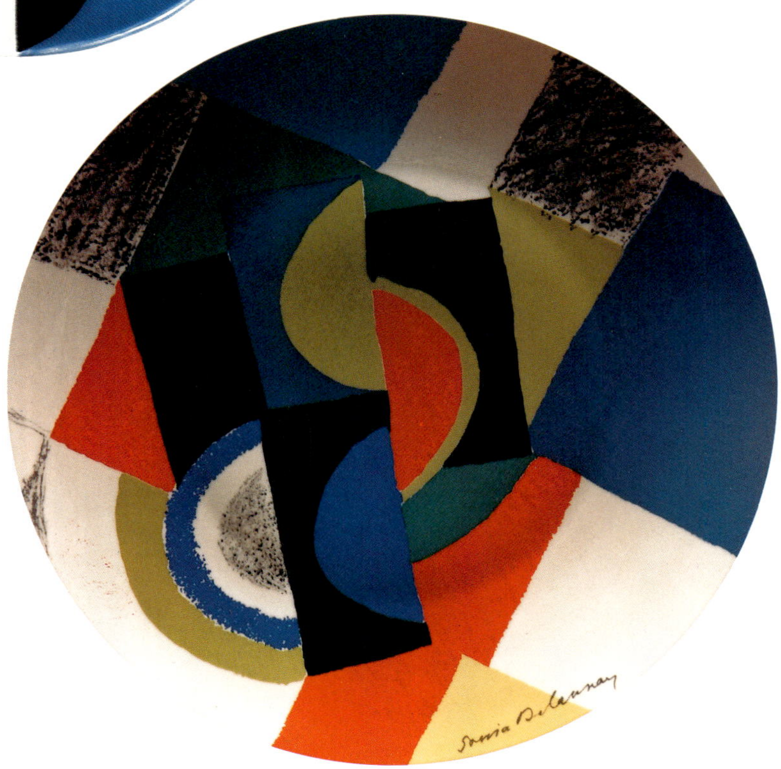

CHAPTER 15

PUTTING SONIA FIRST

Now that Sonia had seen the fruition of her efforts on Robert's behalf, her thoughts began to turn to her own work and her own place in art history. Back in November 1941, shortly after Robert's death, she had recorded a conversation with Delteil, in which he had said that she must start painting again. She replied that, if she did, it would be only for herself, because she did not want people to use her in order to denigrate Robert's work. Once she had put that in order and its value was fully recognized, it would be time for her to look after herself.

Then, in 1948, she was reminding herself that Robert had always told her she had too much talent and worked too little. That was why she was seeking to empty her life of people who prevented her from living entirely for her work. 'I must catch hold of time and devote myself only to my work.' It was a theme that appears frequently in this period. 'I've decided', she wrote, 'to see useless people as little as possible and to work as much as possible in order finally to bring out what I have inside of me.' At the same time, she was a little bitter about the fact that she had been classified as a decorative artist and not a true painter. Yet she remembered Robert telling her to 'make her pictures like her fabrics'.

Both of them, as she remarked more than once, had been misunderstood; indeed, she speaks of a 'flagrant injustice' against them. Only when the art world would learn to understand the basic facts of colour, the poetry and language of colour combinations, would it understand their importance in painting – 'mine as well as Robert's' – and appreciate what they had done.

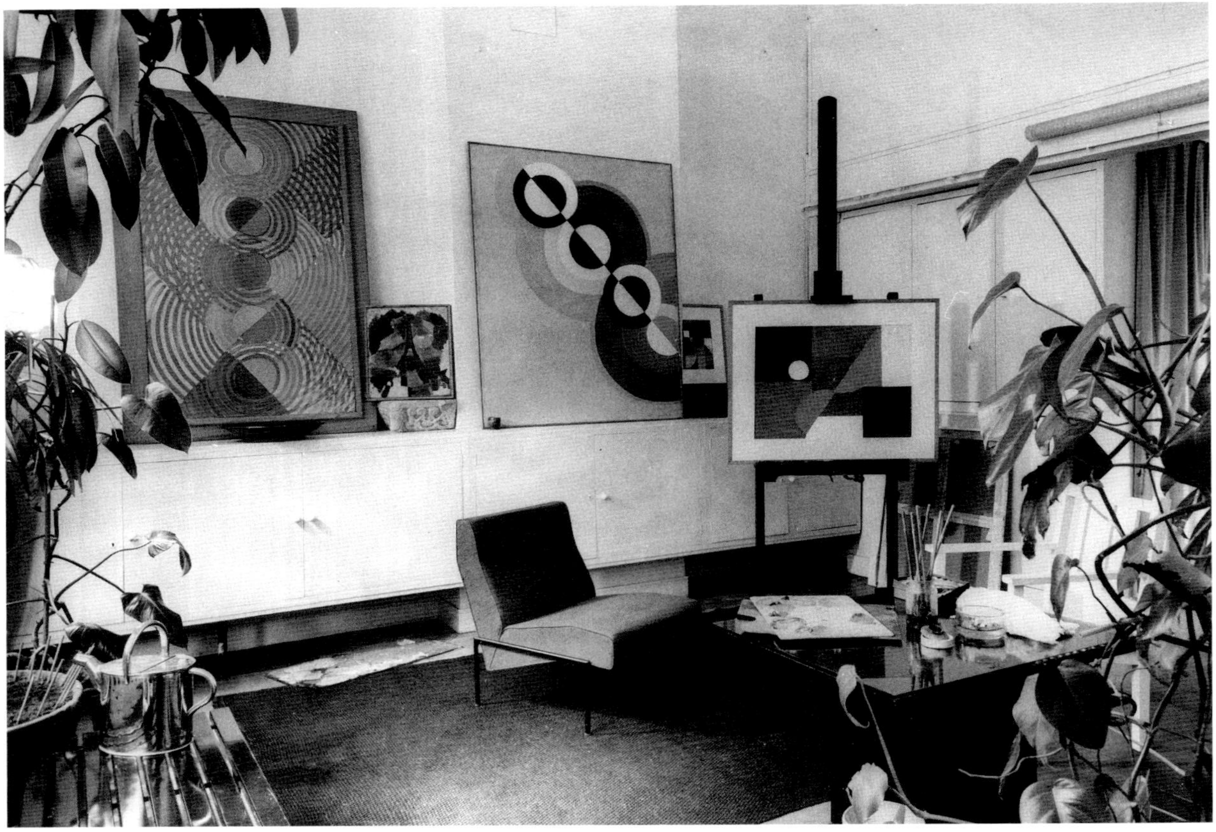

The studio in the rue Saint-Simon apartment, with paintings by both Robert and Sonia on the walls.

In an unusually dissatisfied frame of mind, she told Arp that the world had not been fair to her, because she refused to publicize herself, to push herself forward by dishonest means. She felt that she had been relegated and was not even spoken of as a painter.

But by the 1950s she had learned to put such depressed thoughts aside, and realized that she was beginning to find recognition in her own right. At first she had been labelled the Egeria of Orphism, a decorator, Robert's companion. Then they had conceded step by step – 'collaborator, continuator' and so on – before admitting that her art existed in and by itself.

It was in the Fifties that she produced so many of the gouache paintings on paper that she called *Rhythme coloré*. These brilliant abstracts, illustrating their title exactly, showed a renewed assurance in her work, a joyous explosion of shapes and colours that belied any depression she may have expressed in conversation or writing.

Sonia's pencil sketch for a possible painting, around 1955.

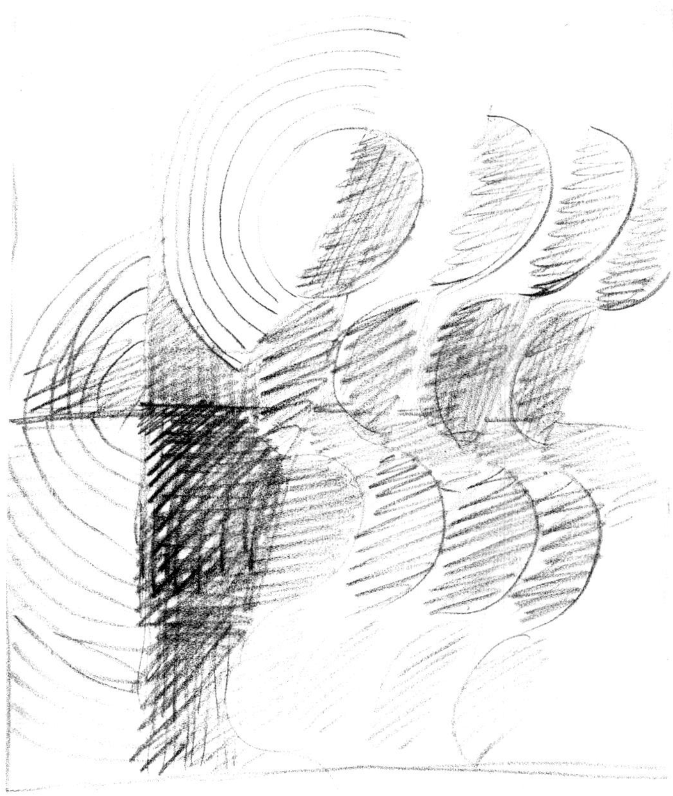

She began to exhibit, particularly in the gallery in Auteuil of Colette Allendy, who had become a close friend of hers but who died in 1960. In 1953, the Galerie Bing mounted a one-man show, which brought her increased attention; in 1955, the Rose Fried Gallery in New York gave her her first one-man show in the United States; in 1958, the Städtisches Kunsthaus in Bielefeld organized a large exhibition of her works, comprising some 260 pieces; and from then on she participated widely in international exhibitions devoted to the work of the Moderns.

In 1950 she made two trips to Italy, one in June, one in October. There does not seem to have been any specific purpose behind these journeys, but she certainly made good use of them to experience again the natural and artistic wonders she had first seen as a young girl. In mid-June the places visited on the way to Florence were Bologna, Parma, Padua. Though there were beautiful things to ravish her eyes, she wrote that only in France (and particularly in

A study for a mosaic design, 1955.

Below, a *Rhythme couleur* of 1959.

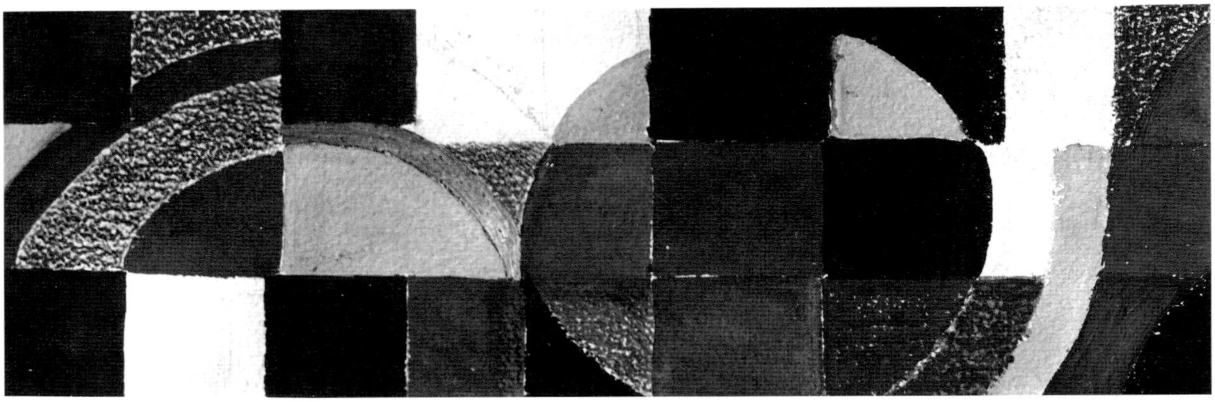

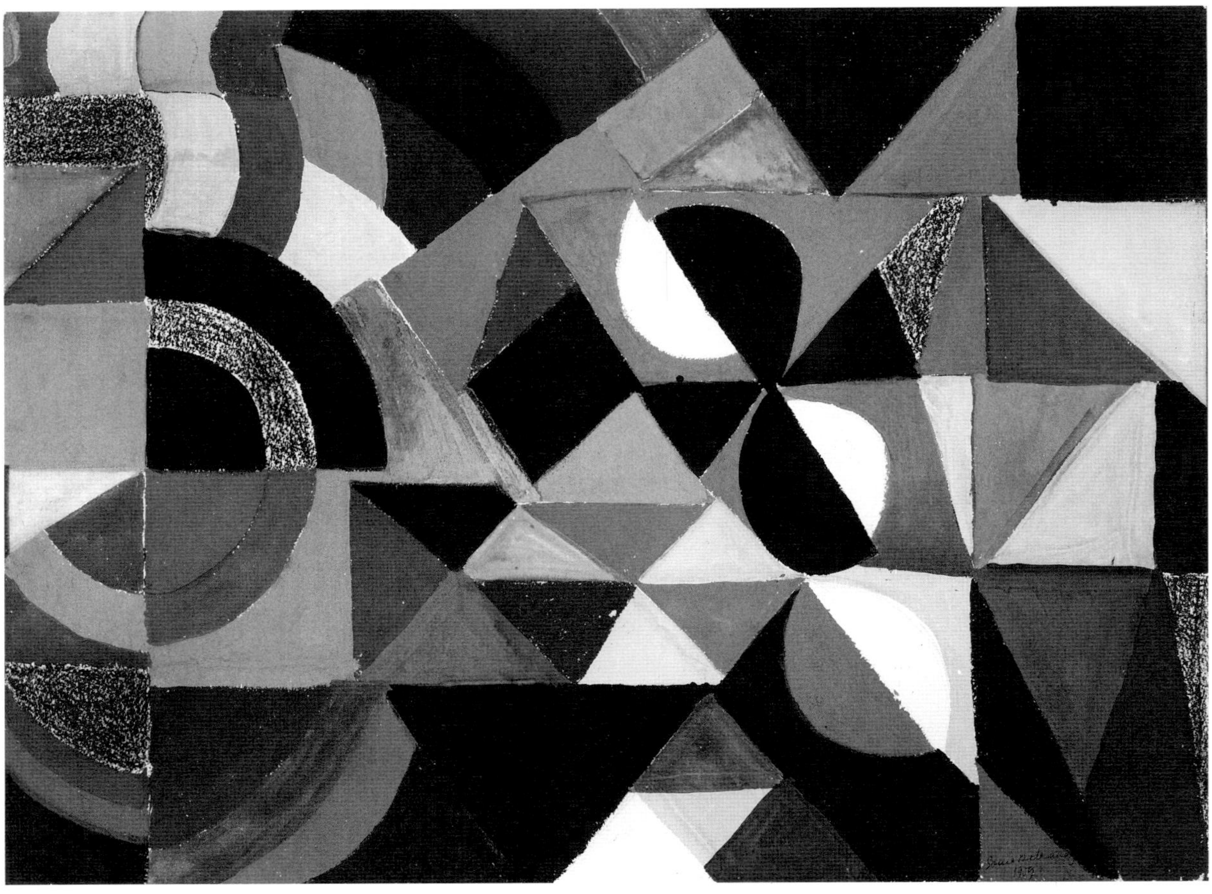

the Ile-de-France) did she feel well. And in Florence she was far less impressed than she had been as a girl of fourteen, arriving for the first time from ugly countries like Germany and Switzerland, 'where the light is heavy and lacking in spirit.' But she realized that in the meantime she had been spoiled by France itself, Spain and Portugal.

During the second trip, she found the terrain more attractive after the train passed through Lucerne, and she was reminded again of the trips with her family when she was a child, reminded of familiar names like Brunnen. They had lived somewhere near there and taken excursions. And visiting the Medici tomb by Michelangelo in the church of San Lorenzo in Florence brought back those earlier visits, which had been 'wrapped in a poetry and mystery which I no longer felt now.' In her imagination there had been a more beautiful light. But in the Accademia she was struck by the Michelangelo statues, especially the unfinished ones; it was clear to her that Rodin's work sprang from them.

What she emphasizes in her particular admiration for the Florentine primitive painters is the rhythm in their pictures. As time went on, this rhythm was unfortunately replaced by what she terms 'description'. She felt that there were things she could learn from those early Florentine and Sienese painters – as well as the Byzantines: 'I believe that what interests me is the rhythm, the construction, a wonderful bareness, a grandeur of vision, also the transition from the Byzantine to the Renaissance period.'

At the beginning of the Sixties, she was again given to bouts of mild depression, even though she participated in shows in London, at the Galerie Denise René in Paris, in Cologne, Ottawa and New York. Much as she claimed to prefer being alone, it is obvious that she was lonely. Even earlier, she had written about visiting Colette Allendy one evening to meet a friend of Gleizes's and then going on to the Magnellis: 'All these people seem to form a united milieu and I don't feel that I belong to them at all. They were always together apart from us, and still are.' Cendrars died in 1961, Tzara in 1963 and Arp in 1966. 'Eventually there's no one you dare talk to, everything becomes gossip instead of a discussion to help one see more clearly. So one ends up being gray and impersonal.'

She also claimed that she had never confided to anyone what she told herself; her journal was the companion of her interior life. And in all her work – fashion, stage, decoration – she had had to make her way alone. 'In my life,

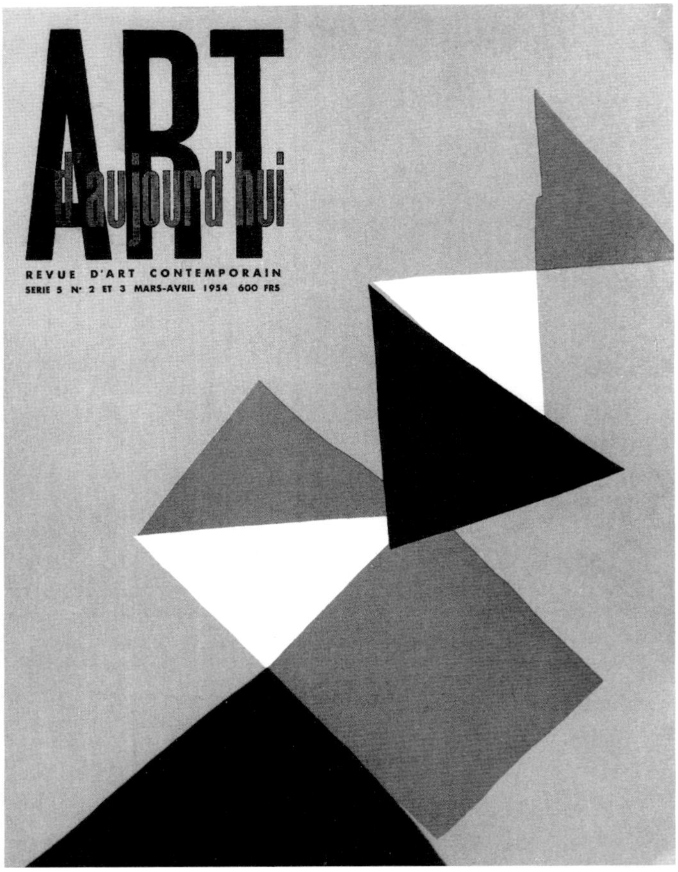

Sonia's design for a cover of the journal *Art d'aujourd'hui*, 1954.

I've hardened myself in order to keep myself intact, to guard myself against being ruled by superficial people, snobs, intriguers.'

In mid-January 1960 she was 'disgusted' with everything but painting; and the cold weather prevented her from going out of doors to refresh her ideas. But little by little she 'gained the upper hand' and recovered her balance and her good humour. When she visited the exhibition of the Salon de Mai, she ran into the painter Pierre Soulages and said to him that there were lots of her enemies in the hall. He replied, 'I know that you have enemies, but you also have great friends.' She was very touched by his words.

CHAPTER 16

WORK AND LONELINESS

IN 1964 she met Jacques Damase, at that time a writer, a poet, an enthusiastic art-lover and editor of the monthly *Maison et Jardin*. Damase jokingly blames their meeting on Chagall, because it took place at the inauguration of the ceiling Chagall painted for the Opéra.

There is never any way to explain why two people should have a natural affinity to each other, but that was certainly the case of Damase and Sonia Delaunay. In her journal she writes that 'in the late phase of my life when I began to be known as a painter, Jacques Damase was in the front rank.' In promoting her recognition, he played the same role she had played in promoting Robert's.

Working together on exhibitions, catalogues, albums, printmaking, they discovered that, by extraordinary chance, they resembled each other in their deepest sensibilities. Never before, she says, had she had 'the weakness to let anyone suspect my true interior life. Even for Delaunay, Apollinaire, Cendrars, I was a force of nature, invulnerable, a bit unreal, the one who smiled at fate, who never complained and who was happy by nature: I would smile, Robert would grumble.'

Damase appeared at a time in her life when she was most troubled by the daily activities and annoyances that she had been able to take completely in her stride twenty, even ten, years before. She was, after all, almost eighty when they met, and though her health continued to be good, even robust for a woman of her age, she had far less energy than before and felt constantly harassed by the behaviour of dealers (particularly *her* dealers), inquiries from museums, domestic squabbles, dishonest cleaning women, conflict with her daughter-in-law, worries over her grandchildren, and the gnawing frustration of feeling under-valued as a painter. In January 1964, for instance, she was speaking to a friend about a curator who had promised to give her a show: 'I told him that if Sophie Taeuber was given an exhibition in a museum – and not I – that was doing me a bad turn – because Sophie meant nothing to France, she was an instructor in decorative art in Zürich. Her pictorial work is very meagre and it was improved by Arp.' She declared herself to be 'very provoked by this situation – having for more than fifty years exercised an influence, worked, leaving an important body of work – to find myself like that because I don't use the methods of a pedlar – it disheartens me.'

She was often annoyed by Denise René, whose gallery seemed to pay much more attention to Vasarely than to her. 'The dealers', she wrote, 'are disgusting and their last concern is the quality of what they are selling.' In the first few months of 1965, she was having the greatest difficulty retrieving some paintings that were still being held by the dealer Bing, who had in fact been in the forefront of those who had supported first Robert and then her. Her dispute with him was complicated by the fact that he had an American collaborator, Leonard Hutton, whom Sonia would have liked to dismiss as her agent. Unable to obtain satisfaction from either Bing or Hutton, she had recourse to a lawyer by the name of Matrasso, but Bing died on the 3rd of June, and presumably that problem at least was solved.

She was in general suspicious of all her dealers, even those, such as Paul and Suzy Feigel in Basel, who seemed to be entirely devoted to showing and selling her pictures. The two galleries with which she felt most comfortable were those of the Gimpels in London and Erica Brausen's in Zürich.

The one satisfying event of 1964 was her donation of 117 works by herself and Robert to the Louvre, which were exhibited in the Galerie Mollien of the Museum. In the catalogue he prepared for the event, Jean Cassou wrote, 'The generous donation of Mme Sonia Delaunay constitutes an inestimable enrichment for the Musée Nationale d'Art Moderne and confirms in a striking way the place Robert Delaunay occupies and at the same time, indivisibly, that of the couple Robert and Sonia Delaunay in the panorama of the spiritual creativity of our times.'

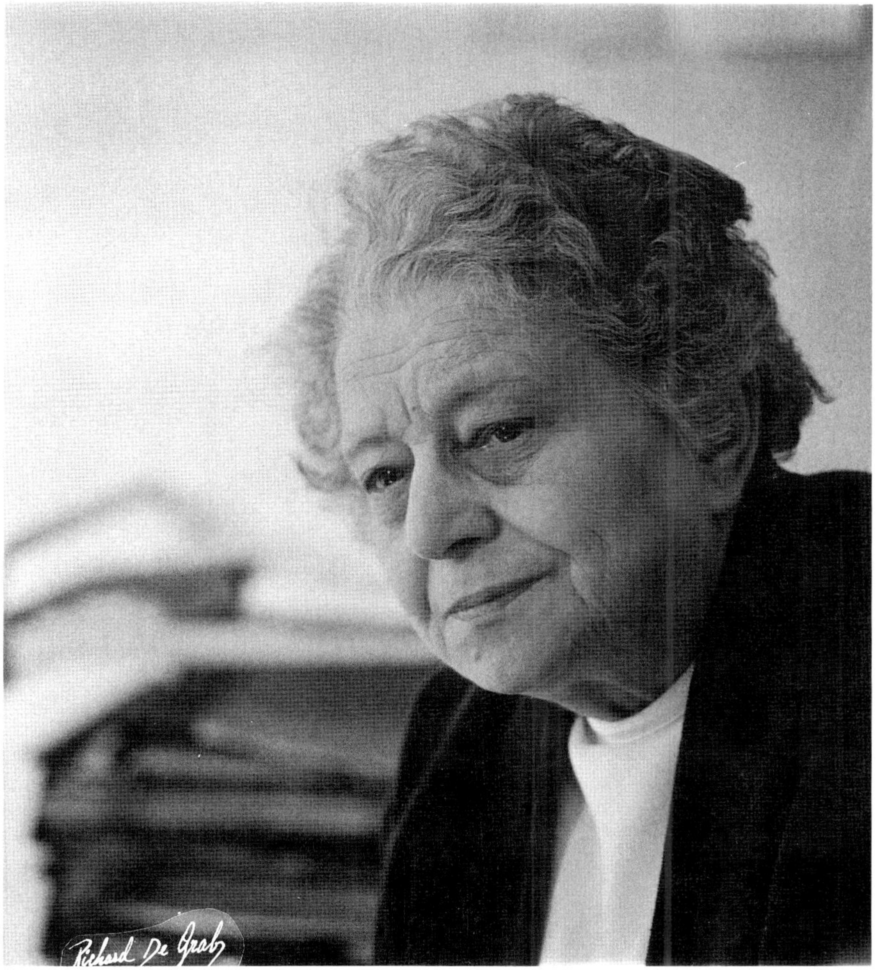

Sonia in her seventies.

On 3 January 1965, though it was a beautiful sunny day, she felt all at once lonely. She wanted to say 'Bonjour Minouche' to her last cat, but the cat had died and left a void. She missed seeing the two boys, Eric and Jean-Louis, and was angry at her daughter-in-law for keeping them from her. ('Minouche had more nobility of soul than she . . .') As usual in such circumstances, she told herself it was time to start painting again.

Her circle of friends was severely reduced as compared to the Thirties. Though she was frequently telephoning the Magnellis she saw little of them. They were, she wrote, 'the rich poor, whereas I am the poor rich.' She made a rare visit to them on 7 June 1965; Magnelli told her that she and Braque were the only living painters to have been shown at the Louvre. Among her new friends were a young Panamanian couple by the name of Altamiranda, whose attentions and solicitude flattered her. For a time she was visited now and then by an American painter, Buffy Johnson, who also sent her letters and postcards when away from Paris.

She was also in close touch with Tim and Eleonore Osborne, though she found Tim, who was a painter, extremely prickly, given to black moods and hard to fathom. In February 1965 Tim brought a brother-in-law, Sidney Cohen, to see Robert's paintings. Cohen reacted with enthusiasm to the paintings she showed him, but he was also taken by the still-lifes she had done in Portugal, and asked her to quote prices. For Robert's *Femme nue lisant* she set the price at 40,000,000 (old-style) francs, for *La Ville* of 1920 she was asking 50,000,000. For her still-life the price was 5,000,000 francs and for what she called her 'Woman in the market' 10,000,000. When Osborne phoned the next day to say that his brother-in-law found the prices high, she told him that she was in no hurry to sell the pictures.

The question of prices rose again in March, when she was visited by a collector from Switzerland, Josefowitz, who had first called in January asking to see works by both Robert and her. He seemed most interested in the Fauve period works, and even phoned that evening for prices – though he did not follow it up. This time he came with his wife and chose *La Ville*; but he, like Mr Cohen, found the price above what he wanted to spend.

On the other hand, when an American couple called Bronstein came to see her work and bought a pochoir she had done for a catalogue of Bing's, they paid $200 without demur. She, however, decided on consideration that she had overcharged them and wanted to return $100. They were agreeably sur-

A happy meeting with Arp around 1960.

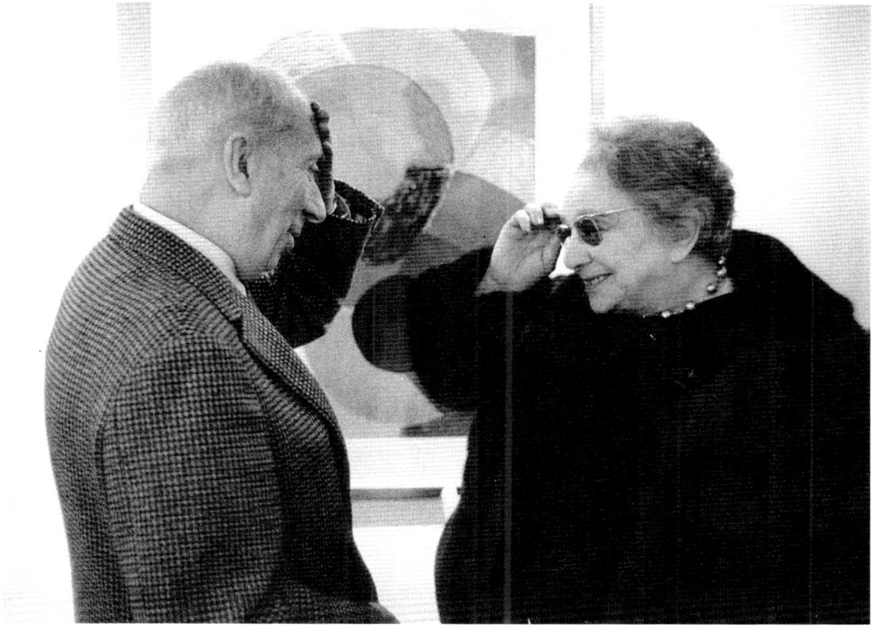

prised when she telephoned their hotel to tell them this, and in the end what she did was to send a small gouache to them in San Francisco.

In March 1965, she participated in a show devoted to women painters, *Salon des femmes peintres*, sending a gouache and an oil. She went to look at the installation on 12 March, and was pleased to find her pictures well-placed just across from the staircase. As for the Salon itself, she decided it was no worse than any Salon, perhaps even better because it was less pretentious. A reporter from the newspaper *Combat* asked for her opinion on women painters; her answer was, 'I don't see any difference. There are good ones and bad ones, the same as men.'

She was always interested to see what her contemporary artists were doing, and found the time to visit all the exhibitions that promised to have any interest at all for her. Her comments in the journals show that she could be generous as well as scathing in her judgments. In the case of Calder, she was always generous. At a show in November 1946 she found many attractive things, especially some of the mobiles. She detected the influence of Arp and Miró. And in July 1965, she wrote that what she liked about Calder was 'the generosity of his art. He gives himself without stint.'

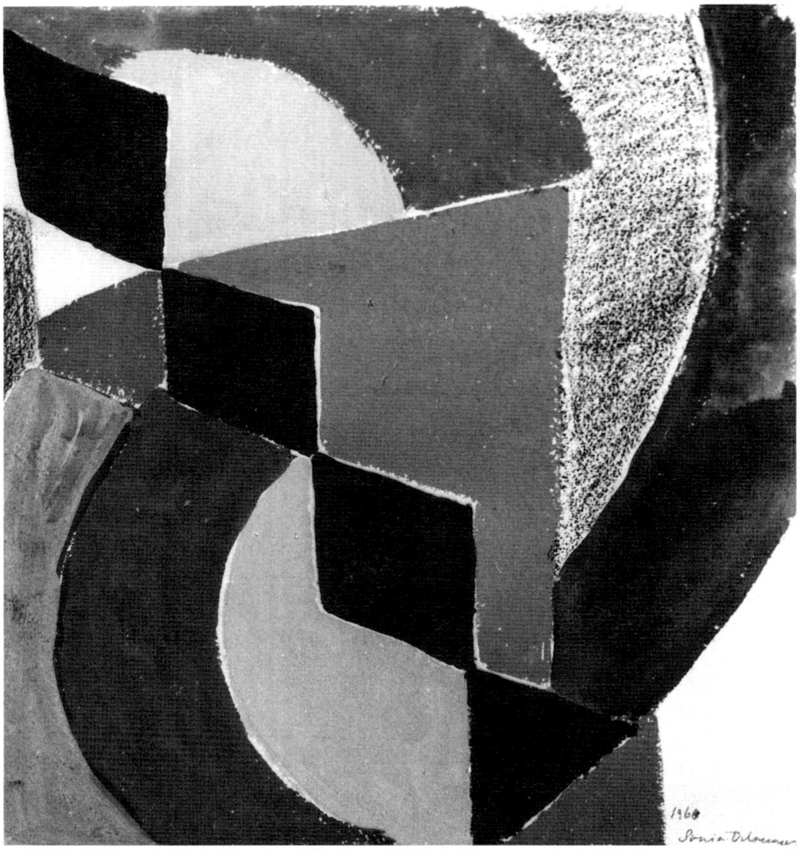

Various paintings and projects of the 1960s.

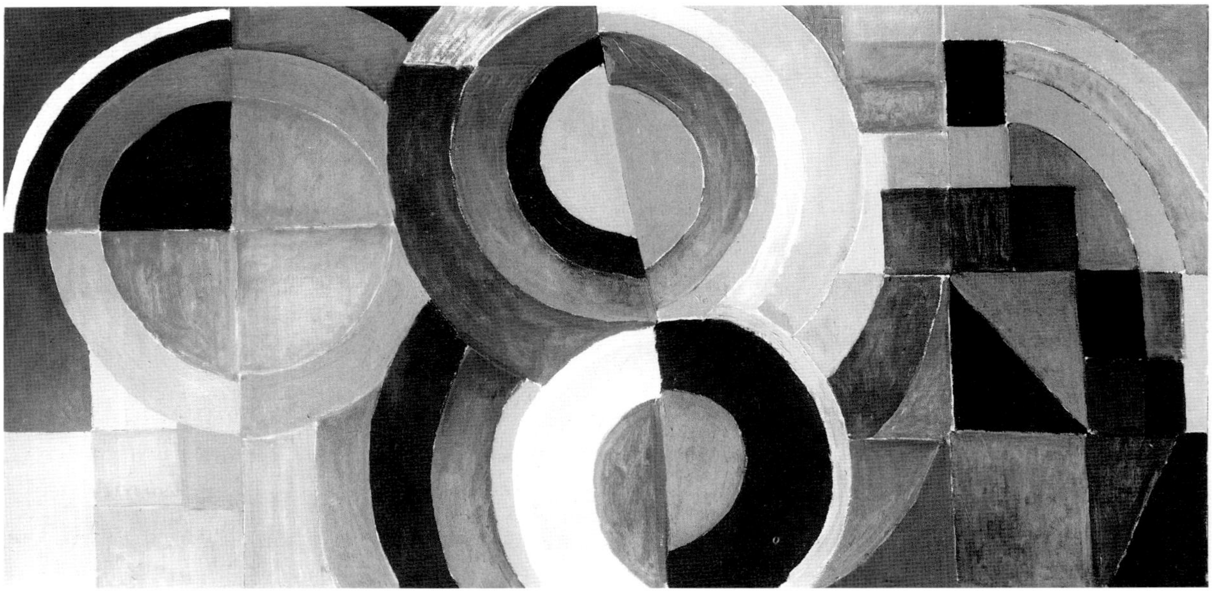

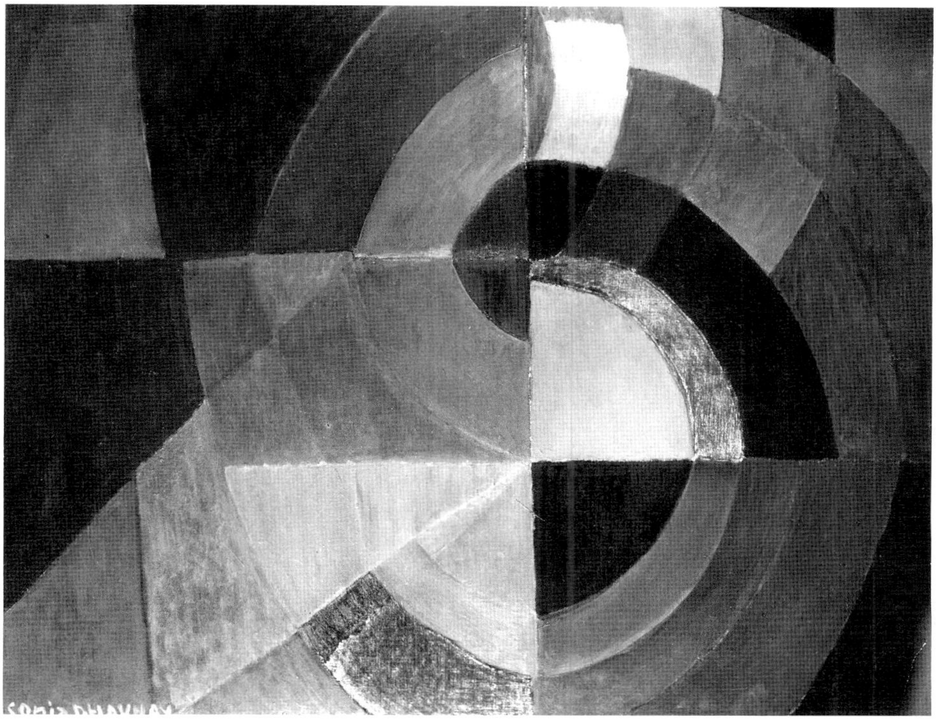

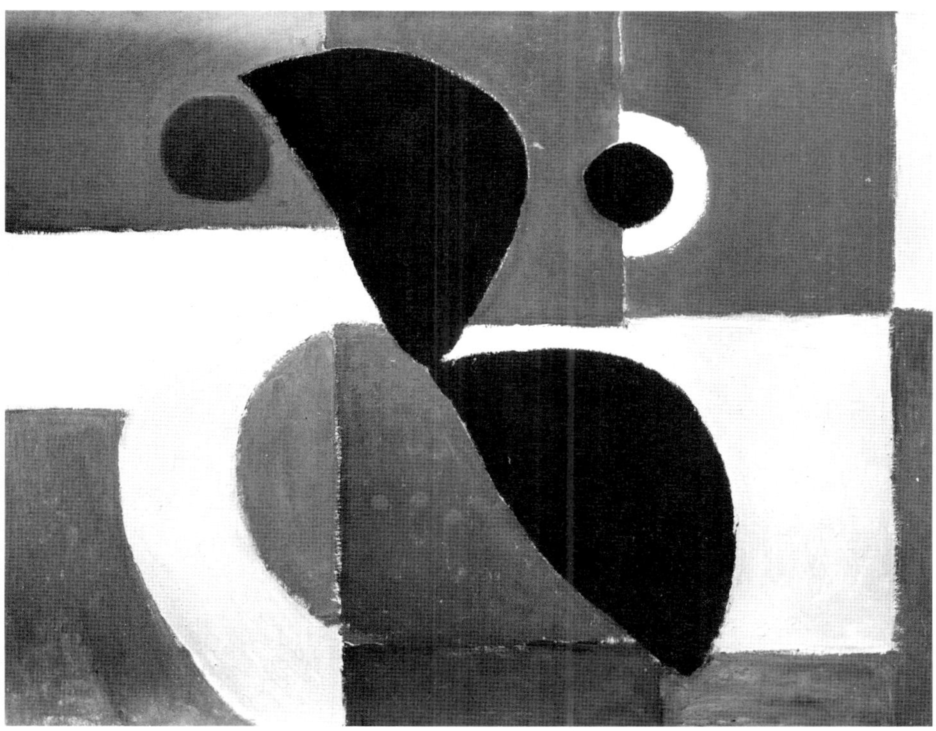

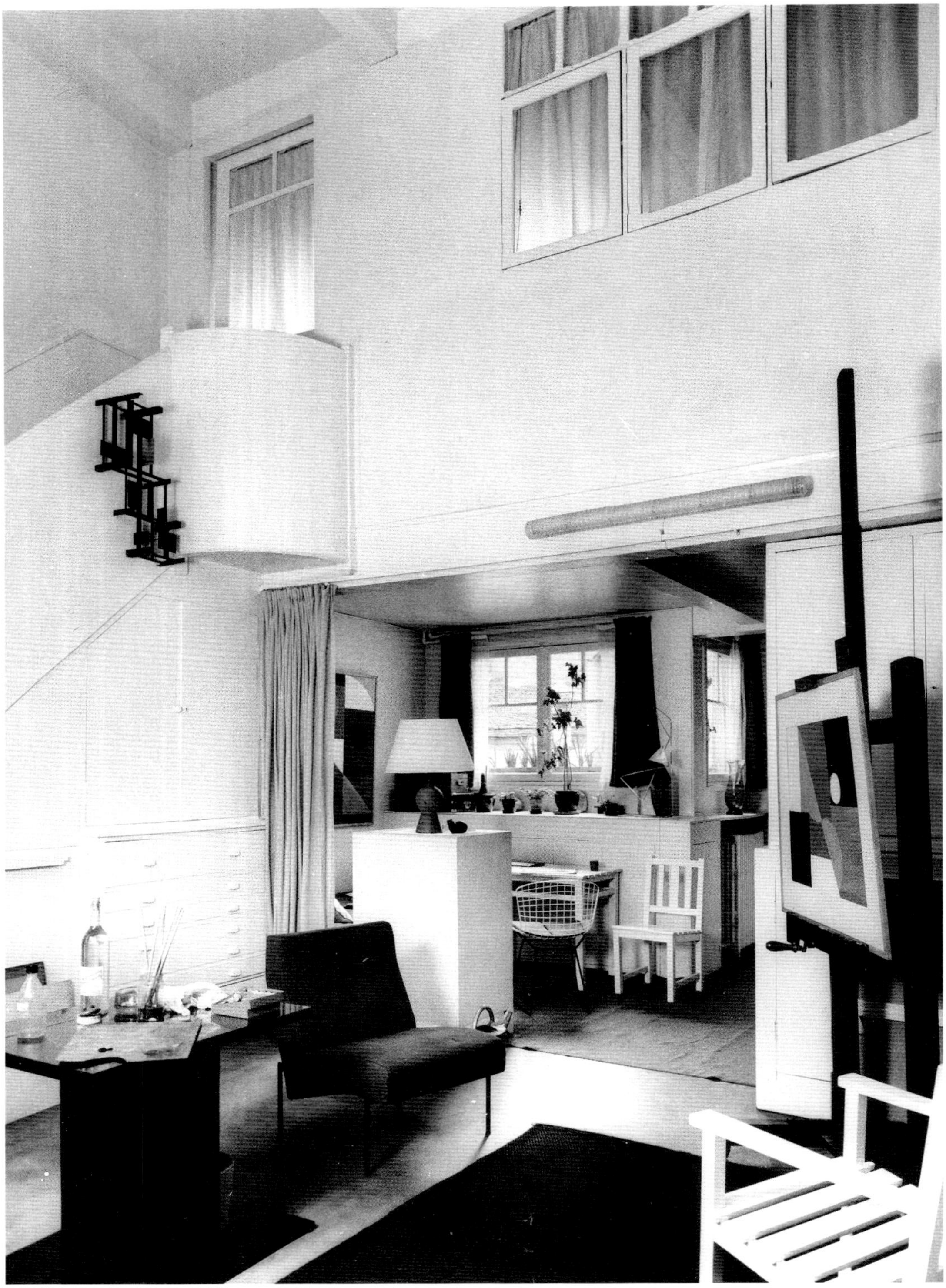

Left, a view of Sonia's studio in the 1960s.

She was less impressed by Michaux and André Masson. Of Michaux's work she said, 'It is authentic and attractive, even though it isn't painting; it's much more a kind of writing, but it's something.' As for Masson, who was sharing an exhibition with Michaux, he was 'nothing, it's empty, he changes all the time, probably a clever fellow . . .' By the same token, she came away from an exhibition of Nicolas de Staël's work in 1965 with the impression that it was 'nothing, and badly painted.' But the dealer Dubourg, who owned a stock of de Staël paintings, managed it all very well.

In April 1965, she had a sudden spurt of painting. On the 19th, after lunch, 'I started a large gouache and painted all afternoon until 7.00 – but not happy with the result – lacks cohesion, any overall conception – but I want to

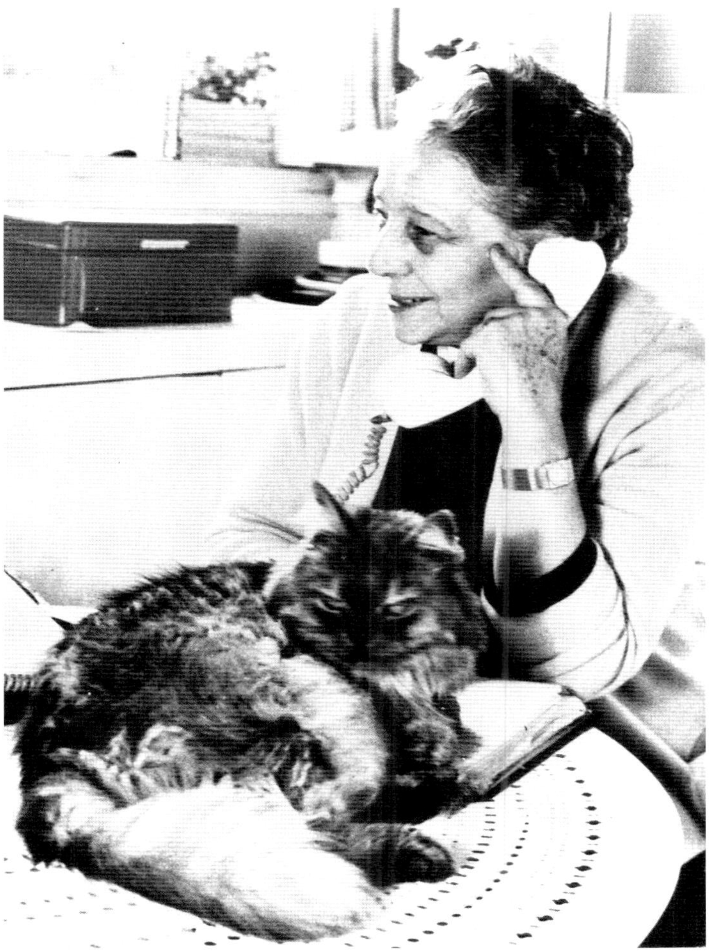

The cat and the telephone: two of Sonia's great attachments.

go right to the end in order to re-enter painting again.' Two days later she worked in the afternoon on a new large gouache: 'finally I'm beginning to find myself again but the weather is depressing and works against the *joie de vivre* I need.' This burst of creative activity was short-lived. Not until the 7th of July did she do anything more, and on that evening she worked on a small gouache, which went well and would serve for a large gouache. She felt that the main thing was to find the equilibrium of work, but for the time being that seemed to elude her.

All the same, she was never short of ideas. In July 1965, she suddenly wondered whether she ought to give Robert's collection of poems by his friends to the Bibliothèque Doucet, another foundation of the man who had bought the Rousseau *Snake Charmer* back in 1922. After meeting with a representative of the library, she got the notion to do a book on that period using the documents in her possession – and she felt that only Malraux could write a suitable introduction. This made her look back on those days of hopes and innovations and joyful creativity: 'We were just a handful of people who lived a dream, Robert with his towers and cities, me with my dresses and the transformation of everything around us, Cendrars with the *Transsibérien* and afterwards *Panama*. And this dream . . . was the basis of a new era which has influenced everything.'

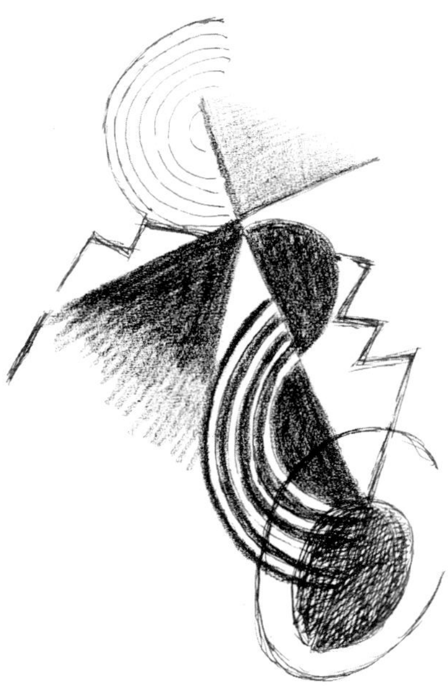

Rhythme, a drawing in pencil and ink, 1969.

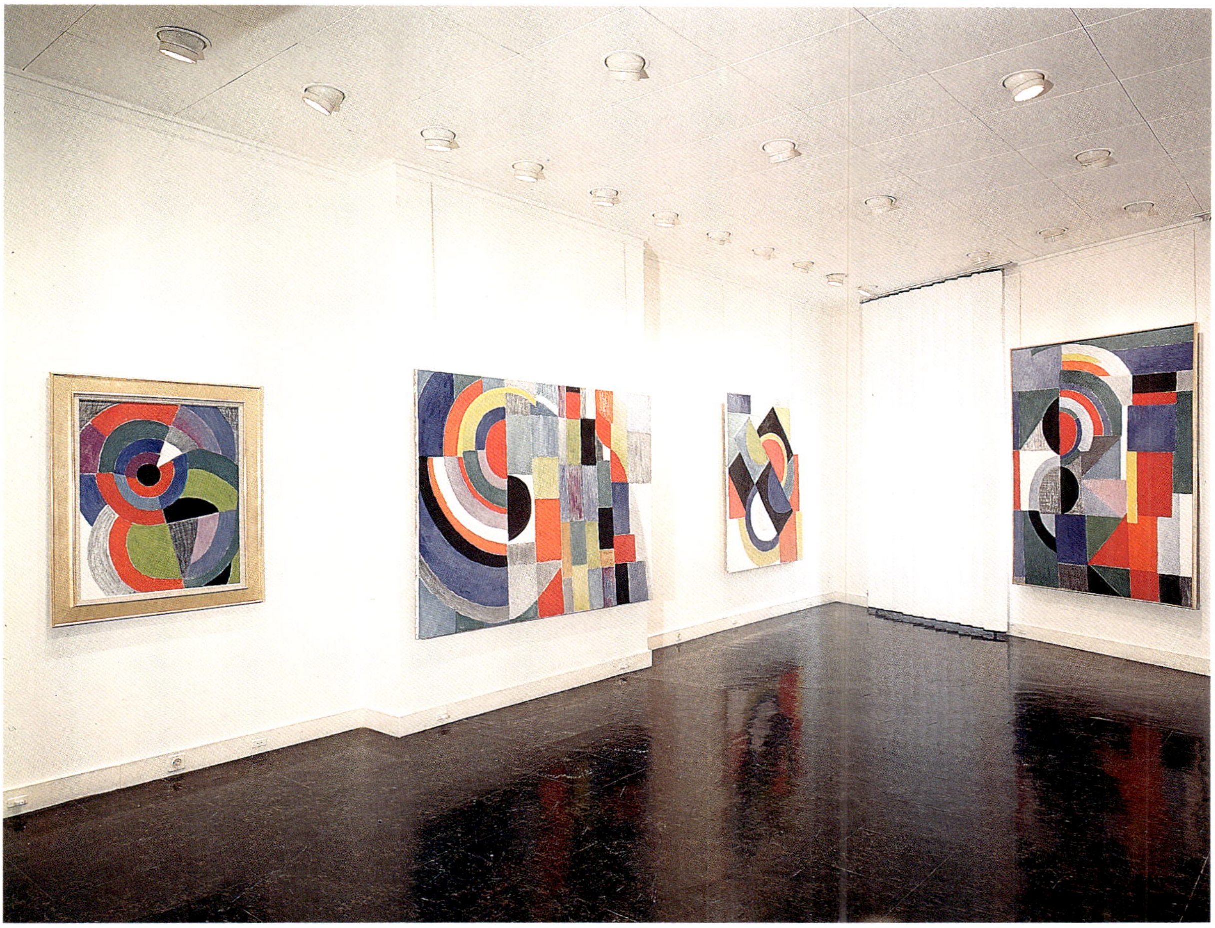

92 An exhibition room at the Musée d'Art Moderne de la Ville de Paris where paintings by Sonia were shown in 1971.

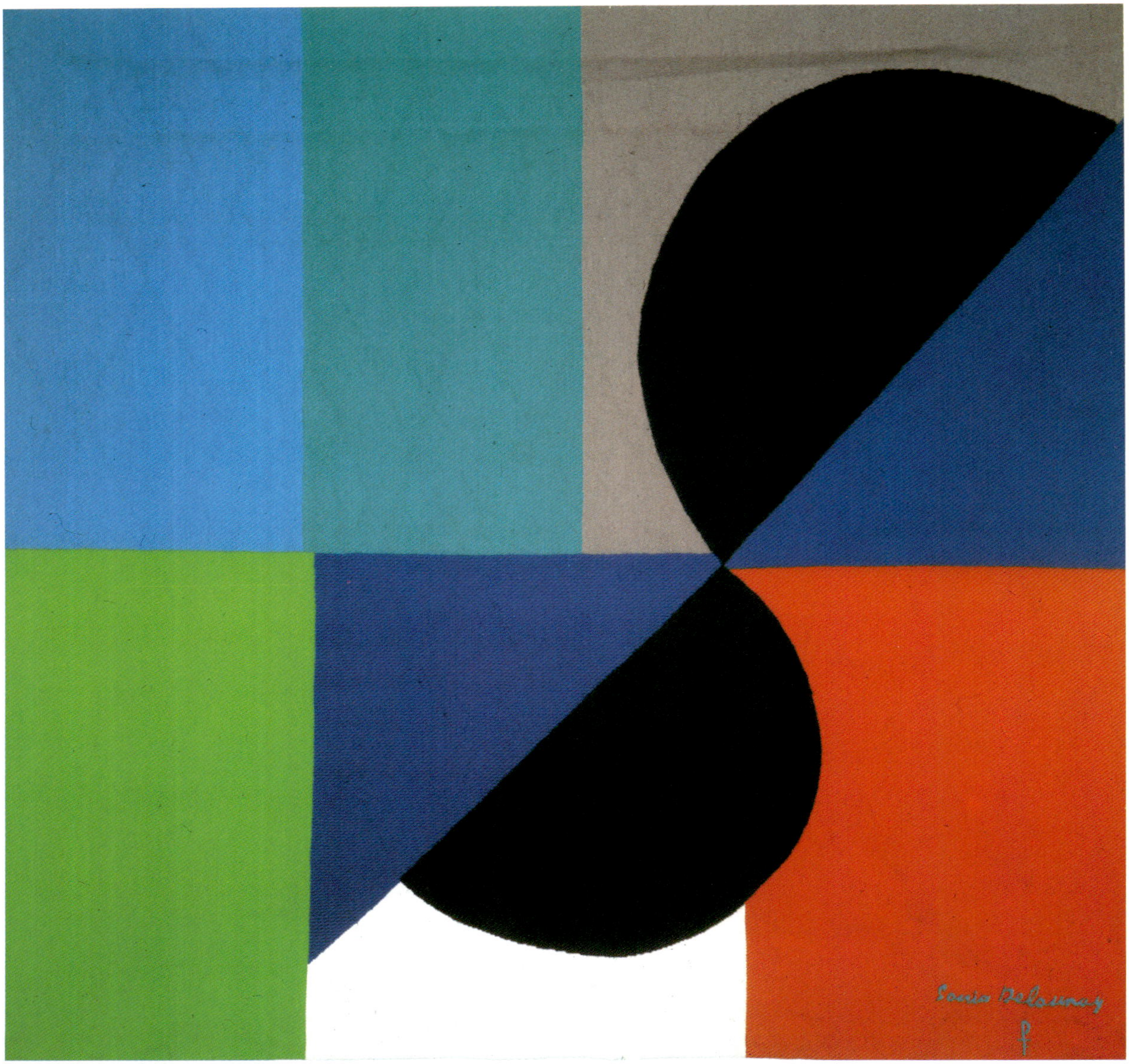

93 *Nocturne matinal*, gouache, 1969.

94 Opposite, *Green squares*, gouache, 1970.

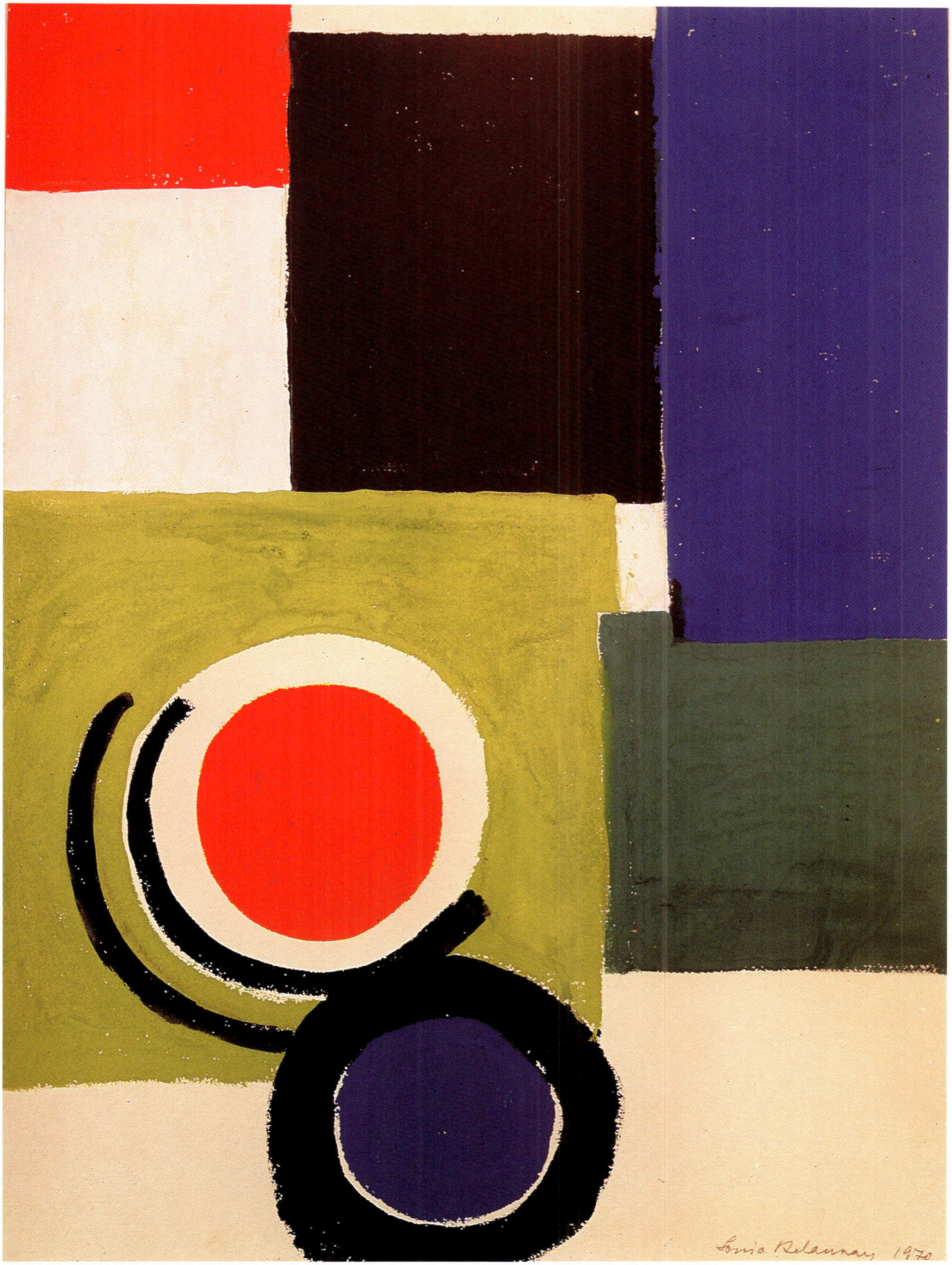
Sonia Delaunay 1970

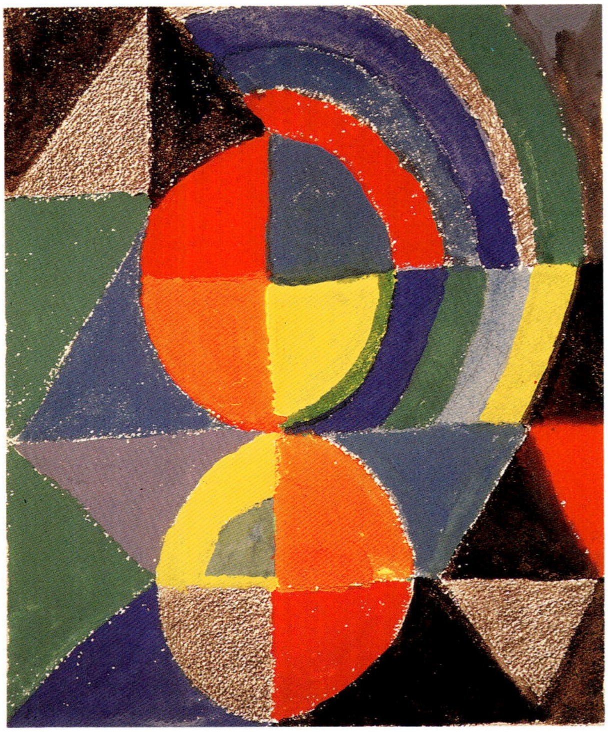

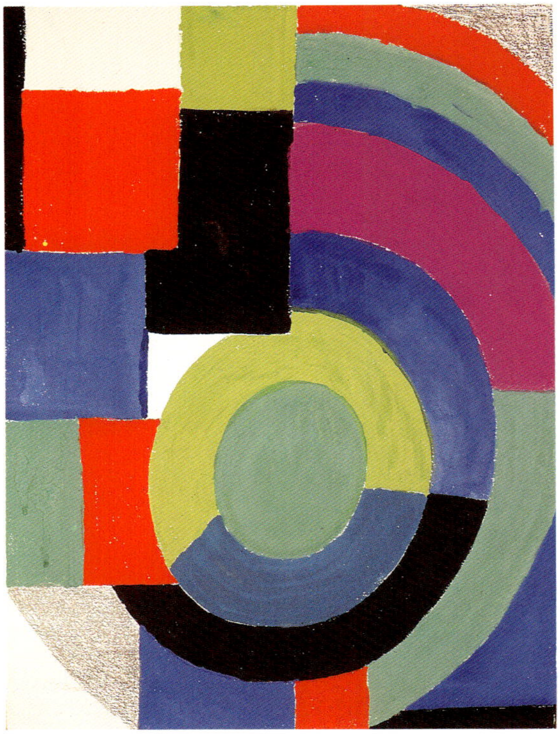

95 *Icone*, gouache, 1965.

96 Gouache of 1970.

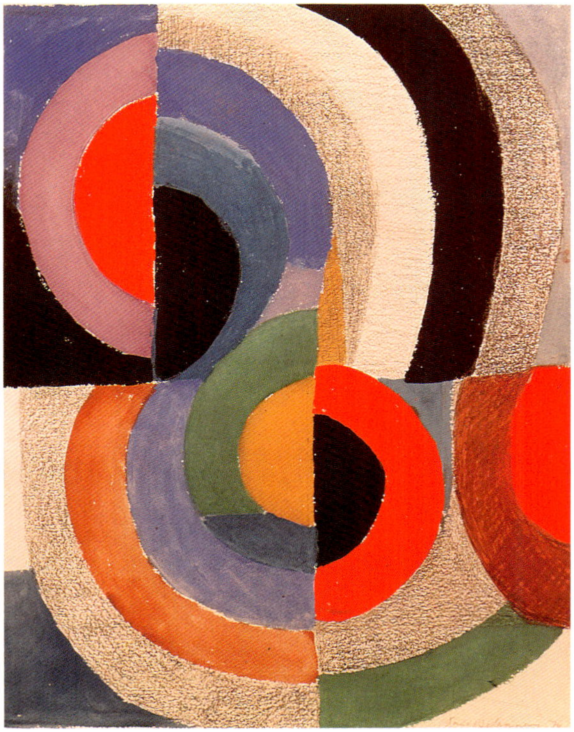

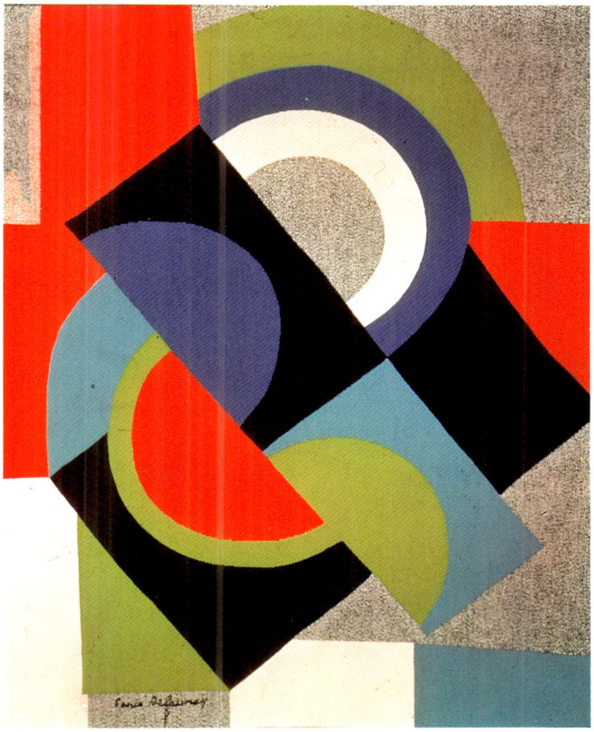

97 *Drakar*, tapestry, 1968.

98 *Contrepoint*, Aubusson tapestry, *c.* 1970.

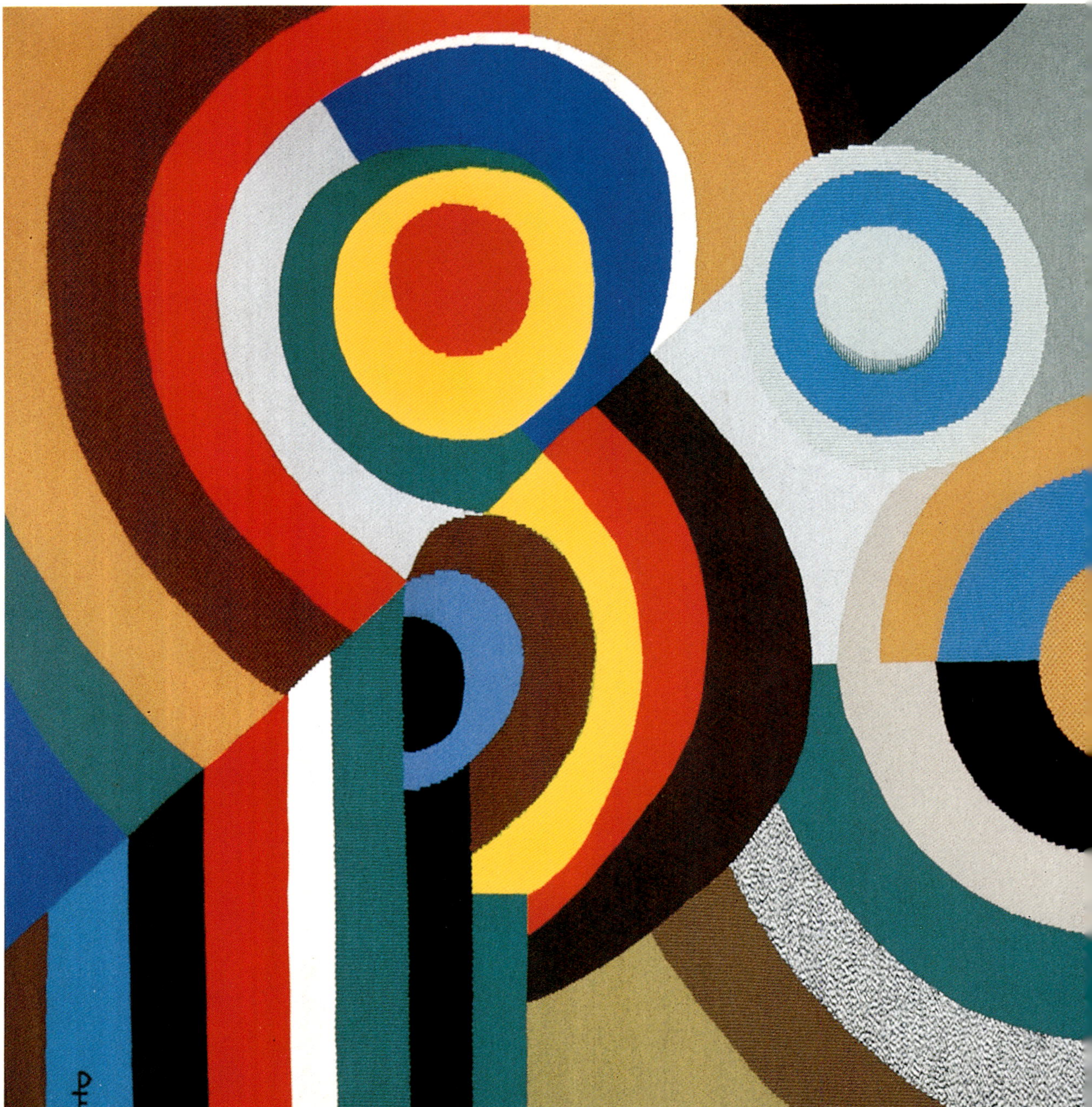

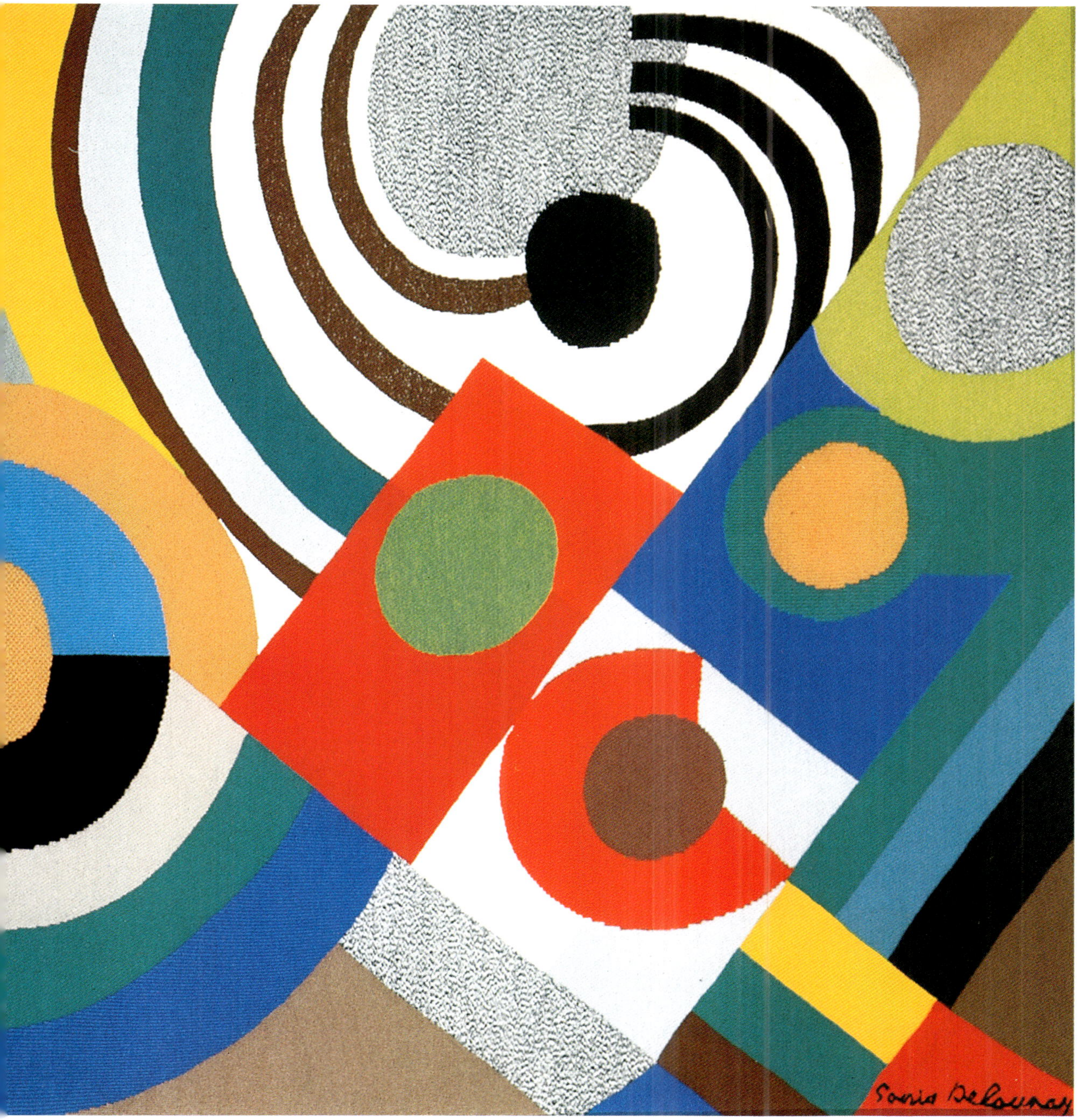

99 Monumental Aubusson tapestry II, 1971.

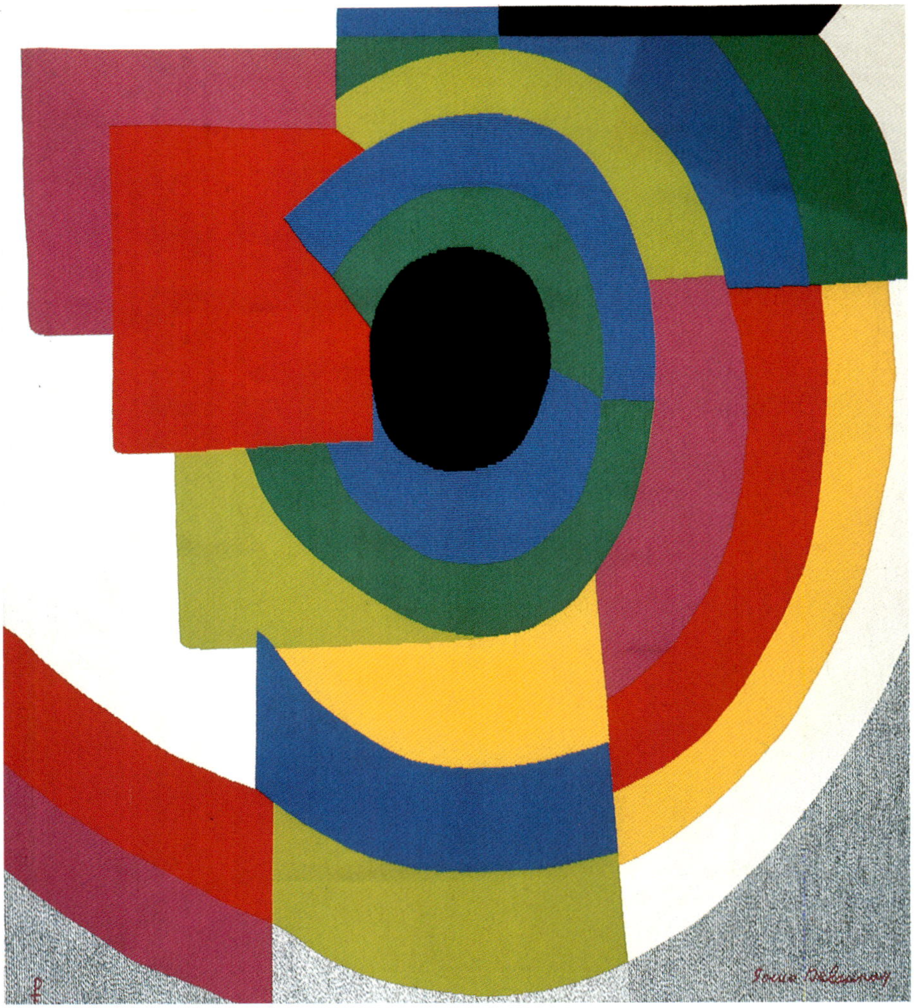

100 *Syncopé*, tapestry, 1970.

101 Opposite, *Jeux d'enfants* (Children's games), Aubusson tapestry, 1969.

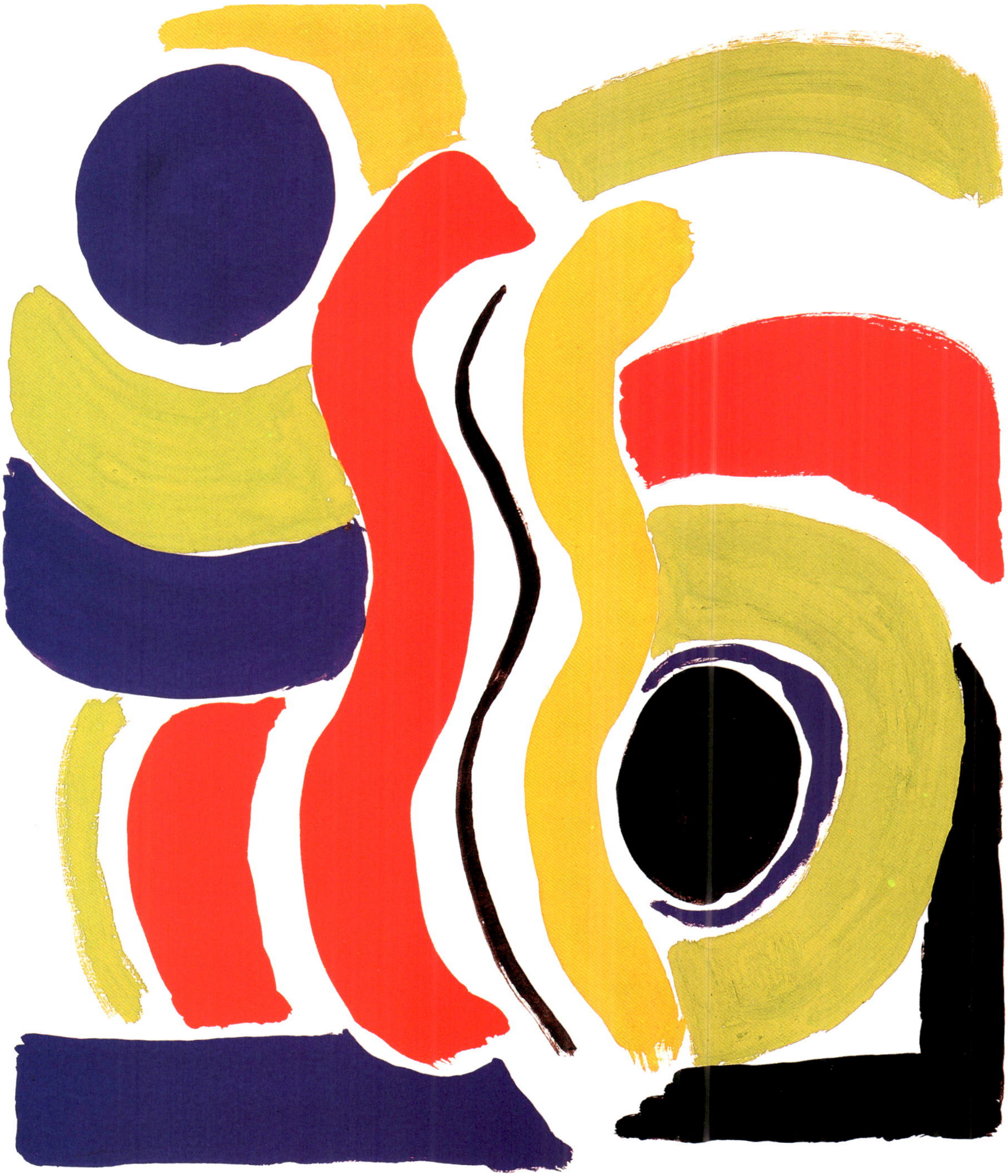

102 Below, *Plougastel* (town in Brittany), lithograph, 1973.

103 Right, gouache of 1970.

104 Below right, *Bow*, gouache, 1971.

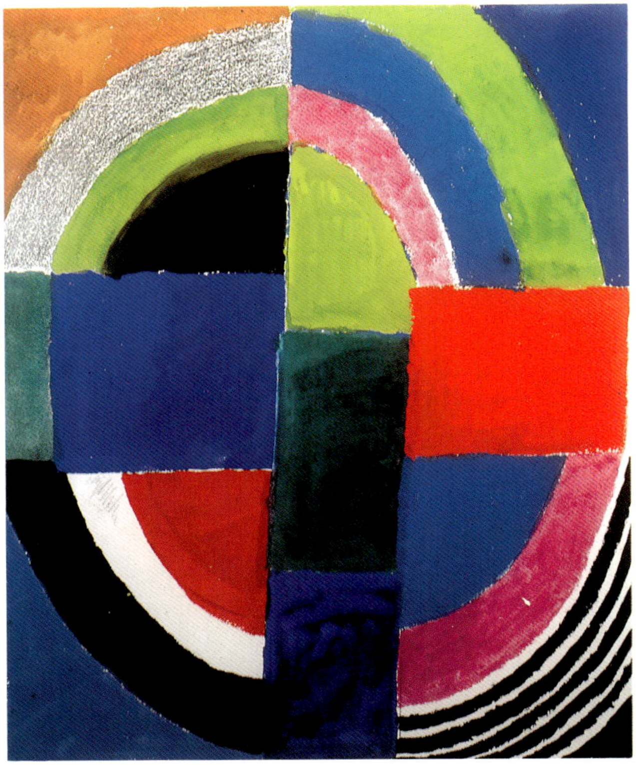

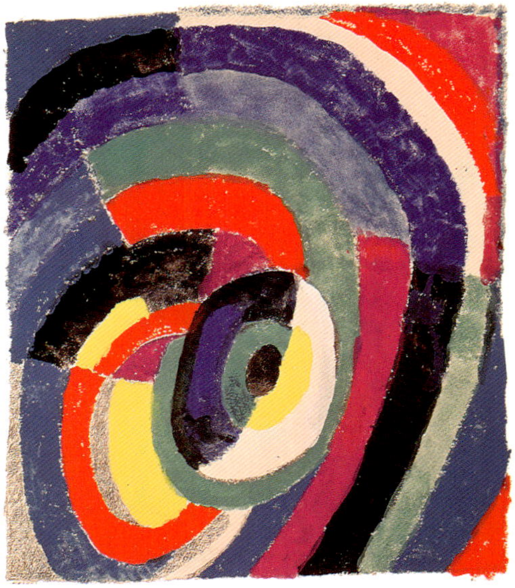

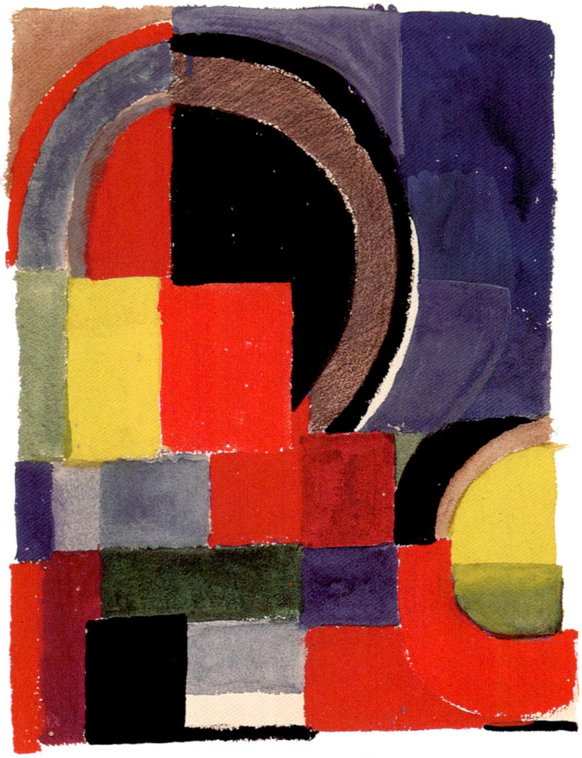

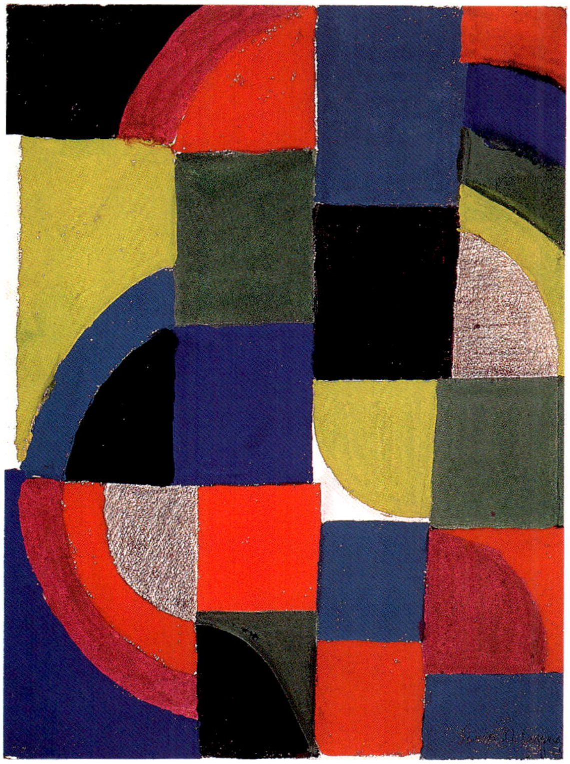

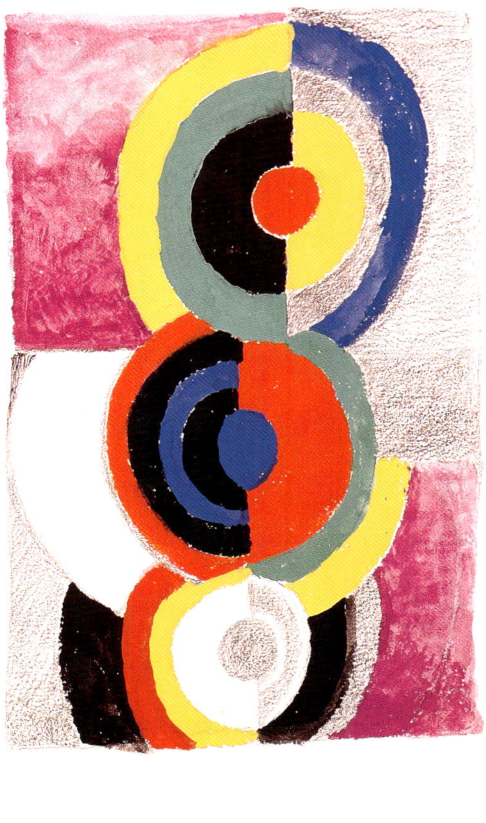

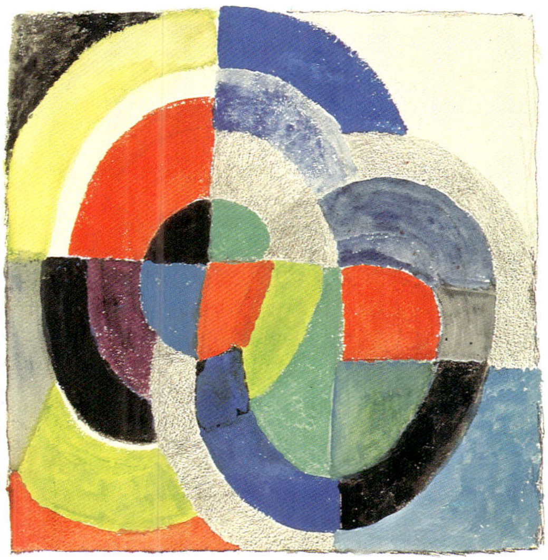

105 Above left, *Rhythme-couleur*, gouache, 1970.

106 Left, *Rhythme sans fin* (Rhythm without end), gouache, 1971.

107 Above, *Russian Easter*, gouache, 1971.

108 Below, Gouache, 1978.

109 Bottom, *Rhythme-couleur*, project for book jacket for Jacques Damase, 1972.

110 Opposite, *Deux têtes*, gouache, 1972.

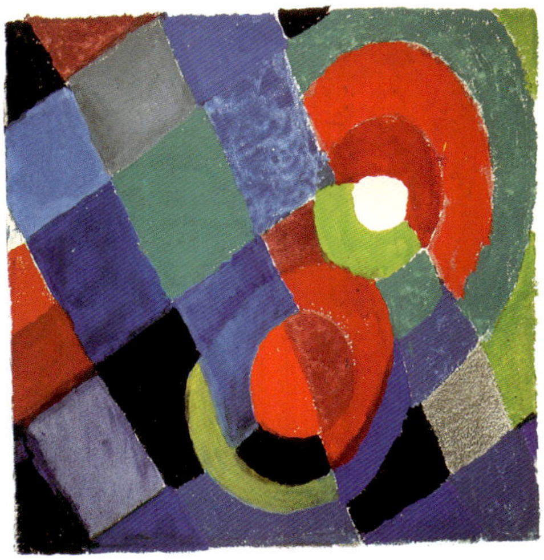

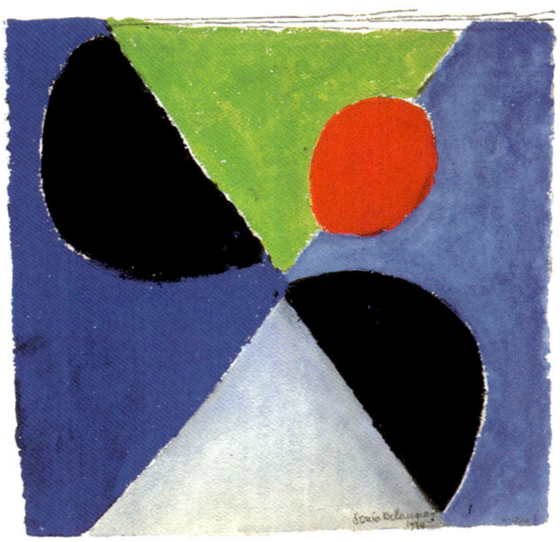

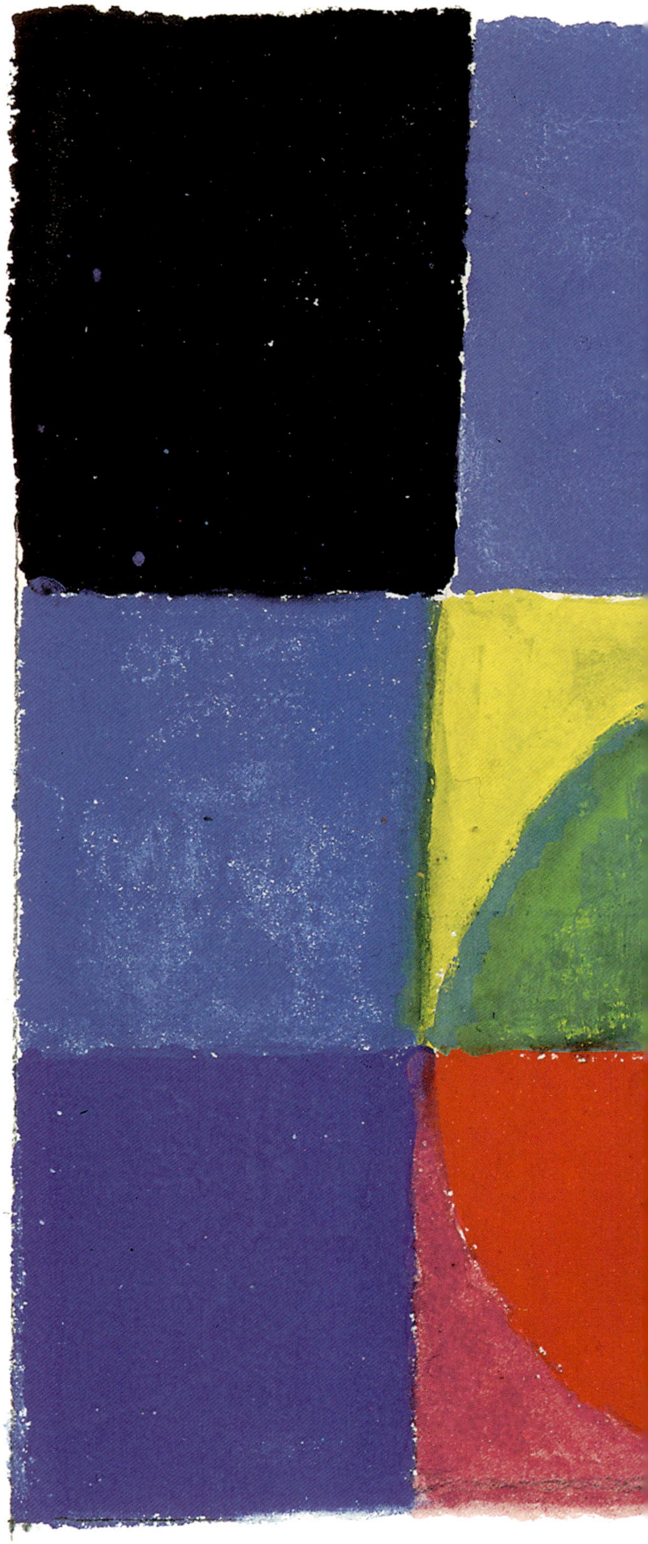

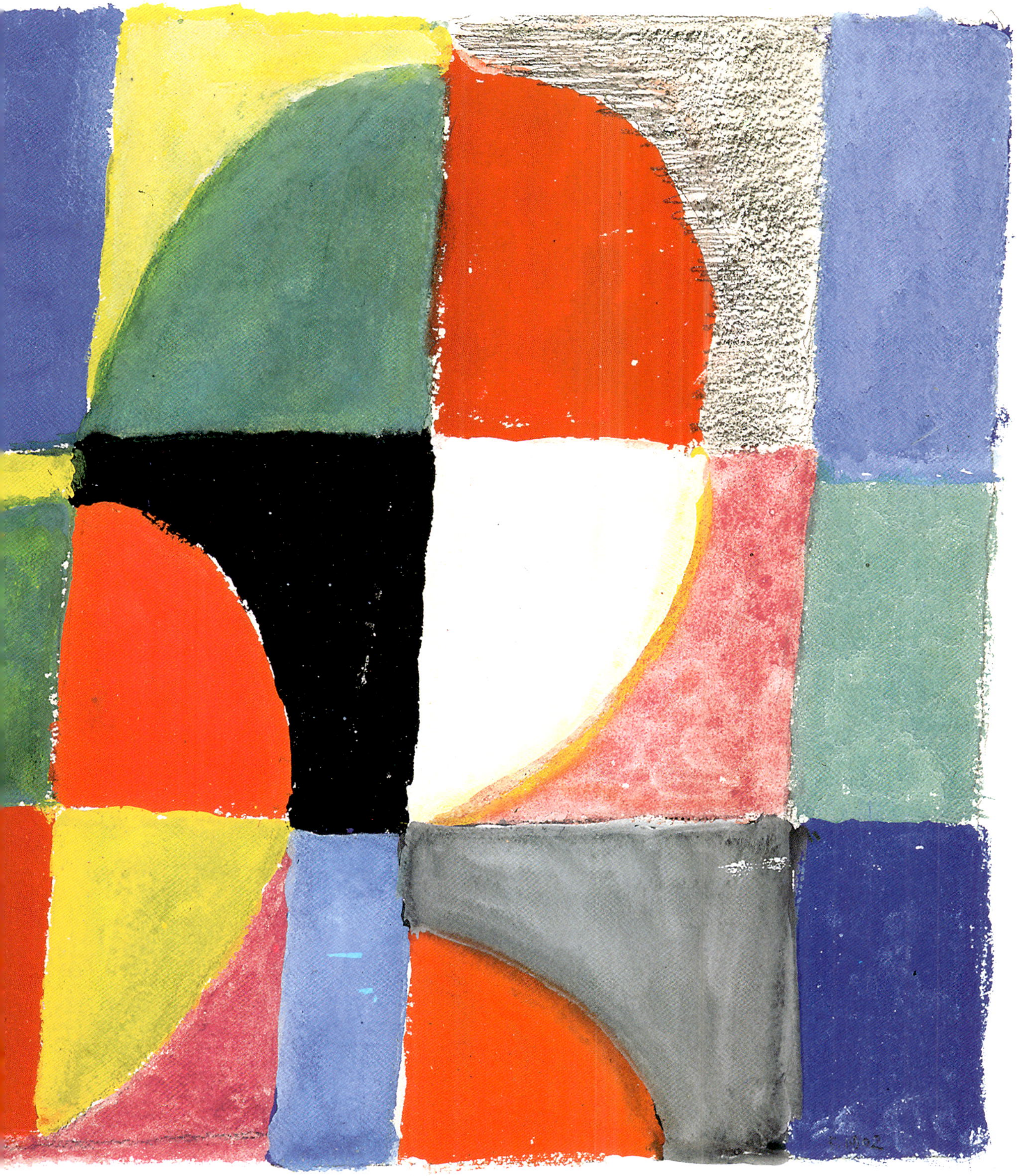

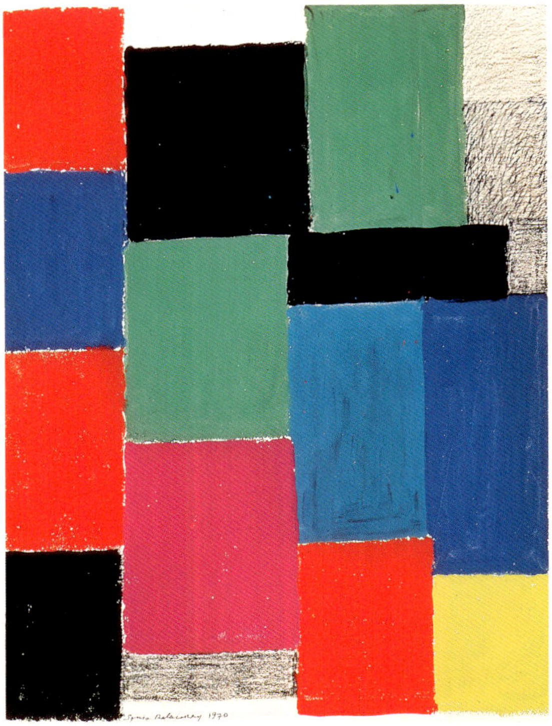

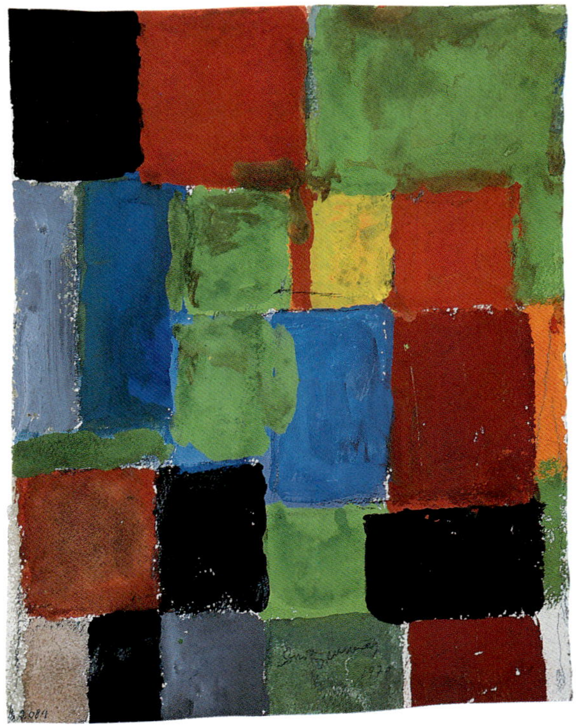

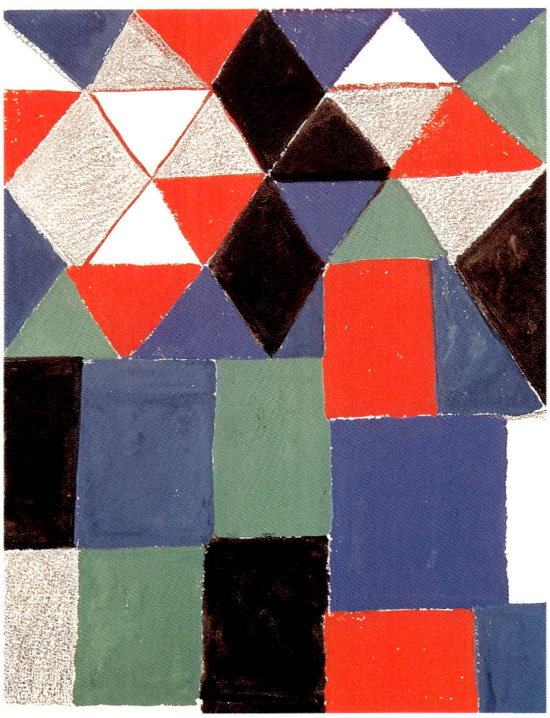

111 Above left, *Squares*, gouache, 1970.

112 Above, Sonia's penultimate gouache, 1979.

113 Left, *Scottish*, gouache, 1970.

114 Opposite, the last gouache, 1979.

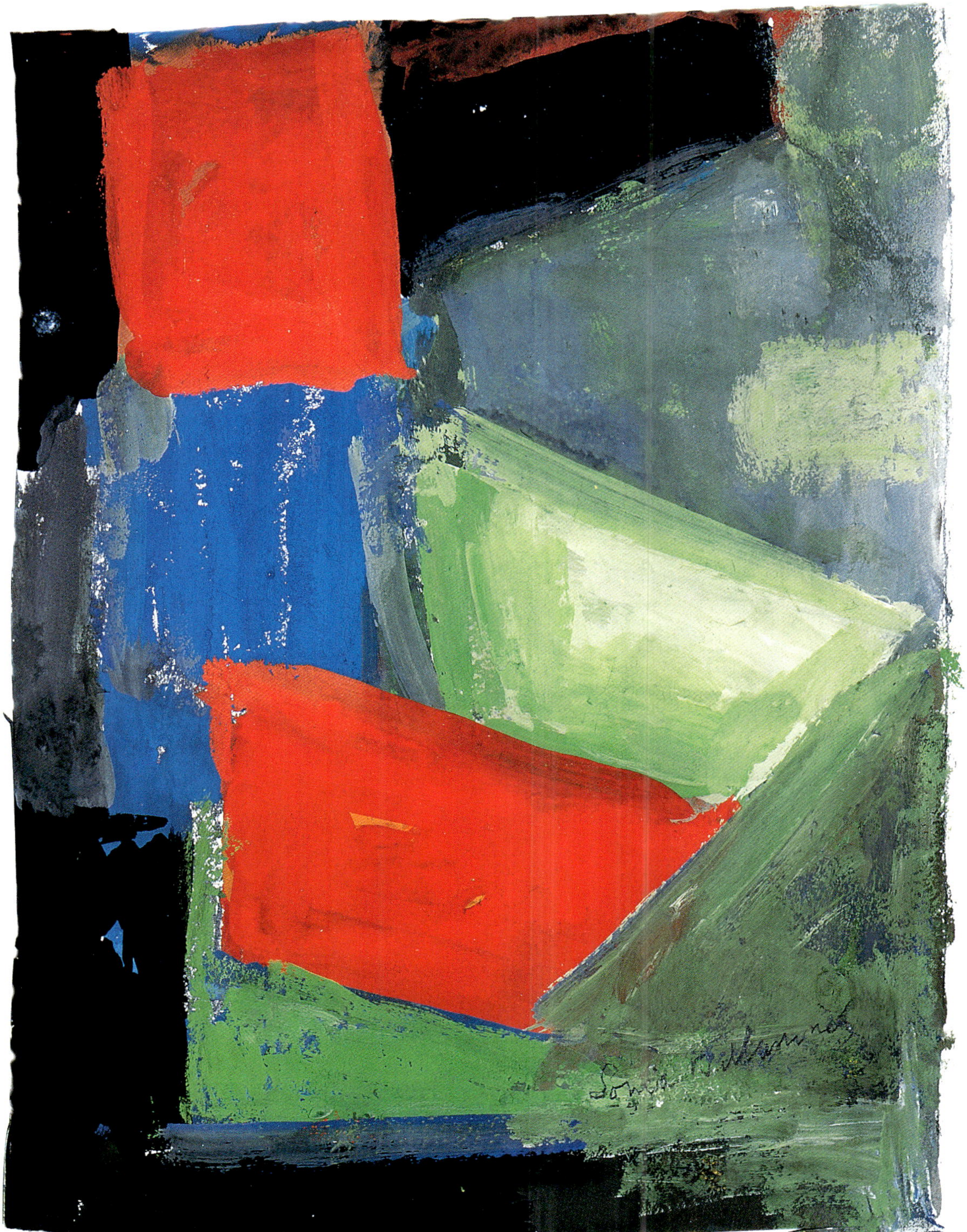

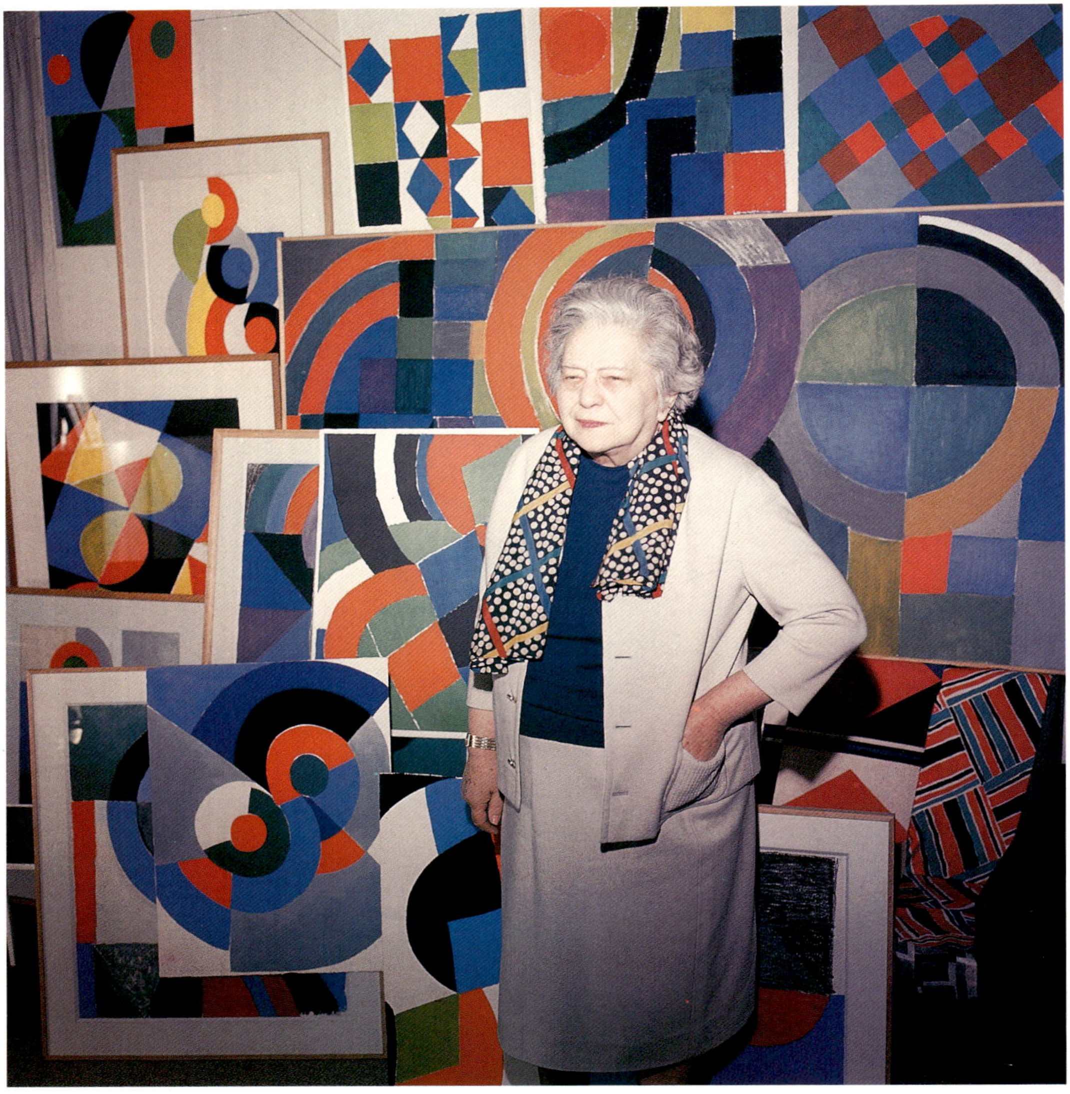

115 Sonia in her studio in 1968, her eighty-third year.

CHAPTER 17

THE LAST TEN YEARS: HAPPINESS AND FULFILMENT

Her main and overriding preoccupation in this period was the turmoil within her own family. She had never been fond of her daughter-in-law Denise, but in the Sixties she began seriously to distrust and suspect Denise of plotting to turn the boys against her and to get her hands on the pictures and other property Sonia would be leaving upon her death. The marriage had not been a successful one, but Charles, at least in Sonia's view, was regrettably weak and unable to take decisive action against his wife, such as divorcing or leaving her.

Charles had been urging Sonia to finalize her will, and make over the bulk of the estate to him straight away. As Sonia was certain that Denise was behind this and wanted Charles to be in possession of the estate so that she could divorce him and claim half the spoils, she was prepared to fight in order to avoid the fate of King Lear. All of this may well have been in Sonia's mind only, but it is clear that she and Denise were by now not on talking terms, and that Denise was keeping the boys from visiting their grandmother. Sonia particularly resented this because of her great love for the younger boy, twelve-year-old Eric, who showed a significant interest in art as well as a certain talent for drawing. He had often stayed overnight with Sonia in the rue Saint-Simon and she encouraged him to use her painting or drawing materials to create things of his own.

But then Denise was persuading Charles to move farther away from Paris, which meant that Eric would be going to another school and his visits to her would become much less frequent, if indeed he would be permitted to come at all. Sonia not only spoke to Charles with great bitterness about these things, but also had frequent meetings with the lawyer Matrasso, seeking the best way to deal with her will so as to ensure that her daughter-in-law would be denied access to the property.

It is no wonder that, when she received a letter from Jacques Damase on 14 December 1964, some months after their first meeting, which broached a project he thought she might be interested in, she should have been eager to see him. They did not meet, however, until early June when Damase came to the house with a maquette of the book he wanted to discuss with her, and they went to have dinner at her local restaurant, the Belles Gourmandes. What he was proposing was a de luxe book of his poems with a certain number of Sonia's gouaches.

Sonia indicated that the idea appealed to her, but first she wanted to read the texts. These he brought to her on 4 August, and by the 23rd she made a note that she was pleased with the texts and already working on the gouaches.

These developments coincided with several visits from the dealer René Gimpel, who came first on 24 June 1965 to talk about putting on an exhibition of Sonia's work in his London gallery and perhaps also in Erica Brausen's Hanover Gallery in Zürich. After looking at her latest paintings, he bought three gouaches.

On the 28th of July, Gimpel came again, very excited about the prospects of the show he had suggested; and on 5 January 1966 he paid a third visit. This time she showed him the gouaches she had prepared for Damase's book, which was to be called *Rhythmes-Couleurs.* Then Damase arrived and the three of them discussed the price for which the book could be sold. Gimpel thought that the first twenty-five copies should not be too expensive, and that the price could be increased once those had been sold. Gimpel also said that he would sell the eleven individual pochoirs separately, and he offered to have a cocktail party on the opening day of the show if Sonia would agree to come to London.

She went over to London, with Damase, on 31 January. It was he who looked after all the arrangements – dealing with her luggage and porters and taxis. She enjoyed the flight, and even though their landing was held up because of fog in the area of the airport, she felt no fear, for they were talking all the time. 'He told me about his origins . . . His father had large properties in Africa. It was very fanciful and told in his usual manner and basically one has to wonder if it was not made up, it is so intricate, so complicated, but in any case sympathetic . . .'

While Damase was obviously not taking on the guise of Othello to mesmerize Desdemona/Sonia with tales of the African anthropophagi he had encountered, from the time of this short journey to London, Sonia was deeply interested in Damase, if not infatuated by him. She stayed at the Grosvenor Court Hotel in Davies Street, he with friends. There was a dinner-party at the house of René Gimpel's brother Charles; Peggy Guggenheim and Erica Brausen were among the guests. Sonia stayed in all only two days in London, but on one of those days Damase gave her a personal tour of one of his favourite cities. In spite of her sometimes hostile ideas about Anglo-Saxons, she found much to admire in London, and as she looked out over the Thames in the late afternoon, all her reading of Dickens came back to her, 'everything very dark, sinister'. Most of the time, she notes, they were talking, because it was so 'curious that Damase's feelings are so much like mine and he understands me like no one else in this respect'.

Once back in Paris, she and Damase began to see each other regularly. She thought he had emotional and drinking problems, and wished to help him. To be useful to another person was something she had not experienced since Robert's death. In an interview with a young woman who was writing a thesis about painting in Paris in the 1920s, she had said, 'I'm fed up with all these people who live off me and won't leave me my freedom.' Damase neither lived off her, nor curtailed her freedom. What he did, in fact, was to look after her. She had been in danger of losing her extraordinary zest for living and most in need of undemanding friendship and companionship. She could hardly help herself from expressing her wonder again and again: 'Jacques' great sensitivity', she wrote in February 1966, 'corresponds to mine, and the way we get on together I have never experienced before and it has been missing all my life. This somewhat cerebral hypersensitivity gets translated in my case into painting.'

One of the first important exhibitions that took place after her meeting with Damase was the one called 'L'Expo 1925', organized by François Mathey in 1965 at the Musée des Arts Décoratifs in Paris. One room was devoted to Sonia's fabric designs and her dresses – which reminded the public of the major influence she had been in those areas of art during the Twenties.

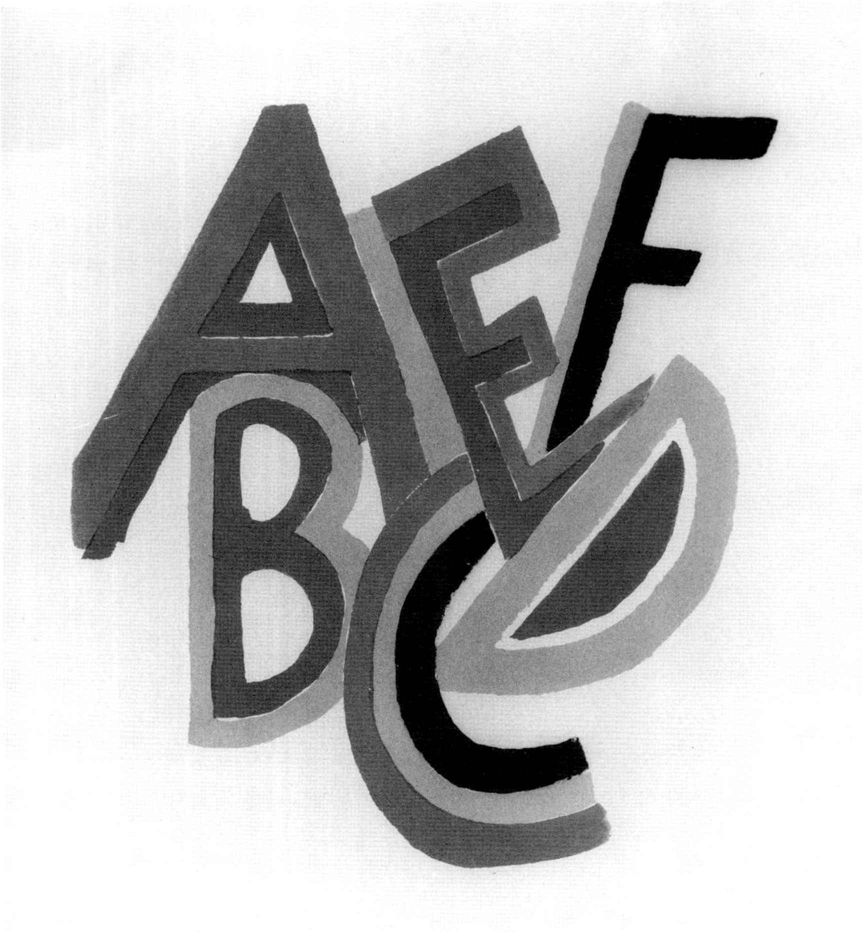

An alphabetic design of 1969.

Coincidentally, it was about the same time that an American Mr Archer came to her in search of fabric designs. He told her how much he regretted not having worked with her before, but said that her designs were much in vogue. They had been created, in fact, forty years too soon. As if to demonstrate that he was not merely flattering her, he gave her an order amounting to 125,000 francs.

In 1967, with Damase's help, she enjoyed her most important tribute, a full-scale retrospective of her work, consisting of almost 200 pieces, at the Musée Nationale d'Art Moderne, which had been managed from 1946 to 1965 by her long-time friend Jean Cassou and was now the domain of Bernard Dorival. It was, by all reports, a spectacular event, attended by the cream of the art world and officially honoured by the eminent author André Malraux, now de Gaulle's distinguished Minister of Culture, who had become quite a good friend of Sonia's. Among the many examples of Sonia's versatility as an artist was a Matra automobile that she had painted in her typical style. Malraux paused to admire this especially on his way out of the museum.

And after that, hardly a month passed without some exhibition all over the world of one of the branches of her activity, whether her rugs, her book covers, her ballet decors, posters, playing cards, masses of lithographs and etchings.

She had attained the recognition she had longed for, even to the extent that when President Pompidou went to the United States on an official visit, he brought as a present from his government a painting of Sonia's. What its recipient, President Nixon, thought of it has not been recorded.

The happiest result of all this admiration and the financial rewards it brought was that Sonia truly enjoyed them, enjoyed being famous and well-off. As she began to experience affluence for the first time since her early years in St Petersburg, she was able to indulge her taste for luxuries. With her almost exaggerated instinct for quality, she derived as much satisfaction from a ripe pear or a perfect flower, from the paper for her gouaches or the large pots of paint she chose at the shops of Sennelier or Lefebvre-Foinat in the rue Vavin, as she

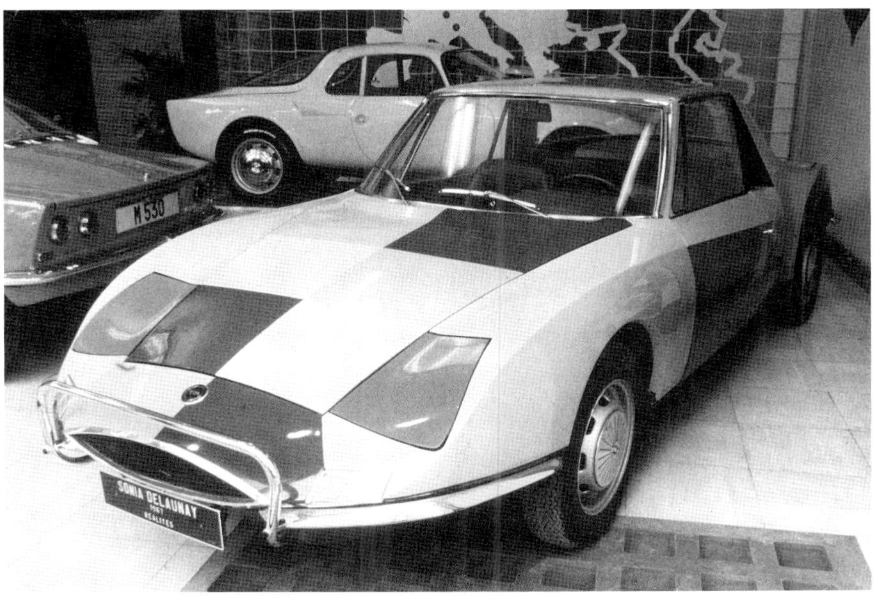

The Matra car painted by Sonia in 1967, shown in her retrospective at the Musée Nationale d'Art Moderne in the same year.

did from the cashmere sweaters at Hermès or the English soap at Old England or the pastries at Fauchon. She began to buy her clothes at Chanel and Givenchy; and most days she was picked up by a hired Rolls-Royce which took her to the Bois for a walk amid the trees and grass, or for a few hours of shopping. She would remain in the car and let the chauffeur go to fetch her usual *vendeuses* who brought out samples for her to choose from. The only thing she demanded of her chauffeurs was that they avoid any streets from which she might catch sight of the new Montparnasse tower, which she detested.

She was flattered and pleased by the attention Malraux paid to her and later by her invitations to dine intimately with Claude Pompidou, the President's widow, in her apartment on the quai de Béthune. The last fifteen years of Sonia's life were filled with official occasions at which either she or Robert was being honoured or exhibited.

For once, in her old age she had a really efficient secretary in Monique Schneider-Maunoury, recommended to her by Damase. She liberated Sonia from virtually all the day-to-day problems of running the household, and dealt with the voluminous correspondence, the booking of appointments, the hounding of galleries and agencies, the issuing of invoices and paying of bills. Since Sonia no longer had to count the linen to make sure the cleaning woman of the moment wasn't dipping into the supply, she had much more leisure time than ever before in her life, and this permitted her to travel extensively with Damase: to Genoa, Florence, Venice, Lisbon (where the Gulbenkian Foundation had bought her larger *Flamenco*), Brussels, Bielefeld and Berlin. And until she was ninety she continued to paint boldly and with total self-assurance. Her pure colours and large patterns in the late works bear even more insistently the internal rhythms that were so vital to her. In some ways, these paintings are like close relatives to Matisse's late non-figurative work.

In addition, she reverted occasionally to some of her earlier interests: in 1968 she created the decor and costumes for a production of the Stravinsky/Balanchine ballet *Danses Concertantes* which was performed by the Ballet-Théâtre of Amiens; she designed a number of rugs; and from time to time she painted important posters such as the one in her ninetieth year for the International Women's Year of Unesco in 1975.

Damase had been publishing books since 1947; after he and Sonia established their friendship, he was responsible for a great number of valuable and beautifully produced books in limited editions. One of these was the first

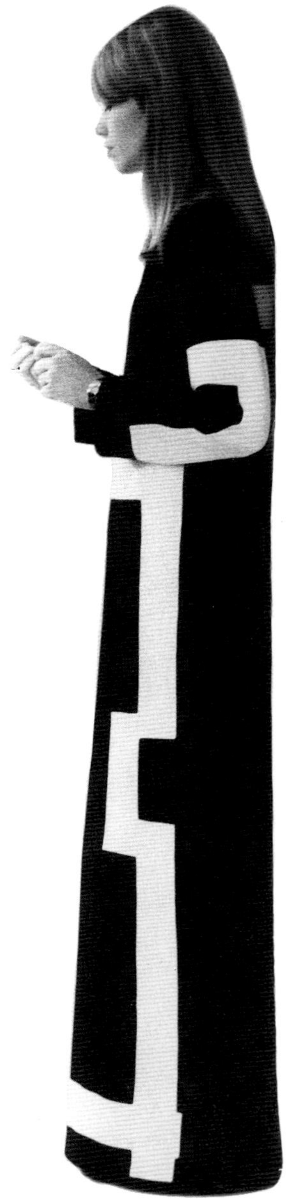

The pop singer Françoise Hardy wearing a Sonia design for Christian Dior in the late '60s.

monograph of Robert Delaunay's paintings by Bernard Dorival. There were other books that illustrated various aspects of Sonia's art; but a large proportion of his production was devoted to literary works of the past, such as Tzara's *Coeur à Gaz* and Rimbaud's *Illuminations*, with gouaches by Sonia. Damase also opened a gallery in the rue de Varenne in 1968 where many special exhibitions were devoted to the wider dissemination of Sonia's work.

It would appear that, at the end of this long, busy life, she had achieved virtually everything she could possibly have wished for when she first chose the career of an artist. Certainly the years after Robert's death and the end of the war, and especially those following the Carré Gallery retrospective, which was the fulfilment of an obsessive drive to make the world appreciate Robert's work, were years of ripeness and increasing satisfactions. It is interesting how often, in the years after the war, she tries in her journals to clarify her thoughts on not just the work she and Robert had done but on the whole basis of modern art. In 1949, for example, she wrote, 'I consider that abstract painting is a logical development in French painting, starting from the Impressionists, the Fauves, the Cubists, and that that's what we have to demonstrate. In doing that, we put our painting into a perspective where it can least be attacked and where we can ask for official patronage.' And a few days later she wanted to write to the journal *Arts*, which had published an article whose author had clearly not understood Delaunay's research. 'I have decided to write to make them understand that there is only Delaunay, and then Mondrian, who are abstract painters on whom the painting of the future can be built, because they provide a new appreciation of the use of colour.'

Then, on 22 August 1949, she wrote out what might stand for her credo:

> Up to the present, painting has been nothing but photography in colour, but the colour was always used as a means of describing something. Abstract art is a beginning towards freeing the old pictorial formula. But the real new painting will begin when people understand that colour has a life of its own, that the infinite combinations of colour have a poetry and a language much more expressive than the old methods. It is a mysterious language in tune with the vibrations, the life itself, of colour. In this area, there are new and infinite possibilities.

On the question of whether she contributed in any way to Robert's painting, she tended to be rather equivocal. In March 1943, when her financial situation was becoming desperate, her friends in Grasse, the Chenus, had suggested buying her 1916 painting *La Danse*. But she felt constrained to keep it 'because it is a witness to something that served for some of Robert's paintings, and it shows many of my instinctive indications which helped in his work.'

Rather than claiming an influence, she preferred to maintain that they had progressed in tandem. And indeed, at certain periods, if one compares the work each was doing, there appear to be mutual influences – certainly during the years in Spain and Portugal, and to some extent during the Thirties. On the other hand, her own development, if one looks at it in total, seems to have been much more straightforward, more instinctive, more human (to use her own word), more consistent. The most important thing, and the most unusual in the circumstances, is that she always had a career of her own, even though it was not recognized as early as it might have been.

She wrote: 'I don't know how to define my painting. That's not a bad thing, because I distrust classifications and systems. How and why define what one has brought up out of one's entrails? Before anyone else, Robert believed in me.'

By the time she died, she was a famous lady, a kind of institution such as the French are especially gifted at creating. She was remarkably healthy, though she was overweight; her only chronic problem in her last years was the pain that resulted from a broken thigh-bone caused by a fall in 1978. Though she began to find walking difficult, this disability did not make her curtail her activities. In that same year, she collaborated in designing the costumes for a production at the Comédie-Française of Pirandello's *Six Characters in Search of an Author*.

In June 1979, the gallery-owner Ernst Beyeler devoted a large space to her at the Basel Festival, for which she produced a series of gouaches remarkable for their youthful agility and quality. She also took part during the summer in the huge exhibition at the Centre Pompidou called 'Paris-Moscou'. And on 15 November (the day after her ninety-fourth birthday) she attended the opening of another Pompidou exhibition devoted to 'Jacques Damase, Thirty Years of Art Publishing'. The poster she painted for this exhibition was the last work she ever did, and it was also her last official engagement.

Sonia at the age of eighty-five.

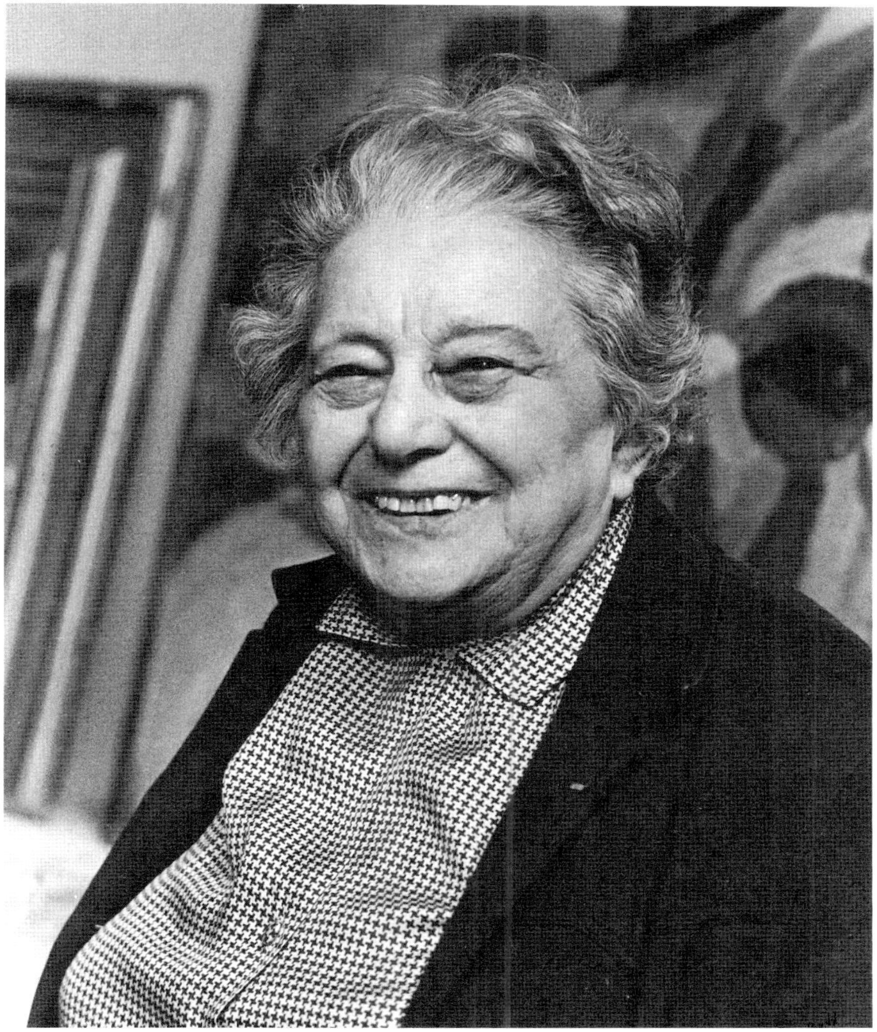

On the 5th of December 1979 she died peacefully in her studio. Wearing the long blue velvet dress that Hubert de Givenchy had designed for her to wear at the reception given at Versailles in honour of Queen Elizabeth, she was buried in the little cemetery at Gambais, next to Robert's grave, which she had visited every year on the anniversary of his death.

It is fitting that Sonia should have written the words that best sum up her life:

> *I have had three lives: one for Robert, one for my son and my grandsons, a shorter one for myself. I have no regrets for not having been more concerned with myself. I really didn't have the time.*

BIBLIOGRAPHY

The basic source for this book has been the private journals kept by Sonia Delaunay between 1933 and 1968, now deposited in the Bibliothèque National, Paris. I take this opportunity to thank the staff of the Manuscript Department for their kind assistance.

As for other sources, the number of books, pamphlets, articles and catalogues devoted to Sonia and Robert Delaunay is surprisingly large. I list here only those publications which I found particularly useful in writing this book.

S.B.

Anscombe, Isabelle *A Woman's Touch: Women in Design from 1960 to the Present Day*, New York/London 1985

Atelier simultané di Sonia Delaunay 1923-1924, Milan 1984

Boyer, Patricia Eckert (ed.) *The Nabis and the Parisian Avant Garde*, New Brunswick, N. J., 1988

Brown, Milton W. *The Story of the Armory Show*, New York 1964

Buot, François *René Crevel*, Paris 1991

Cohen, Arthur A. *Sonia Delaunay*, New York 1975

Damase, Jacques *L'Hommage à Sonia Delaunay*, Paris-Brussels 1976

Damase, Jacques *Sonia Delaunay, dessins noirs et blancs*, Paris 1978

Damase, Jacques *Sonia Delaunay, Rhythms and Colours*, London 1972

Damase, Jacques *Sonia Delaunay. Robes et gouaches simultanés, 1925. L'Art et le corps. Rhythmes-Couleurs en mouvement*, Brussels 1974

Damase, Jacques and Mustelier, Edouard *Sonia Delaunay*, Paris 1971

Delaunay, Sonia *Nous iron jusqu'au soleil*, Paris 1978

Dorival, Bernard *Sonia Delaunay*, Paris 1980

Düchting, Hajo *Robert und Sonia Delaunay: Triumph der Farbe*, Cologne 1993

D'Uckerman, P. *L'Art dans la Vie Moderne*, Paris n.d.

L'Exposition de Paris (intr. Albert Laprade), Paris [1937]

Ferreira, Paulo *Correspondance de quatre artistes portugais, Almada-Negreiros, José Pacheco, Souza-Cardoso, Eduardo Vianna, avec Robert et Sonia Delaunay*, Paris 1972

Hoog, Michel *Robert et Sonia Delaunay*, Paris 1967

Hoog, Michel et Dorival, Bernard *Rétrospective Sonia Delaunay au Musée national d'art moderne*, Paris 1967

Lhote, André *Sonia Delaunay; Ses peintures, ses objets, ses tissus simultanés, ses modes*, Paris 1925

Livre d'or officiel de l'Exposition Internationale des Arts et Techniques dans la vie moderne, Paris 1937

Robert et Sonia Delaunay 1885-1985, Paris (Musée d'art moderne de la Ville de Paris) 1985

Robert Delaunay (Exhibition catalogue), Galerie Louis Carré, Paris 1946

Robert Delaunay (Exhibition catalogue), Orangerie des Tuileries, Paris 1976

Schmidt-Friderichs, Bertram, and Wild, Adolf (eds.) *Jacques Damase Editeur* (Exhibition catalogue), Mainz 1991

Sonia Delaunay (Album for 90th Birthday), Paris 1984

Sonia Delaunay, La Terra impareggiabile, Milan 1971

Sonia Delaunay Rétrospective, Musée National d'Art moderne, Paris 1967-68

Sonia et Robert Delaunay, Paris (Bibliothèque Nationale) 1977

Uhde, Wilhelm *Von Bismarck bis Picasso, Erinnerungen und Bekenntnisse*, Zürich [1938]

Vreeland, Diana *Sonia Delaunay, Art in Fashion*, New York 1986

Zweite, Armin *The Blue Rider and the Lenbachhaus, Munich*, Munich 1989

CHRONOLOGY

1885 14 November: Sarah Stern born in Gradizhsk, Ukraine.

1890 'Adopted' by uncle Henri Terk in St Petersburg. Until 1903, attended school there, spent summers in uncle's cottage in Finland, travelled with aunt and uncle to Germany, Italy, Switzerland.

1899 The German Impressionist painter Max Liebermann, an acquaintance of her uncle, gave her her first box of paints while she was visiting Berlin.

1903 Spent two winters in Karlsruhe studying drawing with Schmidt-Reutter. The composer-to-be Arnold Schoenberg was also studying there.

1905 Went to Paris. Lived with a group of Russian girls and attended art classes at the Académie de la Palette. Worked at printmaking with Grosmann. Produced *Ile Saint-Louis*, a portrait of the Russian poet Chuiko, and other minor works.
First exhibition of Les Fauves at the Salon des Indépendants.

1906-07 Paintings influenced by Gauguin and Van Gogh: *Philomène*, *The Finnish Girl*, portrait of Chuiko, *Nu jaune*. One-man show at Wilhelm Uhde's Galerie Notre-Dame-des-Champs in Montparnasse.

1909 Married Uhde in London. First acquaintance with work of le douanier Rousseau. Met Robert Delaunay at Uhde's gallery.

1910 Divorced Uhde by mutual agreement and married Robert, with whom she moved into an apartment/studio in the rue des Grands-Augustins.

1911 First exhibition of Analytical Cubist painters. Sonia made abstract bed-cover for crib of son Charles, born January.

1912 After the scandal of the theft of the Mona Lisa from the Louvre, Apollinaire stayed with the Delaunays about six weeks. Apollinaire invented the description 'Orphism' for Robert's work.

1913 Electric street lights installed in Boulevard Saint-Michel. Sonia's studies of light: *Prismes électriques*.
Meeting with Blaise Cendrars. Sonia made binding of various fabrics for his *Pâques à New York*.
Collaborated with Cendrars on accordion-type book of his poem *La Prose du Transsibérien et la Petite Jehanne de France*.
Studies for *Bal Bullier* and final painting in two versions.
Sent twenty paintings and objects to Berlin *Herbstsalon*. Learned to know the Blaue Reiter group of painters Kandinsky, Marc, Macke and also Klee.

1914 Showed *Prismes électriques* at Salon des Indépendants. Made various studies for publicity projects (Chocolat, Zenith, Le Rêve gas stoves), which remained unrealized.
Travelled to Madrid, where she and Robert remained throughout World War I. War declared while they were in the Basque border town of Fuenterrabia.

1915 Travelled with fellow-artists Sam Halpert and Edouardo Vianna to the village of Vila do Condo in Portugal. Painted *Flamenco Singers*, *Jouets portugais*, *Disques*.
Moved on to Valença da Minho, where Sonia painted still-lifes and market scenes.
Invited to exhibit at gallery in Stockholm, for which she painted a memorable self-portrait.

1917 Revolution in Russia meant that Sonia's income was lost. Settled in Madrid, she started to engage in interior decoration ('Casa Sonia'), designing clothes and costumes.

1918 Met Diaghilev in Madrid; he invited her and Robert to create costumes and decor for ballet *Cléopâtre*, which opened in London. Sonia designed costume for singer Lahovska as *Aida* in Barcelona.
Death of Apollinaire. Publication of Dada Manifesto.

1920 Delaunays returned to Paris, lived in apartment in

boulevard Malesherbes. Associated with members of Dada and Surrealist groups: Tzara, Soupault, Breton, Aragon, Crevel, etc. Sonia exhibited Portuguese works in Der Sturm gallery in Berlin.

1922 Sale of Rousseau painting *The Snake Charmer* to Jacques Doucet for FF50,000.

1923 Sonia designed costumes for single performance of Tzara's play *Le Coeur à Gaz*. Began to design fabrics for silk manufacturer in Lyons and to create clothes for stylish clientele.

1925 In collaboration with couturier Jacques Heim, Sonia participated in the Exposition des Arts Décoratifs. Publication of a book devoted to her work - *Sonia Delaunay, ses peintures, ses tissus simultanés, ses modes*, with contributions from André Lhote, Soupault, Delteil and Cendrars.
Showed simultaneous fabric designs at the Salon d'Automne and took part in exhibition called L'Art d'aujourd'hui.
Began long-term association with Amsterdam department store Metz & Co.

1926 With Robert, designed costumes and decor for two films: *Vertige* and *Le P'tit Parigot*.

1927 27 January: lecture at Sorbonne on fabric design and fashion.

1929 Designed stage costumes for actresses, and street clothes for Nancy Cunard, Gloria Swanson and Mme Leopold Stokowski.

1930-40 Sonia's so-called 'Years of Liberation': gave up business to resume painting, but forced by financial circumstances to continue design and clothes activities. In 1935 left boulevard Malesherbes apartment and moved to 16 rue Saint-Simon, where she lived the rest of her life.
Support from collectors Delhumeau and Guggenheim.

1936-37 Participation in International Exposition in Paris: prepared large panels for Pavillon des Chemins de Fer and the Palais de l'Air.

1937 27 September-2 October: Motor trip to South of France and back.
6 December: Death of Robert's mother, Mme de Rose.

1939 Bought property in Gambais.
Robert diagnosed as having cancer, but nevertheless instituted his 'Thursdays', meetings with young abstract painters. Organized the first Salon des Réalités Nouvelles at Galerie Charpentier.
3 August: Declaration of war.

1940 Sonia and Robert left Paris by car and rented apartment in Mougins in the Midi. In contact with Magnellis and Arps in Grasse.

1941 October: During short excursion to Châtel-Guyon, Robert became ill and underwent operation in Clermont-Ferrand. Transferred to Montpellier where he died 25 October.
Sonia went to live in Grasse where she remained for the duration of the war.

1944 Sonia went to Toulouse, where she stayed three months before returning to Paris 3 November.

1946 Retrospective of Robert's work at gallery of Louis Carré.

1946-53 Participation in various exhibitions in Paris (Galerie Colette Allendy), Vienna, Knokke-le-Zoute, Jerusalem.

1953 One-man show in Galerie Bing, Paris. Represented in other exhibitions in Paris (Musée National d'Art Moderne, Galerie Suzanne Michel, Galerie Colette Allendy) and Rome.

1955 First one-man show in New York (Rose Fried Gallery).
Various exhibitions in Marseilles, Lausanne, New York.

1956 Exhibitions in Rome, Milan, Venice, Havana, Grenoble.

1958 Major show of Sonia's paintings at Städtisches Kunsthaus, Bielefeld.

1959 Major exhibition of works by Robert and Sonia in Musée des Beaux-Arts, Lyons.
One-man show at Fetscherin gallery, Munich.

1961 One-man show at Brook Street Gallery, London.

1962 Exhibition of 43 recent gouaches at Galerie Denise René, Paris.

1964 Met Jacques Damase.
Donation of 117 works by Robert and Sonia to the Louvre.

1965 Began collaboration with Damase in book of poems and pochoirs to be called *Rhythmes-Couleurs*.

1966 January: Went to London with Damase to attend opening of one-man show at Gimpel Gallery.
Fabrics and designs in exhibition 'Les années 25' at Pavillon de Marsan, Paris.

1967 Major retrospective at Musée National d'Art Moderne.

1968 Designed costumes and decor for Stravinsky/Balanchine ballet *Danses Concertantes* in Amiens.

1969 Awarded International Grand Prize for Women Artists by the Salon International de la Femme, Cannes.

1972 Exhibition at Gulbenkian Foundation, Lisbon: 'Robert and Sonia Delaunay and their friends in Portugal'.

1975 Designed UNESCO poster for International Year of Women. Received Légion d'honneur.
'Hommage à Sonia Delaunay': exhibition organized by Damase in his Brussels gallery to celebrate her ninetieth birthday.

1976 Donated to Centre Pompidou her entire graphic work.
First exhibition of her work in Japan, at Baku Gallery, Tokyo.

1978 Fell and broke thigh-bone in January.
Collaborated with Patrick Raynaud in costume designs for Comédie-Française production of Pirandello's *Six Characters in Search of an Author*.

1979 Took part in exhibition 'Paris-Moscow' at Centre Pompidou.
15 November: designed poster for exhibition at Pompidou: 'Jacques Damase - trente années d'édition d'art'. This was her last work of art and her last public appearance.
5 December: Died peacefully at home. Buried at Gambais on 7 December.

PHOTO CREDITS

Ina Bandy, Paris, p. 144
Budd, New York, p. 201
Robert David, Paris, p. 70 (bottom), 147, 166, 173 (both), 176
Robert Donat, St-Cloud, p. 198
Richard de Grab, Paris, p. 169
Etienne Hubert, Paris, p. 58 (below), 196, 197
Germaine Krull, Paris, p. 79
Studio Lipnitzki, Paris, p. 73
André Morain, Neuilly, p. 171
Marc Vaux, Paris, p. 10, 17, 46, 58 (above), 77, 107, 139, 142, 164

INDEX

Page numbers in italics refer to illustrations